MARKETS IN OAXACA

Special Publication Sponsored by the
INSTITUTE OF LATIN AMERICAN STUDIES

The University of Texas at Austin

Markets in Oaxaca

edited by
SCOTT COOK AND MARTIN DISKIN

Foreword by Sidney W. Mintz

UNIVERSITY OF TEXAS PRESS
AUSTIN

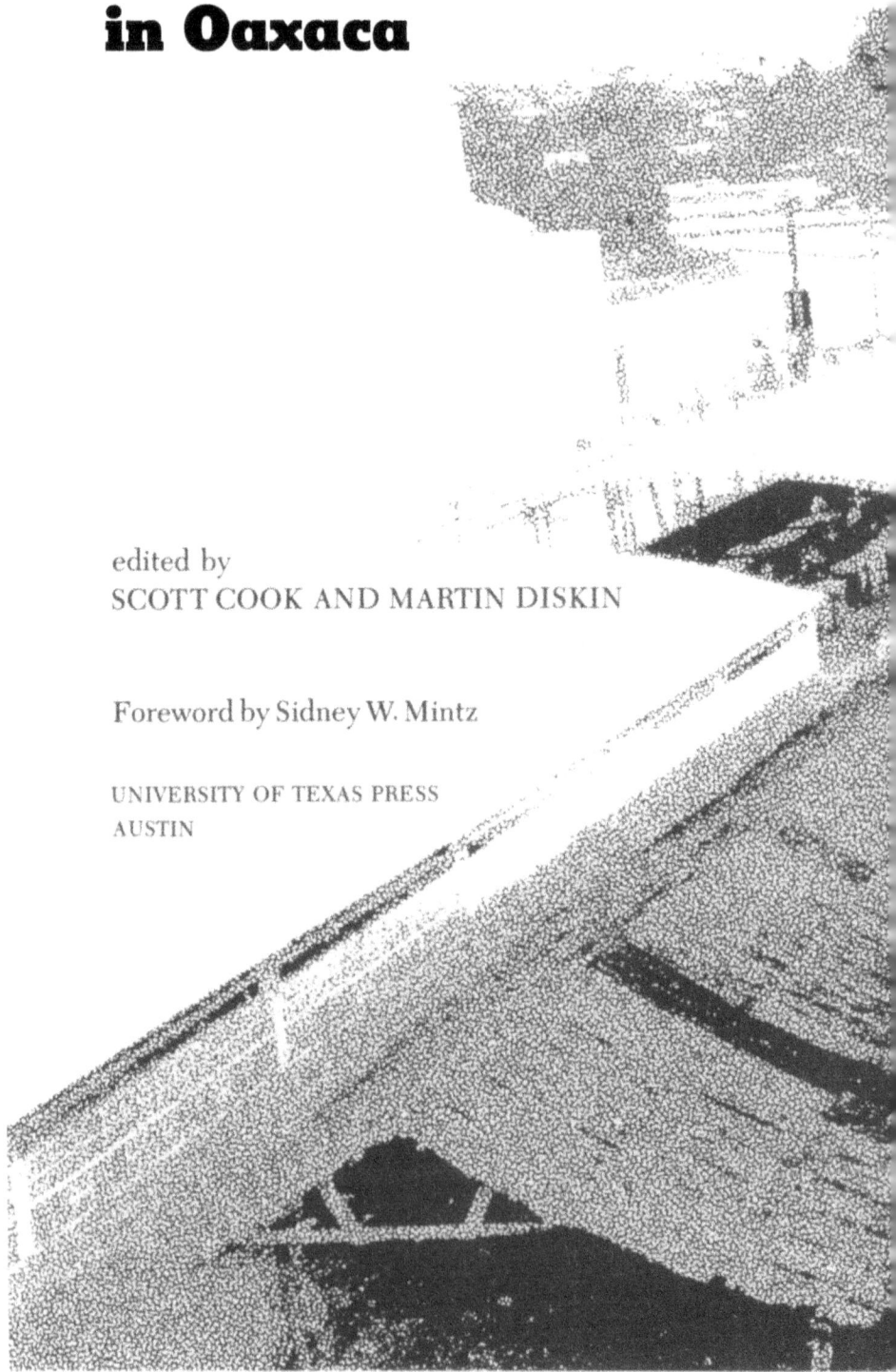

Library of Congress Cataloging in Publication Data

Main entry under title:

Markets in Oaxaca.

   (Special publication sponsored by the Institute of
Latin American Studies, the University of Texas at Austin)
   Edited papers from a symposium held in Tucson, Apr. 30,
1971, sponsored by the Southwestern Anthropological
Association.

   Bibliography: p.
   Includes index.
   1. Oaxaca Valley—Economic conditions. 2. Markets—
Mexico—Oaxaca Valley. 3. Oaxaca Valley—Social condi-
tions. I. Cook, Scott, 1937–   II. Diskin, Martin,
1934–   III. Southwestern Anthropological Association.
IV. Series: Texas. University at Austin. Institute of
Latin American Studies. Special publication.
HC137.027M37   330.9′72′7   75-8518
ISBN 978-1-4773-0116-6

www.utpress.utexas.edu/index.php/rp-form

First paperback printing, 2015

AL PUEBLO TRABAJADOR DE OAXACA

CONTENTS

NOTE TO THE READER

The city of Oaxaca de Juárez, capital of the state of Oaxaca, is referred to throughout the book as Oaxaca City.

The symbol $ is used throughout to indicate Mexican pesos (exchange rate: 12.50 pesos = 1 U.S. dollar).

FOREWORD

The essays which make up this volume mostly originated in research conducted as part of the Oaxaca Market Study Project. Editors Cook and Diskin have worked hard to endow them with greater coherence by providing introductory and final essays that offer the reader a perspective often lacking in collections of this kind. The prefatory remarks which follow touch on several issues only, where it seems to the writer that this collection may mark an advance in our general understanding of the economic anthropology of peasant societies and of complex societies, widely defined.

Studies by anthropologists of exchange and exchange systems now have a very long history. But anthropological studies of the exchange systems of peasant (as opposed to "primitive") societies were practically nonexistent until about twenty-five years ago. The editors point to the work of Marroquín (1957) and Malinowski and de la Fuente (1957), as marking the beginnings of such research among the Mexican peasantry. Approximately the same date would hold for the rest of the peasant world. It was probably expectable that the first such work, as the editors declare, tended to be descriptive rather than analytical, qualitative rather than quantitative, and only rarely aimed at the solution of any particular theoretical issue. These limitations, however, reflect the generally laggard growth of anthropological interest in peasant societies.

Anthropological studies of peasant communities, beginning perhaps with Robert Redfield's *Tepoztlán* (1930), while often revealing a genuine concern with the relationships between the local community and the wider society, also demonstrated at the outset the unpreparedness of anthropology to deal effectively with the analysis of extracommunity or supracommunity institutions in the modern world. The methodological (and theoretical) difficulties surely persist; but now they are better recognized, and some concrete efforts are being made to resolve them, as the following essays demonstrate.

Early attempts to study peasant communities suggest that at least three approaches were employed to cope with the reality of supra-community ties. One might simply confine one's problem area to phenomena of a range sufficiently narrow to minimize (or to eliminate, in the case of some methodological rationales) the significance of such ties. Or one might study the community as if such linkages did not exist, thereby imparting a rather artificial quality of isolation to communities which were not, in fact, at all isolated.[1] Or one might try, however unhandily, to grapple with the problems that became visible as soon as one conceded the lack of such isolation. It was as part of the pioneering efforts to refashion the discipline's tools for this task that a vocabulary long alien to the concerns of anthropological inquiry began to turn up in articles and monographs—"the world market," "the nation-state," "the capitalist [or some other] mode of production," "capitalism," and the like—and these terms have not always been employed with care. Nonetheless, the shift in emphasis in anthropological orientation cannot be written off as merely another passing vogue; its careful development may hold genuine promise for the ultimate future of social-science theory.

Seeing the community as more than itself meant looking for the systems into which its members were articulated and seeking to conceptualize those systems usefully. The study of internal market systems thus provided one of the routes by which anthropologists might attempt to transcend the community, so to speak, in order to grasp more clearly its fit within the region and the nation. But it needs to be stressed that an adequate conceptualization of this kind is not concerned simply with "fitting" or "linking" the community as such to wider systems; to a very substantial degree, it is the nature of that integration which actually *helps to define the community itself*. The view of communities as firmly bounded and isolated groupings, gradually losing their separateness and intactness to outside pressures, while conveying a generally accepted understanding of how change occurs, is not quite adequate, then, in dealing with the reality of larger sociocultural wholes. Surely one of the reasons for the popularity of anthropological marketing studies in recent years has been the growing recognition that the analytical "reality" of communities is no greater than the analytical "reality" of market systems; when employed as heuristic devices, these abstractions may even serve in part to define each other. In this way, "systemic" studies—of internal market systems, say—may have attracted students because of the access they appear to provide to a more ample and imaginative view of occupations, classes, regions, and power blocs in large states, through inquiries that can be made congenial to anthropological methods.

One of the ways in which the contributions to this volume represent a step forward, in my opinion, is in the light they cast upon the mechanics of distribution of influence and power, and not only of economic goods and services. This distribution is neither static nor obvious; moreover, we are entitled to suppose that any regional system of the sort treated here will be marked by distinctive and particular features, as well as by certain general characteristics facilitating comparisons with other whole-systems of a similar kind. When the findings of the present volume are compared to others in recent years which deal with marketplaces and internal market systems, the advantages of treating a single regional system in multi-faceted fashion become visible. The productive arrangements of local inhabitants, whether viewed in terms of kin and domestic groups or larger (community-wide) groups, undergird the distributive system through which needed commodities are allocated; production and distribution, from one vantage point, are at once aspects of a single system and subsystems of even wider sociocultural structures. Viewed from the regional perspective—the Valley of Oaxaca—these subsystems define ongoing relationships among communities, classes, and occupational groups. Viewed from the perspective of the Mexican state, the region is an integer—more or less arbitrarily delimited—in an even larger structure. The struggle to reveal the interior organization of a regional marketing system is thus also a means toward understanding better how nations are put together: how existing institutions may be manipulated for particular goals by contending classes or other groups—how, in the widest sense, cultural forms are employed in an ongoing social system to achieve particular ends. That this is a task fraught with difficulties of every kind simply attests to the pioneering nature of such enterprises.

The present volume may be the first of its kind in a field that might be called—at the risk of pretentiousness—"comparative emporeutics." This is not the study of a marketplace, nor even of a system of marketplaces; nor is it simply a study of the class structure of a region. It is, rather, a composite, synthetic overview of the ecology and economy of a region (with the emphasis clearly on the latter), using distributive patterns of various sorts as a speculum for viewing a wider socioeconomic and political structure, which transcends both individual communities and particular classes. That it leaves a good deal yet to be studied and explained in the Valley of Oaxaca its editors would, I am sure, be the first to concede. But we may look forward to a time when a similar series of investigations in a major region of a wholly different society—Nigeria, say, or Peru—could result in interregional comparisons of a kind never before possible.

In their concluding essay, the editors engage the general issue of the economic relationships of localities, communities, and regions to the national and international capitalist economy. That this issue has bedeviled whole generations of social scientists should hardly occasion surprise; there probably is no single tougher and more complex question confronting the student of economic change. Diskin and Cook have, it seems to me, stated their case well. It is essential, as they contend, to escape from the conceptual limitations of a view that counterposes subsistence and exchange, or folk and urban, or any of the other conventional sociological polarities that may conceal, rather than expose, the uneven, reversible, and ragged processes by which the noncapitalist world becomes asymmetrically "modernized." The editors' insistence that precapitalist forms nurture the accumulation of capital elsewhere and may be protected, by the capitalist sector or by the state, precisely for this reason follows naturally. Accordingly, the relationships between capitalist and precapitalist sectors must be studied in all of their elaborate detail, much as Diskin and Cook suggest.

Yet the fact that *neither* sector is either homogeneous or harmonious cannot be brought to mind too often. While stressing the contrast between precapitalist and capitalist forms, the editors put less weight upon the frequently very competitive claims of different components within the capitalist sector itself. The perpetuation of "traditional" technology, of archaic forms of labor exchange, of "money-barter" and other features of a former way of life may result, at times, not so much from the calculated paternalism of an undifferentiated "capitalism" as from the internecine, long-term struggles among different capitalist groups, with varying but equally intense claims upon the same market or resource. The A's want cocoa; the B's, labor; the C's, rent; together (or rather, *not* together), they may manage to keep the D's startlingly "traditional." Capitalism, in short, is not an entelechy; its social expression implicates particular groups with differing stakes, within the same community, region, or nation. Thus the survival of older economic forms, in some cases, may turn out upon examination to be more the precipitate of conflicting external interests than the intended consequence of the actions of some particular interest group.

But this assertion has little relevance to the book as a whole. Here the reader is afforded a varied and detailed overview of a regional economy, exhibiting in itself much of the social and economic complexity that has so long fascinated students of the Mexican reality. The editors and their fellow contributors deserve credit for having shed much light upon the interior processes of that reality, and upon the energy, verve, and ingenuity of those who must struggle to survive within it.[2]

Sidney W. Mintz

PREFACE

This collection of papers represents the combined effort of several cultural anthropologists and a cultural geographer, all of whom share common scholarly interests in Mesoamerican studies as well as field work experiences in various communities in the state of Oaxaca, Mexico. Most of us were also participants in the Oaxaca Market Study Project directed by Ralph L. Beals between 1965 and 1969 (see Essay 2 below). The editors of this volume, with the encouragement and assistance of Dr. Beals, took the initiative in organizing a symposium for the purpose of stimulating all of us to present some of our research findings and to exchange views about these.[1] The positive response and enthusiasm during the symposium from our colleagues and others encouraged us to undertake the task of assembling and editing the symposium papers for publication.

Despite the fact that most of the authors did field work within the framework of the Beals project, the reader will note that the papers encompass a diversified range of research interests, methods, and types of data. We are also painfully aware of the fact that these papers and our editorial essays leave more questions unanswered than answered and more problems exposed than resolved. Nevertheless, we believe that our over-all understanding of the regional peasant market economy of the Valley of Oaxaca has been substantially enhanced as a result of the symposium and our subsequent editorial labors. At the very least, we now consider ourselves better prepared than at any time in the past to formulate more precise and meaningful strategies for future study of the complex realities of the Valley of Oaxaca economy. We must be satisfied at this point, however, with knowledge that will help to guide continuing research, as opposed to knowledge that provides definitive understanding.

ACKNOWLEDGMENTS

While each contributor to this book owes considerable gratitude to many people whose patience and friendship were significant in helping to learn about Oaxaca, we assume that each instance of field work was done in a spirit of mutual respect and dignity so that the relevant local individuals have already been properly thanked. Let us here point to those people whose support was common to the entire field project.

The people of the villages, the towns, and the city studied were quite consistently open and receptive to our investigations. The same may be said for the officials of each community, whose support facilitated our work by giving us access to documents and by providing legitimation for us. From our side of the border, Ralph Beals is warmly acknowledged as the originator and major force behind the Oaxaca Market Study Project. While not all the contributors to this volume were his students, his guidance, stimulation, and constant interest contributed to the cohesion of the group.

Mexican colleagues and institutions were helpful and supportive throughout. The round-table meeting held in the Universidad Benito Juárez in Oaxaca City in August, 1965, was a useful first evaluation of the project. Dr. Gonzalo Aguirre Beltrán, Dr. Ignacio Bernal, and Dr. Fernando Cámara Barbachano, three distinguished Mexican colleagues, were active participants who helped sharpen our ideas and orient us toward future analyses of the data. We gratefully acknowledge the Instituto Nacional de Antropología e Historia and its regional director, Sr. Lorenzo Gamio, for the numerous kindnesses showed to our project members. Mr. Cecil Welte, of the Oficina de Estudios de Humanidad del Valle de Oaxaca, has been uniformly generous and helpful to the project. His map of the Valley of Oaxaca is the best there is. His compilations of statistics, his constant willingness to verify details, and his good judgment at many places in this book were invaluable.

The experience of editing a book has yielded two noteworthy results for us. First, a genial relationship between two colleagues has
developed into a warm friendship between two families; and, second, through the many discussions we have had during the various
phases of this book, we have come to understand the seriousness of
the anthropological enterprise, involving as it does the exposure to
the world of significant details of the cultural existence of many
people. The only justification for doing this is the hope that works
such as this can have an impact on public policy as it affects the lives
of the people we study. This book is offered as the first step in that
direction.

Scott Cook
Martin Diskin

PART ONE

Introduction

The aims of this section are (a) to delineate the salient structural features of the precapitalist socioeconomic formation in the central valley and outlying regions of the state of Oaxaca, Mexico, and to summarize their development and present functioning; (b) to describe and analyze the position of Oaxaca within the structure of the developing Mexican nation; and (c) to suggest how our Oaxaca research relates to Mesoamerican studies in particular and to economic anthropology in general.

The systematic economic anthropological study of the regional peasant economies of Oaxaca began with the work of Bronislaw Malinowski and Julio de la Fuente (1957), and of Alejandro Marroquín (1957)—the former focusing on the central valley marketing system and the latter on the marketplace system centered in the town of Tlaxiaco in the Mixteca Alta. These studies were essentially descriptive, taxonomic, and synchronic in nature; though limited in their theoretical and analytical aims, they provided us with useful first approximations of the structure and functioning of economic life, especially as reflected in the marketing process, in these peasant regions. The Oaxaca Market Study Project directed by Ralph L. Beals used these pioneering studies as departure points for a more comprehensive investigation of regional economic life. Beals's thoughtful summary of some of the salient preliminary results of this project represents a step forward in the clarification and amplification of our understanding of the preindustrial economy of Oaxaca from the viewpoint of synchronic structural-functional analysis. Our view, however, is that this approach must be supplemented with diachronic and dynamic analysis, and that problems and concepts must be introduced from an economic anthropology which is not bound by the restrictions of the formal-substantive dichotomy and which draws upon the contributions of political economy, history, archaeology, and cultural ecology.

This combination of approaches enables us to understand the dynamics of the evolution of the Valley of Oaxaca economy as a precapitalist formation existing within the matrix of the metropolitan capitalist money-market economy and the international division of labor. The structure and functioning of the Valley economy, whether examined at one point in time or through time, cannot be understood as a mere reflex of extraregional processes and events, nor as the outcome of strictly endogenous or *sui generis* phenomena. From our perspective, metropolitan society and hinterland society are mutually interrelated and their economies mutually interpenetrating; they interact, either cooperatively or competitively, as separate sectors of one system. But there is a fundamental asymmetry: the development of the metropolitan society and economy engenders the underdevelopment of the hinterland society and economy. Nevertheless, "underdevelopment" should not imply "stagnation," and "development" must not imply a monopoly on "dynamism." As an internal colony of the urban-industrial metropolitan centers of the Mexican nation, the Valley of Oaxaca is dependent but not stagnant; and its past or present state of dependency vis-à-vis the metropolises should not imply an absence of structural integrity or internal dynamism.

1. The Peasant Market Economy of the Valley of Oaxaca in Analysis and History

SCOTT COOK AND MARTIN DISKIN

ECONOMIC ANTHROPOLOGY AND THE OAXACA MARKET STUDY

In its thematic focus on marketing this volume falls into the mainstream of economic anthropological inquiry. From its origins in the work of Bronislaw Malinowski, Marcel Mauss, and Richard Thurnwald, economic anthropology has dealt prominently with trade and exchange processes in preindustrial societies (Cook 1973:825–838). As the ethnographic record shows, Malinowski was destined to pursue this interest (which he initiated with his 1922 study of the *kula* trade in the Trobriand Islands, published under the title *Argonauts of the Western Pacific*) into Mesoamerica and, more specifically, into Oaxaca, Mexico. Indeed, it was Malinowski, in collaboration with the Mexican anthropologist Julio de la Fuente, who pioneered the economic anthropological study of the same Valley of Oaxaca marketing system which is the object of analysis in the present volume (see Malinowski and de la Fuente 1957; Essay 2 below).

In the synchronic, functionalist, empiricist tradition of the Malinowski–de la Fuente study, the Beals project held out the possibility of an eclectic, integrative, macroscopic approach to the Oaxaca marketing system, while necessarily devoting much effort to collecting and analyzing an extensive corpus of data dealing with sections or aspects of that system. The project assumed that discrete local communities were not microcosms of regional society but simply units within it, differentially articulated along ecological, economic, social, and cultural axes. The fundamental problem was to determine how the separate sections or units articulated with the regional economy through the marketing system. Consequently, certain essays in this volume deal with specific infrasystem topics (e.g., those of Beverly Chiñas, Scott Cook, Charlotte Stolmaker, and Ronald Waterbury); others are more general and holistic in focus (e.g., those of Ralph Beals and Martin Diskin); and the dominant concern of all the authors is to contribute toward a more precise understanding of the role of the marketing system in regional economic life. The essays by John C. Warner and Richard Berg provide much-needed descriptions of regional marketing systems outside the Valley of Oaxaca—those of the Nochixtlán Valley and the Sierra Zapoteca respectively, whereas Herbert M. Eder's contribution examines another regional economy of Oaxaca from the perspective of cultural geography.

Why are marketing and markets singled out as topics of analysis in these studies and in others of different regional peasant economies in Mesoamerica (e.g., Redfield 1939; McBryde 1947; Foster 1948b; Marroquín 1957; Kaplan 1965; Swetnam 1973)? One of the obvious reasons is that marketplaces are major focal points of regularized social activity for large segments of the rural Mesoamerican population and are indispensable mechanisms of social articulation— serving as arenas for interaction between members of various ethnic groups and classes (Mintz 1959). A second is that through marketplaces certain economic processes are dramatically visible and approachable empirically. As Malinowski and de la Fuente suggest, marketplaces "constitute the principal economic mechanism of distribution; they reveal the form in which people make products available and acquire products for consumption . . . [and] embody the economic organization of each district and locality" (1957:19).[1] Third, marketplaces are indigenous to Mesoamerica and are closely related to the development and elaboration of the division of labor and specialization there. Multiple-marketplace trading systems of the Mesoamerican type presuppose a complex and highly differentiated division of labor and specialization of production on an intra- and intercommunity basis (see Tax 1952:52–56)—a developmental configuration which from the cultural ecological perspective has been referred to as a "symbiotic region" or "ecological mosaic" (see

Sanders 1956; Palerm and Wolf 1957:29–34; Adams 1966:52–54; Sanders and Price 1968:126–138). The Valley of Oaxaca marketing system, with its roots in a pre-Hispanic urban civilization, embodies some well-developed techniques for the movement of goods and ideas and, we believe, is also a fundamental vehicle for socioeconomic development (Diskin 1971:191).

It follows from these and other reasons that the study of marketing is a strategic point of entry into society, economy, and ecology relationships in Mesoamerica. In the various marketplaces, one can study "the people, their material objects, values and customs on exhibit as in an ephemeral, dramatic museum of the day" (Malinowski and de la Fuente 1957:19–20). The marketing system, to paraphrase Eder (see Essay 4 below), can be viewed as a mirror reflecting a representative range of elements comprising a regional sociocultural system. It is clear from our Oaxaca research, just as it was to Malinowski and de la Fuente, that a study of marketing as a phase of the regional economic process must inevitably encompass production, utilization, and distribution; and that production—in its concrete forms of agriculture, animal husbandry, artisanry, etc.—introduces a principle of order and provides the generating force for the regional economy (cf. Malinowski and de la Fuente 1957:85; Cook 1968:4, 8, 29–30, 50).

ASPECTS OF OAXACA'S HISTORICAL DEVELOPMENT AND
SOCIOCULTURAL STRUCTURE

The state of Oaxaca is located in the southeastern part of the Mexican republic, between 15°30' and 18°48' north latitude and between 93°52' and 98°30' west longitude. It shares borders with the states of Puebla and Veracruz to the northeast and north, with Chiapas to the east, with the Pacific Ocean to the south, and with the state of Guerrero to the west (see Appendix, Map 1). With a total surface area of 95,364 square kilometers, equivalent to approximately 4.8 percent of the total surface area of Mexico, Oaxaca is among the most extensive of the thirty-two entities of the Mexican federation (occupying fifth place after Chihuahua, Sonora, Coahuila, and Durango). Oaxaca has 570 *municipios* ("municipalities," roughly equivalent to counties in most of the United States and to "towns" in New England), more than any other Mexican state (25 percent of the national total)—a fact that gives some idea of the extreme degree of political-administrative fragmentation in the state (see UNDP/FAO 1972:4–5).[2]

The Valley of Oaxaca is a principal section of the Central Valleys (Los Valles Centrales) region—the latter being one of the seven traditionally identified regions of the state (see Map A-2).[3] It lies roughly 350 miles south of Mexico City between 16°40′ and 17°20′ north latitude and between 96°15′ and 96°55′ west longitude and has been characterized geographically as follows:

It is drained by two rivers: the upper Río Atoyac, which flows from north to south, and its tributary, the Río Salado or Tlacocula, which flows westward to join the Atoyac near the present city of Oaxaca. The valley is shaped like a Y or three-pointed star, whose center is Oaxaca City and whose southern limit is defined by the Ayoquesco gorge, where the Atoyac River leaves the valley on its way to the Pacific Ocean. The climate is semiarid, with 500 to 700 millimeters of annual rainfall, confined largely to the summer months. The valley-floor elevation averages 1550 meters. (Flannery et al. 1967:446; cf. Lorenzo 1960; UNDP/FAO 1972:5–11; Kirkby 1973:7–25)

While this hydrographic and geological description is accurate and the zone has exhibited cultural integrity, it is too narrowly circumscribed to encompass the present limits of the plaza system. This may be due to the historical expansion of the system through the activities of traders or military conquerors. In any case, the district of Miahuatlán—which lies outside of the Valley of Oaxaca as delimited above—is certainly an integral part of the present marketing system and has been since the fifteenth-century Aztec occupation of the Valley. In fact, when there was royal intervention during the colonial period, with the removal of the marketplace from Miahuatlán to Chichicapan because of the Aztec sale of slaves, complaints about interruption of local marketing patterns led to a successful petition to the crown to restore the plaza to Miahuatlán in 1591 (Diskin 1967:42–43).

Human occupation of the Valley of Oaxaca probably dates back several millennia before the Christian era. Recent archaeological findings suggest that it may have been the site for the domestication of several cultigens (maguey, maize) that are still of basic importance today (Flannery 1968). The urban ceremonial center of Monte Albán, built at the beginning of the Christian era, presents evidence of regional coherence through pottery styles and other artifacts that encompassed most of the territory within the present limits of the Valley of Oaxaca or of the Valley Zapotec region (Paddock, ed. 1966; Spores 1965; Sanders 1972:143–145). Archival evidence dating from the Spanish conquest supports the thesis that the region maintained its integrity after the conquest and also indicates that a marketing system existed by that time (Mendieta y Núñez 1949:xiii–xviii; Diskin 1967:Chap. 2; Taylor 1972:Chap. 1). This system presumably served the Zapotec inhabitants of the region, but was also used by the Aztecs during their phase of imperialist expansion and was taken over by the Spaniards during the colonial period. In fact, the most compelling evidence for the sustained, systemic nature of the region lies in the functional versatility through time of the same basic organizational forms. Today, in the Oaxaca marketing system, services and transactions of political, religious, legal, economic, and medical types all flow through channels that have existed for centuries (cf. Diskin 1971:195).

The Spanish conquest of the Valley of Oaxaca, in contrast to earlier Mixtec and Aztec intrusions, was spiritual and exploitative rather than military. Its spiritual representatives were the friars of the Dominican order; its exploitative apparatus operated through the twin colonial economic institutions of encomienda and repartimiento and their executors, the Spanish landowners, mine operators, settlers, and administrators; under these institutions indigenous land and labor were exploited for Spanish profit (cf. Taylor 1972; Hamnett 1971). Oaxaca City, founded as an Aztec garrison (Huaxyacac —see note 2 above) in the fifteenth century, became the control center of the Spanish colonization effort and exploitative apparatus in the sixteenth century, when it became known as Antequera. The power holders were not exclusively Creole landowners, as was true elsewhere in New Spain (e.g., the Bajío), but *alcaldes mayores* and Spanish peninsular merchants; and, of course, the Dominicans— especially during the late sixteenth and seventeenth centuries. This reflects the fact that the encomienda and repartimiento did not contribute toward the establishment of landed estates to the degree that they did in central and northern Mexico (Chevalier 1963:117–147). The crown was also reluctant to divide the fertile land in the Valley of Oaxaca among the Spaniards for fear that to do so would deprive the dense Indian population of its livelihood (Chevalier 1963:51).

During the colonial period the corporate Indian communities provisioned the city with goods and services necessary for its existence (via tribute and other means). However, given the significant number of landed estates held by various religious orders (especially Dominicans and Jesuits) by 1750 (Taylor 1969:319–358; 1972), it is likely that these also were a source of the urban food supply in the

Valley of Oaxaca as they were elsewhere in New Spain (see Simpson 1970:viii–ix). In any case, Oaxaca City (Antequera) became firmly established as the dominant urban center of an extensive rural hinterland with many peasant-Indian villages, several ecclesiastical and private estates, and a few mestizo towns. As Taylor points out, the city "was first and foremost a politico-administrative community, a patrimonial center" and was of secondary importance as a commercial center; the peasant-Indian communities of the hinterland, during the colonial period, "maintained at least a semi-independent position" and "were largely inner-directed in their economic activities" (1971:11). This inner-direction, however, is not to be confused with self-sufficiency; rather it was a reflection of the extent to which each community had, in fact, become integrated into a multi-community division of labor and specialization of production organized around the plaza.

It should also be pointed out that during the eighteenth century Oaxaca City was an important center in the cochineal trade and that many of the hinterland villages and towns were involved in the cultivation of *nopaleras* and the sale of its precious insect dyestuff (Dahlgren 1963; Hamnett 1971). Likewise, cotton and cotton-mantle trades involved Oaxaca City–based merchants during this period— just as the silk trade had undoubtedly done during the sixteenth century (Hamnett 1971:1–8). Certainly Oaxaca City and, inevitably, its hinterland were brought into the sphere of international market operations relatively early in the colonial period. But the incorporation of the Valley of Oaxaca economy into the European mercantile capitalist system did not deprive it of its own structure and dynamic embedded in a precapitalist mode of production.

Whether one looks at Valley of Oaxaca society as a congeries of separate peasant-Indian communities surrounding a preindustrial city, as an intercultural region, or as a class-stratified metropolis/hinterland system, he or she is apt to view it diachronically in terms of models derived from the study of other regions of Mexico. However, recent studies of Oaxaca suggest that it has developed institutionally in ways that diverge significantly from those in the north, west, and central regions, as well as in other areas of the south. Taylor (1972), for example, argues that land-tenure patterns and related institutions in Oaxaca differed substantially from those described by Chevalier (1963) and other authors for central and northern Mexico; and as noted above Hamnett (1971:3) contrasts Oaxaca to the Bajío and suggests that it was not so much dominated by Creole landowners as by the *alcaldes mayores* and Spanish peninsular merchants.

With regard to marketing arrangements it is tempting to apply to Oaxaca models that emerge from the historical record in the Tarascan area (e.g., Zavala and Miranda 1954:48; Kaplan 1965), where the active intervention of Spanish colonial authorities is well documented and involved, among other things, the establishment of a major new marketplace in the dominant Spanish settlement of Valladolid de Michoacán. According to Silvio Zavala and José Miranda: "The Indian *tianguis* (market) was the first thing that the Spanish sought to introduce in their settlements in order to assure the provisioning of the population. And they even tried on one occasion to impede the operation of markets in some Indian towns so as to improve the market in the Spanish city" (1954:48). As it turns out, a similar policy was followed by the local Spanish administrators in Antequera, where a marketplace was established to meet the needs of the growing urban population. But the pre-Hispanic Indian marketplaces in Ocotlán, Ayoquezco, Etla, and other towns were essentially undisturbed by Spanish meddling. The paternalistic colonial policy of segregating Indians from Spaniards and *castas* led the viceregal government to support the autonomy and independence of the Indian marketing system in the Valley (Taylor 1971:8–9). Thus, what was true for the Tarascan region was only partly so in the Valley of Oaxaca.

Emerging in the Antequera hinterland out of the colonial period was a distinctive socioeconomic formation encompassing (*a*) a series of discrete village social structures in which the component households were stratified in a civil-religious hierarchy consisting of a series of ranked and age-graded posts, or *cargos*; (*b*) a fiesta or ceremonial cycle in which sponsorship of major saints' cult celebrations (*mayordomías*) was often obligatory and always prestigeful in proportion to its cost (thus reinforcing already-existing class relationships); (*c*) obligatory communal labor service (*tequio*) for the performance of work on village projects (e.g., irrigation canals, communal field cultivation and harvesting, construction of public buildings); (*d*) an institutionalized mechanism for reciprocal exchange known as *guelaguetza*; (*e*) intervillage production specialization and the concomitant importance of artisans and traders; (*f*) a cyclical marketplace organization to facilitate intercommunity trade; (*g*) a peasant-Indian labor force conditioned to exploitative work arrangements (peonage, wage labor) and involved in production for exchange as well as for use; and (*h*) a clear-cut division in society between producers and nonproducers, with tribute, taxation, or other mechanisms for the systematic appropriation of the surplus product of the former class by the latter (cf. Carrasco 1951; Mendieta y Núñez, ed. 1949; Wolf 1967). This was, in essence, an advanced precapitalist formation in which the indigenous modes of production—incorporating household and suprahousehold units of production, relations of production, ownership of the means of production, and processes of distribution—were partially integrated with and subsumed by a dominant mercantile capitalist system. Within this colonialized indigenous formation, land and labor remained substantially within the noncommodity or simple-commodity sphere of circulation. By 1800, then, in the Valley of Oaxaca economy the social process of production was still not dominated throughout by exchange value (see Essay 12 for a fuller discussion of this concept). With the rise of free-enterprise capitalism under the "liberal" regimes of the second half of the nineteenth century, the sphere of dominance of exchange value expanded in Oaxaca as it did through Mexico (Aguilar Monteverde 1968: esp. Chaps. 6 and 7; Pozas and Pozas 1973:Chap. 4).

ECONOMY AND SOCIETY IN CONTEMPORARY OAXACA

Today, in a Mexico which during the nineteenth century achieved and consolidated its political independence as a nation and which during the present century has experienced a major social revolution (1910–1920) and its institutionalization, accompanied by industrialization and urbanization as generated by capitalist development, the basic patterns of rural Oaxaca life would not be totally alien to the peasant of the eighteenth or nineteenth century.

There has, of course, been change in Oaxaca, some of it fundamental, especially since 1940. But its rhythm, content, and intensity have been shaped by the dialectic between indigenous production and trading institutions on the one hand and the predatory demands of expanded capitalist reproduction on the other. The metropolitan influence has not been powerful enough to totally commercialize or nationalize every aspect of regional life. This inability, sometimes due to economic reasons, ineffective state policy, or contradictions between metropolitan, regional, and local bourgeoisies, has left a partial vacuum, which has been responded to from the versatile repertory of peasant strategies in the areas of production, exchange, village politics, and the preservation of local autonomy and corporateness (cf. Wolf 1955; 1956).

The over-all picture is one of dynamic equilibrium in social terms, or stagnation in the economic sense. It is also a picture of underdevelopment, with the region bound to national and foreign metropolitan interests in a dependent way (Frank 1969: esp. Chaps. 19 and 20). While, over the centuries, the Valley of Oaxaca population has maintained many indigenous cultural features, these now seem in opposition to national capitalist development. As the Oaxaca case clearly illustrates, a major problem for the future management of national and regional economic growth in Mexico is how to harness classical peasant defensiveness to humane developmental goals (see Avila 1969:Chap. 6; Flores 1970:esp. Chaps. 6 and 9).

This dependent status is reflected in the demographic profile of the Valley of Oaxaca since the eve of the Spanish conquest, when its native population is estimated to have been about 350,000 (Taylor 1972:17). After the conquest the population declined steadily until bottoming out in the 1630's at 40,000–45,000 (Taylor 1972: 18); and by 1960 it had not yet reached its preconquest level again. According to the 1960 census the total population of the combined settlements in the Valley (excluding Oaxaca City) was just over 207,000 (density 57.5 per square kilometer), and Oaxaca City had a population of 72,370 (giving the Valley a total population of 279,467, or roughly one-fourth of the total state population). The 1970 census puts the Oaxaca City population at 100,000 and gives the Valley a total population of 348,000, to finally approximate the 350,000 high mark of 475 years ago.[4]

The Oaxaca economy is dominated by agriculture: in 1968 more than three-fourths of the total state population lived in rural areas— the majority of them (64 percent) in settlements of less than 1,000 inhabitants (contrasted with 43.8 percent of the total population of the Central Valleys living in settlements larger than 2,500) (UNDP/FAO 1972:51). Moreover, approximately 80 percent of the economically active population is involved in some type of agricultural occupation, with most of the secondary and tertiary occupations related to industrial processing or marketing of agricultural products. With regard to land tenure, 30 percent of the total area censused in 1960 was comprised of 13,986 privately owned parcels of more than five hectares, while 138,505 privately owned parcels of five hectares or less accounted for only 3 percent of the total area.

In addition, there were 506 communal land units, which accounted for 38 percent of the total area, and 509 *ejidos* (agrarian reform units), which accounted for 13 percent—the remaining land area being held in the form of federal, state, or municipal property. Only one-fifth of the total land area was cultivated in 1960, and 92 percent of the cultivated land was worked seasonally by rainfall agriculture (*de temporal*); only 40 percent of the latter land is under cultivation during any one year—the remainder lying fallow (UNDP/FAO 1972:51).

In 1968 it was estimated that some 590,000 persons—including producers, unremunerated family members, and employed wage-earners—worked the land in Oaxaca. Together with hunting and fishing, which occupied an estimated 4,000 Oaxacans, agriculture generated 31 percent of the gross product of the state economy in that same year (UNDP/FAO 1972:51). The various industrial and agricultural censuses available for Oaxaca provide a basis for estimating per capita productivity and other measures of the economic performance of the "economically active population" in various occupational categories and sectors of the economy. But such censuses ignore the "tens of thousands of 'marginal producers' who are registered in the economically active population for census purposes, but who in reality belong to the group . . . of self-sufficient agriculturists . . . small artisans, palm weavers, itinerant peddlars; in other words, all those marginal workers who . . . are included in the economically active population for general population census purposes but who are not registered in the economic censuses as employed personnel, and whose production doesn't appear in the statistical computations of regional income" (UNDP/FAO 1972:51–52). It is, of course, the productive labor of these so-called marginal peasant-artisans (two-thirds of whom are categorized as producing no surplus above the subsistence needs of their households [ibid.:28]) which is of principal concern to economic anthropologists and which is the social reproductive engine of the regional economy.

Within this regional agricultural economy, the contemporary peasant-artisan villagers of the Valley of Oaxaca make their living by tilling the soil (cultivating the basic crop triumvirate of maize, beans, and squash, plus a wide variety of other subsistence and cash crops), by practicing animal husbandry (cattle, sheep, goats, pigs, and poultry), and by producing a wide variety of artisan products (e.g., pottery, metates, baskets, sarapes and other woven goods, rope, furniture and other wood products). Wage labor, either within the village or intervillage sector or involving temporary seasonal migration to urban areas in the Valley or in other regions, has provided an important source of cash income for the Oaxaca peasant household for many decades and is becoming increasingly important and widespread. Agricultural technology remains simple, with the ox-drawn plow, the machete, the hoe (*coa*), the sickle (*hoz*), and, perhaps, the crowbar (*barreta*) and the shovel (*pala*) comprising the basic tool kit; tractors and water pumps are available in the region, but their use is restricted because of the limited availability of money and credit. Both channel and pot irrigation, which are pre-Columbian in origin (Flannery et al. 1967; Lees 1973), are widely practiced, but agricultural production still depends heavily on precipitation patterns and *temporal* lands; rainfall is seasonal, with the rainy season occurring from April to September or October each year. Cultivation tends to be limited to fields lying outside the habitation area of nucleated villages, though there is cultivation of garden plots within or near residence lots in most villages. Permanent cultivation occurs only in the presence of irrigation, and irrigated lands yield two crops annually. Manure is used as fertilizer, and seed selection is practiced (though not to the extent that special hybrids are in widespread use) (see Kirkby 1973 for a detailed analysis of agriculture in the Valley).

Guelaguetza is the Valley Zapotec term for reciprocal exchange; and, in the ceremonial context (it also operates in the production sector as a labor exchange mechanism), it operates on the principle that the recipient of goods is obligated to reciprocate in kind when the donor requests him to do so (cf. Martínez Ríos 1964; Cook 1968:113–115, 125–132; Beals 1970). This mechanism is relied upon by most villagers to mobilize wealth to meet expenditures entailed in the sponsorship of celebrations on important ceremonial occasions—usually *mayordomías* (saint's-day festivals) and *fandangos* (wedding celebrations). The typical Valley Zapotec household has a *guelaguetza* account book (*libro de guelaguetzas*) containing an itemized list of its payment claims (loans it has made) and payment obligations (loans it has received) in the ceremonial reciprocity network. *Guelaguetza* obligations are inheritable, and even those debtors who move out of their natal community are expected to meet the obligations they contracted while residing there (or to make new loans). The survivors of a deceased *guelaguetza* debtor are held both morally and legally (in terms of the local judiciary system) responsible for paying his or her debts and have the right to call in loans still outstanding that were made during the deceased's lifetime. Inevitably, the Zapotec villager's participation in the ceremonial exchange network has important implications for his plans and calculations with regard to saving, capital accumulation, and investment. Or, put differently, a household's economizing strategies will reflect the shape of its ceremonial balance of payments (i.e., the relation between its *guelaguetza* payment claims upon other households and its *guelaguetza* payment obligations to other households). One of the reasons why the Valley Zapotec household acquires or accumulates liquid assets (e.g., poultry, pigs, goats) or cash is to enable it to meet *guelaguetza* obligations as the need to do so arises.

Perhaps the outstanding feature of the Valley of Oaxaca economy is its cyclical marketing organization, in which a series of marketplaces operate on a rotating basis on separate days of the week and in different locales (cf. Malinowski and de la Fuente 1957; Beals 1967a; Diskin 1969; Waterbury 1970). It is clear that prior to the arrival of the Spanish in the region there were daily markets in the most important indigenous population centers that facilitated the exchange of agricultural and nonagricultural products (Mendieta y Núñez, ed. 1949:xviii). It is also reasonable to suppose that the emergence of Antequera as a control center of the colonial trade in cochineal and cotton products (see above) reinforced the growth of its *tianguis* (Cámara 1966) in the regional marketing system. We can also assume, in the absence of data to the contrary, that the entire Valley marketing system did undergo significant changes (e.g., nature and volume of transactions, role of credit, types of goods traded, role inventories) in response to the constant dialectical interplay between indigenous precapitalist and the intrusive and developing capitalist modes of production. Today, at any rate, Oaxaca City is the hub of this system, which is maintained through a network of mutually interdependent settlements. The towns and villages of the hinterland supply agricultural and handicraft products, as well as labor services, to the city; and they are consumers of the goods and services that the city produces or distributes as a distribution center for products manufactured in the national industrial economy or from the commercial agricultural sector. Eric R. Wolf presents a succinct description of these marketing relationships in the Valley of Oaxaca:

> Although many transactions in the market are between small-scale producers who in a few cases exchange goods directly . . . or indirectly by converting goods into money and money back into goods, the market is also a place in which buyers from outside collect produce with the pur-

pose of shipping it elsewhere or offer goods for sale which have been manufactured beyond the limits of the region. The market is thus characterized not only by horizontal relationships between individuals or communities, but also contains the vertical channels through which commercial institutions operating at levels higher than the community tap the supplies of purchasing power found at lower levels. (1967:302)

The typical village ties into this organization through the marketplace in Oaxaca City, where trade is conducted daily (although Saturday is the principal trading day, or *día de plaza*), and through the marketplace in a district headquarters town or *cabecera* (e.g., Etla, Tlacolula, Ocotlán, Zimatlán, Zaachila, Ejutla), where plaza is held on a particular day of the week. Many villagers, as buyers and sellers, commute daily between their home village and Oaxaca City and weekly between their village and the district town to transact business in the marketplace. By no means all of the external trade of the typical village, however, is channeled through the formal city and town marketplaces. A significant volume of trade (no accurate estimates are available) is conducted outside the cyclical marketplace system through bypass arrangements on a direct village-to-village basis or between villagers and town- or city-based merchants or buyers.

OAXACA, REGIONAL UNDERDEVELOPMENT, AND THE NATIONAL SOCIOECONOMIC STRUCTURE

Given these salient features of society and economy in the Valley of Oaxaca, how can we characterize the entire region vis-à-vis the regional and class-organized structure of Mexican national society? What is the status of Oaxaca in the Mexican nation's past and present? How has the process of nationalization and national integration in Mexico affected the Valley of Oaxaca population? To answer these questions we must temporarily detach ourselves from the Oaxaca material and examine some of the problems in the relationship between anthropology and society that are currently being debated by Mexican scholars.

The social anthropology of Mexico has developed during the past several decades as an enterprise involving Mexican and non-Mexican practitioners. Though many ideologies and methodological permutations match the variety of interests and interpretations that have manifested themselves in this field of study (e.g., Nash 1967a; Bonfil 1966; Warman et al. 1970; Pozas and Pozas 1973), one basic difference, according to Gonzalo Aguirre Beltrán (1970b), is between *in-*

digenistas and *indianistas*. In his words, the "*indigenista* has focused his attention on the nation as a global entity and not on the Indian as a particular entity" (ibid:284). The *indigenista* orientation first arose with the Spanish discovery and conquest of Mexico, when, to again quote Aguirre Beltrán, "the Spaniard on confronting the reality of the Indian was obliged to adopt a position and to take action with reference to that reality," and it continues today, as shown by the fact that the Mexican national government "has established a way of contemplating and of treating the vernacular populations that maintain a parochial identity and a weak relationship with the wider society" (ibid.). The unit of analysis for the *indianista* has always been subnational and, most typically, subregional, for example, a tribe, village, or *municipio*. *Indianista* descriptive and analytic goals focus on study and comparison of local communities rather than community-nation articulation or general problems of national integration. *Indianista* inquiry is often synchronic rather than diachronic. It is fair to say that most Mexican anthropologists represent the *indigenista* tradition (which, in turn, has its own internal differences, hinging primarily around the issue of the hows and whys of integration of the indigenous peoples into national life), whereas most *indianistas* are non-Mexican (especially North Americans).

What are some of the aspects and implications of the development of *indigenismo*? During the conquest period, social arrangements took shape that reflected the colonialist interests of the Spanish as well as the nature of indigenous society. Ideas or attitudes concerning the conquered Indian population were of great importance in determining the course of development of Spanish-Indian relations. For example, to justify *reducciones*, Spanish administrators labeled dispersed native settlement patterns as uncivilized and proceeded to resettle and congregate Indians as the most expedient means to Christianize, urbanize, and civilize them (cf. Zavala and Miranda 1954:39). Likewise, during the eighteenth century, Spanish ideology concerning the customs and institutions of the indigenous population was important in the dispute over rural administration between the *alcalde mayor–aviador* and the *plan de intendencias* (cf. Hamnett 1971:Chap. 5). According to Brian R. Hamnett: "The Viceroys stated that it was a well-known fact that the Indians were lazy, idle, and degenerate, abhorring all forms of labor. By their nature they were inclined to drunkenness and vice. If they were not forced to work, the fields would be uncultivated, and the mines unexploited. If they were not forced to receive clothing, they would be content to live naked" (1971:20).

At a later time, during the Porfiriate—with the dissolution of village corporate landholdings that had begun with the 1857 Laws of Reform—Mexico's socioeconomic development was said to be impeded by the Indians, who were considered as nonproductive, inferior peoples (Brandenberg 1964:41; Wolf 1969:14). During the postrevolutionary period (after 1920) and until quite recently, the central thesis of the *indigenistas* (e.g., Manuel Gamio and his followers) has been that "all indigenous culture must be replaced by the institutions of modern culture" and that "the ultimate identity of Mexico can only be based on the symbols of Western industrial, capitalist culture" (Aguirre Beltrán 1970*a*:131–132)—or, among some *indigenistas* who did not employ an anthropological concept of "culture" (e.g., Alfonso Caso), the perceived task was to solve the Indians' problems by taking "culture" to them (Pozas and Pozas 1973:14). In other words, the purpose of a whole generation of postrevolutionary Mexican *indigenistas* has been to "replace the negative traits of the Indian cultures with positive modern ones" (Aguirre Beltrán 1970*a*). On the other hand, the *indianistas* have simply documented these changes in segments of the Indian population or have pursued "salvage ethnography" while ostensibly remaining "neutral" in matters of national developmental policy (cf. Pozas and Pozas 1973:Chap. 1).

Aguirre Beltrán has himself contributed a theory of regional structure to the *indigenista* tradition based upon his concept of the "intercultural region" as the unit of analysis (1967). He describes this approach as follows: "The study and investigation of the isolated community, as the facts showed, lacked transcendent importance if its socioeconomic interdependence with another nucleus around which it revolved was not considered and emphasized; such a study and investigation would be inadequate if, at the same time, one did not study and investigate the complex system of regional integration in its totality—[a system] which incorporates within it a dominant mestizo nucleus in whose orbit indigenous and nonindigenous folk communities revolved as satellites" (1970*c*:141). This "intercultural region" comprises a system of interethnic relations operating through a "dominical process," which Aguirre defines as the domination exercised by technically and economically more advanced groups over those with less complex forms of life and organi-

zation (1967:1). In the intercultural regions of Mexico this dominical process operates through the following mechanisms: social
segregation, political control, economic dependence, unequal treatment, social distance, and evangelical action (ibid.:11–17). These
regions, Aguirre argues, are characterized by rigid caste structures
in which the indigenous population is subordinate to the Ladino
nucleus and the indigenous hinterland has strictly defined obligations toward the Ladino city.

The intercultural-region/dominical-process model was derived primarily from research in the Chiapas highlands, where the Ladino
city of San Cristóbal Las Casas dominates a hinterland of Tzeltal-
Tzotzil peoples. A problem arises, therefore, as to its applicability
to the Valley of Oaxaca and its hinterland. Unlike the highland
Chiapas area, the Valley of Oaxaca is not a "refuge region" with a
"hostile ecology" (Aguirre Beltrán 1967); it has been a zone of sedentary occupation for human populations dating back to around
1500 B.C. (Flannery et al. 1967:447), a fact which reflects its diverse
and hospitable ecology.

While the Valley has been an arena for Ladino-Indian interaction
since the sixteenth century, we do not see there the inexorable un-
folding through time of progressively greater control of Indians by
Ladinos. Ladino-Indian relations in the Valley of Oaxaca have not
been characterized by the blatant Ladino exploitation of the Indian
documented for Chiapas (de la Fuente 1967; Stavenhagen 1965)
and the Mixteca (Marroquín 1957:207–214). There was, of course,
considerable abuse of indigenous labor by the Spanish during the
colonial period, which is reflected in the severe population decline
between contact and the seventeenth century (Taylor 1972:28–29).
But, perhaps because of the failure of the hacienda system to develop as extensively here as it did in other areas of Mexico, the bulk
of the Indian population of the Valley of Oaxaca escaped many of
the most directly exploitative and abusive aspects of the dominical
process. The historical records suggest that many of the landholding
villages in the Valley were, from the beginning of the colonial period, very aggressive and skillful in successfully defending their
lands against Spaniards or others who sought to acquire them (cf.
Taylor 1969:373–374, 1971:8; de la Fuente 1965:31–32). However,
the Spanish-mestizo population, during the colonial period at least,
showed little interest in farming or the ownership of arable land and
was content to depend upon the corporate Indian villages for the
bulk of its food supply (Taylor 1971:7). In short, the Valley of

Oaxaca was and continues to be a region in which the indigenous population has exercised substantial autonomy in the realms of production and exchange.

While it is clear that the Valley of Oaxaca is a region of concentrated indigenous population, it is not possible to distinguish easily Indians from mestizos on the basis of the usual criteria of language, dress, local community corporateness, etc. And even if it were possible to do this, the results would be of questionable value, since social relations in contemporary Valley society are not organized along ethnic lines. We share Aguirre Beltrán's view that "the Indian who participates in a community culture must not be considered simply as an individual who belongs to the country's working class" (1970c: 150); but in the Valley of Oaxaca "ethnicity" does not function in interpersonal relations to bind city and town to village.

In the plazas, for example, our observations of interaction between representatives of various segments of the Valley population suggest that it is more accurate to identify strata in terms of place of residence (i.e., village, town, or city) rather than in terms of cultural or ethnic affiliation (see Essay 3 below). There are isolated incidents involving discriminatory pricing by sellers against non-Spanish-speaking buyers (Indians or tourists), but such discrimination reflects the seller's opportunistic pursuit of a profit-maximizing strategy (based on his evaluation of the place of origin of the buyer) rather than systematic exploitation of ethnic differences. Julio de la Fuente, who has included the Valley of Oaxaca in his comprehensive analysis of ethnic relations in Middle America (1967), regularly distinguishes social relations in this region from those in other intercultural regions because they are not based on castelike distinctions between Ladinos or mestizos and Indians (e.g., in access to public facilities, like amusement parks, theaters, or private businesses serving the public, like barbershops or restaurants).

There is still another dimension in which the intercultural-region/dominical-process model does not apply to the Valley of Oaxaca. Although the spatial patterning of settlements follows the village-town-city progression in the Valley, it is not necessarily true that the villagers (or townsmen) are isolated from the so-called "great tradition," or "civilization" in Robert Redfield's sense, which implies that they must come to the city in order to experience "urban culture." It is inherent in the cyclical plaza system that the sociocultural structure of the region is replicated each week in the plaza towns. Indeed, what we mean by saying that the cyclical plaza system integrates the region is that, for any resident of one of the plaza towns or one of its associated villages, attendance at the plaza is functionally equivalent to a trip to the city. To a significant degree, in the Valley of Oaxaca, the city "comes" to the hinterland through the plaza system (cf. Diskin 1971).

As an alternative to a regional model based on interethnic relations, the Chiapas model, or the internal-colonialism model (González Casanova 1965:89–108), Pozas and Pozas's work on interclass relations is suggestive for the Valley of Oaxaca. Use of a class analysis makes it possible to consider the region within the framework of capitalist development (Pozas and Pozas 1973:27–33). Accordingly, Valley of Oaxaca society would be viewed as a dual class (bourgeoisie/proletariat) structure of multiple levels (medium and small bourgeoisie, proletariat proper, semiproletariat, subproletariat, and lumpenproletariat) and sectors (e.g., industrial, commercial, agricultural, artisan) (ibid.:130–155). The peasantry, then, does not comprise a separate class in the Valley social structure; the great majority of peasants are members of the proletariat (semi- or sub-), though some also belong to the bourgeoisie (ibid.:134–136). Land-tenure status (e.g., ownership, usufruct) together with the social relations entailed in working the land must be examined to determine the class level and sector of peasants (ibid.). Some peasants who own substantial amounts of land may lease or rent or sharecrop it or work it with hired labor—establishing themselves in the process as members of the small or middle bourgeoisie; others may be landless or have access to insignificant amounts of infertile land and, therefore, be obliged to turn to wage labor, sharecropping, artisanry, etc., to make a living—thus establishing themselves as members of the semi- or subproletariat. In any event, the populations of Valley communities participate in and circulate through various levels and sectors of the class structure (ibid.:136–137). It should be noted that the operations of the rural bourgeoisie in the Valley (e.g., businessmen, medium to large landowners, small industrial operators, government functionaries) are essentially in the rural sector, even though they reside in urban centers (cf. Stavenhagen 1970:258–268). In the larger towns and villages of the Valley (e.g., Tlacolula, Ocotlán, San Pedro Apóstol, Ayoquezco, Mitla, Zaachila) the resident population includes representatives of most, if not all, of these classes. It is not coincidental, of course, that these larger settlements are usually sites of important marketplaces.

Rodolfo Stavenhagen argues, and we concur, that in the more

underdeveloped regions of Mexico, like Oaxaca, "the oppositions and contradictions between social classes at the local and regional level very often lose their importance as compared with the larger opposition represented by the subordination of the region as a whole to the dominant centers or 'metropoli' of the country, that is, the large cities and the areas of rapid economic growth" (1970:267). That Oaxaca is among these dominated regions with an impoverished rural population is indicated in several macrostudies of the Mexican socioeconomic structure (e.g., Lamartine Yates 1965:19, 41, 79, 103; González Casanova 1965:105–155; Padilla Aragón 1969: 102–103; Singer 1969: esp. 149–153; Stavenhagen 1970:267) and has been confirmed by the field experiences of most anthropologists who have worked in the Valley or other areas of Oaxaca and have observed the occupational destinations of villagers who migrate to the cities (as servants, gardeners, maids, cooks, construction laborers, street sweepers, garbage collectors, prostitutes, etc.).

In a recent socioeconomic survey,[5] Oaxaca was cited as the area of least development in Mexico during the decade between 1950 and 1960; the difference between it and the area of highest development (the Federal District) changed from 11 points in 1950 to roughly 12.6 points in 1960 (ibid.: 61–62). This "stagnant" situation reflects the facts that during the 1950's and into the 1960's more than 80 percent of the total active labor force in Oaxaca was employed in the agricultural sector (compared to just over 50 percent of the total active labor force in Mexico as a whole), that only .5 percent of the total industrial output of the Mexican economy originated in Oaxaca, and that the per capita productivity of the Oaxaca laborer was roughly 25 percent of the national average (Secretaría de Industria y Comercio, Dirección General de Estadísticas 1969; Ibarra et al., eds. 1972:70–71).

The "underdeveloped" state of the Oaxaca economy is vividly outlined in the following concise statement from the recent comprehensive socioeconomic study by the United Nations Development Program and the Food and Agricultural Organization (UNDP/ FAO):

... its population corresponds to 4.5 percent of the total national population; nevertheless, the gross state product of Oaxaca in 1968 was hardly 1.4 percent of the gross national product. Between 1960 and 1968, the Oaxaca population increased at a rate corresponding to two-thirds of the national rate, but the increment of the gross product was less than three-fifths of the national rate; therefore, the relative position of the average inhabi-

tant of Oaxaca has worsened in comparison with the average Mexican. . . .
In 1968, the average per capita output for the economically active Oaxacan
was estimated as $2,209 pesos, or somewhat more than $6 pesos daily,
compared with $20 pesos daily for the average Mexican. The life expec-
tancy of the average Oaxacan is fifty-three years, while for the average
Mexican, it is sixty-one years. (UNDP/FAO 1972:28; editors' translation)

Elsewhere in this same report the following facts are adduced to
portray Oaxaca's relatively impoverished status:

Oaxaca had, in 1967, the second highest general mortality rate and the
highest rate of morbidity in Mexico, and according to the 1960 census, was
seventeenth—among the thirty-two federated entities—with respect to
the proportion of the total population in per capita wheat consumption;
twentieth with regard to consumption of meat, fish, milk and eggs; twenty-
first with respect to the proportion of dwellings constructed of adobe or
wattle and daub; twenty-seventh with regard to the number of persons per
room; and in last place in the index of families without radios, television
sets, electric irons . . . and sewing machines. Oaxaca was in second place in
1960 with respect to the highest rate of illiteracy. (UNDP/FAO 1972:53;
editors' translation)

Within this generalized structure of underdevelopment and impov-
erishment in the state of Oaxaca, the Central Valleys region is
relatively less underdeveloped and impoverished (vis-à-vis national
averages) than other regions. Together with the regions of Tuxtepec-
Choapam and the Isthmus, it is, in the words of the UNDP/FAO
study, of "greater economic importance and greater relative development" (p. 35) in terms of several different quantitative indices (e.g.,
output of principal agricultural products and livestock, total value of
economic transactions, capital investments) than the four other regions of the state, whose economies are substantially more depressed.

Granted that these macroeconomic survey data are only rough statistical approximations of the concrete realities of daily economic life
in Oaxaca, they do show that a large majority of Oaxacans belong to
the "Mexico which has not" rather than to the "Mexico which has"
(González Casanova 1966). Moreover, as census data from the various villages studied in the Oaxaca Market Study Project unequiv-
ocally demonstrate about these specific populations (and enable us
to infer with reasonable accuracy about others), a large proportion
of the people who regularly participate in the Valley of Oaxaca marketing system are *minifundistas* (i.e., smallholders, or members of an
agricultural unit that is too small to give full employment to two
adults and to adequately satisfy the needs of a peasant family [Sta-

venhagen 1970:231–233]) and/or rural semi- or subproletarians who, on a seasonal or part-time basis, engage in nonagricultural wage labor as a necessary complement to their subsistence-geared agricultural activities. These, in essence, are people whose existential situation vis-à-vis other sectors of the Mexican national population (especially those in urban-industrial sectors) is characterized by lack of employment opportunities, low standard of living, low incomes, inferior and limited education, lack of capital and credit facilities, and lower life expectancies.

Given present trends in Mexican national development, which include increasing urban overpopulation as well as unemployment and underemployment in the industrial sector of the economy, it is likely that the *minifundista/jornalero* adaptation of the Valley of Oaxaca peasant-artisan will continue in its present form. This situation will obtain until Mexican national development priorities and policies are radically altered from their present course (cf. Stavenhagen 1970: 257). This is so because, as Stavenhagen notes in his analysis of Mexican agrarian structure, "even though marginalized from the process of economic development," the subsistence *minifundio* "fulfills a function at the present historical moment: it contributes to fix the population on the land to provide minimum subsistence to those who otherwise would perhaps have none" (ibid.). In the absence of a regional economy integrated through a system of periodic marketplaces, our studies suggest that *minifundio* agriculture would probably not be able to fulfill this imperative of social reproduction. In conclusion, we agree with Malinowski and de la Fuente's judgment that, in the underdeveloping regional economy of the Valley of Oaxaca, the "function of the market is closely related to the miserable existence of the poorest [peasants]" (1957:32).

2. The Oaxaca Market Study Project: Origins, Scope, and Preliminary Findings

RALPH L. BEALS

The regional marketing networks of Middle America and the color-ful Indian marketplaces that in some areas function on a rotating weekly basis have attracted the attention of observers since con-quest times. Cortez gave an account of the Tlaxcala marketplace in his second letter to the crown. Bernal Díaz del Castillo and Bernar-dino de Sahagún described Aztec marketplaces and traders in some detail. Recently Manning Nash (1967b) has given a comprehensive overview of Middle American marketplaces, but his generalizations rest on an inadequate informational basis, and the Oaxaca data sug-gest that some modifications may be necessary. Some of the earlier studies by anthropologists and geographers that include material on traditional Indian economies (e.g., Beals, Foster, de la Fuente, Les-lie, Marroquín, Nader, Nahmad, Parsons, and West in Mexico; Mc-Bryde and Tax in Guatemala) are included in the reference list. A number of these works give some data on marketing networks or systems, but the majority are village-oriented rather than system-oriented. A noteworthy exception for Oaxaca is the incompletely published study by Malinowski and de la Fuente (1957); but, as Tax (1953) described the market system of the Lake Atitlán region of Guatemala from the viewpoint of the village of Panajachel, so Malinowski and de la Fuente discussed the market system of the Oaxaca region primarily from the viewpoint of Oaxaca City. Nevertheless, their work was basic to the formulation of the Oaxaca Market Study Project. In addition, Waterbury and I were influenced by our own unpublished field work and observations over several years, in my case extending back to 1933.

Initially, two major points seemed evident: (a) the traditional marketing system of the Oaxaca region retains great vitality and integrity and offers a good opportunity for a study addressed to the nature and operation of such a system; and (b) since the Malinowski and de la Fuente study around 1940, the influence of the modern national economy has expanded enormously. Corollaries to these points are the significance of the adjustments that the traditional marketing system makes to the modern economy and the relevance of these adjustments for enlarging our understanding of processes of modernization and the future of traditional systems. Despite the apparent stress on change, the primary objective was to obtain concrete knowledge of the nature and operation of the traditional marketing system.

Definitions of the traditional system and the modern economy are essential to planning such a study and understanding its scope. Various writers have used the terms *Indian* and *peasant*, when discussing the traditional economy in Middle America, and *Zapotec*, when referring to the Oaxaca region. The term *Indian* is unsatisfactory because many of the component parts of the system are villages where no Indian language is spoken today (although in most cases Indian languages were spoken in the past). The term *Zapotec* is unsatisfactory because, although the majority of the peoples involved do speak Zapotec or did in the past, speakers of other languages, such as Mixe and Mixtec, are an integral part of the system, while Zapotec is applied to a cluster of at least six languages or dialects, in some cases not mutually intelligible. The term *peasant* is more acceptable, and we have used it at times. However, it must be understood that in Oaxaca peasants, or *campesinos* (the local term), include farmers, artisans, rural workers, and traders living in rural settlements that are usually nucleated, essentially endogamous, and partially closed communities. These communities exhibit similar social and cultural characteristics but have distinctive local variations and highly differentiated economies. In many ways Oaxaca peasants do not conform to most of the vague typological definitions of the term *peasant*. They are peasantlike, but they differ markedly from the peasants of Haiti or China or medieval Europe.

The traditional market system of Oaxaca, then, embraces a broad spectrum of producers and consumers residing in rural settlements of a definable region and has minimal extraregional involvements. This system took shape early in the colonial period and has persisted in relatively stable form to the present. Its antecedents are aboriginal, and its history explains some of its present-day features. Because of our limited funds and manpower, we took the system as essentially "given" and did not attempt to explicate its origins and development. The system deals primarily in products of farm, forest, and ocean, a wide variety of village craft products, and a few town or city products used extensively in the villages. The limited nature of the latter is indicated, perhaps, by the fact that some basic metal tools are still forged in villages. Much, but far from all, of the trading in the traditional system takes place in marketplaces, most of them periodic, which serve as centers for the assembly and dispersal of products. Most vendors are either peasant producers or various types of traders or middlemen. Likewise, the majority of retail buyers are villagers rather than town or city dwellers.

The marketing system of the modern economy is characterized by stores, warehouses, wholesalers, and other essentially modern commercial type establishments dealing largely in industrially produced goods from outside the region. The majority of the vendors are town- or city-based mestizos, sometimes from outside the region.

The traditional and modern systems are noncompetitive to some extent, for they deal in different kinds of goods. They also are interdigitated to some degree. Modern products formerly not available or available only seasonally have a limited distribution through the traditional marketing system, while the modern commercial marketing system provides new outlets for some traditional products, especially outside the regional system.

The watershed era that divided a regional economy dominated by the traditional marketing system from the massive introduction of a modern economy of national dimensions began just after the Malinowski and de la Fuente study, coinciding roughly with the period between the opening of the Pan American Highway to Oaxaca City in 1943 and the completion of its paving to Tehuantepec in 1948. In slightly more than a decade the number of licensed commercial establishments in Oaxaca State increased 1500 percent (Tamayo 1960:72). The growth of the modern sector is perhaps symbolized most dramatically by the opening of a Sears, Roebuck store in Oaxaca City.

In designing the project, this modern marketing system also was taken as a "given." We were not concerned with the origins and nature of the modern economy except as these affect the traditional marketing system and its adjustments in recent times.

The decision to focus on the regional marketing system raised methodological problems inherent in any holistic or "systems" type study, particularly one concerned with process rather than with the relatively obvious structural features of the system. As Cook notes in the preface to his paper in this volume, our knowledge of such a complicated system will always be conditional and incomplete. The processes of the system must be studied segmentally, since time, manpower, and funds are finite, and the results can be only a series of approximations of a reality that is dynamic and ever-changing. We must deal with innumerable transactions, which occur in distinctive social and cultural contexts, with a highly differentiated production and supply system, and with a complex, culturally conditioned consumption or demand system. The initial problem, then, was to identify the segments, aspects, or processes for the first stages of a systematic study.

Given the fragmentary knowledge of the Oaxaca marketing system during the planning phase, a number of basic questions had to be answered. These included the range of products marketed, where and by whom they were produced, where and by whom they were consumed, the routes they followed, the sites or locations where they were exchanged, and the personnel involved at various points in the exchange process. It was decided that the investigation of these questions should be accompanied by the accumulation of data on the economics of the marketing system, including not only its transactional aspects but also the related production and consumption systems. Our studies of the total economy were to include such matters as resource control; the roles of capital, savings, and credit; supply and demand factors; facilitating services; prices and price formation; the nature and conduct of transactions; restraints and available options in marketing; and the strategies employed by participants in the marketing system. Data on cultural and social factors affecting any aspect of the marketing system were also to be gathered.

The obvious first step seemed to be a replication of the Malinowski and de la Fuente study of the Oaxaca City marketplace. Not only does this central marketplace offer the widest variety of marketing situations, but it also draws products, vendors, and buyers from all parts of the system. Observation of products sold, interviews with buyers and sellers, and, ultimately, precise counts of vendors selling each item provided firm data concerning the variety of goods traded in Oaxaca City and the number of vendors handling them, as well as information concerning origins and destinations of goods. Similar studies were undertaken at Tlacolula, the second-largest marketplace in the Valley of Oaxaca; at Zoogocho, a small marketplace in the mountains north of the Valley; and in several other large marketplaces in the Valley on their respective market days. Some smaller marketplaces were also examined in varying detail. Special attention was given to the role of these marketplaces in the community and in the local market areas served. The marketplace studies, supplemented by product surveys carried out in the northern Sierra, furnished additional information on the origins of goods and vendors and indicated the relative importance and distinctive characteristics of the various marketplaces. The results allowed us to make a preliminary determination of the geographical range of the marketing system and the variety of products traded. They also permitted identification of types of traders and trading activities as well as the ways exchange is conducted. The investigation of the exchange system was further advanced by a series of village studies, which demonstrated the varied character of villages' involvement in the market system and suggested the extent of exchange activities that do not take place in the periodic markets. The village studies also provided data on production and consumption systems.

The terms *village, town,* and *city* are used in a special regional sense. The only city in the region is Oaxaca de Juárez (Oaxaca City), with a population today approaching 100,000 persons. Five localities in the Isthmus have populations of between 10,000 and 20,000; the rest have populations of less than 10,000. Because of the importance of farming in these communities, none are classed as cities. The term *town* is used in a looser and more ambiguous sense. In the Valley and the Isthmian subregions we have applied this term to localities with secondary marketplaces. Tlacolula, in the Valley, has a population on the order of 7,500; other secondary market towns are smaller. In the Sierra region, marketplace settlements are very much smaller. Zoogocho, a relatively important marketplace town, has a population of about 1,000 (1,083 in the 1960 census,

957 by Berg's observations); Yalalag's population in 1960 was 3,117. The term *village* is even more loosely used. Generally it refers either to a *municipio* (a political unit similar to the U.S. county) or to the principal settlement, or *cabecera*, of a *municipio*. In some cases all or virtually all of the population lives in a single nucleated settlement; in others, there are one or more smaller subsidiary settlements in addition to the *cabecera*. Most of these are larger than the villages recognized as such in other regions of the world. The village of Mitla, for example, in 1960 had a population in the neighborhood of 3,561, and the *municipio* of which it is a part had a population of about 5,500. The Mexican national census recognizes over a thousand towns, villages, and hamlets for the region, but the *municipios* to which they belong are more or less integrated social and cultural systems as well as administrative political units. The line between town and village hence is not clear-cut. Generally, village populations are wholly or primarily Indian in origin and are engaged in farming and craft production, whereas towns are more commercially oriented, have marketplaces, and often include a significant mestizo population. The villages studied in some detail include a farming and metate-making village, studied by Scott Cook; a market-gardening and trading village, studied by Ronald Waterbury and Carole Turkenik; and a pottery-producing village, studied by Charlotte Stolmaker. Cook had earlier and independently studied another metate-making village, and Waterbury had spent some time in a farming and weaving village. A brief study was made of Mitla to discover what had happened to this trading village since 1933.

With the field work completed, we are now in a position to make some preliminary statements about the Oaxaca market system. I will discuss a few of these in summary form. It should be stressed that these are my own interpretations and do not necessarily represent the views of my collaborators.

Extent of the System

The most obvious feature of the Oaxaca market system is the central marketplace in Oaxaca City and its forty-five dependent marketplaces or cyclical plazas (Table 1). The Saturday plaza in Oaxaca City is also cyclical and is often referred to by city dwellers as a *tianguis*, an Aztec term. A dependent marketplace is one that directly or indirectly has most of its intermarket trade centering in Oaxaca City. Each market plaza is the primary exchange point for a varying number of dependent villages, ranging from about ten to more than thirty. A village is considered to be part of the system if 50 percent

Table 2-1
CYCLICAL MARKETS AND MARKET DAYS

	Marketplace (Plaza)	Primary Market Day
Valley subsystem:		
City plaza	Oaxaca City	Saturday
Central town plazas		
of local systems	Ayoquezco	Tuesday
	Ejutla	Thursday
	Etla	Wednesday
	Miahuatlán	Monday
	Ocotlán	Friday
	Tlacolula	Sunday
	Zaachila	Thursday
	Zimitlán	Wednesday
Village plazas	San Pablo Huixtepec	Sunday
	San Pedro Apóstol	Sunday
	Mitla	Saturday
	San Antonino (Ocotlán)	Sunday
	Santa Cruz Mixtepec	Sunday
	(Santa María) Atzompa	Tuesday
	Teotitlán del Valle	Wednesday
	Tlacochahuaya	Sunday
Sierra subsystem:		
Sierra Zapotec	Capulalpan	Monday
	Ixtlán	Monday
	Lachirioag	Thursday
	Natividad	Sunday
	San Juan Yaeé	Sunday
	San Pedro Cajonos	Sunday
	(Santiago) Lalopa	Sunday
	Taléa	Monday
	Villa Alta	Monday
	Yalalag	Tuesday
	Yavesía	Sunday
	Zoogocho	Thursday
Sierra Mixe	Atitlán	Thursday
	Ayutla	Sunday
	Cacalotepec	Friday
	Juquila Mixes	Sunday
	Mixistlán	Wednesday
	Quetzaltepec	Sunday

Marketplace (Plaza)	Primary Market Day
Tlahuitoltepec	Saturday
Totontepec	Sunday
Zacatepec	Thursday

	Marketplace (Plaza)	Primary Market Day
Isthmian subsystem	Juchitán	Daily
	Matías Romero	Daily
	Mogoñé	Daily
	Salina Cruz	Daily
	Tehuantepec	Daily
	Jalapa del Marqués	Information lacking
	Ixtepec	Information lacking
	San Mateo del Mar	Information lacking

or more of its external trade is conducted through a market plaza in the system or directly with other villages in the system. For some villages near the limits of the system our data are too inadequate to be certain of their affiliation with it. This is especially true of the Isthmian region, where all plazas operate on a daily basis and several have not been visited. The Isthmus may have a separate marketing system, but it has close trading ties with the Valley of Oaxaca, some of which are documented for the sixteenth century and probably are aboriginal. Many Isthmian buyers and sellers attend the Oaxaca City *tianguis.* Consequently the Isthmian system is treated as a subsystem of the Oaxaca marketing system. On this basis we can state that the system involves 1,044 localities, of which approximately 370 have 500 or more inhabitants, and a total population, including all localities, in the neighborhood of 750,000 persons. These figures are conservative. It should be noted, however, that the population figures include a number of towns such as Salina Cruz, which have major commercial ties outside the system. They are included because they are fed within the traditional system and also today depend substantially on the modern wholesale suppliers of Oaxaca City.

Some further inferences may be made. Evidence is fairly clear that the average number of persons per household in this area is

little more than five. In the Valley most informants suggested that
$20 (pesos) a day is necessary to maintain a household with a de-
cent standard of living, including social and ceremonial obligations
but not including exceptional expenditures, as for a *mayordomía*.
Data collected on household budgets for the Valley indicate that a
majority of households achieve or surpass this minimum, although
the figure may be somewhat lower in the mountain regions. If the
undoubtedly large figure of six persons per household is used, there
are at least 125,000 households for the region, and the value of
goods and services consumed annually within the market system is
of the order of $912,500,000. How much of this is autoconsumption,
that is, consumption of food or goods produced within the household, is still problematical. However, our consumption budgets and
other data suggest that half or more of this amount flows through
the marketplace system, via money-mediated transactions.

Marketplace Classifications

On first acquaintance, the main marketplaces of Oaxaca are characterized by the existence of periodic plazas, or *tianguis*, which appear to have a hierarchical aspect. It is tempting to apply the typology developed by Skinner (1964) for Chinese marketplaces or to
refer to them as a solar system, as Nash and others have done. These
terminologies conceal the special complexities in Oaxaca. The plazas
may be arranged in a rough order according to relative size and
marketing activity and the extent of the area and clientele served.
On this basis the marketplaces of the Valley have been ordered by
Malinowski and de la Fuente as "primary," "secondary," and "tertiary." However, when details are examined, this order often is vio-
lated. Tlacolula, for example, is a primary marketplace for parts of
the Sierra. Ocotlán is the primary marketplace for cattle for the entire Valley region. Of the tertiary plazas, San Pedro Apóstol appears
to be a primary marketplace for wooden building materials (planks,
beams, rafters, and stringers). Of the villages in San Pedro's standard trading area, a number trade alternatively at Ocotlán, depending on market conditions and commodities involved. Therefore, we
classify the plazas of the Valley subsystem according to the three
categories of city plaza, central town plazas of local systems, and
village plazas.[1]

The problem is compounded by what Waterbury has called the
urban component of the traditional system, a permanent marketplace often distinguished from the plaza by the local term *mercado*.
It is best developed in Oaxaca City, where it is housed in two large

public market buildings and a number of neighborhood market buildings. Several general characteristics may be noted. The *mercado* operates on a daily basis with a permanent group of vendors occupying permanent locations. Except on plaza days, most of the buyers are city people. Many vendors are of village origin, but some are completely mestizoized and urbanized. All occupy a low social status within the city in contrast to the owners of larger stores and commercial enterprises. The vendors are specialized, dealing in distinct classes of merchandise, and are grouped in sections of the *mercado* with others selling similar commodities. The commodities handled include most local peasant foodstuffs, often bought from peasant vendors, and some craft products, but imported fruits and vegetables bought from wholesalers are also sold. Some vendors specialize in various types of imported or industrial goods, such as groceries, cloth, clothing, footwear, hardware, and household equipment. Many establishments are able to buy directly from factory representatives and receive direct factory shipments. For groceries and non-food items the majority of the customers are either peasants or urban proletarians.

Most towns and villages with plazas (and a few without plazas) also have permanent market structures, but these vary somewhat in character. In many cases the daily vendors number only five to a dozen or so, and the buildings are fully utilized only on plaza days. The existence of market buildings appears to be correlated with the size of the communities in which they occur, and the buyers on nonplaza days seem to be local residents. Establishments selling nonfood items often seem to differ from the larger stores outside the *mercado* mainly in the variety of goods and size of stocks carried.

The *mercado* is associated with the plaza and perhaps is an outgrowth of it; the development of a permanent marketplace is probably related to increasing urbanization. In Oaxaca City its development goes back at least to the last century. As a contemporary form it may be viewed usefully as a type of marketplace institution intermediate between the recurring plazas and the developing modern commercial system of distribution. The local terminological distinction between *plaza* and *mercado* relates to significant institutional and functional differences and may usefully be retained here.

Types of Market Exchange

The following types of exchange can be identified (see Table 2-2):

Table 2-2
TYPES OF EXCHANGE

1. Intravillage
   a. Household to household
   b. Household to store
2. Intercommunity
   a. Village to village
   b. Village to marketplace
   c. Marketplace to village
   d. Marketplace to marketplace
3. Interregional

1. *Intravillage exchange.*
a. Much intravillage household-to-household exchange involves loans, gifts, or the special reciprocal system of the *guelaguetza.* There are, however, some sales and barter transactions in which values or prices are established by the market.
b. A minor type of intravillage exchange is from household to local store. The importance of it varies from village to village and according to the commodity. In one weaving village a substantial part of the production is sold through one dealer.

2. *Intercommunity trade.*
a. Village-to-village trade is relatively small in amount, and most of it is carried on by village-based middlemen.
b. Village-to-marketplace exchange is the principal type of route followed by commodities leaving the village. The goods are transported and sold by producers or by middlemen. Although some of these goods are consumed in the towns and city or are exported, a very large proportion flows back to villages.
c. Marketplace-to-village trade is the principal way in which village products are redistributed to other villages and by which town or city or imported commodities are distributed. Village dwellers constitute a very large proportion of the buyers in the marketplace.
d. Marketplace-to-marketplace trade deals to a large extent with traditional products. Through it, peasant-produced commodities are transported by middlemen from one plaza to another for resale to peasant buyers in different trading areas.

3. *Interregional trade.* This involves bringing products from outside

the regional system and exporting goods—and in some cases labor—outside the regional system. Interregional trade has been significant in the traditional market system in the importation of cacao, iron, and iron tools, and, in colonial times, in the export of cochineal and silk, succeeded in the last century by coffee. In modern times interregional trade is increasingly important. Imports still tend to pass through the traditional market system, although stores and shops handle an increasing share of the industrial goods. Traditional exports, including coffee, still pass through the regional marketplaces. However, some handicrafts, such as pottery and woven products, are greatly influenced by the new national markets and the tourist trade, and part of the goods are now bought by agents or buyers from outside the system who bypass the traditional market.

Types of Vendors in the System

1. *Propios or producer-vendors* may sell to fellow villagers, shopkeepers, or traveling buyers. Most of the latter are from within the system, but for a few products, for example, the fairly new avocado trade, buyers may come from outside the region and bypass the traditional system entirely. A few *propios* may visit neighboring villages to sell. The majority, however, sell in the traditional plazas either to *regatones* or at retail.

2. *Regatones* are middlemen (literally, bargainers) who buy and sell either as a part-time or as a full-time occupation. The term has wide application: it includes shopkeepers, wholesalers, and operators of stalls in daily markets. Many, however, are individuals who lack a permanent sales location. All tend to specialize in particular classes of goods, and they operate in a variety of ways:
a. *Village-to-village regatones* are usually small-scale operators who carry goods from a specializing village to one or more neighboring villages, where they either sell in the town square or peddle goods from house to house.
b. *Plaza-to-village regatones*, often called *viajeros*, or travelers, carry goods, usually purchased in a traditional cyclical plaza or from wholesalers and similar distributors, to villages. Often they combine this operation with that of buying goods in villages to take to plazas. They usually have fairly regular routes. Formerly they carried their goods on burros or mules; today, where roads exist, many use public transportation, either trucks or buses. In some parts of the region

today they may own their own trucks. Many of these intervillage traders are based in a village and often have other sources of income.

c. Interplaza regatones limit their operations to moving from one cyclical plaza to another. Today some own small trucks; otherwise they use public truck and bus transportation. Dealers in bulky articles may rent storerooms, where they leave some unsold products between plaza days rather than transport them from plaza to plaza. Most of these traders have a base in a plaza town. In the Valley most live in Oaxaca City. They usually visit five cyclical plazas during the week, including the Saturday plaza in Oaxaca City, where they spend one or two days "resting."

d. Ambulantes are small-scale street hawkers, mostly found in larger towns, who carry their small stock of goods from place to place through the streets.

e. Fixed-location regatones are vendors with fixed locations or *puestos* in *mercados* or with stores. In the city they usually are full-time marketeers: in the villages they usually have other sources of income.

Function of the Market

The existence of a market depends upon an unequal distribution of goods and services in relation to wants. In peasant Oaxaca, the primary unit of production and consumption is the household. Consumption wants, at least for most things, are fairly uniform from household to household. However, the production and exchange systems are characterized by a very large number of different economic roles, calling for differences in knowledge and skills. Even within each village, households differ in the production and service roles they exercise. Moreover, many villages specialize in particular goods or services, partly because of differences in soils, elevation, climate, water supply, or access to various other natural resources, and partly because of a long-standing tradition of specialization. Consequently, villages differ not only in kinds of crops produced but also in handicrafts and services.

Probably no village, even in the past, was completely self-sufficient in foodstuffs demanded by the consumption system. Certainly most villages did not produce tomatoes or chili peppers aboriginally. The region did not produce cacao, although the demand for this may have been for ritual rather than for subsistence in times past. Today not all villages produce onions or garlic, which are regarded as basic foods. Many do not meet their consumption needs for maize; still more do not meet their own demand for beans, squash, or animal products. Except for *ixtle* fiber, none of the few weaving villages produces all its raw materials. For a period far into the past, almost no village has produced all the cloth for its clothing, and today many do not produce all their clothing. Few villages now or in the past have produced pottery. Many depend on the market for essential house-construction materials, metates, and most of their tools and capital equipment.

As a result, the majority of the buyers of peasant products are peasants, and the most striking characteristic of the Oaxaca market system as compared with many other peasant systems is that its primary function is to facilitate the exchange of goods between villages. As in other parts of the world, it also serves to feed the towns and the city with peasant-produced crops and to supply peasants with goods imported from outside the region (metal tools, for example) and with goods produced in the city and towns. Until recently, however, very few products were manufactured in Oaxaca City or the Spanish-mestizo towns. Their principal commercial function in colonial times was as intermediaries in the trade between central Mexico and the trans-Isthmian south, including the Peruvian trade through the Isthmus, and as bulking centers for the few Oaxaca exports.

Impact of the Modern Economy

The effects of the modern economy in part are the expansion of markets for Oaxaca products and an enlargement of the quantity and kinds of goods available from outside the region. Some of this expansion makes available some seasonal products throughout the year and, indeed, involves the importing of basic foodstuffs to provision the rapidly increasing population. As a whole, the region today is a maize deficit area, so that the modern economy supplies part of this most basic staple. The importation of wheat and wheat flour has virtually ended local wheat and flour production. Tomatoes, onions and other vegetables, and many fruits are now available the year round and not just seasonally. Many more industrial products are available at prices the peasant can afford.

The most important factor in this change appears to be the improvement in transportation over the growing network of roads and truck trails. Shops have expanded in the peasant villages both in numbers and in variety of goods. Stores in towns do more business with peasants, and wholesalers, both bulkers and breakers, have become more important. Relatively, the traditional peasant market-place has declined somewhat in importance, at least in Oaxaca City. Nevertheless, the traditional marketing system remains an efficient, low-cost method of distribution for peasant needs because it re-quires little capital or equipment and is served by vendors with a low standard of living. Until a large percentage of the people pres-ently engaged in marketing occupations can find more attractive occupational opportunities, the traditional marketplace system will survive, not only for the exchange of peasant-produced goods but also as an important mechanism for distributing many kinds of goods manufactured in the modern industrial economy.

FUTURE RESEARCH POSSIBILITIES

Although the Oaxaca project has enabled us to make many gen-eral statements about the marketplace system, we are still far from adequately understanding how that system articulates with other aspects of the regional peasant economy. Among the areas needing further study, a few may be mentioned. We need much more in-formation about the economics of production on a firm quantitative basis for different kinds of product specializations, such as the data Cook has collected on metates. Studies of additional types of villages and their integration with the market system are needed. The small markets of the Valley merit more attention, as does the entire sub-region of the Isthmus. More attention should be given, too, to the integrative functions of the market system in a region of consider-able linguistic and cultural diversity, where, to paraphrase Chiñas, heterogeneity is viewed as natural. The system also should be studied as a channel of culture and as a means of individual social mobility. The Oaxaca labor market deserves more detailed investi-gation, perhaps coupled with studies of the influence of urban migration.

The role of the individual in the marketing system has been little examined by the project. We have a good deal on the choices in-dividuals make but very little on why they make them or on possible psychological differences involved. It is tempting to invoke a vague concept of entrepreneurship or a "risk-taking" personality to ac-count for why some individuals dedicate themselves to marketing or achieve success in it. On the other hand, there is some evidence that people dedicate themselves to marketing activities because there are insufficient alternatives. Farming and some types of handi-craft production also are high-risk activities. There is some evidence from our project that some of the risk takers would gladly take steady jobs if they were available. Whether psychological or socio-logical variables are at work is still an open question. Also in re-lation to the individual, we need more information on how decisions are reached, including not only career decisions but also such things as how people operate in a situation of negotiated prices.

The problem of price formation has many inadequately explored ramifications. The Oaxaca market system comes very close to the economist's mythical "perfect" or open market, the model on which so much economic theory and analysis rests. Oaxaca offers many opportunities to see how such a market might really work. How, for example, does a market price emerge from a large number of inde-pendent dyadic negotiated-price transactions? How do such factors as distance from the supply point, the existence of alternate supply points, or the presence of multiple markets affect prices for different kinds of goods? For the investigation of these and many other problems, the Oaxaca project has laid the basis for a great deal of further fruitful research.

Few theoretical implications have been offered either for the com-pleted research or for possible future research. In particular, the substantivist-formalist controversy has not been mentioned. My own feeling, perhaps not shared by my associates, is that this controversy is quite irrelevant to the study and analysis of the Oaxaca marketing system. Oaxaca peasant economies present examples of gifting, re-ciprocation, and leveling mechanisms, just as does every economy with which I am familiar, but the peasant economy of Oaxaca is predominantly a "market" economy in Karl Polanyi's sense. Almost certainly it was so for many centuries before the first European contacts. The market is characterized by many impersonal trans-actions, although personal relationships are important at all levels of its functioning. The market implies some constraints on economic behavior but is essential to the continuance of the diversified peasant economies of Oaxaca. Buyers and sellers in the market may be cheated or exploited, but the market is not per se exploitative; that is, it is not the marketing mechanism that is exploitative but rather the people using the mechanism. The effects of possible exploitation are limited, however, because of the open character of the Oaxaca system, its relatively free competition, and the large number of alternatives open to individuals at each step of the marketing process from production to consumption. Further development of these points may be useful in the substantivist-formalist debate, but their investigation calls for the eclectic use of theory, without the systematic, almost ideological commitment of some economists and anthropologists.

PART TWO

The Valley System and
Related Regional Systems

In this section we describe the plaza systems of the Valley of Oaxaca as well as three important geographically contiguous regions: the Pacific Coast, the Sierra Zapoteca, and the Mixteca Alta.

For the Valley, in Diskin's paper the plazas are examined in order to describe their operation in terms of schedules, size, relation to the annual cycle, specially occurring ones, and as a significant demonstration of regional social structure. This is presented in terms of three profiles: village, town, and city—each exhibiting a distinct complex of sociocultural attributes. Through a quantitative description of the plazas, precise meaning is given to several concepts, such as the peasant market, the sectional-network distinction, and the dynamics of marketplace role behavior. Finally, the significance of the region as a unit of observation and analysis is discussed.

In Eder's paper we see a zone, embracing a diverse mix of productive organizations, exploitative activities, and community types, being "mirrored" in the marketplace. This account shows how several kinds of local subsistence arrangements, involving maritime and agricultural techniques, are giving way to greater emphasis on cash-producing techniques while, at the same time, through the development of roads, goods are brought in from other parts of Mexico. The total effect, as in so many other regions, is the reduction of subsistence activities and the greater involvement in the wider cash economy.

Berg's paper is an effort to map the paths through which goods flow between local production sites and the national economy in both directions. While the plazas are quite significant here, as in the other regions, other distributive arrangements are described, such as the *casatienda*, the household, and ambulatory vendors.

Finally, for the Mixteca Alta, the Nochixtlán Valley plazas are described by Warner. This careful account enables us to observe the day-to-day workings of the plazas with respect to their cyclical

nature, use of space, geographical interrelation, specialized functions, and role composition. The emergent picture is one of a system
of plazas that effectively integrates a large zone in a manner quite
similar to its counterpart in the Valley of Oaxaca.

This section, then, points out the convenience and necessity of
regional analysis. The plazas discussed below are coordinated in a
systemic fashion, knitting together communities of varying sizes,
ecological adaptations, and social structures. The regional organization of marketplaces perpetuates itself mainly by distributing goods
produced within the region, staffed by local people, and implies
something like self-sufficiency at levels higher than the village. Such
an organization seems to have considerable flexibility in responding
to changes in productive patterns, economic forces, and politics.
Looking at all the regions included in this section, we see that, while
each one is describable in somewhat different terms (with respect to
size, ecological adaptation, social structure of communities), each
one has elaborated techniques that provide for local household-
based production to find regular sale outlets and for peasant producers to satisfy their wants at the same time. The one exception is
the coast, where, in the absence of a plaza system, the channels for
converting local production to cash and for buying goods from outside the local zone are often different. This exception highlights
more vividly the relationship between the plaza system and regional
integrity.

3. The Structure of a Peasant Market System in Oaxaca

MARTIN DISKIN

The peasant market system in the Valley of Oaxaca is composed of a series of marketplaces (plazas), each of which is active once a week. This essay illustrates certain ideas developed in the continuing discussion of the links among the social components of complex societies. Within the plaza, representatives of different social segments can be observed in regular and direct contact. The marketplace displays the interaction of community-oriented and nation-oriented groups (Wolf 1956) and exhibits techniques for the distribution of goods and the articulation of the social segments represented (Mintz 1959). A study of the plaza, then, can yield information on the internal but nonlocal composition of modern complex societies.

There are three goals of this essay. First, we must be clear about

NOTE: An earlier version of this essay was published as "Estudio estructural del sistema de plaza en el Valle de Oaxaca," *América Indígena* 29, no. 4 (October 1969):1077–1099. The field work for the essay was done while I was a member of the Oaxaca Project, National Science Foundation Grant G570, directed by Professor Ralph L. Beals, UCLA. My participation lasted from October, 1964, to November, 1965. I wish to thank Dr. Sidney Mintz, Dr. Arthur Kaledin, and Mrs. Eugenia Kaledin for their careful reading and thoughtful criticisms of an earlier draft.

the nature of the interaction occurring in the plaza. Before generating hypotheses about social structure, or integration, or development of regional systems, one must first carefully identify and count the constituent parts of the system. In the field this is an essential (though complicated and exhausting) procedure; a description of the kinds and quantities of social constituents of the marketplaces is the most important objective of this paper.

Second, we should assess the systemic quality of the market system and demonstrate how the plazas distribute goods produced within and outside of the territorial limits of the system.

Finally, the plaza system must be seen in terms of its capacity to change through time. Involved in this latter discussion is the role of regions in national economic development.

The Area of Study

The Valley of Oaxaca region (see map in Appendix) has historical and, to some extent, geographical unity. It consists of a series of highland valleys converging at the point where Oaxaca City is found. Environmental variation in this area seems to have facilitated diversity of village production without hindering the movement of people necessary to exchange these goods: in short, the conditions for regional trade are present.[1] Archaeological evidence corroborates this view (Paddock 1966:151, 236). Site surveys and surface collections of pottery suggest that the present valley area has exhibited noticeable cultural uniformity for a considerable time.

Within the region there are eight towns, spaced rather evenly, and almost always lying in adjacent valleys separated by average distances up to about twenty miles or by ranges of hills. The most important location for market activity from the standpoint of business volume is Oaxaca City. Oaxaca City has a population of approximately ninety thousand people and lies along the major land route between the national capital and the important southern part of Mexico that includes the Isthmus of Tehuantepec and the Soconuzco coast of Chiapas.[2]

The Plazas

Every town plaza meets once a week (see Table 3-1). The bulk of the people in attendance characteristically come from the villages that surround the town and from the town itself. A small percentage of people come from other plaza towns or from the city and occasionally from other regions in Mexico. Every time a plaza is held—that is, every week—a large spectrum of goods and services becomes available to those who attend. The social and economic composition

Table 3-1
SCHEDULE OF OPERATION OF MAJOR PLAZAS
IN THE VALLEY OF OAXACA SYSTEM

Day	Plaza
Sunday	Tlacolula
Monday	Miahuatlán
Tuesday	Ayoquezco
Wednesday	Etla
	Zimatlán
Thursday	Ejutla
	Zaachila
Friday	Ocotlán
Saturday	Oaxaca

of the whole region is, so to speak, replicated once each week. Between the *ixtle* vendor from the village of San Bartolo Quialana and the yard-goods dealer from the city of Puebla lies the whole continuum of economic activity, from traditional to modern, from small scale to large. Within the marketplace one notes roles, modes of exchange, and social and economic functions performed by a variety of actors, including everyone from peasants whose sale of goods is directly related to household and ceremonial wants not satisfied by subsistence production to highly specialized individuals whose livelihood depends upon the accurate computation of costs and whose behavior attests to an "entrepreneurial" sense of adventure.

Every community in this region responds to one or more plaza schedules. People in the small villages of the area time their commercial activities so that virtually all their buying and selling takes place in the nearest town plaza once a week and sometimes in the Saturday plaza in Oaxaca City as well. Some slightly larger villages have their own plazas daily, usually in the morning, where food is bought and sold. At these small plazas, goods may be offered that were purchased at the larger weekly plaza in town. In general though, the daily plazas do not duplicate the functions of the weekly plazas. Several villages, also of intermediate size, such as Teotitlán del Valle (population 2,849, 1960 census) or Mitla (3,651), have weekly plazas, in which a wider variety of goods is available, but their stocks are still concentrated heavily on food products.

Throughout the region there is a series of religious holidays, celebrated in communities of all sizes. Often these places are not large enough for plazas. However, during the annual fiesta, whether in honor of a patron saint or in connection with Holy Week observances, sufficient numbers of people converge so that some of these communities are transformed into plazas. At such times people appear offering the goods and services that pilgrims might require. At local fiestas, where people come only from surrounding communities, the marketing is mainly concerned with immediately consumable foods, often of a festive nature, such as special *tacos, tamales,* or *buñuelos.* When the fiesta attracts visitors from distant places, particularly from places across environmental boundaries, such as the coastal region, then the plaza typically offers a very wide range of goods. These large fiestas tend to have considerable antiquity (e.g., the Virgin of Juquila in November, Santos Reyes Nopala in January) and appear to attract people from different ecological zones. There is not enough evidence to speculate on the primacy of the religious as against the commercial, but these fiestas certainly have a more diverse flavor in terms of the people and goods seen than do the weekly plazas that occur regularly all year.

Structure

It is customary in the anthropological literature to include within the notion of "structure" the sense of stable, continuous groupings that reflect a principle, or principles, of organization, such as age, sex, descent, political affiliation, or residence. However, for some scholars, such as Raymond Firth, structure is located in the "fields of social relations" rather than in clear-cut, formally organized groups. Such a formulation is a natural outgrowth of Firth's studies of the market networks of Malayan fishermen (Firth 1946), where the boundaries of the field were fluid and changing. In spite of this fluidity—which holds for the Oaxaca case as well—the phenomenon under study is structured in the sense that it reflects particular productive arrangements and regular social relations among participants throughout a territorially delimited market system. The plaza, while cyclical and repetitive in function, is not the sort of grouping usually dealt with by anthropologists, since it has no corporate functions, no unifying ritual, and no definitions for membership that set off one segment of the population from the rest. It is in many ways dependent upon cultural, social, ecological, and political events that occur elsewhere. Where, then, does one look for evidence of structure? My approach has been to study the distribution of positions whose content is specified in terms of goods, activities, cultural constellations, and ideology. Every actor is related to some good, whether as buyer or producer (craft or agriculture) or specialist in the roles of marketing or transport. Every actor has a center of operation that may be specified in terms of community type—village, town, or city.[3] These components of role—relationship to goods and community type of origin—were studied intensively in Tlacolula and recorded for all the plazas in the system. Two results emerge from this procedure: a profile of each plaza in terms of the nature and intensity of economic activity and a sense of the structure of a fairly large region, the Valley of Oaxaca, as a summation of many small local units whose major participation in a network occurs in the plazas.

The observation technique was as follows: With the help of local people, I began to identify the salient characteristics of all participants in the Sunday plaza at Tlacolula. These characteristics usually consist of items of dress, speech, and, occasionally, products peculiar to certain places. In addition to these data, I determined by direct questioning whether these people were primary producers (*propios*) or middlemen (*regatones*), according to culturally standardized categories. Then, with an assistant,[4] I counted the sellers in every plaza in the system, during peak hours, on two occasions: once, during a time of ordinary or moderate activity, in most cases around the last week of September (see Table 3-2 for exceptions); and the second time, during the largest plaza of the year, the Plaza de Muertos (which falls on the market day preceding November 1, the actual day of the celebration of the Day of the Dead).

General information concerning the communities that contribute to the plaza was obtained by visiting numerous villages and while residing in the market town of Tlacolula.[5] This information is arranged in terms of three broad social categories or levels. Each "level" is an abstraction from data organized according to four criteria: (a) cultural boundaries, (b) sociopolitical structures, (c) production organization, and (d) ideology.[6] Observations were made in communities in the region, and the three "levels" that emerge may be conveniently called the *village, town,* and *city* levels. These levels are the "sources" of people and goods that participate in the market system. They are the articulating units of the system and the contexts within which individuals act either inside the system or to effect change. The levels may now be described.

Level 1

Cultural Boundaries. The communities on the first level are villages whose inhabitants are distinguishable from each other through commonly recognized clusters of customary behavior (*costumbre*). Dialect differences in Zapotec (in the Tlacolula Valley and, to some extent, elsewhere) are noticeable from village to village. In addition, informants recognize distinctions between community styles of dress, community ceremonials such as marriage (*fandangos*), the sponsorship of saints' celebrations (*mayordomías*), specific religious village observances such as patron-saint feast days, Lenten celebrations, peacemaking rituals (*contentadas*), and the functions of ritual specialists (*huehuetes*). The validity of these cultural boundaries is generally agreed upon by the local people.

Sociopolitical Structures. To a large degree these villages regulate their internal public affairs through local officials chosen by means of customary techniques. Some form of the civil-religious hierarchy survives in an attenuated form throughout the whole region. While the villages are no longer landholding corporations, they do exercise considerable pressure on individual landowners and thereby qualify private ownership in the direction of community responsibility.

Production Organization. While all villages in the area are predominantly agricultural, most are specialized in the production of particular crops. In addition, many villages engage in crafts, such as sandal making, weaving, ropemaking, basketry, pottery, and stoneworking. The full list of these craft and agricultural specialties constitutes the culturally standardized inventory of necessary goods.

Ideology. Most activities on this level—social, political, and economic—are seen as reinforcing community boundaries. Production and distribution have as their goal the maintenance of an approved lifestyle. People try to make enough *por el gasto* (to meet expenses); this includes the "replacement fund" (agricultural implements, animals, and housebuilding) and the "ceremonial fund" (hospitality and gift giving at *mayordomías*) (Wolf 1966:6–7). This may be characterized as a consumption ideology, since internal consumption is the goal for any goods produced.

Level 2

Cultural Boundaries. At Level 2 are the market towns—the fixed points of the weekly round of economic activities. These towns are not homogeneous entities in any cultural sense, exhibiting instead some measure of internal differentiation into modern and traditional sectors. The criteria that differentiate the sectors are language (whether Spanish or Zapotec as main language), dress, ceremonial and political participation, and occupation. There are also residential qualifications. The "traditionalists" tend to live farther from the commercial center of the town than those attracted by a "modern" lifestyle and economic activities (Diskin 1967:Chap. 5).[7]

Sociopolitical Structures. Here most public affairs are controlled by officials whose offices are in accordance with state dictates. The presence of a central administrative authority is felt more keenly than in Level 1. While there are ceremonial offices (*mayordomos*) and ritual specialists (*huehuetes*), their function is not so much that of social regulation as of maintenance of the cultural integrity of the traditional sector of the town. Political activity is mainly framed in terms of state and national organization. The community exercises no jurisdiction over land.

Production Organization. The number of production specialties increases on this level, and there is a considerable amount of occupational diversity. Some activities, such as baking and butchering, flourish because of steadier demand and a larger buying public than in the villages. More services may be sold here because of the weekly markets and their need for part-time labor. There are also a large number of nontraditional employment opportunities for townsmen: jobs connected with the government offices located in town; jobs relating to the transportation of goods and people (bus drivers and helpers, auto mechanics, taxi drivers, truckers); and special services dealing with maintenance and repair of modern goods (watch repairmen, radio repairmen, electricians). In addition to this expanded list of occupations, there is greater opportunity for job mobility here than on Level 1.

Ideology. The ideology of consumption is represented on this level by those people who engage in agricultural and in traditional occupations (ropemaker, basketmaker, metate producer, baker) and also by those who engage in some forms of nonagricultural wage labor (mason, brickmaker, water carrier, porter). However, the notion that economic activity can be cumulative and expanding is widely held. What might be called an ideology of capital formation is expressed by many people and is openly contrasted by these people with the consumption ideology (Diskin 1967:Chap. 5).

Level 3

Cultural Boundaries. The Level 3 community is Oaxaca City. Its cultural distinctiveness is seen only in contrast with other regions of Mexico. The central Oaxaca area is felt by Mexicans from other parts of the country to be unique with respect to the physical type of its inhabitants, certain typical foods, and, possibly, musical styles. Participants in the plaza system who come from this level identify themselves more with the nation than with local communities. Although the merchants often make conscious efforts to adopt local cultural styles, this is in order to sell more effectively in the plazas.

Sociopolitical Structures. The legal system, administrative procedures, and political processes that affect life on this level are virtually identical with those that pertain throughout the nation.

Production Organization. Economic activity is geared toward profit. Cash is universal. Within the limits set by the general level of industrialization, there are a great number of occupations and an accompanying increase in occupational mobility. Economic activity is responsive to the changes of the national and international market.

Ideology. Those whose activities are located within Level 3 are concerned primarily with capital formation. They organize their activities in line with capital accounting and rational procedures involving the measurement of units of labor, costs of transportation, and margins of profit.[8]

The data are presented in two tables: (*a*) according to economic role (Table 3-2); and (*b*) by levels (Table 3-3).[9] These are both recognized dimensions of plaza systems as reported for the general Middle-American area (Malinowski and de la Fuente 1957; Foster 1948*b*).[10] The tables provide a quantitative description and also help show the systemic relation between plazas.

Considering the plaza breakdown according to levels (Table 3-3), each level constitutes a "group" in Wolf's sense, and it is possible to locate "community-oriented groups" (Level 1) and "nation-oriented groups" (Level 3) precisely. Level 2 presents some problems, since both sorts of groups are found there. This means that the whole community cannot be characterized in one way only; rather, the criteria for the level must be observed in their distribution among the relevant population. Such a study based on sample survey techniques was done in Tlacolula (Diskin 1967:Chap. 5).

Seeing a plaza system as the regular interaction of these levels relates to the question of cultural brokers: persons who mediate between levels (Wolf 1956). They can be identified in terms of the criteria that impart character to any level. They can be pinpointed by considering the modal behavior at each level (see Table 3-4) and examining those actors whose behavior diverges from the mode. One notes that at Level 1 the modal economic role is that of the small-scale *propio*; at Level 2 there is a split between large-scale *propios* and medium-scale *regatones*; and at Level 3 there is a split between medium-scale and large-scale *regatones*. Several broker positions are

Table 3-2
BREAKDOWN OF *PUESTOS* (STALLS) BY ECONOMIC ROLE

	Time 1 (Ordinary Market Day)				Time 2 (Plaza de Muertos)			
	Date	P	R	Total	Date	P	R	Total
Tlacolula	10/10ᵃ	974 60.3%	641 39.7%	1615	10/31	773 55.2%	627 44.8%	1400
Miahuatlán	9/27	344 53%	304 47%	648	10/25	543 57.3%	405 42.7%	948
Ayoquezco	9/28	146 66.9%	72 33.1%	218	10/26	150 53.4%	131 46.6%	281
Zimatlán	9/29	219 52.8%	196 47.2%	415	10/27	420 59.4%	310 40.6%	707
Etla	9/29	215 47.9%	234 52.1%	449	10/27	318 50.3%	314 49.7%	632
Zaachila	9/30	478 65.2%	255 34.8%	733	10/28	No data		
Ejutla	9/23	286 47.7%	313 52.3%	599	10/28	354 43.4%	452 55.6%	816
Ocotlán	10/1	650 56.6%	498 43.4%	1148	10/29	729 51.8%	678 48.2%	1407

NOTE: The study was done in 1965.
ᵃ This plaza was held during the annual patron-saint celebration. It is not meant to characterize ordinary plazas during the year.
P: *propio*
R: *regatón*

possible. First, at Level 1, there are individuals who are not small-scale *propios*, that is, *regatones* whose activities involve them in movements outside of their villages, requiring them to alter their worldview and their knowledge of different communities. These Level 1 *regatones* must divert energy to marketing and away from agriculture (and also possibly from participation in village politics). At Level 3, those people who deal in highly traditional goods, such as pottery, dried chili, sandals, and rope, while full-time market specialists, still have considerable similarity of experience with Level 2 and Level 1 people and perform brokerage functions. On the town level, intensive field work can be done to determine the bases for choice in participating in community-oriented activities, such as subsistence agriculture, or nation-oriented pursuits, such as white-

Table 3-3
BREAKDOWN OF *PUESTOS* BY LEVELS

	Time 1 (Ordinary Market Day)				Time 2 (Plaza de Muertos)			
	Date	Level 1	Level 2	Level 3	Total	Date	Level 1	Level 2	Level 3	Total
Tlacolula	10/10[a]	639	595	381	1615	10/31	596	518	286	1400
		39.7%	36.8%	23.5%			42.5%	37%	20.5%	
Miahuatlán	9/27	292	210	146	648	10/25	478	302	168	948
		45%	32%	23%			50.4%	31.8%	17.8%	
Ayoquezco	9/28	142	42	36	218	10/26	125	104	52	281
		65.1%	19.2%	15.7%			44.4%	37%	18.6%	
Zimatlán	9/29	143	182	190	415	10/27	328	284	95	707
		34.4%	43.8%	21.8%			46.4%	40.1%	13.5%	
Etla	9/29	102	225	122	449	10/27	160	323	149	632
		22.7%	50.1%	27.2%			25.3%	51.1%	23.6%	
Zaachila	9/30	342	270	121	733	10/28	No data			
		46.6%	38.2%	15.2%						
Ejutla	9/23	135	290	174	599	10/28	204	431	191	816
		22.5%	48.3%	29.2%			25%	51.6%	23.4%	
Ocotlán	10/1	539	329	280	1148	10/29	608	538	261	1407
		46.9%	28.6%	24.5%			43.2%	38.2%	18.6%	

NOTE: The study was done in 1965.
[a] Plaza held during the annual patron-saint celebration.

collar jobs. Through an effort to identify brokers at all three levels, the boundaries of social mobility can be found. This view of market structure yields a quantitative description of what Sidney Mintz calls "articulation" (1959). From this one can gain a precise appreciation of "horizontal" or "vertical" movement of goods (ibid.). Thus, in gross terms, we can see that no plaza in the system has less than 43.4 percent contribution of *propios*. I would argue here that such a relatively large contribution of primary producers in the marketplace is an essential characteristic of peasant markets. It seems clear that the "horizontal" nature of movement is greatest where *propios* and Level 1 people actually enter the marketplace. In part, this is so because these same people also constitute a buying public for other village *propios*. The scale of each individual's activity is adapted to householders' needs rather than to large-lot buying and selling.

When examined more closely, each plaza shows particular varia-

Table 3-4
MODAL ROLE BY LEVELS (TIME 1)

Plaza	Level	Role[a]	Contribution[b]
Tlacolula	1	s-p	67
	2	l-p, m-r	56
	3	m-r, l-r	87
Miahuatlán	1	s-p	93
	2	m-r	52
	3	m-r, l-r	86
Ayoquezco	1	s-p	81
	2	l-p	48
	3	m-r, l-r	78
Zimatlán	1	s-p	65
	2	s-r, m-r	51
	3	m-r, l-r	81
Etla	1	s-p	82
	2[c]		
	3	m-r, l-r	85
Zaachila	1	s-p	81
	2	l-p, m-r	61
	3	m-r	51
Ejutla	1	s-p	90
	2	m-r	39
	3	m-r	63
Ocotlán	1	s-p	78
	2	l-p, m-r	54
	3	m-r, l-r	78

[a] The first letter refers to stall size: small, medium, or large; the letter after the hyphen refers to *propio* or *regatón*.
[b] Percent of contribution of the corresponding level.
[c] Roles were evenly distributed among all possibilities.

tions that occur because of local production specialties and transportation factors. For example, in the plaza at Ayoquezco roughly two-thirds of the sellers are *propios*, while in Ejutla slightly less than half of the vendors are *propios*. In Ejutla (and Etla as well) one observes more middlemen who buy local produce in bulk or who sell manufactured goods to the local people. Here one may identify "vertical" movement in several ways. First, there are more town and city dwellers whose activities are geared toward national and international markets. They bring in goods from distant places, and they sell local production elsewhere too. Vertical movement exists in a more subtle sense. Those people that come to the plaza mainly as buyers have earned cash, usually by selling what they produce directly to middlemen, often in large lots, or by finding relatively new sources of income, such as wage labor in Oaxaca (near Etla there are jobs on the railroad). Thus, the middleman's function in the plaza becomes more important in distribution as the vertical spread of goods and social articulation increases.

A quantitative appreciation of peasant markets is aided by Eric Wolf's distinction between "sectional" and "network" markets (1966: 40–43).[11] In his view, the sectional market describes a regional system where, "although the communities form independent bodies outside the market, in the network of exchanges each community is a section, and the act of exchange relates each section to each other" (ibid.). The relationship that exists between sections is at least an economic one, that is, "the act of exchange," but may also be more embracing, including such things as religious celebrations, so that the sectional market is the cultural expression of a region. This type of market structure corresponds to Mintz's horizontal movement of goods. The network type of market, an extension of John A. Barnes's image of a social network (1954), refers to the situation where goods flow from production sources to even wider social spheres through increasingly specialized mechanisms of bulking, storage, transport, and marketing. Here production flows into national and international markets, often being ordered in advance of planting or production, commonly with credit arrangements, advances of seed, materials, and cash. Here the usual sort of contact is vertical, with members of different social classes exchanging goods and money. Wolf argues that under such conditions more universalistic criteria for prestige and social mobility pertain. Display of the symbols of wealth and status, a general spirit of the negotiability of social relations, and fluidity of stratification characterize this "open" situation (Wolf 1955:461–466).

The data presented here suggest that it is difficult to characterize the entire internal market system of a country. Mintz recognizes this when he specifies classes of goods in his discussion of directions of exchange (1959:22), but it is difficult to judge any contemporary societies by these criteria. Wolf, on the other hand, while not restricted to forms of exchange in his 1955 article, discusses the impact of exchange forms on communities of his "open" and "closed" types. Here, the problem is to be able empirically to describe and identify these types in the field. In the Oaxaca market system the general tendencies described by Mintz and Wolf appear in certain cases, although numerous intervening factors complicate the matter.

The plaza at Ayoquezco is the best example in the system of the sectional market. Here one sees very localized forms of production (such as pottery and mountain fruits) that do not circulate continually throughout the system. Certain items, such as sugar cane, which normally lend themselves to large-scale production and distribution, are sold here in small quantities by the peasants that cultivate them. Middlemen constitute a minute proportion of the sellers because they require a certain scale of capital holding in order to make such economic activities worth their while. The plaza at Ayoquezco gives the impression that it could be self-sufficient and independent of the rest of the system. Villages use the plaza literally for exchange; there is still some barter practiced, especially in the case of food and commonly in the morning. The plaza here is a place where buyers and sellers know each other; and, as a result, the sections are related through the act of exchange.

In the case of Etla and Ejutla, mentioned before, while there is considerably more vertical movement than in any other plazas, the sectional spirit is not absent. Village people deal with many people in a personal and cordial manner, especially those buying and selling prepared foods, maize, and some craft items. However, as the tables indicate, there are many more middlemen in these cases. Some are merchants who come mainly to buy in bulk for warehousing and resale in Oaxaca City or possibly in other parts of the country. Some of the large middlemen come to sell manufactured goods, such as ready-made clothes. Neither of these kinds of large merchants acts to cement socially the communities that comprise the market area. Rather, they tend to individuate transactions and to erode any sense of regional integrity. They are the vehicles for the introduction of items that carry status in recent years: transistors, plastic items, shoes, porcelain and enamelized kitchenware, and the like. This entire system of plazas looks somewhat different from the perspective of the large-scale, city-based middlemen. From their standpoint the factors of significance are the general volume of business that a plaza represents; the particular production specialty of its surrounding region; and certain situational factors, such as religious and other celebrations, that can attract large crowds. For the short run it does not seem to be important whether a plaza relates to its surrounding villages in a network or a sectional fashion, particularly when seen from the city. The long-range effects of the network system will be of great importance, however. The intensification of the middleman role and the organization of production for the external market will probably reduce the importance of the plaza as the locus of exchange for the region. With changes in production, the inventory of traditional goods needed to maintain the appropriate peasant lifestyle will also change, so as to make the region another market for manufactured goods coming from the capital and from the world outside. Since the price determinants will change and the aspects of social articulation inherent in the plaza will be reduced in significance under these conditions, stores will probaby increase greatly in importance, selling more nonlocal goods at fixed prices. For the present, however (and to some degree, independently of the nature of a specific plaza system), the entire Valley system is joined into one structure through the activities of urban-oriented (or nation-oriented) merchants who regularly visit each plaza. This condition would probably change with any general drift toward a network market system and concomitant improvement of transportation and centralization of market functions.

Flexibility of the Plazas

Since the reasons for attending the plaza are quite varied—ranging from the satisfaction of household consumer wants to bulk purchasing for wholesale reselling elsewhere—the size of the plaza changes throughout its annual cycle and sometimes from week to week. These fluctuations may be accompanied by a change in the functional mix or in the contributions of various levels; by market glut or scarcity of certain commodities; or by a poor or especially abundant crop, with accompanying price fluctuations. By observation of the plazas in operation during their fullest extension, something can be learned about their possibilities for change over time.[12]

The Plaza de Muertos, preceding El Día de los Muertos on November 1, is the largest plaza of the year because the demand for cash on the part of the average villages is then at an annual high and because, due to the harvest, the peasant participants have a maximum of goods for sale. In order to observe the occasion properly, every household must have special dried chilies, turkeys, fruits, copal incense, cacao for special chocolate, new clothes, new pottery, and mezcal. Villagers obtain the cash they need to buy these necessities through the direct sale of livestock, fowl, maize, and craft products. Townsmen, who also participate in this celebration, rent sleeping and storage space to villagers coming to the plaza, and enter the plaza selling orchard fruits, ready-made foods, and artisan ware. The general volume of activity is greatly increased, and larger-scale merchants respond to this change. This is revealed by comparing the figures for Times 1 and 2 in Tables 3-2 and 3-3. Considering the distribution of roles (Table 3-2) at both times, it might be said that a well-integrated plaza does not change its proportion of *propios* to middlemen, even during periods of intense marketing, since the typical plaza has a fairly high level of activity, and the levels of the region interact with great regularity. Zimatlán exhibits the largest increase of *propio* activity for the Plaza de Muertos, since many producers then enter the marketplace for the first time, and some regular village middlemen enter the market as *propios*—that is, instead of selling in bulk to town and city merchants, they set up stalls in the plaza. The Miahuatlán plaza increases in activity because peripheral villages within its general region participate only at this time of year, and some regular participating villages are represented by more people than usual. Ayoquezco declines in its relative contribution of *propios* because middlemen become interested in this plaza during this week and almost double their usual representation, while *propios* remain constant in absolute terms.

The large fluctuations in numbers of participating sellers in the plaza point out that there is considerable room for change in economic roles. Individual producers may either sell in bulk directly to middlemen (who often set up their scales on the paths leading into town), or they may set up stalls in the plaza. For the peasant this decision often depends on whether he has a pressing need for cash or is compelled to use his time and labor in alternate efforts. The significance of this role fluidity is that the network quality of a plaza has not become so established even at Etla and Ejutla that it cannot alter quite a bit. In quantitative terms it probably means that the network structure requires roughly two-thirds of all sellers to be *regatones*, or specialists in distribution (bulking, transportation, storage).

A factor that should be considered by social and economic planners is the quality of cohesion and regional integrity implied by the plaza system. Such association and group feeling will be quite important in mediating the impact of the central government and its developmental agencies. The region—that is, the full territorial extension of the plaza system—might be a convenient administrative unit for developmental schemes, and its present flexibility might make possible the kind of experimentation useful in the early stages of development. Should such a regional system turn out to be a convenient and useful unit for development, then the deliberate effort to create such structures might be undertaken as a practical measure in other parts of the country.

Summary and Conclusions

This paper discusses a regional peasant market system. It presents data on the role composition of the participants and on the contribution to the structure of plazas of various sectors of the area. Village, town, and city are distinguished from each other by constellations of traits including cultural boundaries, sociopolitical structures, production organization, and ideology of production, as they occur in communities on these levels. From these considerations several general statements may be made about this system of plazas.

1. The most important quality of the plaza system is the fact that approximately half of all participants are primary producers of the goods they sell.

2. Moving from village to city means intensifying middleman activity, increasing the scale of operations, and increasing physical mobility within the system.

3. Each local system has a unique mix of levels, product specialization, and role interaction. The differences may be characterized in terms of the sectional versus network market distinction, and they provide an idea of the direction of social change.

4. The system as a whole is extremely flexible, with respect both to its constituent parts and to its character over time.

The data give rise to problems and suggest areas for further study in systems of this sort. First, which aspects of each level might promote economic actors who would be influential in economic development and change? The data suggest that individuals can be identified in the plaza whose role performance is not in accord with modal expectations, given their level of origin, the nature of the goods they sell, and other considerations. Such atypical cases could be useful in erecting a typology of roles that would deal with positive and negative chances for change.

Another broad area of consideration is to use the plaza system as a model for a regional social system and thereby to test hypotheses about social change or regional development. The region as here described has certain attractive features, such as established communications and opportunities for interaction of individuals and groups, location within a national political framework, intermediate size, and cultural uniformity but with occupational and craft diversity. These combine to provide an atmosphere that seems relatively free of what may be termed a "colonialist mentality," such as exists under plantation conditions in the coastal regions or where the indigenous population is held in low esteem, as in the Mixteca (Marroquín 1957). Given such circumstances, political experiments in greater self-rule and community development might bear some fruit.

This paper is an effort to use quantitative data to describe a regional system that is slightly different from those usually dealt with by standard anthropological techniques. I also intend it to be a contribution to the study of economic aspects of peasant life in their relation to complex, modern societies.

4. Markets as Mirrors: Reflectors of the Economic Activity and the Regional Culture of Coastal Oaxaca

HERBERT M. EDER

Markets can be viewed as microcosms containing a representative array of the elements comprising a regional environment. Markets provide a compressed display of an area's economy, technology, and society—in brief, of the local way of life. Until recently, few scholars, particularly social scientists, have recognized the potentialities of markets as laboratories in which to gain perspectives of broader biophysical and human milieux.[1] For a cultural geographer attempting to understand the interplay of man and the landscape, markets function as admirable schoolrooms and tutors, serving as objects of study in themselves and as springboards for investigating the location and its surroundings.[2]

I became aware of the research possibilities above in the summer of 1964, through my introduction to southern Mexican marketplaces, their variable contents, sources, and participants. I was very intrigued by the persistence of the market as an element of the Mesoamerican cultural landscape (Peterson 1959). A reconnaissance of markets in and around the Valley of Oaxaca and south through Central America was conducted in the summer months of 1965.[3] The opening of the Pacific *tierra caliente* highway drew me to the coast of Oaxaca for a year of field work in 1966–1967[4] and an additional three-month period in 1968–1969.[5] My interests focused on the transformations in the regional landscape resulting from the modernization of traditional patterns of economic activity and resource utilization. I found the markets to be the best places to learn about the modes of livelihood, cultivated crops, collected and extracted foodstuff, tools, and other cultural paraphernalia, as well as about the various social and cultural groups occupying the coastal region.

The principal contribution of this essay may be the observations and generalizations about a regional market system adjacent to those of the highlands of Oaxaca and other portions of southern Mexico. The information may, hopefully, provide points of comparison and contrast with the detailed analyses of the highland Oaxaca market system, its segments and problems, presented in the works of other participants in the volume. The noncyclical aspect of coastal markets and the decreased significance of marketplaces as economic and social transactional settings are two major points of contrast with the highland market systems; there are many more.

The paper is organized in two parts. The first part describes the role of the coastal region in the highland market systems, stressing (a) coastal products and their provenience and (b) seasonality, transportation, and points of interchange. The second part discusses the characteristics of the coastal markets, including (a) location, marketplaces, structure, and calendar; (b) contents of markets and their sources; (c) cultural and economic characteristics of vendors; (d) horizontal and vertical movement of goods and vendors; and (e) effects of modernization on the environment, economy, culture, and regional markets.

The coastal dwellers or *costeños* of Oaxaca perceive their wet and dry tropical habitat as divided into two areas: the narrow coastal plain, or Costa Chica, of the west and center, and the broad Isthmus of Tehuantepec plain, or Istmo, to the east (see Fig. 4-1). Less emphasis will be placed on the Isthmus urban markets herein, since I am familiar with them only from a "survival" standpoint, that is, as places to make daily purchases of necessities. However, the economic outposts of women marketeers, the Tehuanas, in the Pacific Chontal and Huave culture areas will be noted.

THE ROLE OF THE COASTAL REGION IN HIGHLAND MARKET SYSTEMS

Coastal Products and Their Provenience

The products of the coastal region on sale in the markets of highland Oaxaca and southern Mexico derive from three environmental zones: the hills and plains of the tropical lowland; the marine zone offshore; and the land-sea interface of lagoons and beaches.

Salt may well have been the principal, if not the first, commodity extracted and traded inland from the coast (Wolf 1959). Salt making as an economic activity was mentioned in the sixteenth-century *relaciones geográficas* for the coast (Paso y Troncoso 1905). The association with salt production has earned the people of Pinotepa Nacional the nickname *los salineros*, by which they are known not only in the region, but also in the mountains and valleys to the north (Tibon 1961). Today, salt is collected from the lagoon margins, or *salinas*, near Pinotepa Nacional, Salina Cruz, and Juchitán, employing technologies that vary from pre-Hispanic to modern. Salt remains a major export of the coast, crudely processed at the *salinas* and further refined in plants in the towns named above. I have seen bags of salt with coastal trademarks in the markets of the Mixteca, southern Puebla, the Valley and Sierras of Oaxaca, and as far south as San Cristóbal Las Casas in Chiapas.

Salt, sunlight, and often smoke have been used to preserve fish and shrimp taken from the coastal lagoons and offshore waters. Fish, salted and dried, as well as fresh turtle eggs, supply the highland markets via collecting centers at Pinotepa Nacional and at Jamiltepec, in the west. A greater variety of lagoonal and marine products come from the central section of the coast, from Puerto Escondido and Puerto Angel, and from the eastern section of the coast, from the Lagunas Superior and Inferior, the Mar Muerto, and the Pacific Ocean itself. The fish and shrimp, destined primarily for highland markets, are processed in the isolated fishing camps or in the dooryards of the several small communities. Fresh turtle eggs (*huevos de caguama*), collected in ever-decreasing amounts on the sandy beaches, are sold seasonally in the local public markets, though the largest quantities go to the highland markets, wholesalers, and barkeepers (Eder 1969).

Fruits form a large and varied class of products supplied to highland markets from the coastal lowland.[6] The assortment is great, but if one considers only those produced in marketable quantities throughout the entire annual cycle, the variety is reduced to avocados, hog plums, *nanche*, oranges, limes, mangoes, papayas, pineapples, watermelons, and sapotes (see Table 4-1), since most of the *tierra caliente* fruits are easily damaged and highly perishable. Nonperishable tree crops, such as gourds, or *jícaras*; coconuts; and *coquitos*, or palm fruits, are trucked over the sierra to market, where

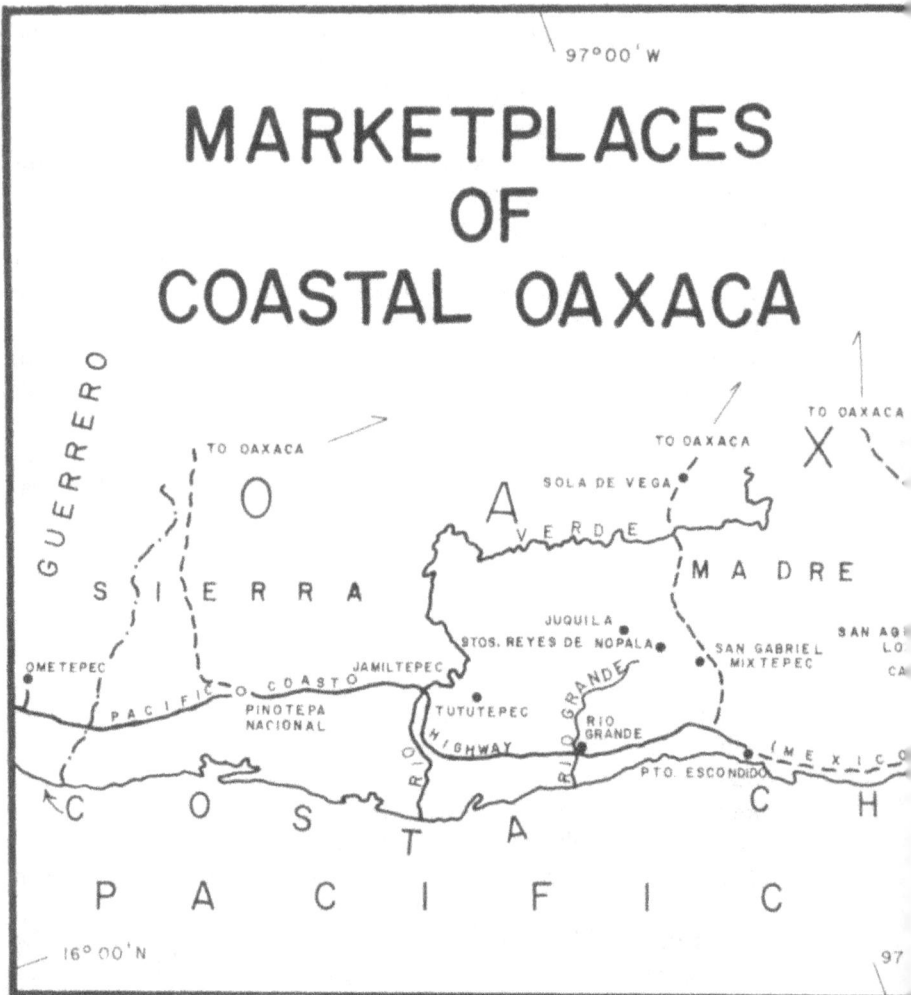

MARKETPLACES
OF
COASTAL OAXACA

they are purchased in decreasing amounts, as plastic containers, vegetable oil, and petroleum products replace their traditional uses (Eder 1970). Moreover, as surety and rapidity of transportation develop with better vehicles and expanding road connections, both the variety and quantity of tropical fruits appearing in the highland markets may be expected to increase.

Chilies from the Costa Chica have been in constant demand in the markets of the Mixteca and Oaxaca. The small, dark green pep-

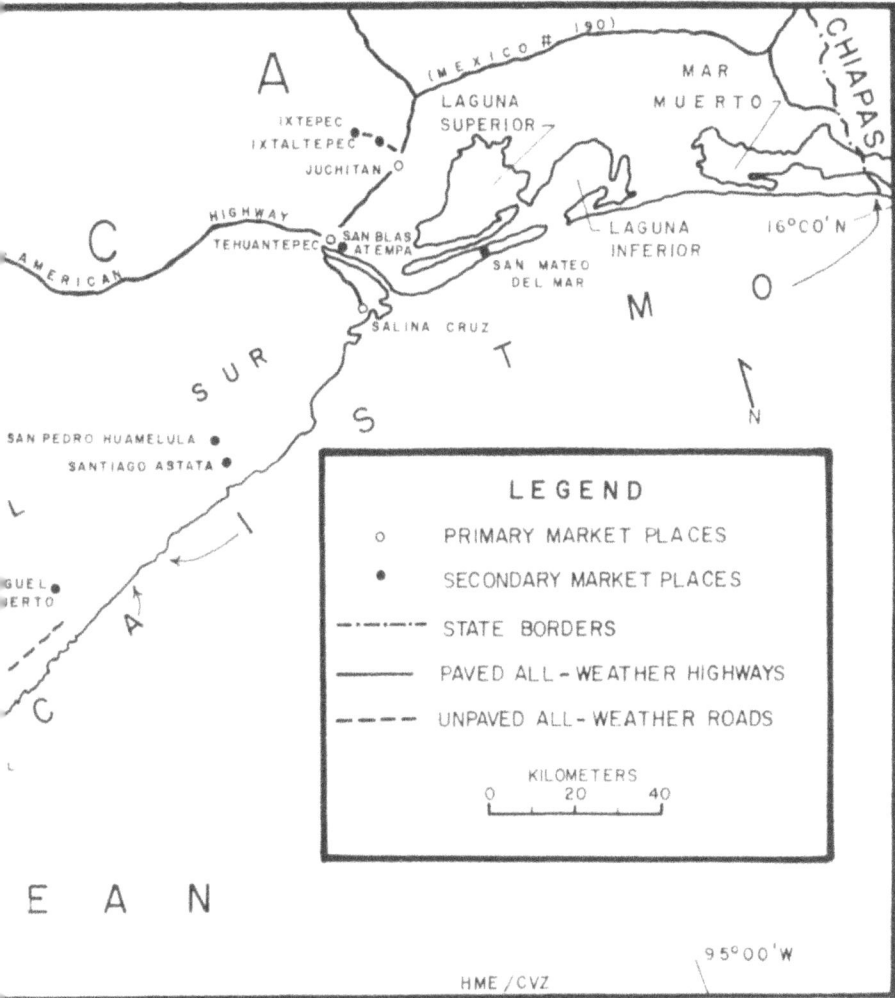

Figure 4-1. Marketplaces of coastal Oaxaca.

pers, or *chiles costeños,* have the well-deserved reputation of a quality condiment. The capsicums have been exported dried or fresh
since colonial times, when they were carried on pack trains, or *re-
quas,* to the Mixteca and from there were sent on to Puebla and
Oaxaca City. Today chilies are trucked north to the same destinations.

Cattle, goats, and pigs have been traditional exports to the Mixteca and to Puebla markets and pastures. Raised on the rolling

Table 4-1

MAJOR COASTAL CROPS SOLD
IN HIGHLAND OAXACA MARKETS

| Common Name | | Taxonomic Name |
English	Spanish	
Avocado	Aguacate	*Persea americana*
Calabash gourd	Jícara	*Crescentia cujete* L.
Canteloupe	Melón	*Cucimus melo* L.
Chili pepper	Chile	*Capsicum frutescens* L.
Chocolate	Cacao	*Theobroma cacao*
Coconut	Coco	*Cocos nucifera* L.
Coffee	Café	*Coffea arábica* L.
Hog plum	Jocote	*Spondias mombin* L.
Lime	Lima	*Citrus aurantifolia*
Mango	Mango	*Mangifera indica*
Nanche	Nanche	*Byrsonima crassifolia* L.
Orange	Naranja	*Citrus sinensis*
Palm fruit	Coquito	*Acrocomia mexicana*
Papaya	Papaya	*Carica papaya* L.
Pineapple	Piña	*Ananas comosus*
Sapote	Zapote negro	*Diospyros ebanaster*
Watermelon	Sandía	*Citrullus vulgaris*

grassy plains of southwestern Oaxaca and in the surroundings of towns, the livestock used to be driven north in mixed herds or transported as dried meat—*tasajo* (beef) or *cecino* (pork). Now the animals are trucked to feedlots or slaughterhouses in Oaxaca City, Acapulco, Puebla, Mexico City, or other urban centers. A similar story can be told of the Isthmian livestock, with destinations as far away as Chiapas, Veracruz, and Tabasco.

Seasonality, Transportation, and Points of Interchange

The seasonality, or timing in relation to changing conditions of the environment, of the bulk of production on the coast is synchronous with the dry season, or *seca*, of the tropical wet and dry climate. Salt making, fishing, crop harvesting, and thinning of livestock herds are all concentrated in the six months from the end of the rainy season, or *temporal*, in November to the end of the dry period in late May. During the wet season the energy and attention of the coastal population is absorbed with planting and cultivating crops, for this is overwhelmingly an agricultural region.

The pack trains and ox-drawn cart trains, which historically carried produce from the coast across the Sierra Madre del Sur to the interior, not only were limited in cargo capacity and range, but also were slow and seasonally restricted, by and large, to the dry months. The construction and maintenance of the first all-weather truck roads linking the isthmus and the coast with interior Oaxaca were achieved only recently. The Pan American Highway from Oaxaca to Tehuantepec was not fully paved until the middle 1950's. The three highland-to-coast roads from Miahuatlán to Puerto Angel, from Sola de Vega to Puerto Escondido, and from Tlaxiaco to Pinotepa Nacional were completed in the middle 1960's. The Pacific Coast Highway (Carretera del Pacifico, Mexico #200), which will link Acapulco and Salina Cruz, has been completed to Puerto Escondido on the west-central coast. When finished, the coast highway and the truck and bus traffic flowing over it will enormously influence the production and marketing of regional goods, perhaps more than any other single factor. Air transportation connected the coast with the urban centers of southern Mexico, especially Oaxaca City, as early as the 1930's. But the small carrying capacities and high costs of planes have restricted the economic effect of air transport and will continue to do so in the future.

The points of interchange, that is, market towns between the coastal region and the highland-valley economic centers of Oaxaca, have changed through time and are still in a state of flux. The markets of the Mixteca, for instance, those of Juxtlahuaca (Romney and Romney 1966) and Tlaxiaco (Marroquín 1957), have functioned as trading locales and linkages between the coast and the highlands. The sierran market towns of Juquila, Santos Reyes, Nopala, San Gabriel Mixtepec, and Candelaria Loxicha have been points of collection and northward transferral of both coastal and mountain products. The three highland-to-coast roads mentioned above, with daily vehicular traffic, are reducing the importance of these traditional interregional points of interchange (with the exception of San Gabriel Mixtepec, located on the Sola de Vega–Puerto Escondido route, and Candelaria Loxicha, located on the Miahuatlán–Puerto Angel road). Future points of interchange will be the closest spots along a road to a production site, where trucks or buses will stop for additional cargo on their way from the coast to Acapulco or Oaxaca

City. In clear contrast with many markets of the highlands, those of the coast play little or no role in the interregional exchanges; that is, tropical and marine products moving to the highlands, principally in the hands of middlemen with the facilities to carry through the exchanges, usually bypass the lowland marketplaces.

THE CHARACTERISTICS OF THE COASTAL MARKETS

Location, Marketplaces, Structure, and Calendar

Well-developed markets are found in the Costa Chica at Pinotepa Nacional, Jamiltepec, and Pochutla. They are surpassed in size by the Istmo markets of Tehuantepec, Juchitán, and Salina Cruz. The markets of coastal Oaxaca are located on or near the margins of the town squares, called *plazas* or *zócalos*. Markets are found adjacent to the cathedrals, government offices, hotels, bars, and restaurants. Consequently, there is the same historical and functional grouping of major economic, religious, political, and social institutions as in highland settlements. Small, rapidly expanding markets in the western towns of Río Grande and Puerto Escondido adjoin the bus terminals, underscoring the increasing importance of transportation as a locational factor. Many villages and some towns of the Pacific Coast, containing only a few small all-purpose stores, or *tiendas*, are marketless. In the smaller settlements, these general stores are reminiscent of the *tienda de raya* of the hacienda, with their monopoly on trade, extension of credit at exorbitant interest rates, and practices of offering *campesinos* goods on credit in return for exclusive purchase agreements on harvests at deflated prices.

The marketplaces of coastal Oaxaca vary in scale from imposing market buildings through open plazas to a few palm mats at a roadside. Formal enclosed marketplaces are seen in the urban centers of the coastal region, for example the Mercado Pedro Rodríguez in Pinotepa Nacional. Inside the walls, separate tin-roofed *puestos*, or enclosed stands, dominate the scene, their interstices filled with sellers attending their wares displayed on small counters and on woven palm mats, or *petates*. The entranceways to the *mercados* or marketplaces are often lined with Indian women selling tortillas, turtle eggs, small piles of fruit, or the like. A few smaller towns built during the colonial epoch have open-sided market platforms with tile roofs. Other settlements possess only a collection of portable wooden counters or tables covered with tarpaulins to protect the vendors and their goods from the tropical sun and occasional downpours. One interesting variation is the Tehuana marketplace in the center of San Mateo del Mar, the Huave capital. Goods are bought and sold under thatched sunshades or *ramadas*, with the entire market enclosed by barbed-wire fencing. In contrast, such trading enclaves in the Pacific Chontal, west of Salina Cruz, are unfenced.

Marketplaces of the western and central portions of coastal Oaxaca do not exhibit the distinct grouping by product or residence of vendors characteristic of the markets of highland Oaxaca. There are some recognizable aspects of structure in the placement of meat stalls, hardware sellers, pottery, merchants, and tortilla hawkers. However, in the Costa Chica markets there is no clear grouping of vendors of perishables, such as fruit, vegetables, or seafood, in designated sections. The resultant lack of pattern reflects a general absence of specialization and a mixture of goods in the hands of each vendor. Moreover, there is a "general store" appearance to most *tiendas* and *puestos*. The urban markets of the Istmo more closely parallel the highland model of market structure, with clustering of products by kind. Whether there is a relationship between the place of residence of the vendors and their location in the Isthmian markets, as there is in many highland markets, I could not determine, owing to the taciturnity of the female sellers. In the trading outposts of the Chontal and Huave territories the displays of the Tehuanas take on an unspecialized look.

Markets on the tropical lowlands of the Pacific Coast meet on a daily basis, with no specifically designated market day or *día de plaza*. This is a major point of disparity with the cyclical markets of the Valley of Oaxaca, of the Mixteca, and of the Zapotec or Mixe sierras. One can enter the markets of the Costa Chica or Istmo any given day and buy the same goods, supply and seasonality excluded as limiting factors. On Saturdays and, particularly, Sundays, increased numbers of rural folks travel to market to sell their negotiables, make purchases, socialize, sight-see, and occasionally attend Mass. In the yearly cycle of fiestas there are expansions of markets in size and variety or specialty of goods depending upon the holiday. For example, during the Lenten season, *la cuaresma*, fish, shrimp, turtle meat and eggs, cheeses, poultry, and eggs are featured commodities.

Contents of Markets and Their Sources

Products of tropical or marine origin expectably compose the largest proportion of goods in the markets of coastal Oaxaca. Locally or regionally produced staples of maize, squash, and chilies combine with other vegetables and tropical fruits to provide dietarv and economic self-sufficiency, though complete dietary autonomy is nonexistent.

Town butchers provide daily supplies of beef, pork, and processed meat products to the retail stalls of the region's markets. Preserved fish and shrimp and, from time to time, fresh fish and turtle eggs are sold by Mixtecas and *morenas*, women of African descent but mixed racial background, in the west, and Tehuanas and Juchitecas in the east. Boys peddle fresh-caught fish in Puerto Escondido and Puerto Angel, where the sale of marine products is in the hands of the fishermen rather than the women.

Coffee and cacao, the makings of hot beverages taken with the morning and evening meal, are available in limited quantities, albeit with excellent qualities. On the Costa Chica, south of the coffee-growing regions of Juquila–San Gabriel Mixtepec, on the west, and Pluma Hidalgo–San Miguel del Puerto, on the east, a few vendors in each market offer small stocks of the renowned *café caracol* and *café oro*. Similarly limited amounts of cacao beans, produced in the shaded *huertas*, or orchards, of the southern slope of the Sierra Madre, are handled by the same vendors. In the markets of the Isthmus, coffee and cacao are imported from the neighboring Sierra Mixe and from Chiapas, Tabasco, or Veracruz.

The items that combine to form the dietary foundation of Mexican life, maize tortillas and salt, are constant elements of the coastal markets, being produced and processed in the locale. Both are sold by women and girls whose stations are in the entrance of the *mercados*, where they sit quietly with their baskets of tortillas or small sacks of salt—in striking contrast to their highland sisters, who attract customers with gestures, whispers, and promises.

Pottery of local or regional manufacture can be bought in the markets of the coastal region. The earthenware associated with the western area is produced in Pinotepa Nacional and Jamiltepec; Juchitán is the pottery-making center of the Isthmus.

Tools employed in agricultural pursuits by *costeños* and manufactured within the region are sold in specialty shops in the market-places. The centers of hand-forged iron and steel tools, Ometepec, Guerrero, and Jamiltepec, produce the distinct humpbacked machetes; the straight-bladed hoes, or *coas*, and the larger *coas tarequas*, both of pre-Hispanic design; and the heavy, pointed iron bars used to break soil, *barratines* and *barratillos*. Local blacksmiths repair the tools and supplement the output of forge towns, but their products rarely enter the *mercados*. Imported agricultural implements have begun to crowd the products of local and regional manufacture off the market. Some forges have closed; others have made the transition to the production of ornamental knives and machetes.

A walk through the marketplaces of lowland Oaxaca will provide one with ample evidence that goods from outside the region are becoming important. Products brought into the coastal zone originate in other parts of Oaxaca and Mexico, as well as the manufacturing centers of North America, northwestern Europe, and, recently, Japan. Luxuries, which have become necessities, now come to the south coast by way of Acapulco, Oaxaca City, or Veracruz, bypassing the former transit centers of Ometepec, Tlaxiaco, Miahuatlán, and Tehuantepec.

Machetes, axheads, spades, and files are imported to meet increasing demands. Handmills for grinding maize, batteries for transistorized radios, replacement parts for gas lanterns, and munitions are increasingly commonplace despite their high cost. Cloth and ready-to-wear items brought to the coastal markets from the textile centers of Puebla, Mexico City, and Orizaba have gained acceptance as the production of homespun materials and the use of traditional costumes have declined.

Increasing quantities of highland fruits and vegetables are carried to the coast from the Valley of Oaxaca, the Sierra de Juárez, the Mixteca, and other agricultural regions of the Mexican plateau and its escarpments. These imports include potatoes and chilies from the Sierra, red and black beans, garlic, onions, radishes, and lettuce from the Valley of Oaxaca and the Mixteca. Small lots of apples, apricots, and peaches are brought from the foothills and mountains in and around Oaxaca, Puebla, and Orizaba (see Table 4-2).

Soft drinks and beer, by volume the principal imports, come from bottling plants as close as Oaxaca City and Acapulco. However, some beer is imported from as far as Mexico City, Monterrey, and Tecate, Baja California! Bottlers of soda pop in Pinotepa Nacional and on the Pan American Highway near Juchitán do not produce enough to quench the thirst of even their local population.

Cultural and Economic Characteristics of Vendors

The vendors of the Costa Chica markets are predominantly mestizos. Many of the tradesmen, or *comerciantes*, are men from local middle-class families or immigrants with limited capital from highland Oaxaca, Guerrero, or Puebla. A minute fraction are of Middle Eastern or Chinese background, but these usually operate as independent merchants outside or on the margins of the *mercados*. In

Table 4-2
MAJOR HIGHLAND VALLEY AND SIERRA CROPS
SOLD IN COASTAL MARKETS

| Common Name | | Taxonomic Name |
English	Spanish	
Apple	Manzana	*Pyrus malus* L.
Apricot	Chabacano	*Prunus armeniaca*
Chili pepper	Chile	*Capsicum annum* L.
Garlic	Ajo	*Allium sativum* L.
Kidney bean	Frijol	*Phaeolus vulgaris* L.
Lettuce	Lechuga	*Lactuca sativa* L.
Onion	Cebolla	*Allium cepa* L.
Peach	Durazno	*Prunus persica*
Potato	Papa	*Solanum tuberosum* L.
Radish	Rábano	*Raphanus sativus* L.

1966, I estimated that three-quarters of the marketeers of Pinotepa Nacional, Jamiltepec, Río Grande, Puerto Escondido, and Pochutla were mestizos; the remainder were Mixtec or Zapotec; a small fraction were *morenos*. The cultural composition of the Istmo vendors is Zapotec, comprised of female marketeers of Tehuantepec, San Blas Atempa, Juchitán, and Ixtaltepec. Small numbers of mestizos and foreign-born merchants have shops near the urban markets. Except in Salina Cruz, these men are scarcely represented within the marketplaces.

The vendors of the Oaxacan coast are petty entrepreneurs characteristically operating with limited capital and small inventories. The activity of marketing runs counter to the economic grain of the region in two ways: it is commercial in an otherwise agricultural setting; and it is specialized in a locale where lack of occupational specialization is conspicuous. The 1960 statistics suggest both the small population engaged in marketing and the differentiation of occupation by area. The percentages of commercially active population for Costa Chica, based on large colonial census tracts, or *ex-distritos*, were 2 percent for Jamiltepec, 3 percent for Juquila, and 2 percent for Pochutla; in contrast, those of the Istmo amounted to 5 percent for Tehuantepec and 4 percent for Juchitán (Secretaría de Industria y Comercio, Dirección General de Estadísticas 1963*b*). But these percentages are misleading, as many marketeers classify

themselves as primary producers, homemakers, or economically inactive, therefore appearing in other statistical categories or not at all.
Horizontal and Vertical Movement of Goods and Vendors

The traditional horizontal movement of goods and vendors in the cyclical markets of highland Oaxaca and other southern Mexican systems has no parallel in the coastal region. Daily schedules, restricted mobility, and small buying populations deter the movement of internal and imported products and their sellers from market to market in the Costa Chica. A few men walk out from Jamiltepec to trade in the isolated settlements of the Mixteca Costa and Baja for two or three days at a time. Mobile vendors, or *ambulantes*, from outside the region visit the settlements of the west and central coast as roads to and along the lowlands are improved and extended. The tradition of the *arrieros*, or muleteers, doubling as traveling salesmen provides historical preconditioning for the growing numbers of itinerant peddlers. More horizontal movement has been customary between the urban and rural markets of the Isthmus. With improvements in transportation, women from Tehuantepec, San Blas Atempa, and Juchitán make forays of a few days to a week to Santiago Astata or San Pedro Huamelula in the Chontal or to San Mateo del Mar in the Huave country to sell, buy, and trade wares.

The vertical movement of coastal products is restrained, save for the provision of highland markets in Oaxaca and elsewhere in southern Mexico with previously mentioned tropical and marine commodities. Marketeers from the Istmo regularly travel to Oaxaca City to sell supplies to wholesalers or attend the markets of the Valley of Oaxaca with stocks of salt, dried fish and shrimp, fruit, or vegetables brought up from the lowland tropics. Minor, but long-term, commercial patterns in trading ornamented gourds, pottery, and spindles, or *husos*, have joined the Mixtecan towns and villages to the north with those of the Costa Chica (Ravicz 1965). Trafficking in tourist souvenirs and folk art is a recent development. Commodities include hand-forged machetes and knives, Indian costumes, and hand-woven fabrics. These goods, purchased in limited quantities on the coast and in the sierra, are transported to Oaxaca City, Mexico City, or Acapulco for exportation or resale to tourists.
Effects of Modernization on the Environment, Economy, Culture, and Regional Markets

Modernization is a recent process in the *tierra caliente* of Oaxaca; isolation, conservatism, and resistance to innovations have been much more the rule since the human occupation of the Pacific Coast.

In recent decades the rate and direction of change and its visible effects on coastal environment, economy, and culture have accelerated. Modernization has been encouraged by various agencies of the state and national government operating in the coastal region. The National Indian Institute (Instituto Nacional Indigenista, or INI), the Secretariat of Public Education (Secretaría de Educación Pública, or SEP), the Secretariat of Health and Welfare (Secretaría de Salubridad y Asistencia, or SSA), and the Secretariat of Communication and Transportation (Secretaría de Comunicaciones y Transportes, or SCT) are working to improve education, health, sanitation, water supply, and communications in the Oaxacan lowlands. However, some of the agencies have not always understood the forceful process of modernization at their disposal, nor have they foreseen the possible negative effects of these processes on the environment, economy, and culture. The disappearance of regional varieties of maize brought about by the introduction of hybrid maizes from the Secretariat of Agriculture and Livestock (Secretaría de Agricultura y Ganadería, or SAG), the ecological impact of the Tehuantepec or Río Verde irrigation projects of the Secretariat of Hydraulic Resources (Secretaría de Recursos Hidráulicos, or SRH), and the diffusion of squatter settlements along the *vías de penetración* of the Secretariat of Public Works (Secretaría de Obras Públicas, or SOP) were revolutionary effects scarcely envisioned by their engineers or planners. Our knowledge of individuals as agents of change remains incomplete. Nevertheless, we can hypothesize that linking the Oaxacan coast with other regions of the state and republic will increase the flow of goods and ideas. In this new connectivity, the exchange will be overwhelmingly one-sided, with the coastal region receiving the material and technological benefits of the national economy and culture. The benefits of introduced modernization are already visible in the marketplaces with their supplies of plastic shoes, toys, and utensils; tinned foods; packaged white bread and cake; and detergents and pesticides. The long-term result of decreased isolation most certainly will be the dissolution of existing modes of livelihood and patterns of resource use. Over the next decade or two, the marketplaces of coastal Oaxaca will continue to function as reflectors of the regional conservative ways and the extraregional modernizing ways; they could and should be used as sites to record those artifacts and ways of life, developed over several hundred years of near isolation, which otherwise may be forever lost.

5. The Zoogocho Plaza System in the Sierra Zapoteca of Villa Alta

RICHARD L. BERG, JR.

This essay describes the Zoogocho plaza system that exists in the Sierra Zapoteca district of Villa Alta in the state of Oaxaca and shows how it is an integral part of what I call the "greater Oaxaca marketing system." Most of the data on which my description and analysis are based were elicited from monolingual Zapotecan and bilingual Zapotecan- and Spanish-speaking people living in San Bartolomé Zoogocho, a village located high on a mountainside in the southern Sierra Madre range of Mexico, where I conducted field work in 1967–1968. Zoogocho is approximately 112 kilometers by truck from Oaxaca City by way of Ixtlán and Natividad, a trip that takes twelve hours under optimum conditions.

Zoogocho has the largest weekly plaza (marketplace) of the eight plazas found in the Villa Alta district, all of which are integrated to form a periodic system, in which marketers and their goods and services are able to move to and from separate plazas because most operate on different days of the week (see Table 5-1). Within this system, five "plaza-areas" can be identified (Camotlán–Villa Alta, Yaté-Yalalag, the Cajonos, the Rinconado, and the Zoogocho *rumbo*),[1] each of which may also be considered as a separate

Table 5-1
PLAZA SCHEDULE IN THE SIERRA ZAPOTECA
OF VILLA ALTA

Plaza	Day	Vendors
Zoogocho	Thursday	350–400
Talea	Monday	233
Yalalag	Tuesday	175
Villa Alta	Monday	171
San Juan Yaeé	Sunday	73
San Pedro Cajonos	Sunday	56
San Pedro Cajonos	Wednesday	36
Lachirioag	Thursday	30
Lalopa	Saturday	6

Total 1,155

Peripheral Plaza in District of Ixtlán		
Natividad	Sunday	Unknown

plaza system or as a subsystem within the larger region which I call
the Sierra Zapoteca of Villa Alta (SZVA). In this essay I will focus
on the plazas of the Zoogocho *rumbo* (see Table 5-2) as a subsystem
of the SZVA; Zoogocho is the eighth largest of the fifty-one villages
that comprise the SZVA region. I should also note that three villages
(Laxopa, Yahuío, and Guiloxi) in the neighboring district of Ixtlán
are included as part of the Zoogocho plaza subsystem (also including
eleven additional villages in the Villa Alta district) because all participate regularly and actively in it.

Municipalities in this region (SZVA), of which there are twenty-
six, have three ecological zones: cold, temperate, and hot (from
pine-forest woodland to cornfields to semitropical vegetation). *Ixtle*
products, coffee, and avocados are the main cash products that are
exported from the SZVA to the greater marketing system of Oaxaca. Coffee and avocados are most abundant in the northern section, where more rainfall occurs; and in the lower and drier southern section *ixtle* predominates. Each village has its own unique ecological characteristics in comparison with other villages, a factor
that provides the basis for intravillage specialization in production
and for intervillage exchange.

Table 5-2
VILLAGES IN SZVA

Villages in Zoogocho Rumbo (ZR)

1. Guiloxi	6. Xochixtepec	11. Yohueche
2. Laxopa	7. Yahuío	12. Yojovi
3. Solaga	8. Yalina	13. Zoochila
4. Tabaá	9. Yatzachi Alto	14. Zoochina
5. Tavehua	10. Yatzachi Bajo	15. Zoogocho

Villages in SZVA minus ZR

16. Betaza	28. Roayaga	40. Yaá
17. Camotlán	29. San Francisco Cajonos	41. Yaté
18. El Porvenir	30. San Pedro Cajonos	42. Yalahui
19. Gertrudis	31. San Miguel Cajonos	43. Yetzecovi
20. Juquila	32. San Mateo Cajonos	44. Yaeé (San Juan)
21. Lachirioag	33. Tagui	45. Yalalag
22. Lachitaá	34. Temaxcalapan	46. Yetzelalag
23. Lachichina	35. Talea	47. Yagallo
24. Lachixila	36. Tanetze	48. Yatzona
25. Lalopa	37. Tonaguía	49. Yatoni
26. Otatitlán	38. Villa Alta	50. Yaganiza
27. Reaquí	39. Xagacía	51. Yovego

Zoogocho and the communities related to it through the plaza, as a unit, produce and exchange, buy and sell goods from the region as well as imports from outside the region. The mechanisms that control this flow and regularize it are the significant aspects of this subsystem. The flow of goods and services through the Zoogocho plaza reflects supply and demand conditions, and the rate of flow is definitely regulated through pricing. However, there are several economic activities that are embedded in local peasant institutions conditioned by nonmarket factors. For example, a social obligation derived from a person's status at a particular time and place is the generating factor for some goods and services to enter a different sphere than that regulated by the supply-demand-price mechanism. Moreover, both social obligations and prices may and do exist together as influential pressures in other economic activities. It cannot be overemphasized that both market (supply-demand-price) and nonmarket (social-obligation) factors operate to shape economic conduct in Zoogocho. I have tried to express this schematically in the flow diagram of the circular flow of wealth in "modern" and "traditional" economies (Fig. 5-1).

For purposes of this analysis, a "plaza" is a place where some of the goods and services circulating among a regional peasant population are aggregated for a short period of time—one day a week in our case. In Zoogocho, activities related to the flow of goods and services are handled by the peasants themselves in a relatively closed, traditional marketing network in which many commodities circulate under varying degrees of accordance with general supply-demand principles. This is a network in which the locus of economic decision-making resides in the household management unit, although decisions made within the latter are affected indirectly by regional and extraregional market conditions. Indeed, in viewing the peasant household as a management unit I am implying that it differs in degree rather than kind from nonhousehold management units (businesses) operating in the regional economy. Consequently, it is important to determine how much of the flow of local consumables is produced by household as compared to nonhousehold management units. With this type of data we should be able to determine quantitatively the structure of the regional peasant economy as schematized in Figure 5-1.

What follows is neither a macro- nor a microanalysis but a mini-microanalysis; that is, to ascertain the magnitude and content of the total flow of goods through the Zoogocho plaza system I had to trace each and every item consumed by the 825 households of the fifteen villages in the Zoogocho *rumbo* (see Table 5-4). Thus, I obtained information on all 516 items consumed throughout the marketing network: where each was produced and how it was marketed and consumed. As it turns out, 295 of these items are or were traditionally produced in the SZVA region. These are classified into eight categories: (*a*) fruits; (*b*) plant products gathered; (*c*) plants partially domesticated; (*d*) annual crops; (*e*) domesticated animals; (*f*) household-modified foods; (*g*) household-manufactured non-foods; and (*h*) household and industrially manufactured candles and clothing. The remaining 221 items are classified separately as one heterogeneous category, (*i*) industrial manufactured items. As a result of this analysis, I found that 63% of all goods consumed were produced by the household that consumed them or were acquired directly from other producing households. The remaining 37% of the goods consumed were acquired through the plaza or the *tienda-casatienda* system, and 1% of the latter was acquired outside the SZVA.

One major question I had to answer was, "How important is the Zoogocho plaza for the population of the Zoogocho *rumbo?*" To answer this question I had to compare the plaza with the household and *tienda-casatienda* management units—the three major suppliers of goods operating in the area. *Tiendas* (stores) and *casatiendas* (vendors who operate out of their homes) are similar in operation, but *casatiendas* have smaller and less varied inventories. A list was compiled to identify the types of industrial manufactures available in the *tiendas* and *casatiendas* in Zoogocho as well as in the permanent and semipermanent *puestos* (stalls) in the plaza proper. In 1967 every village in the area had at least a *casatienda*, if not a *tienda*; and there were specific items common to the typical *casatienda* or *tienda* inventory. Moreover, the *tiendas* generally sold one specialized line; for example, *tienda* 1 specialized in cloth, yarns, and threads; *tienda* 4 specialized in mescal and beer; and *tienda* 5 specialized in cloth and bulk wax from Oaxaca City.

Table 5-3 contains a breakdown of these inventory items and shows the relative importance of the plaza and the *tienda/casatienda* in the marketing of them. Among other things this table shows that nearly 40% of the items were not marketed through the plaza (i.e., the sum of columns 3 and 5, items sold more by the *tienda* and those sold only by the *tienda/casatienda* respectively, minus the sum of columns 2 and 4, items sold more regularly or exclusively in the plaza); and that more than 18% of the items were marketed equally through the plaza and the *tienda-casatienda* routes (column 1). Finally, the 8% of the items not marketed through either of these routes (column 6) involved a small demand crowd and required a large amount of cash investment—which placed them out of reach for the typical retailers in this peasant economy.

What is clear, then, from my study is that the *tienda-casatienda* routes were dominant in the marketing of industrial manufactures in the Zoogocho-*rumbo* economy. However, this was a relatively recent phenomenon, since the first *tienda* to operate in the area was not established until the 1920's, and the plaza remained dominant in the marketing of industrial manufactures long after that. By the time my research was conducted, however, the role of the plaza had been reduced almost exclusively to the marketing of locally produced goods. Nevertheless, it should be emphasized that all of the

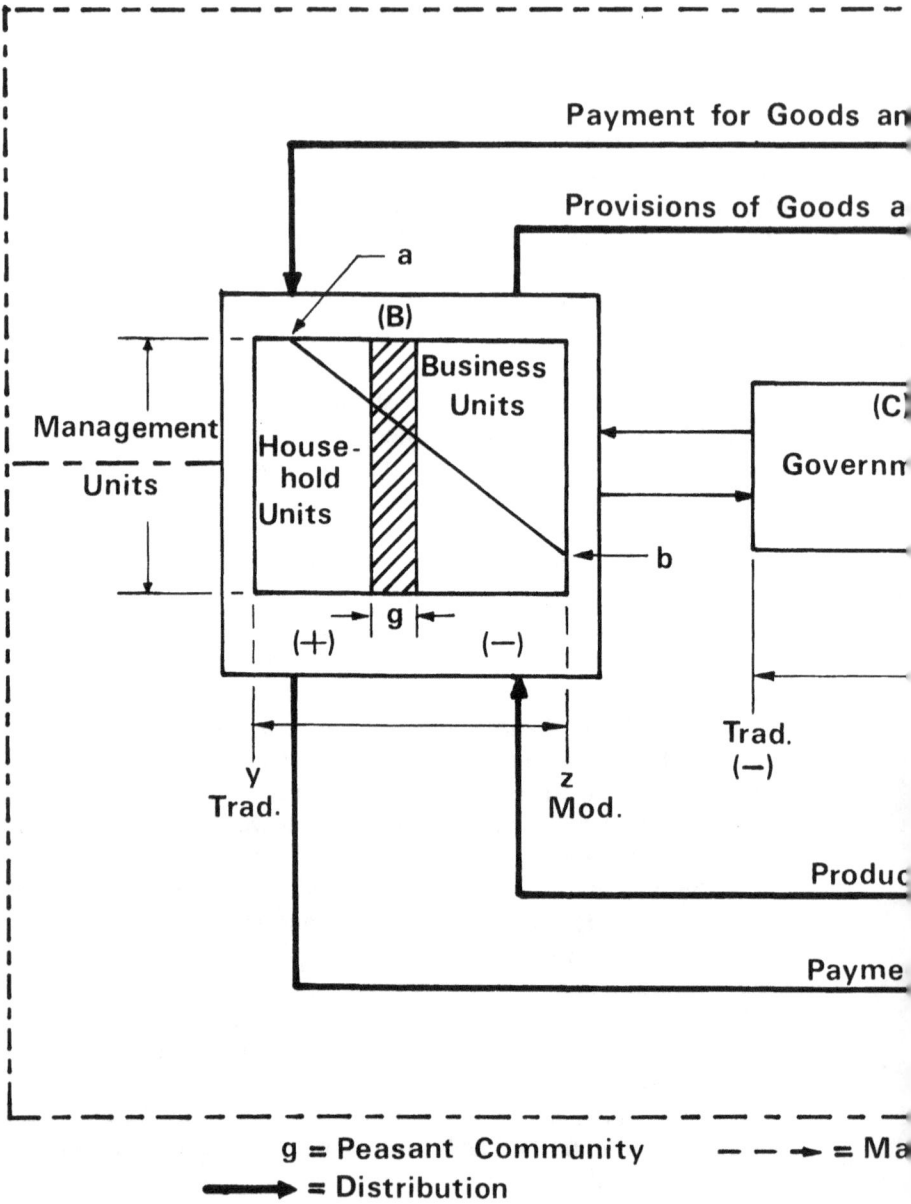

g = Peasant Community   — — ➤ = Ma

➤ = Distribution

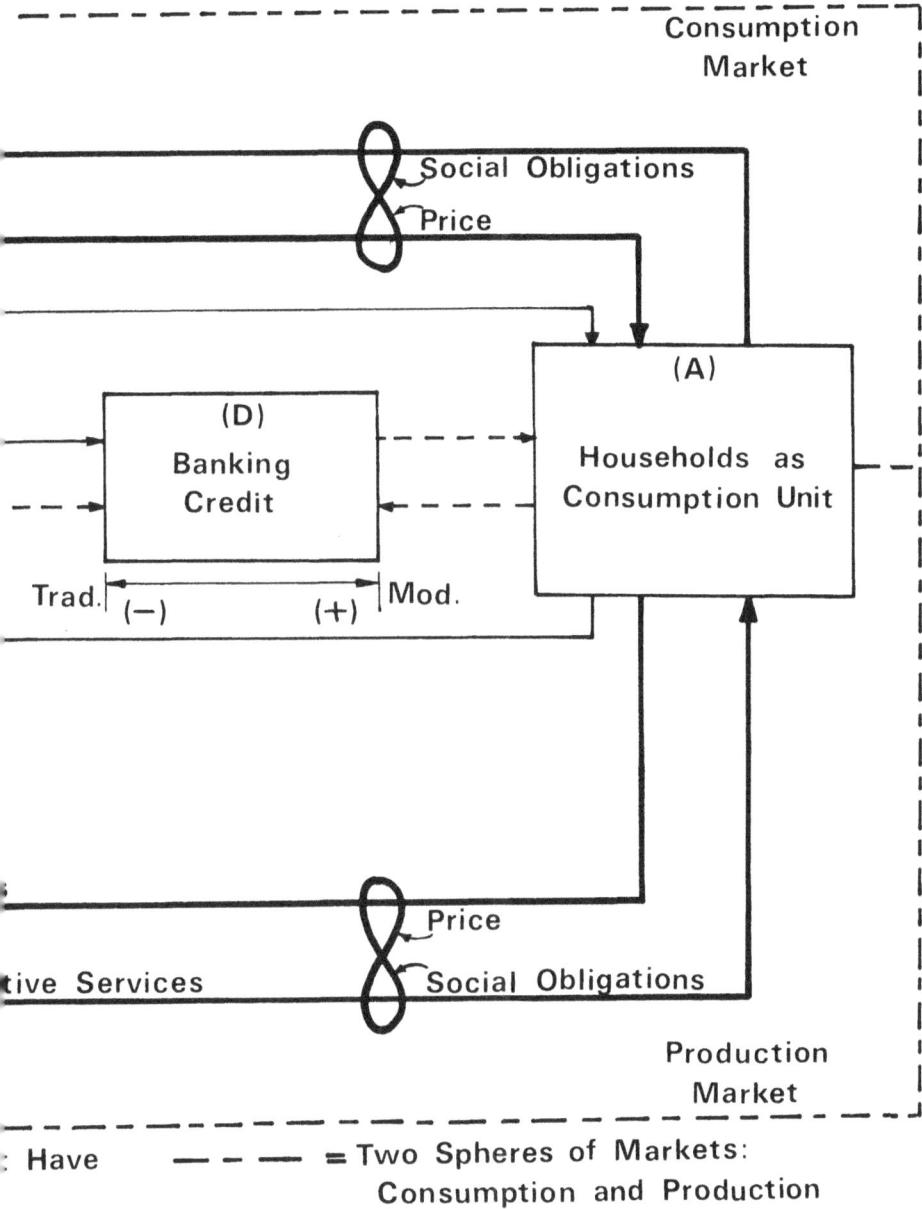

Figure 5-1. Flow diagram illustrating modern (Mod.) and traditional (Trad.) economics.

Table 5-3

RELATIVE IMPORTANCE OF PLAZA AND *TIENDA/CASATIENDA*
IN DISTRIBUTION OF INDUSTRIAL MANUFACTURED ITEMS

Items	1 P=T	2 P>T	3 P<T	4 P	5 T	6 N
A. Clothing and materials	12	3	3	3	1	3
B. Construction supplies	—	—	—	—	1	9
C. Drinks: manufactured	—	—	3	—	4	—
D. Food items	1	—	10	—	7	—
E. Haberdasheries	5	6	10	1	6	—
F. Hardware	4	1	4	4	16	—
G. Laundry and cleaning supplies	2	—	3	—	2	—
H. Recreational and religious supplies	5	—	2	7	5	1
I. Pharmaceutical supplies	3	—	3	—	15	—
J. Plastics	7	2	—	9	—	—
K. School and stationery supplies	1	—	10	—	4	—
L. Tools	1	1	1	—	7	4
M. Miscellaneous items	—	1	3	1	3	1
Total	41	14	52	25	71	18
Percentage	18.55	6.33	23.53	11.31	32.13	8.15

P=T: items sold in equal quantities in plaza and *tienda/casatienda*
P>T: items sold more in plaza than in *tienda/casatienda*
P<T: items sold less in plaza than in *tienda/casatienda*
P: items sold only in plaza
T: items sold only in *tienda/casatienda*
N: items sold neither in plaza nor in *tienda/casatienda*
    (procured directly by consumer, or ordered)

present *tienda* operators got their start in the plaza trade, and the plaza still served as a mechanism for capital accumulation for would-be store operators (e.g., the largest supplier of plastic goods in the Zoogocho *rumbo*, the haberdasher in puesto F-25 in the plaza, had intentions of opening a *tienda* in Zoogocho as soon as he had accumulated sufficient capital).

The total relative percentages of all nine categories of items acquired in the households, plazas, *tiendas*, *casatiendas*, and by order or directly by the user from outside sources have been calculated and listed in Table 5-4. This table includes 516 of the 537 items used by the Zoogocho *rumbo* population (21 items have been excluded for lack of quantitative data). As would be expected from a predominantly peasant population, the largest percentage (63%) of the 516 items used originated in local household production. At first, I was surprised to find that 25% of all goods were obtained in the plaza, as compared to 11% in *tiendas* or *casatiendas*. This is not so surprising, however, when one realizes that these figures deal only with absolute numbers of items and do not consider relative proportional quantities between items.

Column K in Table 5-4 indicates that there were a total of 516 products consumed by the Zoogocho *rumbo's* populace (in addition to the 21 items not included in the table.) From this total, 225 (43.6%) of the products were industrially manufactured items, 204 (39.5%) were household-modified, and 87 (16.9%) were unmodified. The 225 industrial products were marketed through the plaza, the *tiendas* or *casatiendas*, and by order or direct purchase from outside the SZVA region. Under columns C, D, and E, one finds that the *tiendas* and *casatiendas* supplied 65.8% of the industrial products, compared to 26.0% supplied by the plaza and 8.2% supplied by the individual consumer (as producer) or by order.

Here is evidence that the role of the *tienda* and the *casatienda* was essentially to supply industrially manufactured items. In other words, it is clear that the *tiendas* and *casatiendas* were not competing with household management units. They did compete, however, with those few *puestos* in the plazas that sold similar items.

On the other hand, Table 5-4 shows that the plaza supplied more than 59% of the 186 household-modified food items (category 6) and household-manufactured nonfood items (category 7). In addition, it supplied between 26% and 40% of the 259 items that comprise categories 2, 4, and 9 (gathered plant products, annual crops, industrial manufactures). A small percentage of the remaining 71 items were sold in the plaza. It is obvious, then, that the plaza handled a large number of both household products and industrial manufactures; it was an arena in which both the private producer-consumer and the highly capitalized merchant could buy and sell products.

All categories of items in Table 5-4 had a household procurement percentage higher than 34% (except industrial manufactures, which had a zero procurement rate). The total percentage of household procurement was 62%. This high percentage of goods locally produced for local consumption is a quantitative indicator of a peasant economy. In column F, under "Area Where Item Is Obtained," we find that 139 of the 291 locally consumed products were pro-

Table 5-4

COMPOSITE TOTALS OF ITEMS CONSUMED
IN THE ZOOGOCHO *RUMBO*

| | How Item Is Marketed | | | |
Categories of Items	Hshd Average (%)	Plaza Average (%)	T&CT Average (%)	N Average (%)
1. Fruits grown on trees	97.92	1.78	0.30	0.00
2. Plant products gathered	51.33	40.33	8.34	0.00
3. Plants partially do-mesticated	97.87	2.13	0.00	0.00
4. Products grown annually	45.28	33.25	21.47	0.00
5. Domesticated animals	97.87	2.13	0.00	0.00
6. Household-modified foods	37.38	60.74	1.88	0.00
7. Household-manufactured nonfood items	34.64	59.21	5.42	0.73
8. Household and industrially manufactured candles and clothing				
Candles	4th	3rd	2nd	Most[b]
Men's clothes	Most	2nd	2nd	3rd
Women's clothes	97.98	1.11	1.11	0.00
9. Industrially manufactured items (excluding candles and clothing)	0.00	26.01	65.84	8.15
Total				
Percent of total (of those with figures)	62.23	25.19	11.60	0.99

Total unmodified items (rows 1–5): 87 items from total of 516
(16.87%)
Total household-modified or -manufactured items (rows 6–8): 204
items from total of 516 (39.53%)
Total industrially manufactured items (rows 8–9): 225 items from total of 516 (43.61%)

Area Where Item Is Obtained				Cash Crop to Oaxaca City or Manufactured Item	Total Number of Items Consumed in ZR
Z	ZR minus Z	ZVZA minus ZR	Outside SZVA		
19	25	6	3	3	25
2	2	1	1	0	5
5	5	2	0	0	12
16	20	2	18	1	33
12	11	9	5	0	12
15	22	3	7	0	28
33	83	43	32	32[a]	158
4	2	0	5	0	9
6	6	5	4	0	4
9	9	0	1	0	9
18	18	?	221	0	221
139	203	71	297[c]	36	516

[a] The 33 *ixtle* products have been included in this figure as one unit.
[b] Manufactured by the Church (a corporate unit).
[c] The 297 goods include 225 not produced or manufactured in SZVA; 72 of these are similar to those manufactured in SZVA.
Hshd: household
T&CT: *tienda* and *casatienda*
N: neither household, plaza, nor *tienda/casatienda*
Z: Zoogocho
ZR: Zoogocho *rumbo*

cured within Zoogocho, 203 of the 291 items were available within the Zoogocho *rumbo*, and 71 of the 291 items were imported into the Zoogocho *rumbo* from elsewhere in the SZVA region. In other words, the Zoogocho peasant was not self-sufficient but was involved in a network of intervillage trade rooted in a system of intervillage specialization in production of handicrafts and agricultural products. With regard to imports and exports to and from SZVA, over 43% of the different types of items used by the regional population were imported, and only 7% of items produced regionally were exported (coffee, *ixtle* products, and avocados). It must be emphasized that the latter figure can easily be misinterpreted as quantitatively insignificant. This is not the case. If we look at the two major cash crops of the region, avocados and coffee, we find that a grand total of $765,000 (pesos) was paid by Oaxaca City–based buyers for approximately 8,500 *bultos* of avocados from SZVA and the district of Choapan (that enter Yalalag); this was on an annual basis for the mid-1960's. An estimated 3,012 members of the regional population received this revenue in different proportions (see Table 5-5). For example, 29 of the 3,012 individuals received 38% of the total avocado sales revenue; I am certain that 11, and possibly 14, of these 29 were not peasant producers but truck owners and drivers, and the other 15 were *comerciantes*. My records indicate that the average peasant producer of avocados earned sufficient cash income from the sale of avocados to buy an equivalent of a one-to-two-month supply of maize for his family.

A similar analysis was made of coffee, the dominant cash crop of the SZVA region. Using $200 as the average net return per quintal, I estimate that $2,000,000 flowed into the district of Villa Alta from annual coffee sales. This yielded an average of $210 (or forty-three *almudes* of maize) in cash returns per coffee-producing household in the SZVA for the year. In other words, a typical regional peasant family could buy a forty-three-day supply of maize if we assume that the cash return from every pound of coffee was exchanged for maize and distributed equally to each household. Since the average percentage of locally grown maize consumed by the typical household in the Zoogocho *rumbo* was 44.6%, we can see that the greater portion of cash income received by the peasant from coffee sales was spent, directly or indirectly, on buying maize imported from the outside (often from the coffee buyers, or *mayoristas*, who also sell maize).

Let us now examine the circulation of goods in the Zoogocho

Table 5-5

ESTIMATED DISTRIBUTION OF GAINS PER YEAR
ON AVOCADOS FROM SZVA AND CHOAPAN

	Amounts in Pesos	Approximate Number of Persons	Average of Pesos Received per Person
Received by *comerciantes*	$172,750	15	$11,517
Received by speculators	10,000	50	200
Total	$182,750		
Received by sellers in plaza (peasants)	137,500	833[a]	164
Received by sellers by trees (peasants)	180,000	2,000[a]	90
Trucking:			
Received by drivers ($200 per trip)	34,000	8[b]	4,242
Overhead ($300 per trip)	51,000		
Owners' profit	85,000	6[c]	14,167
Gross (@ 25¢ per kilo)	170,000		
State tax	85,000		
Personal costs for *comerciantes* and *viajeros* for trips	9,750		
Totals	$765,000[d]	2,912 persons[e]	

[a] Part from Choapan.
[b] Not peasants.
[c] Three do not work land—possibly five.
[d] Amount paid for 8500 *bultos* of avocados in Oaxaca City (=$90 per *bulto*).
[e] All but eleven to fifteen of these are either full-time or part-time peasants.

plaza system. We have learned that 63% of all goods consumed by the Zoogocho *rumbo* population were produced locally and distributed directly among the household producer-consumer units. There is, however, a percentage of household consumer items produced by local households that entered the plaza and *tienda* distribution channels. The data presented in Table 5-6 enable us to determine the percentages of various household-produced goods that were marketed through these extrahousehold channels.

In this table the household, the plaza, and the *tienda-casatienda*

Table 5-6

MOVEMENT OF GOODS
IN THE ZOOGOCHO PLAZA MARKET SYSTEM (ZPMS)

Distribution Channels	Items Used		1 Fruits Grown on Trees	2 Plant Products Gathered
	As Percentage of 291[a]	Total Number		
1. $H_L \rightarrow H_L$[b]	82.13	239	25	3
2. $H_L \rightarrow P_L \rightarrow H_L$	58.76	171	23	1
3. $H_L \rightarrow T_L \rightarrow H_L$	3.78	11	—	—
4. $H_A \rightarrow H_L$	0.00	0	—	1
5. $H_A \rightarrow P_L \rightarrow H_L$	9.28	27	—	1
6. $H_A \rightarrow T_L \rightarrow H_L$	4.81	14	3	—
7. $i_A \rightarrow H_L$	3.09	9	—	—
8. $i_A \rightarrow P_L \rightarrow H_L$	2.75	8	—	—
9. $i_A \rightarrow T_L \rightarrow H_L$	0.34	1	—	—
10. $I_A \rightarrow H_L$	0.69	2	—	—
11. $I_A \rightarrow P_L \rightarrow H_L$	3.44	10	—	—
12. $I_A \rightarrow T_L \rightarrow H_L$	4.12	12	—	—
13. $H_L \rightarrow Int \rightarrow MES$	1.72	5	3	—
14. IPCI (all consumed in plaza)	4.47	13	—	—
15. IPCI (some consumed in plaza)	6.19	18	15	—
16. Producer-consumer items	15.81	46	23	1
17. Church-produced items	1.03	3	—	—
Totals		295	25	5

Different Types of Goods Used in ZPMS

3 Plants Partially Domesticated	4 Products Grown Annually	5 Domesti-cated Animals	6 Household-modified Goods	7 Household-manufactured Nonfoods	8 H&I Candles Clothing
12	23	12	23	124	17
5	20	7	22	90	3
—	—	—	2	6	3
—	—	—	—	—	—
—	17	5	4	—	—
—	5	—	2	—	—
—	—	—	—	9	—
—	—	—	—	8	—
—	—	—	1	1	—
—	—	—	—	2	—
—	—	—	—	5	5
—	—	—	—	7	5
—	1	—	—	1[c]	—
—	8	—	5	—	—
—	1	—	2	—	—
3	17	2	—	—	—
—	—	—	—	—	3
12	33	12	28	158	22

[a] Four of the 295 items are manufactured only outside SZVA.
[b] Includes both goods produced in one household and consumed in another and goods produced and consumed in the same household.
[c] Includes all 32 *ixtle* products.
H: household
I: industrial
P: plaza
T: *tienda*
i: handicrafts
Int: intermediators
MES: modern economic sector
IPCI: immediate plaza-consumption items
Sub-L: local (within SZVA)
Sub-A: from outside SZVA

marketing channels have been broken down further into thirteen channels, which are represented in the first column from row 1 through row 13. Because, at this point in our analysis, we are interested in quantifying flows through the household management unit, only those products in categories 1–8 are included. It should be noted that 4 of the 295 products in the first eight channels were not manufactured locally; therefore, 291 is used as the total in calculating the percentages in the table.[2]

In each of the first twelve rows the final symbol H_L signifies that the ultimate destination of products being marketed was local household consumption. The marketing channel represented in row 13 indicates that local products were destined for use in the "modern sector" of the extraregional economy; in essence, it shows the local household as the cash-crop producer, with its products being handled by an intermediary for sale in extraregional markets (e.g., Oaxaca City). The first twelve marketing channels encompass three distinct types of movements: (a) the movement of goods directly to local households—represented by rows 1, 4, 7, and 10; (b) the movement of goods through the Zoogocho plaza—represented by rows 2, 5, 8, and 11; and (c) the movement of goods through the local *tienda-casatienda* system—represented by rows 3, 6, 9, and 12. In addition, the first twelve rows are ordered in four groups of the above three types of movements. Each group of three is identified by the nature of the production unit: H_L, household consumables locally produced; H_A, household consumables produced outside SZVA; i_A, handicrafts produced outside SZVA; and I_A, modern manufactures produced outside SZVA.

This description of the various marketing channels gives us a clearer perspective on the destinations of consumer goods produced by local households. Diagnostic of the "peasant" nature of this economy is the fact that 63% of the consumption goods procured by local households (Table 5-4) flowed through the $H_L \rightarrow H_L$ channel shown in row 1 of Table 5-6. To emphasize this in another way: 239 types (82%) of locally produced goods were consumed by the producing household or by other local producer households. However, most of the 147 household-modified or -manufactured products (out of the 239 products distributed between households) were modified by specialists. Moreover, most of the 115 household-modified or -manufactured products (out of the 171 products that entered the plaza—see row 2) also fell into this category. In other words, the peasant households of the Zoogocho *rumbo* remained viable because of their involvement in a regional system of intervillage (and inter-household) specialization.

In Table 5-6 we also find that approximately 59% (171) of the 291 locally produced products flowed through the $H_L \rightarrow P_L \rightarrow H_L$ marketing channel. Of these 171 items, 46 (16%) were brought to the plaza by producer-consumer vendors (see row 16). As a general rule these products moved in greater volume through the $H_L \rightarrow H_L$ channel. But they were produced seasonally, and each village had slight seasonal variations in output due to ecological differences; this resulted in restricted flows into the plaza from the "haves" to meet the demand of those who had exhausted their own supplies of these products, whose crops were not yet ready for harvest, or who simply didn't produce these particular products. It should be noted that these products were all in categories 1–5 and that category 1 (tree fruits) and category 4 (annual crops) comprised 40 of the 46 different products. Also, 8 of the 40 products were sold in the plaza for immediate consumption, which means that demand for them was plaza-specific; and 16 more of these products were partially for immediate consumption in the plaza (i.e., some were taken from the plaza for home consumption). In addition, 7 household-modified foods (category 6) were sold as immediate plaza-consumption goods, and 5 of the 7 were totally consumed in the plaza. Thus, a total of 31 (10.6%) of the 291 household-produced goods were sold to feed the plaza crowd on plaza day (in addition to the four small restaurants that operated on plaza day).

It is clear from row 3 in Table 5-6 that few household products entered the *tienda-casatienda* marketing channels (i.e., only eleven products or 3.8% of the total, and all were from categories 6, 7, and 8). The availability of credit made it possible for these products to flow into the *tienda-casatienda* channels. Relatively speaking, the eleven locally produced products marketed through the *tiendas* were negligible compared to the 67% of industrial manufactures (see categories 8 and 9, Table 5-4) marketed through the *tiendas* out of the total of 225 industrial manufactures imported by Zoogocho *rumbo*. The primary role of the *tiendas*, then, was the marketing of outside industrial manufactures in the local economy. It should be noted that four products were manufactured in the Zoogocho *rumbo* in modern factories (wooden boxes, tar, chemicals for fireworks, and paper). These products were marketed through channels $I_A \rightarrow P_L \rightarrow H_L$ and $I_A \rightarrow T_L \rightarrow H_L$ (see rows 11 and 12 in Table 5-6). Handicraft products marketed through the channel were generally gifts sent to the *rumbo* by relatives living in cities. Several different categories (1, 2, 4, 5, 6) of nonhandicraft household products with origins outside the SZVA region were marketed through the $H_A \rightarrow P_L \rightarrow H_L$ and $H_A \rightarrow T_L \rightarrow H_L$ channels. These were mostly annually grown food products, such as dried chilies, green jalapeños, onions, tomatoes, etc. They were sold in the plaza rather than in the *tiendas* because most were perishable and not easily stored (a problem that the stores may have solved with refrigeration after the completion of the federal electrification program in 1970).

The goal of this analysis is to illustrate quantitatively that the household is the basic production unit in Sierra Zapoteca peasant economy, and it was toward the achievement of this goal that we identified and measured the nature and volume of product flows from producer to consumer. By referring to the Production Unit diagram in Figure 5-2 we can relate this analysis to some of the broader issues of peasant economic studies.

In Figure 5-2 line *ab* represents linear change and segregates the household from the nonhousehold business management units. Linearity is employed for heuristic purposes. In reality it is likely that this change is nonlinear; it may be exponential or have some other form

Figure 5-2. Production units.

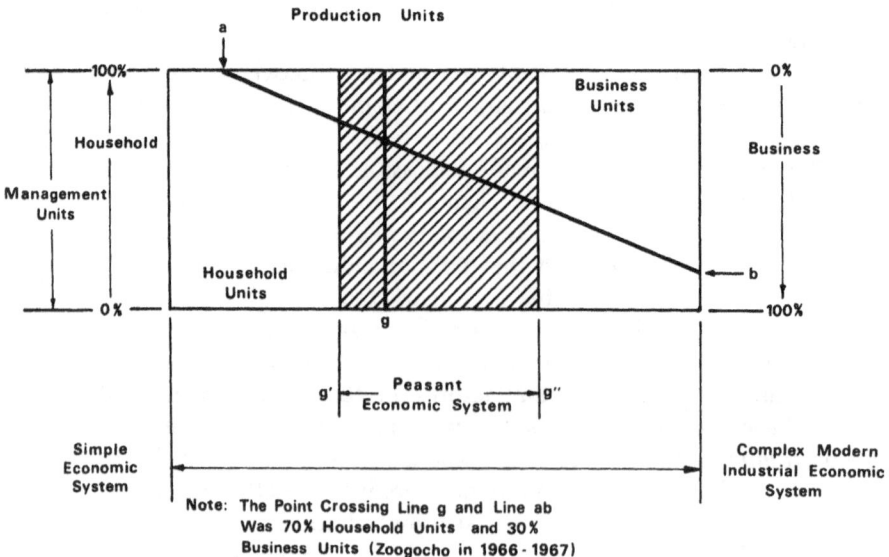

Note: The Point Crossing Line g and Line ab Was 70% Household Units and 30% Business Units (Zoogocho in 1966-1967)

of nonlinearity. Moreover, different regional peasant societies will be characterized by different rates or rhythms of change, and possibly a family of curves would have to be analyzed in order to approximate a single line of change for the peasant economic system. In the diagram, the increment $g'g''$ is defined as the unknown boundary of the area where the peasant economy lies between the hunting-and-gathering economy at one pole and the complex industrial-market economy at the other. Through this study of the peasant economy of Zoogocho *rumbo* I have tried to determine quantitatively where the boundaries of this peasant economy are on a hypothetical continuum of polar types of economies. The point estimated by this study is located at g; that is, 70% of the goods locally consumed in 1967–1968 were produced locally by household management units. This estimate includes goods produced by local household units, H_L, as well as by household units outside SZVA, H_A.

In pursuing the analytical goal, it was necessary to identify and measure the supply (output) and demand (consumption) of each product that circulated through the regional economy for the exclusive consumption of the regional population. The same was also done for regionally produced cash crops (coffee, avocados) that were exported from the region and represented the dominant sources of cash income for the regional population (though unequally distributed). There were, of course, other outside influences on the economic life of the region; for example, the state government had a tax collector stationed in Zoogocho to collect taxes on all products produced locally and on several that were sold locally. We were unable to obtain an estimate of how much money left the regional economy in taxes, but we verified through observation that little was received back in the way of government facilities or services. No conscious state or federal program for progressive economic change existed for the region. There were a few public health programs, a potable-water program, partial financial backing for the construction of a road linking the Sierra Zapoteca (Yalalag) with the Valley of Oaxaca (Tlacolula), as well as an electrification project scheduled for completion in 1970. But there had been no attempt to initiate industrial or agricultural projects to increase regional productivity and income. Aside from a few record-keeping officials for the state government who resided in the district town, none of the local officials was paid for rendering services in any civil post (*cargo*). In other words, the predominant proportion of commodity and money flows in this regional peasant economy circulated re-

Table 5-7

PRODUCTS GROWN ANNUALLY: DATA

Plants	Time Used	Plaza Section	Zoogocho Processed-Planted?	Vendors?
1. Maize husks	All yr.	—	Yes	—
2. Maize spikes	All yr.	J, Q	Yes	Yes
3. Squash	June–Dec.	a	Yes	—
4. Pumpkin seeds	All yr.	F, O	Yes	1
5. Sweet potatoes	Sept.–Dec.	F	Yes	3
6. *Chile onza*	All yr.	F, O, P	Yes	?
7. Fodder	All yr.	J, Q	Yes	5
8. Sugar cane	All yr.	F, G, I, L	Yes	Yes
9. Bean vines	Apr.–June	b	Yes	—
10. Black bean leaves	May, June	b	Yes	—
11. Squash vines	June, July	a	Yes	—
12. Squash flowers	June, July	a	Yes	—
13. Chives	All yr.	P	No	—
14. Broad beans	Sept.–Jan.	B, F	No	—
15. Peas: Dried Green	All yr. Oct.–Dec.	A, B, F	No	—
16. Onions	All yr.	P	Yes	2

SZVA minus Z		Area Pro-cured Outside of SZVA	Total Number of Vendors	Number Sold in Plaza Each Year
No. of Vendors	Vendors' Village			
—	—	—	—	
—	—	—	1–2	42 loads
1	5	—	1	1–2 squash
5	All villages in ZR	—	6	2,288 lbs.
7	3, 4, 22	—	10	2,842
?	All but 1, 2, 7, 8, 14	—	16	442 *arrobas*
2	14	—	7	416 loads
?	3, 4, 5, 15	—	Few	Few stalks
5–6	2, 8, 13	—	5–6	Few vines
1–2	5, 11, 12, 13	—	1–2	Few bunches
1	5	—	1	Few vines
1	5	—	1	Few flowers
8	42	—	5	36,400 bunches
Several	1, 2, 7	—	2	520 lbs.
Several	2, 7	—	5	200 lbs.
1–2	10	Oaxaca, by SPC vendors; *tienda* 6	4	16,900 lbs.

NOTE: This is an example of how products were treated for analysis.
a Ambulatory.
b Wherever the person has been selling other goods; could be in any section.
c Vendor is from this village but product is not.
d Few people sell each week—generally different people from different pueblos each week.
e There are 10½ *arrobas* of green maize spikes sold annually in the plaza for feeding pack animals.
f There are 147 large animals in Zoogocho; 98 persons have animals; 221 *almudes* of pasture are used.
g Fodder used for pack animals brought to the plaza.
h Estimated figure.
Z: Zoogocho
ZR: Zoogocho *rumbo*
SPC: San Pedro Cajonos
exp: experimenting

Plants	Time Used	Plaza Section	Zoogocho Processed-Planted?	Vendors?
17. Pineapples:				
Local	All yr.	I, O	Yes	—
Oaxaca	March–June	E, F, P	No	2
18. Maize	All yr.	H	Yes	Yes
19. Beans	All yr.	F, G	Yes	Yes
20. Potatoes	Sept.–Nov.	A, B, F, G	No	—
21. Tomatoes	All yr.	E, P, R	Yes (exp)	3
22. Marjoram	All yr.	B, H, E, F	Yes	—
23. Watermelons	Feb.–May	G	No	2ᶜ
24. Pepper and cloves	All yr.	E, H	No	—
25. Jalapeños and local green *chile*	All yr.	P	No	—
onza	Apr.–Aug.	F	Yes	—
26. Cacao	All yr.	H, E, F	No	—
27. Cinnamon sticks	All yr.	E	No	—
28. Garlic	All yr.	E, F, H, O, P	No	—
29. Peanuts	All yr.	E, P	No	—
30. Sesame	All yr.	*Tienda* 1	No	—
31. *Chile ancho*	All yr.	E, H, P	No	—
32. *Chile guajillo*	All yr.	E, P	No	—
33. Cantaloupes	March–May	E	No	—

SZVA minus Z		Area Pro-cured Outside of SZVA	Total Number of Vendors	Number Sold in Plaza Each Year
No. of Vendors	Vendors' Village			
4	4, 12		4	208
2	(15, 31)c	Veracruz via Oaxaca	4	40
d	All ZR	Oaxaca	7	1,500 kilos
d	All ZR	Oaxaca	22	5,408 lbs.
Few	2	Oaxaca; Yatuni	2	1,144 *almudes*
Few	4, 6, 12	Oaxaca, by SPC	2	5,772 lbs.
Few	1, 2, 7	Oaxaca, by *tienda*	12	104 kilos
—	—	Oaxaca, by Z	2	50
—	—	Oaxaca	5	2,275 ounces
—	—	Oaxaca		
d	4, 6, 11, 12	—	3	6,084 kilos
—	—	Oaxaca	5	?
—	—	Oaxaca	4	?
—	—	Oaxaca	10	20,800 heads
—	—	Oaxaca	2	104 kilos
—	—	Oaxaca	1	—
—	—	Oaxaca	9	?
—	—	Oaxaca	5	416 kilos
—	—	Oaxaca	2	50

	Total Number Consumed Annually (Avg.)	
Plants	In One Household	In Zoogocho
1. Maize husks	3.2 *bultos*	771.2 *bultos*
2. Maize spikes	4.0 *arrobas*	964 *arrobas*
3. Squash	15 squash	3,615 squash
4. Pumpkin seeds	4.5 lbs.	1,084.5 lbs.
5. Sweet potatoes	2 potatoes	482 potatoes
6. *Chile onza*	0.5 *arroba*	118 *arrobas*
7. Fodder	*t*	*t*
8. Sugar cane	4 stalks	964 stalks
9. Bean vines	1–2 meals	361.5 meals
10. Black bean leaves	3–4 meals	843.5 meals
11. Squash vines	2–3 meals	602.5 meals
12. Squash flowers	0.5 meals	118 meals
13. Chives	26 bunches	6,266 bunches
14. Broad beans	Few	Few
15. Peas	1 lb.	241 lbs.
16. Onions	39 lbs.	9,399 lbs.
17. Pineapples	4.5 pineapples	1,084.5 pineapples
18. Maize	1,274 kilos	307,034 kilos
19. Beans	130 lbs.	31,330 lbs.
20. Potatoes	Few	Few
21. Tomatoes	Few	Few
22. Marjoram	3 oz.	723 oz.
23. Watermelons	—	—
24. Pepper and cloves	2 oz.	482 oz.
25. Jalapeños and local green *chile onza*	13 kilos	3,133 kilos
26. Cacao	6 lbs.	1,446 lbs.
27. Cinnamon sticks	135 grams	32,535 grams
28. Garlic	52 heads	12,532 heads
29. Peanuts	Few kilos used for snacks; very little for *mole*	
30. Sesame	Few pounds bought by breadmakers	
31. *Chile ancho*	1.5 kilos	3,615 kilos
32. *Chile guajillo*	1.5 kilos	3,615 kilos
33. Cantaloupes	First year in Zoogocho: immediate	

In Zoogocho Rumbo	Household Potential ZR/Yr. from Plaza	Approximate Percentage of Items Procured from		
		House-hold (%)	Plaza (%)	Tienda/ Casatienda (%)
7,552 bultos	—	100.00	0.00	0.00
9,440 arrobas	—	100.00	0.00e	0.00
35,400 squash	0.0006	99.996	0.004	0.00
10,620 lbs.	0.97	78.46	21.54	0.00
4,720 potatoes	1.20	39.79	60.21	0.00
1,156 arrobas	0.19	61.76	33.24	0.00
f	g	100.00	g	0.00
9,440 stalks	—	100.00	—	0.00
8,260 meals	—	100.00	—	0.00
8,260 meals	—	100.00	—	0.00
5,900 meals	—	100.00	—	0.00
1,156 meals	—	100.00	—	0.00
36,400 bunches	15.42	0.00	100.00	0.00
Few	0.22	?	?	0.00
2,360 lbs.	0.11	89.00	11.00	0.00
92,040 lbs.	7.161	5.00	92.00	3.00
10,620 pineapples	0.11	97.66	2.34	0.00
3,006,640 kilos	0.64	44.54	0.05	55.45
306,800 lbs.	2.29	70.00	1.76	28.24
Few	0.49	3.00	97.00	0.00
Few	2.45	5.00	90.00	5.00
201 kilos	0.44 k.	20.00	51.74	28.26
—	—	—	—	0.00
4,720 oz.	0.96	0.00	48.20	51.80
30,680 kilos	2.58	80.17	19.83	0.00
14,160 lbs.	?	0.00h	15.00h	85.00h
318,600 grams	?	0.00h	15.00h	85.00h
122,720 heads	8.81	0.00	16.95	83.05
—		0.00	0.00	100.00
—		0.00	100.00	0.00
35,400 kilos	?	0.00h	15.00h	85.00h
35,400 kilos	0.18	0.00	1.18	98.82
plaza-consumed	—	0.00	100.00	0.00

gionally and could be identified and measured locally with the tools of microanalysis.

What does the future hold for this regional peasant economy of the Sierra Zapoteca? For one thing the plaza will probably decrease gradually in size and function. For example, with the completion of electrification in 1970, refrigeration was introduced; this means that the *tiendas* are now able to handle a larger variety of items that have traditionally been sold in the plaza. Nevertheless, the level of income of the regional population, which is, of course, low, is a crucial variable in considering the possibility of changes in plaza activity. My analysis shows that 87 (17%) of the 516 items consumed in the Zoogocho *rumbo* in 1966–1967 were unmodified goods; that 204 (40%) of the total were household-modified goods; and that 225 (44%) of the goods consumed were industrial manufactures. But, in terms of volume, unmodified goods were still more important than industrial manufactures in the annual consumption of the regional population. More important is the fact that the household-modified consumables are potentially replaceable by industrial manufactures. The latter often become available at a lower price and are of better quality (e.g., more durable) than local manufactures; consequently they gain rapid acceptance by regional consumers (as plastic goods are doing today). The Zoogocho peasant does not hesitate to buy competitively so as to stretch his limited income. But in the absence of a general rise in the regional income level, the replacement of local manufactures by industrial manufactures would, other things remaining equal, cause a recession in the regional economy (i.e., local producers would lose income as a result of reduced sales for their products). One conclusion emerges clearly from this discussion: the fate of the regional economy is the fate of the peasant producer-consumer.

6. Survey of the Market System in the Nochixtlán Valley and the Mixteca Alta

JOHN C. WARNER

The weekly Sunday Nochixtlán market, or *plaza*, while a definable unit in itself, is an integral working part of a much larger system of markets. The purpose of this essay is to define and discuss, first, the role of the Nochixtlán market in relation to itself and the Nochixtlán Valley, and, second, its role in relationship with other markets in northwestern Oaxaca, especially the Mixteca Alta. I will primarily discuss the basic questions of the why, what, where, who, how, and when of the market.[1]

The town of Asunción Nochixtlán is the political, economic, social, and religious center of the *distrito* of that name, located on the Pan American Highway approximately equidistant from Huajuapan de León to the northwest and Oaxaca City to the southeast (Fig. 6-1). Politically, the *distrito* is composed of thirty-two *municipios*, with the *municipio* of Nochixtlán, the largest, having a population of 7,406 (1960 census). The town of Nochixtlán, near the geographic center of the Mixteca Alta, has a population of 3,172, more than 2½ times that of the second-largest town, Yanhuitlán, fifteen kilometers west on the highway. It is the largest town in the area bounded by Tamazulapan (3,390) fifty kilometers (by road) to the northwest,

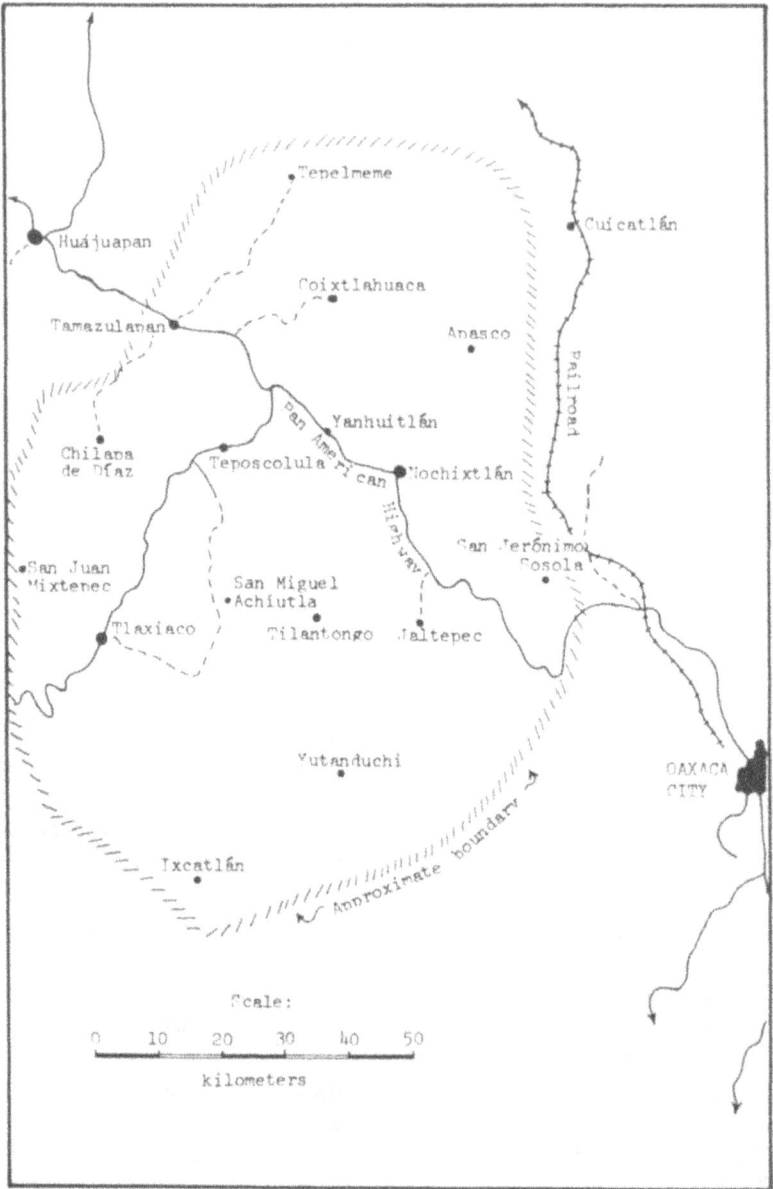

Figure 6-1. The Mixteca Alta.

Tlaxiaco (6,082) one hundred kilometers to the southwest, and Oaxaca City (90,000) one hundred kilometers to the southeast. Of more direct concern here, Nochixtlán is the most important market town within the same area in terms of exchange volume, number of patrons, and the size of their area of origin.

THE NOCHIXTLÁN MARKET

The functions that the Nochixtlán market serves are many. Most obvious and principal to all markets is that of providing a stage for the exchange of goods, and this paper deals primarily with this function.

The market also provides a time and a context for extramarket business. For example, a cattle buyer from Puebla, as well as buying cattle brought into market by Valley locals, often arranges there to buy cattle outside the market on the following day to avoid the heavy market tax. There are also distinct correlations between market day and activity in the town's business establishments. Many essentials, such as kerosene and other supplies, are not available (or are available only in small amounts) in the market, and the town's *tiendas* enjoy their most active trade on Sunday. Many of the *tiendas*, such as general-supply stores and those that sell mescal, transact as much as one-third to one-half their weekly volume on that day. Although many of the market vendors undersell the *tiendas* in like goods, other low-investment vendors buy their goods in the *tiendas* for resale in the plaza with a healthy mark-up—and everyone does a lively business.

The market situation also serves an essential social function as a meeting place for people to gossip, talk over crops, get drunk together, and so on. Also, the occasion presents an opportunity for many to participate in religious or civic functions. Thus, an out-of-town marketer is able to attend church service, usually a rare event in the smaller communities, and all the government offices—mayor's office, tax offices, etc., as well as the post office and telegraph office—experience their busiest day of the week. Monday is the only day of the week that many of these offices are closed.

Determining what goods enter the market and what goods bypass it, and why, is an interesting problem. As a general rule, the marketplace is the main medium for sales of perishable goods, such as fruits and vegetables, and manufactured consumer items, such as clothes and pottery. The market is often the only place of exchange for certain regional subsistence handicrafts and farm produce. Some

Table 6-1

PRODUCT SPECIALIZATIONS

Product	Nochixtlán Area
Canastas (stiff reed shopping baskets)*	Chindúa, Colonia Guadalupe
Piscadores (large reed baskets)*	Jaltepectongo, Tilantongo, Nejapilla
Canastas chiquihuites (small reed baskets)	Santa María Añuma
Cohetes (fireworks)	Jaltepectongo,* Nochixtlán
Cal (burnt lime)*	Rancho La Unión of San Bartolo Soyaltepec
Cotones (ponchos)* and *sarapes* (blankets)*	Yodocono, Nochixtlán, Santa María Peñoles, Chicahua, Cántaros, Tidaá
Blacksmith goods*	Nochixtlán, Llano Verde, Yodocono, Jaltepec
Metates	Yucuita, Jaltepec, Ranchos San Miguel and San Isidro of Jaltepec, Yodocono, Nuxaño, Rancho Los Angeles of Etlatongo, Tilantongo,* Río Verde, Nejapilla
Laja (building stones)	San Juan Sayultepec
Velas (candles)	Nochixtlán, Topiltepec, Tlachitongo, Yodocono*
Pulque* and tepache* (fermented cactus drinks)	Quilitongo, San Miguel Adéquez, Rancho La Luz of Etlatongo, Nochixtlán
Cattle (buyers and sellers)*	Yucuita, Tillo, Añañe, Nochixtlán
Pieles (goat and sheep skins) (buyers and sellers)*	Yanhuitlán, Nochixtlán, Tlatayapan
Quesos (cheese)*	Nochixtlán, Etlatongo, Tinú
Guarachis (sandals)*	
Pottery: *comales* (tortilla griddles)*	San Miguel Adéquez, Santa Inés del Río, Rancho Buenavista of Jaltepec

NOTE: An asterisk by the name of a product indicates that the product is a marketplace item in at least most of the markets in the area of the places listed. An asterisk by the name of a place indicates that the product is a marketplace item in that place or the nearest marketplace.

Cyclical Market Area

Santiago Río Delgado

Huajuapan*
Estancia, Rancho San Miguel of
Jaltepec, Ojo de Agua and Ca-
ñada María near Tlaxiaco
Tlaxiaco, Yolomécatl, Santa Cruz
Tayata, Santa Catarina Tayata

Tlaxiaco, Tamazulapan, Teposcolula

Chilapa de Díaz*

Huajuapan, Teposcolula
Santo Domingo Tonaltepec, Ran-
chos Vistahermosa and Río Blanco of Tonaltepec, Magdalena

Product	Nochixtlán Area
Pottery, other	Cántaros (before), Nochixtlán (glazed ceramic tiles)
[Other pottery that reaches the area*	
Rebozos (shawls)*	
Ladrillos (fired bricks) and tejas (roof tiles)	Nochixtlán, Yodocono, Chindúa, San Miguel Adéquez, Nuñú
Porcelana (porcelain)	Nochixtlán
Huevos (eggs)*	Etlatongo, Jaltepectongo
Flores (flowers: marigolds)*	Zahuatlán
Tortillas de trigo (wheat tortillas)*	Jaltepectongo, Etlatongo, Nuxaño
Pan (bread)*	Nochixtlán, Añañe, Yanhuitlán, etc.
Sombreros (palm hats)*	(too many to mention here)
Tenates (palm baskets)*	Zachío, Tilantongo, Nejapilla, etc.
Petates (palm mats)*	Zahuatlán, Jaltepec, San Miguel Adéquez, Santa Catarina Adéquez, Santa Inés Zaragoza, Tidaá, El Cortijo, Huauclilla, etc.
Sopladores (palm fire fanners)*	Zachío, Jaltepectongo, Tidaá
Escobas (palm brooms)	Nochixtlán (factory), Zachío,* Añuma*
Escobitas para comales (palm brushes for tortilla griddles)*	Zachío
Mecate (palm rope)*	Ranchos San Miguel and Buenavista of Jaltepec

Cyclical Market Area
Peñasco, San Juan Mixtepec, Rancho Morelos of Tinú
Tonaltepec,* Río Blanco,* San Antonio Nduajico,* Santa María Juquila,* Atatlahuca,* San Juan Numí*
Oaxaca City, Atzompa, Coyotepec, Puebla, Acatlán, Nduajico, Santa María Juquila, Juquililla, San Jerónimo]
Santa María Juquila and area, Juquililla
Ajalpan, Tamazulapan

(too many to mention here)
San Andrés Lagunas, San Jerónimo Sosola, Llano Verde, Yolomécatl, etc.
San Miguel Piedras, San Mateo Sosola, Yutanduchi, Teozacoalco, Cavacuá, Sindihui, Apasco, Guadalupe Vistahermosa, San Pedro Jaltepectongo, Nuxaá, Nuxiño, Barranca Chindella, Yolomécatl, San Marcos de León, etc.
Santiago Mitlatongo, San Andrés Lagunas, San Miguel Piedras
San Andrés Lagunas,* Huajuapan,* Llano Verde,* San Jerónimo Sosola*

San Pedro Nopala, Teotongo

Product	Nochixtlán Area
Bosales (palm ox-muzzles)	Nochixtlán (jail), Zachío, etc.
Yugos (ox yokes) *	Cántaros, Tidaá, Diuxi, Tilantongo
Madera para yugos (wood for ox yokes)	Santa Catarina del Río
Manceras para arados (wooden plows) *	Cántaros, Tidaá
Cabos (wooden ax handles) *	Tidaá, Tilantongo
Cucharas de madera (wooden spoons) *	Tilantongo, Tidaá
Molinillos (wooden chocolate beaters) *	Tilantongo
Carretas (wooden ox carts)	Amatlán, Cántaros (Yododeñe)
Timones (wooden plow shafts) *	Tidaá, Diuxi, Tilantongo
Fustes (wooden donkey saddles)	Huauclilla, Cántaros
Arneros and *sarandones* (grain winnowers)	Huauclilla, Yodocono
Leña (firewood) *	Amatlán, Cántaros, Tiltepec
Ocote (pitch pine) *	
Carbón (charcoal) *	Cántaros, Amatlán, Ixtaltepec, Tilantongo
Bateas (wood wash basins)	Tidaá
Carpentry goods: *sillas* (chairs), *puertas* (doors), *camas* (beds), *mesas* (tables), etc.*	
Tablas (boards) *	
Polines (wood poles) *	
Baúles (wood trunks) *	
Tejamaniles (wood shakes) *	
Tortilleras (wood tortilla presses) *	

Cyclical Market Area

Tamazola
San Juan Mixtepec,* Tamazula-
    pan,* Tilantongo

Tamazola, Yucuxina, Llano Verde,
    Teotongo
Yucuxina
Nuxaá, Nuxiño, Teotongo

Ojo de Agua*
Santa Cruz Nundaco

Nundaco, Santo Tomás Ocotepec,
    Tamazola
San Juan Numí
San Miguel El Grande
Guadalupe Victoria, Itundujia
Nundaco

items, such as pottery, are sold almost exclusively in the market-place, while some durable factory-manufactured items, such as bicy-cles, never enter the marketplace at all.

Table 6-1 indicates all of the area's known nonagricultural prod-uct specializations in two columns. The first column lists the products produced in the Nochixtlán Valley and surrounding mountain vil-lages, while the second column lists those products produced in vil-lages within the Nochixtlán cyclical market area, as defined below. An asterisk indicates those products that are marketplace items. The marketing of these items is dealt with in greater detail below in the discussion of all the area's markets.

Goods for sale in the market come from a wide range of origins. Many goods can easily be identified as coming from Nochixtlán itself, the Valley, the Mixteca Alta, or other areas of Oaxaca and Mexico. Other items are imported, like many plastic articles and cheap hardware items from the United States and Japan. Also made in the United States are the automobile-tire soles of the Huajuapan- and Oaxaca City–made *guarachis* (sandals).

Vendors come from as far away as Oaxaca City to the southeast, Tlaxiaco to the southwest, and Huajuapan and Puebla to the north-west. Sometimes fruit wholesalers come from as far away as Vera-cruz. Some of the Oaxaca City vendors sell Valley of Oaxaca woven goods—cotton rebozos and woolen sarapes—while several others sell *guarachis*. Another Oaxaca City man sells *pan bolillo* (buns), and he arrives on a pick-up truck with a man from Etla who sells *queso* and *quesillo* (cheese). Another Oaxaca City man and his wife sell veg-etables, with *chile Tampico* ("Tampico" peppers) as their main item. Two men from Tlaxiaco and another from Teposcolula sell Tlaxiaco-area woodwork items. Several men from Huajuapan sell *guarachis*, and another man sells medicinal herbs. Sometimes Huajuapan men set up *puestos* of *mercería* (notions). Most of the Puebla vendors sell clothes or blankets, though most clothes and yard goods are sold by Tamazulapan vendors. Occasionally a man from Teozacualpan de Amilpas, Puebla, sells Puebla pottery.

The Nochixtlán market draws its consumers from a smaller area. It serves primarily all of the Valley communities north of Jaltepec, northeast of Yodocono, and east of Yanhuitlán, and its influence to the north and east of town penetrates much farther because there are no other nearby markets in those directions (Fig. 6-2). However, not all customers are consumers. Many people buy goods like vege-tables and fruit or woven *palma* products for resale elsewhere. Much

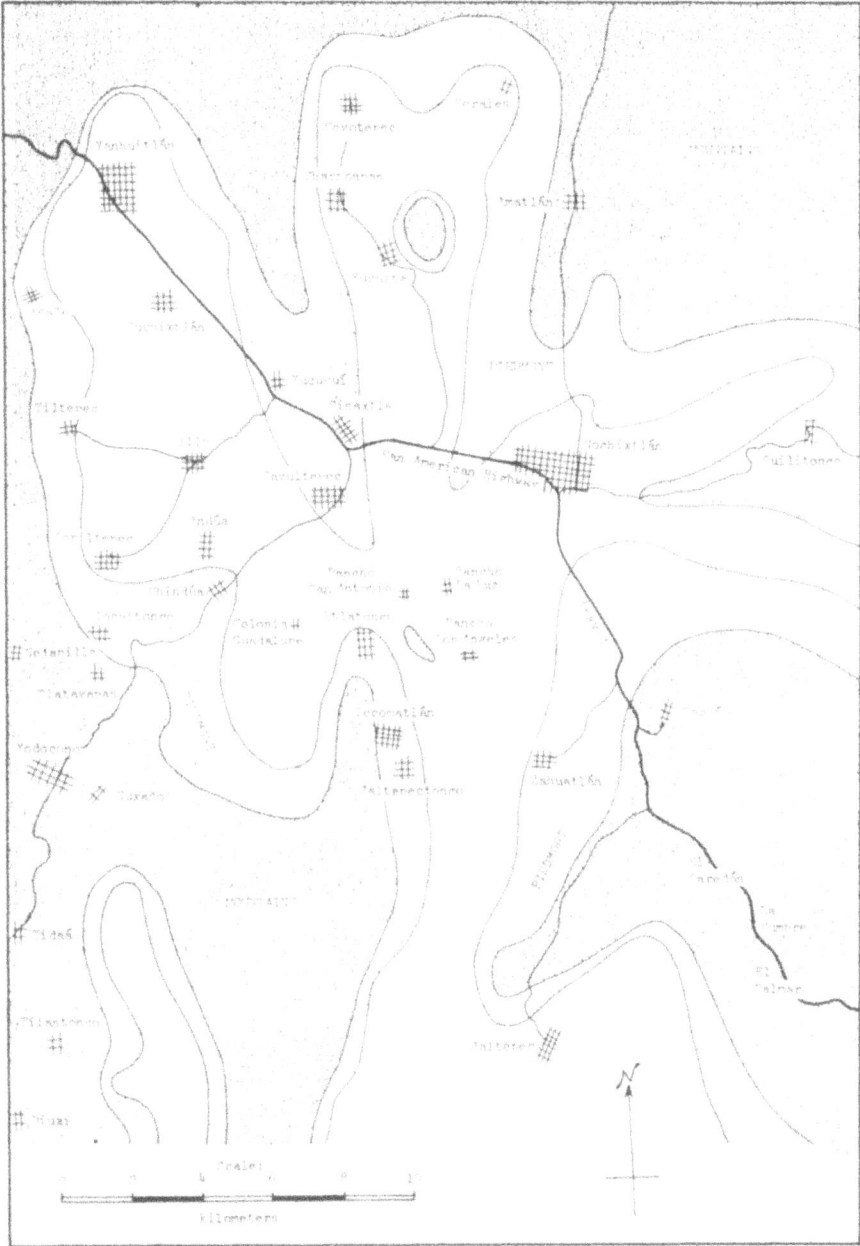

Figure 6-2. The Nochixtlán Valley.

of the former is bought for resale in the area's secondary markets that are outside the cyclical system, like Yodocono and Tilantongo, and much of the latter is bought by people from outside the Nochixtlán area for resale in the Tamazulapan and other markets.

The matter of who are the sellers and buyers has already been partially discussed. Briefly, sellers can be classified as *propios* (producers-sellers), wholesalers, *comisionistas* (commission agents), and retailers. They may be *caseteros*, *puesteros*, or *ambulantes*. (*Caseteros* occupy permanent stalls, or *casetas*; *puesteros* set up and occupy provisional stalls, or *puestos*; *ambulantes* are roving peddlers.) They may, like many *propios*, be subsistence-oriented. For them, selling their goods is not looked on as a means of maximizing profit —or even making money at all; it is considered as a kind of delayed-action barter, with subsistence as the goal in mind. This subsistence orientation is more typical of the large indigenous segment of the society. Or the sellers may be profit-oriented, as in the case of wholesalers and most retailers, such as clothes vendors. Capital accumulation and profit are the main goals of these more commercially sophisticated, often full-time merchants.

The question *how* has several ramifications—how goods are acquired, how they get to the market, how they are marketed once they are there, how prices are determined, and how the exchanges take place are all points of interest. Goods are acquired either by growing them (agricultural or livestock goods), gathering them (as in the case of *tunas* [*nopal* fruit]), making them (*petates*), or buying them for resale. Goods bought for resale may be bought from the producers early on Sunday morning for resale later in the same day, or they may pass through several markets before reaching Nochixtlán. Some *palma*, for example, from the Teozacoalco and Yutanduchi area, passes through the Santa Inés Zaragoza and then the Jaltepec markets before reaching the Nochixtlán market. Grapes from as far away as Chihuahua pass through Mexico City and on to Oaxaca City before appearing at the *puestos* of some of the larger *recauderos* (vegetable and fruit sellers).

Many goods, usually hand-made items of low capital investment and low return or goods from relatively inaccessible areas, are brought to market on donkey back or on foot. For example, pottery from Santo Domingo Tonaltepec is taken first either by donkey or on foot to either Cieneguilla or Yanhuitlán. If to Cieneguilla, the trip is usually completed by bus or truck; if to Yanhuitlán it continues either by burro or by local trucks that provide a kind of auxiliary bus service on Sundays. Many other goods, such as clothes, are characteristically marketed by vendors who either have their own trucks or regularly travel with ones that do.

Most goods are sold in *puestos* and *casetas* in the marketplace proper or in the streets adjoining the marketplace. Generally speaking, most of the smaller *puesteros* are *propios*, while the *caseteros* and most of the larger *puesteros* are retail or wholesale intermediaries. The wholesalers, customarily tropical-fruit vendors, are usually in the street and carry on a simultaneous wholesale-retail business directly from their trucks. Some goods, ranging from sweet bread to flypaper, are sold by *ambulantes*, many of whom are *comisionistas* (commissioned agents). Other goods, such as chickens, charcoal, and firewood, seldom reach the market at all, being sold in the streets by the sellers as they walk through town toward the market.

Although a few items have fixed prices, selling prices for many goods are arrived at only through bargaining, with the initial seller's quotation usually much higher than the final selling price. Depending on the item in question and the situation, the selling may end up as an even compromise (i.e., seller and buyer give ground equally) or else very close to the offered or asked-for price—or, if the buyer and seller are unable to close the gap between bid and quotation, there may be no sale at all. In the Nochixtlán market most purchases are made with cash, though buying *al fiado* (on credit) and through *cambio* (barter) also occur. Barter and credit buying are more common in some of the smaller markets.

Also under study is the growth and decrease of market activity throughout the day, on both Sundays and weekdays. Some Sunday market-goers sell all of their goods by dawn, while others are still selling past dark. Examples of the former are people who walk into town on Saturday night from places like Apasco and Apoala to sell their *petates* and *tenates* the next day for enough cash to buy their weekly necessities and arrive back home that evening. Examples of the latter are a couple of *recauderos* who string up light bulbs by their *puestos* to gain an hour or more selling time, as well as some of the *comedor casetas* that stay open past midnight to serve the late-to-leave. Generally speaking, however, the hours of most intensive activity are from about 10:00 A.M. to 3:00 P.M. The livestock market, where mostly cows, oxen, and pigs are sold, doesn't get under way until 10:00 A.M., and usually all the animals are sold by 1:00 P.M.

There is always some activity in the marketplace on every day of the week (Fig. 6-3). Almost all of the vendors who sell during the week (vegetables and fruits, meat, *barbacoa* [pit barbecue of mutton or goat], tortillas, bread, etc., and sometimes Atzompa and Oaxaca pottery) also sell the same goods on Sunday, though the locations of most of their *puestos* are changed. The decrease in size of the weekday market from 8:00 A.M. (the weekday's busiest hour) to 3:30 P.M. can also be seen in Figure 6-3.

There is also a seasonal variation of many of the marketplace items. For many items, such as agricultural goods, the factor for variation may be as simple as harvest time—though even this isn't as simple as it may first seem, because some crops may be stored after harvest with the idea of saving them until prices go up. The sale of other items, such as religious pictures, certain kinds of bread, and fireworks, fluctuates in close correlation with community or *barrio* religious celebrations. Indeed, on the Sunday after the Día de los Muertos there is virtually no market at all, and it is known as a *plaza muerta*, or dead market, while the two Sundays in October preceding that day are perhaps the most active of the entire year.

MIXTECA ALTA AND OTHER MARKETS

The next largest market unit is the grouping of markets that comprise the Nochixtlán cyclical market circuit. These are the six markets that make up the unit of market towns most regularly visited by the area's motorized market vendors (see Fig. 6-4). These towns and their market days and their town and *municipio* populations (1960) are as follows (asterisks indicate *cabeceras* of *distritos*):

Sunday	Nochixtlán°	(3,172; 7,406)
Monday	Yanhuitlán	(1,253; 2,136)
Tuesday	Coixtlahuaca°	(1,479; 4,938)
Wednesday	Tamazulapan	(3,390; 4,308)
Thursday	Teposcolula°	(2,146; 4,489)
Friday	(none)	("*palma* market" in Jaltepec)
Saturday	Jaltepec	(694; 4,219)

An amplification of this unit includes other smaller markets, which, although they are located roughly within the same area as the cyclical circuit (Fig. 6-4), do not function as a part of that or any other cyclical circuit. These markets, with village and *municipio* (if applicable) populations, are as follows:

Sunday   Tilantongo (135; 3,507), Llano Verde (217), Santa

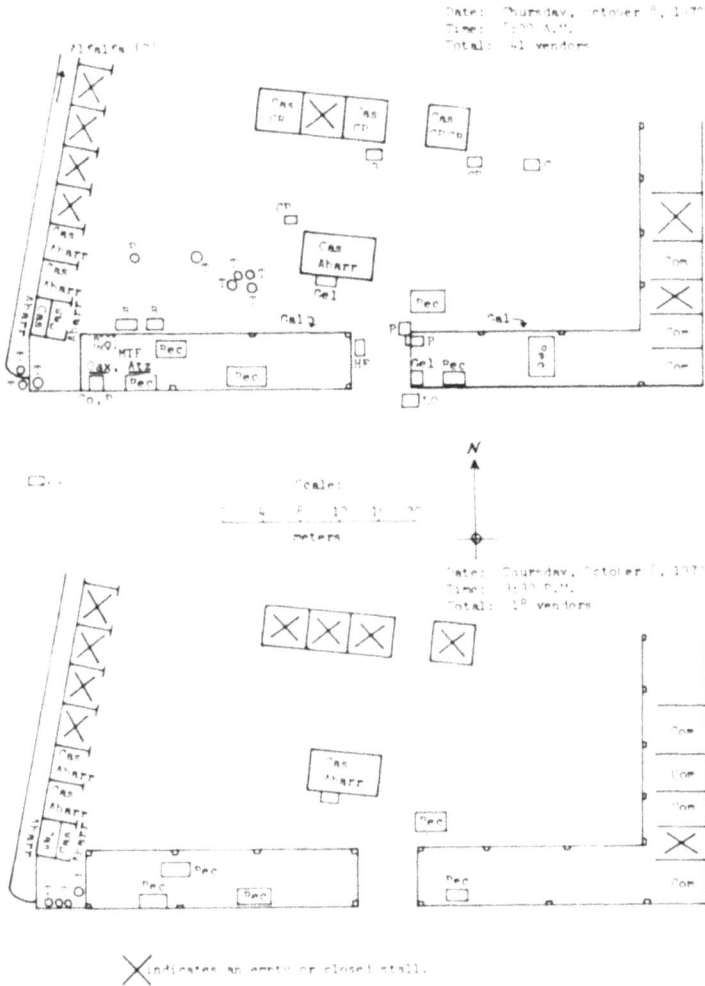

Figure 6-3. Nochixtlán weekday market.

Abbreviations: Abarr, *abarrotes* (groceries); Atz, Atzompa; B, *barbacoa* (pit-barbecued meat); C, *carne* (raw meat); Cas, *caseta* (permanent stall); Co, *comida* (prepared food); Com, *comedor caseta* (eating stall); CP, *carne de puerco* (pork); CR, *carne de res* (beef); Gal, *galera* (roofed area); Gel, *gelatina* (gelatin); HF, *huevos y frijol* (eggs and dried beans); LC, *leche y caña* (milk and sugar cane); Lo, *loza* (earthenware pottery); LQ, *leche y queso* (milk and cheese); MTF, Monday, Tuesday, and Friday only; Oax, Oaxaca City; P, *pan* (bread); Rec, *recaudo* (vegetables and fruit); T, tortillas. Only the southern edge of the plaza is shown; the Sunday market occupies a much larger area.

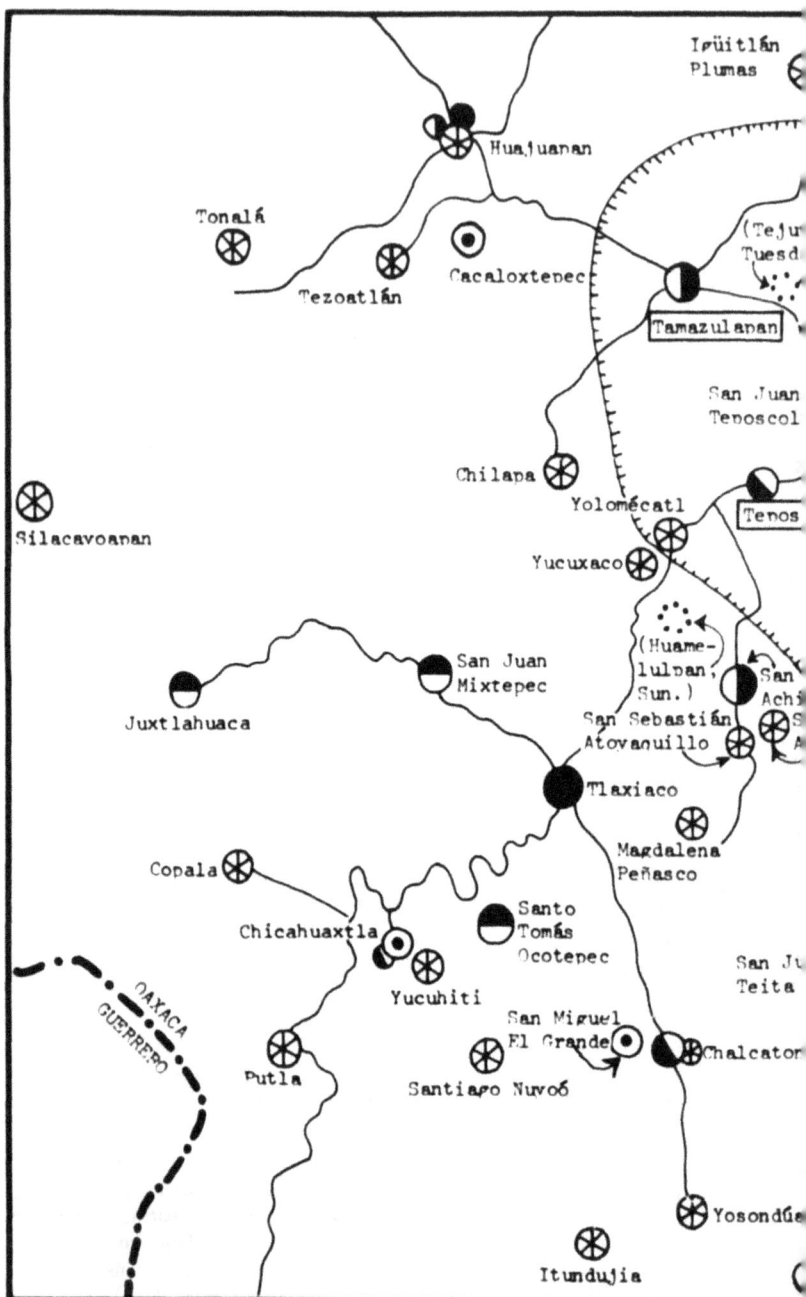

Igüitlán
Plumas

Huajuapan

Tonalá

Tezoatlán

Cacaloxtepec

(Teju
Tuesd

Tamazulapan

San Juan
Tenoscol

Chilapa

Yolomécatl

Tenos

Silacayoapan

Yucuxaco

(Huame-
lulpan,
Sun.)

San
Achi

San Juan
Mixtepec

San Sebastián
Atoyaquillo

Juxtlahuaca

Tlaxiaco

Magdalena
Peñasco

Copala

San Ju
Teita

Chicahuaxtla

Santo
Tomás
Ocotepec

OAXACA

GUERRERO

Yucuhiti

San Miguel
El Grande

Chalcaton

Putla

Santiago Nuyoó

Yosondú

Itundujia

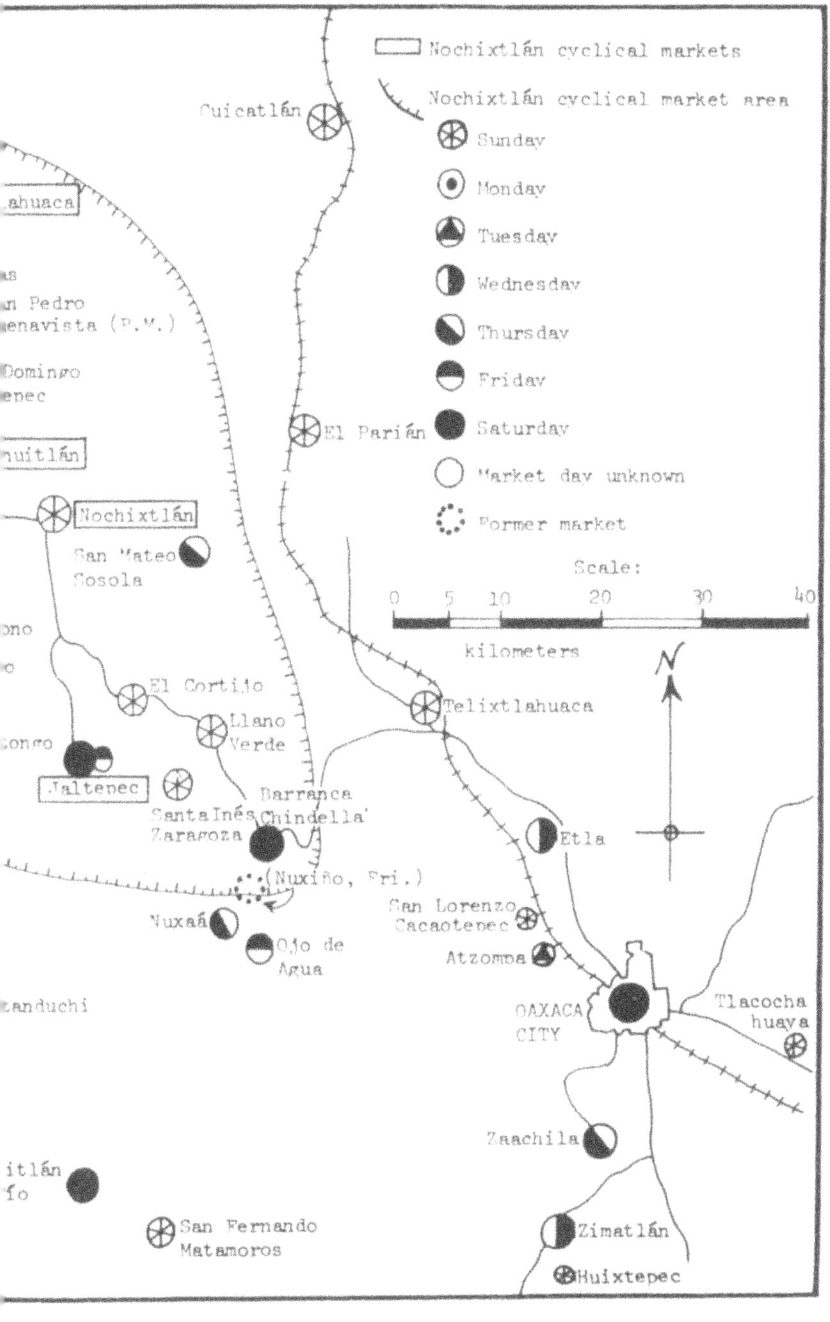

Figure 6-4. Oaxaca market towns.

Inés Zaragoza (804; 2,119), Santo Domingo Tonaltepec (349; 942), La Batea (not in census), Yolomécatl[2] (1,995; 1,995), El Cortijo (309)

Monday   San Pedro Tidaá (2,209; 2,209)

Tuesday   Marcos Pérez (600) (June–August only)

Wednesday   San Juan Teposcolula (1,205; 2,683), Natívitas (1,316;
                2,220) (Market day varies from time to time.)

Thursday   San Mateo Sosola

Friday   (none) (The El Cortijo market had been on Friday,
                and San Juan Teposcolula is considering changing
                to Friday.)

Saturday   Yodocono (1,220; 1,220), Barranca Chindella (502)

Unknown   San Pedro Buenavista (467) (Market day varies from
                time to time.)

The largest unit of markets under discussion here includes the
remaining markets of the Mixteca Alta as well as the markets in
other areas of Oaxaca and adjoining states that are either directly or
indirectly connected to the market network of the Mixteca Alta.
The following list, though undoubtedly incomplete, is an attempt
to document the market days of all the known market towns and
villages within the area shown in Figure 6-4:

Sunday   Huajuapan (also Saturday and Wednesday), Tezoa-
                tlán, Tonalá, Igüitlán Plumas, Tepelmeme (eve-
                nings), Silacayoapan, Chilapa, Yucuxaco, San Mi-
                guel Achiutla, San Sebastián Atoyaquillo, Magdalena
                Peñasco, Tataltepec, San Juan Teita, Chalcatongo
                (also Thursday), Yosondúa, Itundujia, Santiago
                Nuyoó, Yucuhiti, Putla, Copala, San Fernando de
                Matamoros, San Lorenzo Cacaotepec, Telixtlahuaca,
                El Parián, Cuicatlán

Monday   Cacaloxtepec, Chicahuaxtla (also Thursday), San Mi-
                guel El Grande

Tuesday   Atzompa

Wednesday   Huajuapan (clothes and yard goods only) (also Sun-
                day and Saturday), San Juan Achiutla, Yutanduchi,
                Sindihui, Etla, Zimatlán

Thursday   Chalcatongo (also Sunday), Chicahuaxtla (also Mon-
                day), Nuxaá, Zaachila

Friday   Juxtlahuaca, San Juan Mixtepec, Santo Tomás Oco-
                tepec, Ojo de Agua

Saturday   Tlaxiaco, Oaxaca City, Huajuapan (also Sunday and
                Wednesday), Zapotitlán del Río
Unknown   Santa Catarina Cuanana

DISCUSSION

Together, all of the above markets offer a broad spectrum of responses to the basic questions posed above for the Nochixtlán market. I will now discuss some of these varied answers, indicating the
various markets to which they apply. Unless specifically stated otherwise, discussion will pertain only to those twenty-one marketplaces
located within the Nochixtlán cyclical market area.

To the question of what is sold, certain items are almost sure to
be available in all markets. Vegetables and fruit are always sold,
and among the markets visited, *palma* was also sold in all. Atzompa
and/or Oaxaca City pottery was sold in all except Santo Domingo
Tonaltepec. Other markets are noted for the goods exchanged in
them. The Oaxaca City market is the prime source for wholesale
vegetables for the eastern Mixteca Alta, with Nochixtlán as the
principal local distributing point. On the other hand, vegetables
from Atlixco, Pue. (Saturday and Tuesday markets) and Puebla
(Thursday and Sunday markets) compete strongly with Oaxacan vegetables for the western Mixteca Alta, with Tamazulapan (Wednesday market) as the principal local distributing point. Most tropical
fruits from Veracruz are distributed wholesale through the Nochixtlán market. Carpentry items like tables and chairs are distributed
through the Tlaxiaco market. Livestock make up a large percentage
of total market sales in Ocotlán and Jaltepec, and the Sindihui market exists almost exclusively for its *palma* trade. The Barranca
Chindella ("La Herradura") market serves principally as an outlet
for locally made *petates* (many also take charcoal to the community
bodegas [storehouses] on Saturday), Llano Verde is an outlet for
petates, *tenates*, and brooms; Natívitas and San Pedro Buenavista
for *sombreros finos* (finely woven palm hats); and San Juan Teposcolula for *sombreros corrientes* (roughly woven palm hats).

As mentioned earlier, barter (and also "delayed barter") and
buying on credit are common at some of the smaller markets. For
example, a chili and vegetable vendor from Oaxaca City who sells
his produce for cash in the Nochixtlán market also goes to Yanhuitlán the following day if he has any unsold produce, and there he
completes his sales through barter. The exchange items are either
meals or items he later takes to Oaxaca City for resale. I call the

process that takes place in Barranca Chindella, Llano Verde, and San Juan Teposcolula "delayed barter" where woven *palma* goods are taken to market and sold for cash to wholesale middlemen. This cash is then immediately reinvested in more *palma*, and any money left over is then spent on maize and other staples. Buying on credit is common in many markets, such as Jaltepec and Yanhuitlán, and it is even predominant for sales above two pesos in Santo Domingo Tonaltepec and San Juan Teposcolula.

The question *when* has several dimensions—days of the week, months of the year, and times of day. It should be noted that cyclical market circuits can and do change with time. For *comerciantes* with a team of burros thirty years ago, the Nochixtlán circuit was as follows: Sunday, Nochixtlán; Monday, Yanhuitlán; Tuesday, none; Wednesday, San Juan Teposcolula; Thursday, (San Pedro y San Pablo) Teposcolula; Friday, none; and Saturday, Jaltepec. Markets today elsewhere are strategically placed within the week. The abundance of Sunday markets in the Tlaxiaco area is better understood once it is realized that these markets depend heavily upon the large Saturday Tlaxiaco market as a supplier of goods, many of which are perishable foodstuffs. And, as noted above, the Nochixtlán and Tamazulapan markets are similarly placed in relation to the market days of their principal suppliers, Oaxaca and Atlixco respectively.

The very phenomenon of weekday markets, while usually the ideal arrangement from the full-time *comerciantes'* point of view, is not always the most workable system for other areas of Mexico. In the cyclical market areas of Oaxaca a large percentage of the buyers and small part-time sellers are self-employed *campesinos*. Being their own bosses, they are free (except for a few strategic weeks during the planting and harvest seasons) to take any day or days of the week to go to market. On the other hand, in some areas, like south-central Veracruz, a large portion of the population are peons, and almost all the markets are on Sunday, the day after payday. To further illustrate this point, in addition to its Sunday market, Tierra Blanca, Ver., has a market on the fifth and twentieth of every month, which are the railroad's paydays. Also Orizaba's two biggest industries, breweries and textiles, pay their workers on Wednesday and Saturday afternoons respectively, and its market days are Thursday and Sunday.

While discussing market days it should be noted that the day of the market is not immovable. Many market days are known to have changed in the past, and several are planned for change in the near future. The Copala market was changed in about 1965 from Monday to Sunday because the nearby Chicahuaxtla Monday market had become too competitive with the completion of the Tlaxiaco–Pinotepa Nacional road, which passes within a few hundred meters of Chicahuaxtla. The Coixtlahuaca market day was changed in May, 1969, from Sunday to Tuesday in a successful attempt to revive the market, which had been dwindling for several years with the greater mobility of the area's residents. The tiny market at El Cortijo, which has had two starts in its rocky twenty-two-year history, was changed from Friday to Sunday in January, 1971, and the municipal officials of San Juan Teposcolula are waiting only for the opportunity to cheaply print up flyers to announce the change to Friday of their dwindled forty-five-year-old Wednesday market.

Although transportation factors are usually the main causes, directly or indirectly, for market day changes, there are sometimes other reasons. For example, the very existence of the Natívitas and San Pedro Buenavista markets depends almost entirely upon the arrival of the Coixtlahuaca sombrero buyers, and the market days in these two communities are constantly changing to accommodate these buyers.

Finally, there are some towns, usually the larger ones, that hold their markets on more than one day of the week. The Oaxaca City marketplace is very active all week long; and, although intensified activity is (and traditionally has been) on Saturday, many people in the Mixteca consider that it no longer has any one market day. Tlaxiaco has the Mixteca Alta's largest weekday market; but, although it has a large permanent building in which vegetables and fruit, some pottery, and a few other goods are sold daily, it is of minor proportions when compared to either its own Saturday market or Oaxaca City's weekday market. The Mixteca Baja's weekday market in Huajuapan lies midway between these latter two markets in this respect. Furthermore, Huajuapan has three recognized market days of greater importance. The largest is Sunday, the next smaller is Saturday, and Wednesday is the day that most clothes and yard goods enter the market. A further example of multiple market days is the Chalcatongo market, which was officially changed from Sunday to Thursday before 1950, but where the local people still hold a small Sunday market.

The seasonal dimension to market activity also has several interesting comparative aspects. For most of the cyclical markets, activity is sharpest from September through January, after people have harvested their crops and have cash on hand for more than the staple maize. Activity is slowest from May through July because "All the people are out in their fields [some of which may be holdings far from the market centers] planting." The opposite phenomenon is often the rule for isolated markets, such as Tilantongo. There, the most active markets are from March through June, when a large segment of the migrant population returns from Mexico City and other areas to plant the crops.

A more extreme form of seasonal variation takes place in the mountain village of Marcos Pérez. As with the Natívitas and San Pedro Buenavista markets, the very existence of the market depends upon the arrival of a sombrero buyer from Tejupan. Since he comes from June through August, there is a Tuesday market only during these months. During the rest of the year the area's residents take their sombreros to other markets for sale.

The third dimension, the time of day of market activity, also varies from market to market. Most of the cyclical markets are under way by 8:00 A.M., and activity, though peaking in the early afternoon, is maintained until around 5:00 P.M. The Coixtlahuaca market activity is about one and a half to two hours later, due to its difficult accessibility; for the same reason the Santo Domingo Tonaltepec market doesn't get under way until noon, and activity, maintained at a high level until 3:00 P.M., is stopped almost completely by 5:00 P.M. The Sunday Tepelmeme market is in session from around 4:00 P.M. until 11:00 P.M., due to the fact that the vendors are the same ones who spend the morning and early afternoon in the Igüitlán Plumas market. For similar reasons the San Pedro Buenavista market, when held on the same day as the Natívitas market, is also in the evening, allowing the sombrero buyers time to arrive from Natívitas.

The time of day of activity of a particular market also often changes with improved accessibility. For example, before the road reached Teposcolula the market there didn't get under way until Thursday afternoon, and it continued into the night, with many people staying all night and some even buying and selling on Friday morning. With the completion of the road, however, both buyers and sellers could rapidly get to and from the market and on to the next, and now its active hours are similar to Nochixtlán's.

The question *where* also has three dimensions—where the goods are from and where they go before reaching the consumer, where the vendors are from and where they go, and where the customers are from (areas served by the individual markets).

The first dimension has been treated above to a limited degree in the discussion of the Nochixtlán market. Also, as stated above, many goods pass through several markets before ultimately reaching their consumer. Another example of this is the *ocote*, or pitch pine, from Yucuxino, which enters the Jaltepec market, is sold to buyers who resell it in the Nochixtlán market, then in turn is bought and resold as far away as the Tamazulapan market.

Origins and routes of vendors are another widely varied phenomenon. Mentioned above are the cyclical-market circuit vendors. Other vendors from certain areas of the circuit periphery, such as Teposcolula and Yolomécatl, may spend the week among villages comprising parts of two cyclical market areas. Other common variations in marketing patterns are exemplified by the Nochixtlán vegetable lady who sells only in the Nochixtlán marketplace all week long to avoid the expense of transportation, the Yanhuitlán vegetable lady who sells only in Yanhuitlán and Santo Domingo Tonaltepec (traveling by donkey), and the Rancho San Miguel (*municipio* of Jaltepec) couple who sell only in Jaltepec (white bread) and Tilantongo (vegetables and fruits), also traveling by donkey, and also to minimize expenses. A Nochixtlán lady sells patent medicines only on weekends and when her children are out of school and can help tend the *puesto*. She sells in Jaltepec on Saturday and in Llano Verde on Sunday—less competition than Nochixtlán, and she likes to "get away." A Teposcolula man who makes a unique style of *guarachi* sells in Yolomécatl on Sunday to avoid the competition of the Huajuapan and Oaxaca City *guarachi* vendors in Nochixtlán. He also sells in the Tlaxiaco and Teposcolula markets. Most *barbacoa* vendors sell only in the market of the town in which they live, but one sells in Yanhuitlán, Tamazulapan, Jaltepec, and Nochixtlán.

Most pottery makers in Santo Domingo Tonaltepec and Río Blanco take their own pots to market, but although these pots have a wide market distribution (Jaltepec, Tilantongo, Yolomécatl, Tamazulapan, Huajuapan, etc.), each vendor has only one or two markets in which he (or she) regularly sells pots, while the next market always has certain other vendors. Another man who sells Puebla-area pottery has two circuits that he takes on alternate weeks. One is the Valley of Oaxaca circuit (opting for Zimatlán and Ejutla and selling in Nochixtlán on Sunday), and the other is in the Puebla area itself, where he sells either in the Cuautla or Teozacualpan market on

Sunday, the daily Puebla market on Monday, the San Martín Texmelucan market on Tuesday, the Puebla market again on Wednesday and Thursday (market days are Thursday and Sunday), the Tepeaca market on Friday, and the Atlixco market on Saturday. For comparison, most of the vendors in the Yolomécatl market are residents of that town, and most of the pottery sold there is from the Tlaxiaco area. On the other hand, Yodocono is a unique market in that very few of its vendors are residents, and perhaps roughly half of the vendors (and most of the *recauderos*) are from nearby Chindúa.

The third dimension, the areas served by the individual markets, has also been partially discussed above (Oaxaca, Atlixco, Nochixtlán, and Tlaxiaco markets), though mostly in consideration of resellers. The Yodocono market draws most of its consumers from south of the village, though its livestock, being cheaper than that in Nochixtlán, attracts buyers from all over the Valley. Tilantongo and Jaltepec draw most of their consumers from the south and west of their communities, though *palma* entering both markets has wide distribution in all directions.

The *why* of the various markets has also been explored—why their particular day was chosen, why the days change, and why the markets were even established at all. The first two questions have been discussed above. Reasons for the existence of markets are often complex and varied. Probably most of the older, well-established markets were founded for the same reason as the Santo Domingo Tonaltepec market in September, 1970—and that was to fill a void: to bring certain goods within closer access to the consumers and to provide an outlet for local products. Considering these basic common functions that they perform, the manners in which markets are born may vary greatly. For example, the San Juan Teposcolula market was founded in 1925 because the village had such a violent border dispute with San Pedro y San Pablo Teposcolula that the former's residents found it too dangerous to visit the latter's markets, while by contrast the Yanhuitlán market was founded by decree of King Philip of Spain.

However, it should be understood that a market is not only a thing or a time, it is a process; all markets have experienced birth and growth, some have receded, and some, like the Huamelulpan and Tejupan markets, have died. Others, like the El Cortijo market, have died and been reborn, and others, like the Nuxiño (Friday) and Teozacoalco (Sunday) markets have "moved"—the former to

Barranco Chindella and the latter to Yutanduchi. Presumably the relative functions of these markets have altered with the fluctuations their histories record.

SUMMARY

This essay has explored the functioning of the Nochixtlán market in several roles—as the principal Nochixtlán Valley market, as a market within a cyclical market system, and as an integral working part of larger regional and national networks of distribution of goods.

It is hoped that this essay, though necessarily brief and superficial in many areas, will provide a foundation for further study of the market system(s) throughout the Mixteca Alta. Of prime importance at this stage is effort toward accurate and objective descriptive analyses of the many and varied phenomena that together comprise the market and market systems of Mexico. Only then will we be in a position to understand and deal with this very large and important aspect of Mexican society and economy.

PART THREE

Producers and Marketers: Case Studies

In this section we examine the activities of two separate categories of actors in the Oaxaca economy: producer-sellers (*propios*) and middlemen-traders (*regatones*). It is important to remember that underlying these different strategies of adaptation and differential involvements in the marketing process is a similar involvement in discrete household production-consumption units. A large majority of these actors expend time and labor in the production of use and exchange values destined to the provisioning and maintenance of their household units, and not to the expansion of their business assets and profits in a systematic, cumulative way. Exchange values are sought and acquired by these "peasant" actors (most of them do cultivate the soil for subsistence purposes) as indirect means to acquire use values produced by others; they do not seek them as direct means to accrue profits for reinvestment in profit-making enterprises. This is, then, production and exchange embedded in a process of petty commodity circulation, where maintenance of the household unit (i.e., funding of subsistence, rent, capital reaccumulation, and ceremonial needs) is the rule, and expansion of business activities is the exception.

The essays by Cook and Stolmaker deal with village-based peasant-artisan *propio* populations in the Valley of Oaxaca: *metateros* (metate makers) and *alfareros* (potters) respectively. Cook's essay describes and analyzes the marketing process in the Valley of Oaxaca metate industry. His approach is comparative: data from two village-based sections of the industry that are involved in two separate marketplaces are examined to ascertain similarities and differences in market organization, performance, and the quantified results of performance. To facilitate analysis a basic conceptual distinction is made between *market*, *marketplace*, and *market area*—the market referring to a transactional state of affairs, the marketplace providing a locational context for the conduct of trade, as well as for its systematic observation, and the market area encompassing the distributional routes of products flowing through the marketplace into the market and toward the consumer household. An important implication of this study is that the production and labor process is employed as a focal point for understanding marketing. The market area is viewed as the dependent distributional hinterland of a discrete production center and not of a marketplace; the latter is viewed simply as a way station in the flow of products between producers and consumers. Exchange or marketing relations are viewed as social relations of production—the circulation of use and exchange values through the system is interpreted on the basis of the role of labor and capital in the circulatory process.

Stolmaker examines the impact of an expanding, modernizing economy on the practitioners of a traditional craft—pottery making. An overview of production and exchange processes, consumption patterns, and investment trends highlights areas in which there has been considerable stability, notably ceramics manufacture, and areas that have undergone significant modification, for example, pottery marketing and the development of economic opportunities outside of pottery manufacture. She provides some evidence of the potential for significant capital accumulation and movement from simple commodity circulation to capitalist circulation in the pottery industry. For example, we learn that the village's first trucker "began as a potter, then became a pottery dealer, large-scale landowner, [and] storekeeper" before acquiring a truck. She also suggests that there have been significant developments in the local class structure that are presumably attributable to the investment of profits mobilized from the pottery business (e.g., in the past two generations the village has produced one lawyer, two engineering technicians, sixteen schoolteachers, and several accountants). Unfortunately, it is not clear what role, if any, these members of the bourgeoisie play in the village social structure.

The papers by Waterbury and Chiñas deal with trading populations in two different regions of Oaxaca—the Valley and the Isthmus respectively. Waterbury analyzes the results of a comprehensive household survey in the large village of San Antonino; this census was designed to identify, among other things, the "marketplace-oriented" occupations in the village occupational repertory, namely, those entailing regular buying and/or processing and selling in the marketplaces. This paper provides precise quantitative data to support the thesis, which is often asserted without sufficient documentation, of widespread multiple occupational involvement among these villagers—with agricultural occupations predominating. Chiñas, on the other hand, employs the case-study method to describe in detail the trading operations of Zapotec traveling women vendors, or *viajeras*. What is notable about her cases is the magnitude of the profit accruing to these traders, from sixty to well over one hundred percent of initial outlay, combined with the nonentrepreneurial uses to which it is put (e.g., paying debts, meeting ceremonial obligations, constructing new houses, paying for medical expenses, buying new supplies). In other words, capital is accumulated by these *viajeras* to maintain or improve immediate life conditions or to meet requirements of community and family life, rather than to expand business assets and profit potential. A keen sense of entrepreneurship is required to "make it" as a *viajera*, but the exchange value acquired by the application of entrepreneurial skills is basically channeled into use-value rather than processional-value paths of circulation. In other words, we are once again confronted with a precapitalist form of entrepreneurship in which exchange value is accumulated and circulated to reinforce, not transform, the prevailing mode of production.

Many of the problems and implications raised in the papers of this section will be discussed in greater depth in Part Four.

7. The "Market" as Location and Transaction: Dimensions of Marketing in a Zapotec Stoneworking Industry

SCOTT COOK

Insofar as this essay has a thesis it is that the marketing process in peasant-artisan economies displays regularities through time and across space; that the anthropologist can draw upon Marxist and bourgeois economics, cultural geography, and other nonanthropological sources as deductive departure points for discovering and analyzing these regularities; and finally that convergence and divergence of theoretical principles and empirical patterns infuse economic anthropology with verifiable content and operational efficacy.

Expressed briefly, my view of the marketing phase of the economic process is as follows: it begins as the final stage of production (creation of commodities) is reached, encompasses and operates through exchange, and ends as the initial stage of utilization (destruction of commodities) begins. As an intermediate phase in the economic process, marketing depends upon production to generate and sustain it, just as it, in turn, facilitates and sustains utilization. To conceive of marketing formally as a substantive economic process is to conceive of people and commodities circulating between sites in patterned ways and measurable quantities—a material flow propelled by a series of acts of communication and decision-making.

A marketing system, then, implies regularized, interdependent relationships between people, commodities, and sites in a circulatory process coordinated and animated by flows of information (see below, Part Four).

The following discussion pertains only to one microscopic segment of the Valley of Oaxaca economy and relates to a tiny sector of its peasant-artisan population. And because it focuses on a commodity which has a rather unique status in this economy, that is, the metate, which is the only durable consumer good displayed in the contemporary peasant marketplace that has its origins in the pre-Hispanic economy of the region, the extent to which aspects of its marketing situation will be applicable elsewhere is problematic. My feeling is that what is characteristic of metates may also be characteristic of pottery and other artisan products, all of which are produced and circulated by and among peasants as what Wolf terms "compensatory economic reactions" (1955:458); but that when we turn our attention to agricultural products the relevance of metate-specific patterns diminishes. In any case, I wish to clarify beforehand that I am not advocating the fallacious view that what is true of metates is necessarily true of all other products in the Oaxaca economy, or even of a limited range of them.

THE MARKET CONCEPT AND METATE MARKETING

Marketing is the process of the physical transfer of commodities in space and time from producer to consumer or, more specifically, from place of production to place of exchange to place of use. For the sake of clarity and analytical precision in the study of this process, it is necessary to employ three distinct notions of the term *market*. First, it refers to a theoretical or ideal state of affairs relating to transactions between abstract categories of suppliers and demanders and focusing on the behavior of prices and quantities, as well as on the allocation of rewards to producers and marketers. Second, it refers to a particular time and place where flesh-and-blood buyers and sellers meet to trade, and concentrates on their behavior and the observable, quantifiable results of that behavior. Finally, the market concept may denote a distributional area for products which is dependent upon particular marketplaces and/or upon the production centers that supply products to marketplaces (see Part Four below).

Given these preliminary distinctions and focusing on a single class of commodities like metates, it is legitimate to posit a metate market as being generated through a series of multiple buyer-seller transactions occurring in marketplaces and resulting in the distribution of metates into various market areas. The locus of such transactions need not be (nor is it exclusively so in the case of metates) a particular marketplace or series of marketplaces. In the Valley of Oaxaca economy, however, a large majority of metate sales transactions are marketplace-mediated. Or, expressed differently, each market area is supplied through market transactions occurring in a particular marketplace. Theoretically, of course, a market for a particular commodity can be posited independent of either a marketplace or a market area (i.e., simply as a transactional arena where the forces of supply and demand converge and are manifested in trading behavior), although empirically in the Valley of Oaxaca, as in other regional peasant economies of Mesoamerica, it is usually associated with both.

The Valley of Oaxaca metate industry encompasses four discrete production centers (the Teitipac villages of San Juan and San Sebastián, the village of Magdalena Ocotlán, and the town of Tlacolula de Matamoros). These production centers supply at least one of three specific marketplaces; and the marketplace itself provides an interactional context for the operation of a series of potentially competitive markets. These latter, in turn, are the transactional bases for creating and sustaining a series of partially overlapping metate market areas. One such market area centers on the Oaxaca City marketplace and is supplied by the Teitipac villages; another centers on the Ocotlán marketplace and is supplied by the Magdalena producers; and the third centers on the Tlacolula marketplace and is supplied by the Teitipac producers together with a group of locally resident producers.

It should be noted that in a single commodity–oriented study, such as mine, the observer-analyst starts from the production center and looks forward and outward at the marketing system, rather than starting with the latter (or with one of its component marketing centers) and gazing backward and inward toward the production center. From this perspective, the market area is viewed as the dependent distributional hinterland of a discrete production center and not of a marketplace—which is, so to speak, viewed simply as a way station in the flow of products between producers and consumers (or sellers and buyers).

Given this perspective, I interpret the metate industry data as indicating that metates produced in the two Teitipac villages follow marketing paths that overlap only partially, so that, in effect, the

Oaxaca City marketplace (to a larger degree than the Tlacolula marketplace, where both of these producer-seller groups also compete) is an intermediary marketing site (i.e., bulking and dispersing station) for two metate market areas. This is apparently a reflection of the fact that the Oaxaca City marketplace encapsulates a structurally (and spatially) bifurcated metate market: a wholesale market involving most San Sebastián sellers and a retail market involving most San Juan sellers (although the bifurcation is complicated by product transfers between San Sebastianos and San Juaneros and by occasional dual participation by both sets of sellers in wholesale/ retail transactions). I will discuss these market areas in more detail later in the essay; what I will attempt to do now is to delineate the general structure of the metate market, that is, the transactional arena in which metate suppliers meet metate demanders.

ON THE GENERAL STRUCTURE OF THE METATE MARKET

Single Market or Multiple Markets?

My earlier reference to a series of potentially competitive metate markets implies that I have rejected the notion of a single industry-wide competitive market, that is, one transactional network that integrates all buyers and sellers of metates and crosscuts localities. It is possible to define such a market a priori as encompassing all buyer-seller transactions in which a Valley of Oaxaca metate changes hands—implying that transactions in the Oaxaca City, Ocotlán, and Tlacolula marketplaces (not to mention those occurring outside the marketplace) occur in the same market. But this assumes contact (direct or indirect) between buyers and sellers in the separate marketplaces and the concomitant transmittal of current market information between them, a situation that does not obtain in the metate industry.

On the contrary, the metate data suggest that the intermarketplace circulation of market information, like the circulation of metates and their marketers, is irregular and discontinuous. There are, to be sure, both potential and actual buyers and sellers of metates who move between the Tlacolula and Oaxaca City marketplaces or between the Ocotlán and Oaxaca City marketplaces. But, to my knowledge, there is no buyer or seller who circulates, regularly or occasionally, between all three marketplaces—or between any two of them—to trade in metates. As might be expected, the Oaxaca City marketplace does serve as a conduit for the flow of market information between Tlacolula and Ocotlán (and vice versa), and the same persons who transmit this information presumably are also informed of conditions in the Oaxaca City marketplace. Theoretically, then, at any given time there could be potential transactors with direct or indirect knowledge of prevailing metate market conditions in all three marketplaces. But, to reiterate, I have no evidence to suggest that such knowledge is employed to support activity in the purchase and sale of metates that could function to regularly and systematically link together metate price negotiations in the three separate marketplaces (or even in two of them)—even though their periodicity would be conducive to this. In short, the data indicate that metate transactions occur in three essentially separate and independent site-confined markets rather than in a single site-free market that crosscuts localities and integrates metate trading in discrete marketplaces.

Perfect or Imperfect Competition?

The issue of a single market versus multiple markets for the metate industry dovetails with the issue of whether the inter- and intramarketplace marketing situation is characterized by perfect or imperfect competition. The above discussion of the intermarketplace situation implies that on an industry-wide basis metate marketing is conditioned by various imperfections that tend to create a series of potential perfectly competitive submarkets, rather than a single industry-wide imperfectly competitive market. It is appropriate here to identify and discuss some of the conditions that contribute to the compartmentalization of the metate market at the intermarketplace level.

What, for example, are some of the empirical generalizations that derive from an analysis of the metate price data that bear on the competition issue? Data collected over an eight-month period in 1966–1967 in the Tlacolula, Ocotlán, and Oaxaca City marketplaces show a marked differential in the average monthly price levels between these markets. The widest gap was between the price level in the Oaxaca City market and those prevailing in Tlacolula and Ocotlán—the combined average price curve for the latter two was consistently around fifteen to twenty pesos above the Oaxaca City average price curve. On the other hand, the Tlacolula and Ocotlán markets never displayed an average price curve difference as high as fifteen pesos, and only for two months did they display a difference greater than ten pesos. As we will see, these price differentials reflect a variety of factors, including imperfect buyer/seller knowledge, moderate product differentiation creating quasi brand loyalties, transportation costs, and wholesale versus retail trade volume.

That the Oaxaca City plaza has a larger volume of total metate sales and a higher proportion of wholesale transactions than the Ocotlán plaza is clear from the following figures: between September, 1967, and June, 1968, a total of 307 metates were sold by Magdalena sellers in 297 transactions in the Ocotlán plaza, whereas a total of 865 metates were sold by San Sebastián sellers in 301 transactions in the Oaxaca City plaza.

In the marketing of metates in the Valley of Oaxaca, transportation costs (i.e., bus and/or truck fare plus whatever is required to compensate the individual who carts metates between locations) represent one important factor in discouraging intermarketplace trade. Given the price differences between the Oaxaca City and Tlacolula and Ocotlán metate markets, together with their relative locations vis-à-vis each other and the metate production centers that supply them, arbitrage (i.e., buying metates in the most favorable price location and transporting them for sale in locations of higher prices) would only be feasible from Oaxaca City to Tlacolula or Ocotlán. On the basis of transport costs alone such an arbitrage might appear to be profitable in the short run. But, in reality, other factors intervene to alter the situation. For example, any middleman who acquired metates in Oaxaca City for resale in either Ocotlán or Tlacolula would have to compete against the producers who supply these marketplaces; in the case of the Tlacolula marketplace he would, in many instances, be competing with his own suppliers. While the arbitrager would not be operating under this disadvantage in the Ocotlán marketplace, other factors discourage a Oaxaca City-to-Ocotlán trade. For one thing, the sales volume is much smaller in Ocotlán (and in Tlacolula) than it is in Oaxaca City, so that even if the trader could successfully conduct business in the market his cash returns would be low. Also, the metate-buying public in Ocotlán (and in Tlacolula) has developed strong preferences for particular traits in metates (special qualities of workmanship, type of stone, size, color) which are usually not present in the lower-priced metates sold in Oaxaca City. In sum, there are many factors that minimize the intermarketplace trade of metates in the Valley of Oaxaca.

One important difference, alluded to earlier, between the Tlacolula and Ocotlán metate markets and the Oaxaca City market is that the former involve mostly retail transactions at a relatively low volume of total sales per given time period, whereas the Oaxaca City market involves a larger proportion of wholesale transactions at a higher volume of total sales. Thus, out of a total of 624 separate transactions (transferring 1,320 metates) recorded for a period of one hundred trading days between 1966 and 1968 in the San Sebastián sales area of the Oaxaca City marketplace, approximately 62 percent were purchases of two or more metates for resale purposes. A single big-lot buyer who resells in Ejutla and Miahuatlán purchased 45 percent of the metates sold (582); another 24 percent of total metate sales during this same period were to several big-lot buyers from the Isthmus; 8 percent were to one middleman from Ocotlán who resells along the Ejutla-Miahuatlán-Pochutla axis; and 7 percent were purchased by middlemen from San Juan Teitipac for resale in the Oaxaca City marketplace. In other words, about 84 percent of total metate sales by San Sebastián sellers in the Oaxaca City marketplace were to resellers who purchased in lots of two or more metates per transaction and who might acquire as many as a dozen or more metates on any given trading day. This is in marked contrast to the situation in the Ocotlán and Tlacolula marketplaces over the same period, where more than 95 percent of all recorded sales were to individual buyers for private use and involved only one metate per transaction. Obviously, then, the role of wholesale buyers in the Ocotlán and Tlacolula metate markets is minimal.

If one considers for a moment the possible implications for metate trading in the Oaxaca City marketplace of regular and massive wholesale buying, he will probably infer that competitive market advantage rests with the buyers. Such an inference would, after all, support the case for imperfect competition in the metate industry. Yet when one looks at the supply side of the market with special reference to the problem of freedom of entry of potential suppliers, the impact of market imperfections is properly recognized to have another aspect. It is an axiom of economic theory that natural or cultural conditions can produce monopoly—that is, the position of the seller of a commodity with no near substitutes. Within the total market area served by the Valley of Oaxaca metate industry (or within each of the three market areas supplied by particular production centers), it can be argued that the *metateros* as a collectivity occupy a semimonopoly position. This does not mean that the *metateros* are in a formal collusive posture with respect to the buyers or that they have complete control over price; there is ample data to demonstrate that neither of these conditions exists. What it does mean, however, is that certain natural and cultural factors are present in

peasant-artisan economies of the Valley of Oaxaca type to significantly restrict entry as a supplier into the market for any locally
produced good.

In the metate industry case, for example, a prerequisite of production is the availability of or accessibility to exploitable deposits of
the proper kind of stone. Moreover, for any individual to gain entry
into the metate-production sector of a village economy he must first
satisfy a whole series of particularistic requirements (e.g., citizen-
ship rights in a corporate village, acquisition of the necessary technical knowledge and skills). It is very difficult for a nonnative of a
metate village to acquire ownership or usufruct rights to land for
purposes of cultivation, quarrying, or other use; it is also difficult for
a non-*metatero* native villager who wishes to learn the craft to gain
acceptance among the *metateros* as an equal partner in quarry exploitation and metate production. In essence, as one of the many examples in the Valley of Oaxaca economy of production specialization by community, coupled with a tendency toward intracommunity
occupational specialization by family, the metate industry is well
insulated against possible competition from new producers.

The lack of cooperative marketing organization within and between metate-producing communities precludes a formalization of
these natural monopolistic elements into a collective market strategy. Nevertheless, these factors do function indirectly as counter-
vailing forces to offset substantially the price-negotiating power of
big-lot buyers and to make the individual producer somewhat less
vulnerable to the rigors of competition than he would be otherwise.
Furthermore, just as the producer-seller is competing against many
other producer-sellers in the market, so the big-lot buyer is competing against several other big-lot buyers. The absence of a collusive
posture on the supply side of the market is matched on the demand
side. In the context of price formation it is probably true that the
big-lot buyer has a short-run advantage over the small-lot seller. But
considered in the broader context of the organization of production
in the Valley of Oaxaca economy, it is the big-lot buyer who is dependent in the long run upon the small-lot producer-seller as his
only viable, direct, and regular source of metates. Coupled with the
presence of competing buyers and the relative freedom of entry into
the trading sector of the economy, it can be argued that the middleman-trader, not the producer-seller, is most vulnerable to the forces
of competition (cf. Cook 1970:786–787).

Differential Atomistic Competition at the Intramarketplace Level

Up to this point in the essay, I have presented data and arguments in support of the thesis that, at the intermarketplace or industry-wide level of analysis, the structure of metate marketing is imperfectly or monopolistically competitive. Locational factors, including location of production sites vis-à-vis primary marketing outlets and the relative locations of the latter, together with transportation costs, are certainly of demonstrable importance in determining the compartmentalized structure of metate marketing. When we concentrate our attention on the marketplace-specific market, however, several nonlocational factors are operative that tend to reinforce compartmentalization of the intermarketplace structure. In this context metate trading tends to approximate the economist's model of "differentiated atomistic competition" (Dorfman 1964:89). This is a situation in which producers (or sellers) of moderately differentiated products like metates sell at different prices because "the customers have come to perceive differences in the qualities of the products . . . and, while some customers avail themselves of the cheaper variant, others are willing to pay a premium for the one they consider superior" (ibid.).

Such characteristic differences in metates as size, style, fineness of finish, handsomeness of decoration, color and hardness of stone (major indices of the expected durability of a metate as well as of its status as a prestige good) are all factors over which the *metatero* has varying degrees of control and provide criteria by which buyers perceive, judge, and purchase metates. The Tlacolula *metateros*, for example, limit their work to prime stone (as measured in terms of hardness, composition, texture, and color), which is relatively difficult to cut but which yields large, durable, high-quality metates. Moreover, these *metateros* exercise special care and patience in finishing and decorating their products. This combination of factors, which results in a larger input of man-hours per unit of output, has given the Tlacolula metate a deserved reputation for style and quality; it has also been reflected in the relatively high average price level for metates in that market. A comparable situation exists in Ocotlán, where several of the Magdalena *metateros* have created and maintained a large clientele on the basis of the durability and quality of their products.

To propose the presence of brandlike configurations in metate marketing is not to imply the absence of heterogeneity in marketplace inventories. In fact, on any given trading day in each of the marketplaces the inventory of metates is varied—ranging from poorly made small utility metates to expertly made large luxury or gift metates—and the range of final selling prices is wide. Yet, the central tendencies of product traits, prices, and buyer/seller behavior incline each marketplace situation toward a distinctive market configuration. Despite the intramarketplace heterogeneity, buyer preferences and loyalties to a particular type of metate are reinforced in the marketplace by seller behavior. In the bargaining situation buyers are often reminded of the positive attributes of, for example, a Magdalena or a Tlacolula metate vis-à-vis those produced elsewhere; differences between metates of the seller's own group are not emphasized as much as differences between these and metates produced elsewhere. Thus, the occasional appearance of a seller in the Ocotlán marketplace with metates produced in the Teitipac villages invariably elicits criticism from the local sellers, focusing on the putatively inferior quality and workmanship of their competitors' products. This is not to imply an absence of competition between sellers from the same producing group, which does occur regularly if in more subtle ways; rather it emphasizes that between marketplaces (and between separate producer-seller groups) there are a series of real and fictive differences among metates of the same general type that function to limit substitutability and to provide a partial basis for differential pricing.

Disregarding for a moment moderate product differentiation within and between marketplaces, and attempting to understand the nature of competition in metate marketing from a somewhat different perspective, the following state of affairs can be posited as typifying each of the three markets: on any given trading day metates with similar characteristics tend to be sold at different prices (though the differences will be larger between metates with dissimilar characteristics). This is true because transactions in these markets occur as a series of semi-independent events, partially independent of past and contemporary transactions in the same market. Individual transactions are conducted through bargaining but are not unique and wholly independent of each other. Any individual entering into a bargaining sequence is aware that there are other potential buyers or sellers of metates in the marketplace and may, in fact, have already negotiated with one or more of them in previous bargaining sequences on that or another trading day. This knowledge and/or experience does not imply that he has an understanding of supply and demand concepts but does imply his awareness of the possibility of a better deal for a similar metate with another trader. Consequently, if a potential buyer perceives a particular seller's minimum selling price as being too high (even if the quotation is below his own maximum buying price) he may withdraw from negotiations and seek a seller whose minimum selling price is lower. It is, of course, entirely possible that nonprice considerations will also have a bearing on a buyer's decision in such a situation.

One of the few notable exceptions to this pattern is a tendency among some traders to establish semiformalized trading partnerships to minimize risk in the wholesale market—a tentative sort of gentleman's agreement typically linking a San Sebastián small-lot producer-seller (*propio*) to a big-lot buyer. These arrangements tend to be rather brittle and are characterized by seasonal discontinuities—especially from the supply side. Even in these relationships, however, the ritual of haggling, together with other competitive posturings, is often engaged in by the partners prior to their consummating a transaction on any given trading day.

SPATIAL PATTERNS IN METATE MARKETING

On the Structure of the Metate Market-Areas

I have compared the Tlacolula, Oaxaca City, and Ocotlán centered metate markets in several basic dimensions of marketing analysis. But how may the market areas that they supply be characterized and compared? As is the case with price levels, Ocotlán and Tlacolula resemble each other more than either of them resembles Oaxaca City; that is, the market areas centered in Ocotlán and Tlacolula contrast sharply in structure and size with the Oaxaca City–centered market area. A large majority of the buyers who purchase metates in Ocotlán and Tlacolula either reside in villages within the judicial-administrative districts of which they are the head towns (*cabeceras*) or are residents of these head towns. Indeed, out of a total of 380 transactions recorded (390 metates sold) in the Ocotlán marketplace on sixty-two trading days over a two-year period, 64 percent of the metates sold were bought by persons living within the *cabecera* jurisdiction of Ocotlán, 20 percent by persons from the contiguous jurisdiction of Zimatlán, and 4 percent by persons from the contiguous jurisdiction of Ejutla. All told, buyers from sixty-eight different communities purchased metates from Magdalena sellers in the Ocotlán marketplace; 71 percent of total sales were to buyers representing seventeen different communities of origin—the

six most important being San Miguel Tilquiapan, Ocotlán de More-
los, Santiago Apóstol, Asunción Ocotlán, San Pablo Huixtepec, and
San Baltazar Chichicapan (only one of which is not within the Ocotlán district). Even though the market-area boundaries are not co-
terminous with the jurisdictional boundaries of the *cabecera*, the
total area supplied is culturally homogeneous and geographically
continuous—if diverse in ecology and economy. The data from Tlacolula reinforce this pattern: out of a total of 80 transactions recorded over a twelve-week period, only 11 percent involved buyers
from outside the *cabecera* jurisdiction.

The Oaxaca City–centered metate market area contrasts sharply
with the Tlacolula-Ocotlán pattern. Approximately 53 percent of all
metates sold in the Oaxaca City marketplace by San Sebastián sellers over the two-year period were distributed beyond the Valley of
Oaxaca proper, either in the southern highlands (e.g., Ejutla, Sola
de Vega, Miahuatlán, Juquila) or in the Pacific coastal region of the
state (e.g., Pochutla, Candelaria Loxicha); another 24 percent were
distributed in the Isthmus (e.g., Salina Cruz, Tehuantepec, Juchitán,
Matías Romero); and the remaining 23 percent were distributed in
the Sierra de Juárez, in the Sierra Mixteca, and in areas of the Valley
not included in the Tlacolula and Ocotlán market areas (e.g., Zaachila, Etla). In short, the Oaxaca City–centered market area is spatially discontinuous and culturally heterogeneous; it also is more extensive in territory and supplies a much larger population than the
other two market areas. The specialized wholesaling function of the
Oaxaca City metate market, combined with the magnitude and diversity of its market area, demonstrates the existence of a centralized
and rationalized distributional system underlying the apparent chaos
and unpredictability of weekly trading activity in the marketplace.

The Circulatory Routes for Metates

As durable consumer goods, the metate and mano follow routes of
exchange that terminate only as they enter into the process of utilization in the individual consumer household. However, there are several alternative routes of circulation for these products which are
associated with contrasting spatial, social, structural, behavioral, and
statistical patterns. Figure 7-1 schematizes the spatial patterns in
the marketing of metates and serves as a point of departure for discussing related features.

Before turning to a discussion of the diagram and in order to cut
through some of the semantic ambiguity characterizing popular
usage among Oaxacans in the labeling of marketing roles, it is use-

ful to distinguish between and among the roles originating on the producing-village side of the marketplace (i.e., those associated with circulatory routes 1 and 2) and those originating on the distributional or market-area side of the marketplace (i.e., those associated with route 3). In the former context the *propio* is an individual producer who sells products that he personally has manufactured; the term is also employed to refer to the buyer who purchases products for use in his own household (not for resale)—and to avoid confusion I have used the term *comprador* to refer to this private buyer-consumer. *Regatón* is another term with multiple referents among the Oaxacans. In the village context it refers either to an individual who regularly buys metates from *propios* for resale in the extravillage marketplace or to an individual who is not a native of the producing village and who buys metates for resale in his home village or elsewhere. Customarily, it is only the first kind of *regatón* who is also a finisher (*labrador*) of metates and who acquires semi-finished products.

In the producing villages there are some individuals who combine activities as *propios* and *regatones*, but this occurs sporadically and involves only a minority of *propios*. Most *regatones* are also *labradores* (finishers) of metates, but this does not make them full-fledged *metateros* or *propios*; the latter status implies that its occupant works in the quarrying and prefinishing stages of manufacture, as well as in the finishing stages. The distinction between *propio* and *regatón* is made by the villagers themselves; they do not use a hyphenated term like *propio-regatón* or *metatero-regatón* to refer to those individuals who do combine two roles. Such an individual will invariably be identified by his role in manufacturing (i.e., as *propio* or *metatero*). In summation, the following generalization can be made about metate marketing roles on the producing-village side of the marketplace: whereas only a minority of *propios* occasionally enter the market as *regatones*, a majority of *regatones* regularly work as finishers (*labradores*) of the metates they acquire to resell.

On the distributional or market-area side of the marketplace, the word *regatón* is employed by the metate sellers as a cover term to refer to three basic types of middlemen: (a) those who are regular big-lot buyers of metates for resale on a wholesale or retail basis in distant marketing centers (e.g., Salina Cruz, Tehuantepec, Juchitán, Miahuatlán, Pochutla); (b) those who are regular small-lot buyers of metates for resale on a weekly retail basis in the Oaxaca City

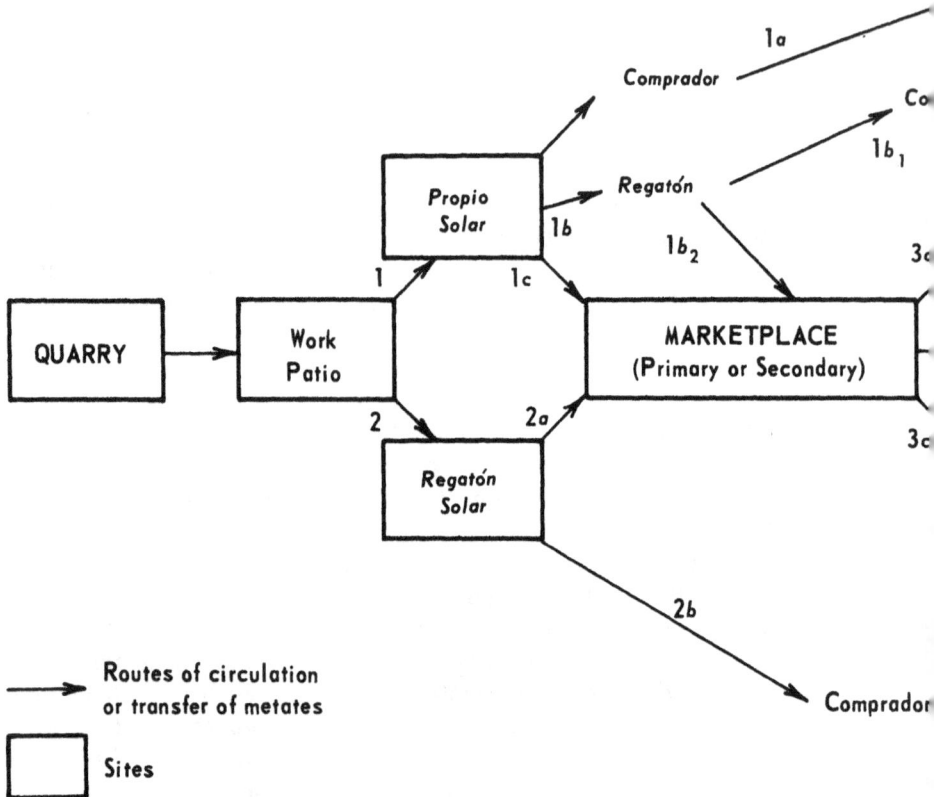

Routes of circulation
or transfer of metates

Sites

marketplace, in secondary or tertiary marketplaces in the hinterland
(e.g., Zaachila, Zimatlán, Sola de Vega, Ayoquezco), or periodically
in fiesta marketplaces held in the valley or beyond (e.g., San Pablo
Huixtepec, Juquila, Candelaria Loxicha); and (c) those who periodically buy small lots of metates for resale on a daily retail basis in
the marketplace as one line of their shop (caseta) or stall (puesto)

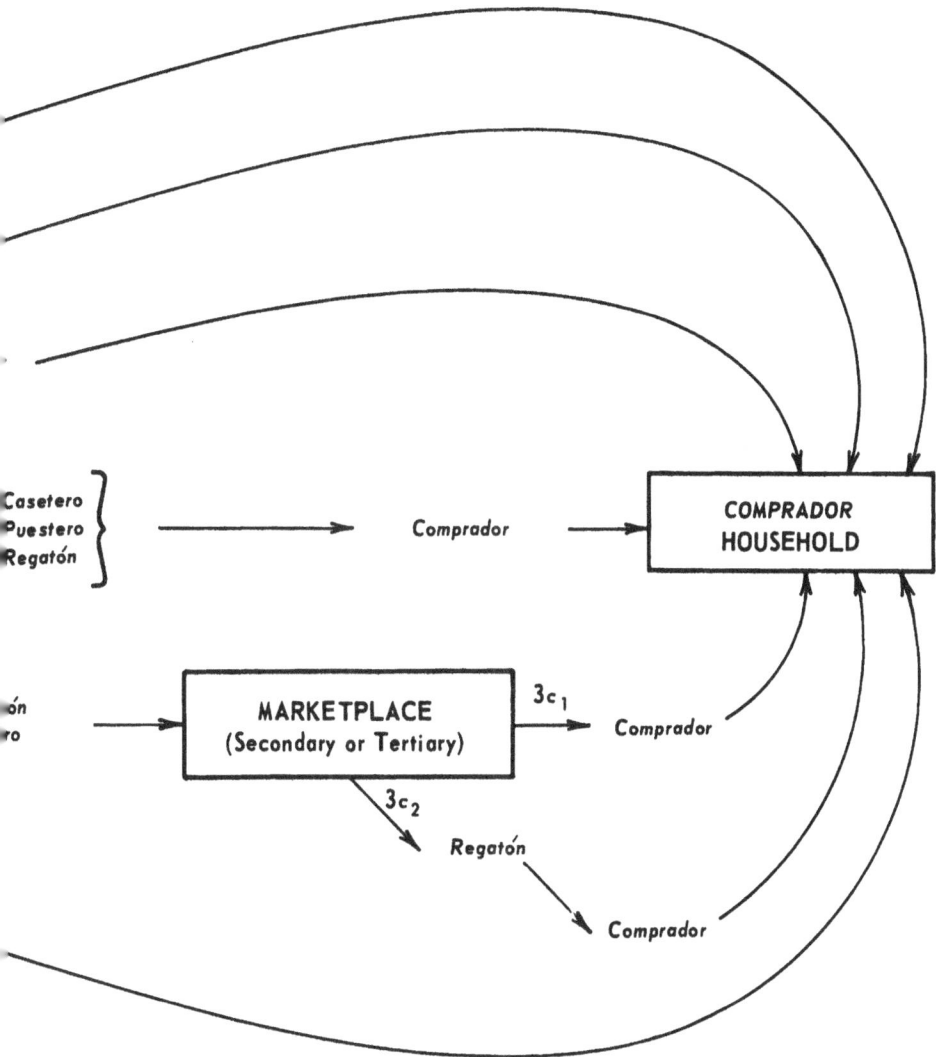

Figure 7-1. Spatial patterns in metate marketing.

based trade. In contrast to their counterparts on the other side of the marketplace, these middlemen deal only in finished products; they perform no manufacturing or finishing tasks whatsoever (except for an occasional touch-up job).

With these terminological distinctions in mind it is appropriate to focus attention once again on the diagram. Two principal circulatory routes for metates, each with alternatives, are illustrated: the *propio*-centered route with two extramarketplace alternative routes (1*a* and 1*b*) and two marketplace-mediated alternative routes (1*b*₂ and 1*c*); and the *regatón*-centered route with one marketplace-mediated alternative route (2*a*) and one extramarketplace alternative route (2*b*). All routes, it should be noted, originate in the work patios adjacent to the quarries, and transfers from there to residence-lot workplaces in the village involve semifinished metates. A majority of metates transferred from either *propio* or *regatón* residence lots are finished and ready for use. However, finishing tasks are sometimes performed in the marketplace sales area (especially in Ocotlán).

The route with the highest volume of circulation is that in which the *propios* transport their own semifinished products from the quarry work patios to their village residence lots for finishing and then transport the finished metates to the marketplace. This route (1*c*) accounted for approximately two-thirds of total sales (approximately 606 metates), in 1967–1968 by San Sebastián sellers in the Oaxaca City marketplace. Or, alternatively, the *propio* sometimes transfers (by sale, gift, or barter) his finished metates directly to consumers without going to the marketplace. This alternative (route 1*a*) typically involves *encargos* (special orders) or ceremonial transfers (e.g., a *propio* presents a gift metate to a bride who is his relative or godchild) but may also involve direct cash sale (usually to a fellow villager or to a buyer from a nearby village). Still another alternative route (1*b*) is for the *propio* to sell (finished or unfinished) metates from his residence-lot inventory to *regatones* (from his own or a nearby village) who, in turn, resell them in the marketplace (1*b*₂) or in extramarketplace transactions (1*b*₁). That these are important routes quantitatively is shown by the fact that from August, 1967, through June, 1968, approximately 27 percent of San Sebastián–produced metates (255 metates) were sold by *propios* to *regatones* from other villages (especially San Juan Teitipac), and that just under one-third of all transactions in the Oaxaca City marketplace involved San Sebastián *regatones* as sellers. So much, then, for the *propio*-centered routes for the transfer of metates.

The *regatón*-centered routes (2*a* and 2*b*) are those originating with the acquisition by local *regatones* of semifinished products in the quarry work area. These metates are then transported to village residence lots for finishing. Typically the *regatón* himself, either with members of his own family or with hired help, finishes these metates for subsequent transfer to the marketplace (2a) or directly to the consumer in extramarketplace transactions (2b). Those *regatones* who take physical possession of semifinished metates in the quarries have usually acquired a prior claim to a given *metatero's* output by having paid him a cash advance (*adelanto*). The *regatón's* trip to the quarry is made to assure prompt repayment and to enable him to choose a metate he wants. Certainly no more than one-fifth of all metates marketed by local *regatones* are directly appropriated in the quarries.

It is interesting to note that by no means all metates which pass from *propio* to *regatón* in the producing village do so through purchase or sale (i.e., via cash-mediated transactions)—although this is the predominant mode of transfer there and is the exclusive mode of transfer of metates in the marketplace. While I have only limited and random data on metate transfers within the producing village completed in the absence of money payment, I do have records of some gift transfers and of twelve instances of barter between *propios* and other villagers (usually *regatones*) in which metates were exchanged for other goods or services. Of these twelve recorded transactions (occurring in San Sebastián Teitipac in 1967–1968), six saw *propios* exchanging semifinished metates in the quarry for prepared food (*chicharrón*) or beverages (*tejate*). One of these metate-for-food exchanges was a multiple transaction: various *metateros* in a work company drank *tejate* offered by a vendor, then each contributed labor toward the semifinishing of a metate; when the tasks were completed the metate was given to the *tejate* vendor (a woman from the village who was also a *regatona*). Of the six remaining instances of barter, two involved the exchange of semifinished metates for the use of an ox team for plowing the *propio's* fields; one involved the transfer of a metate for a quantity of dried beans; another saw one semifinished metate exchanged for finishing services on three other unfinished metates; and the last entailed the exchange of one small finished metate for one *barreta* (crowbar). In most of these cases, the metates exchanged were eventually brought into the marketplace for resale by the village *regatones* who either originally or subsequently acquired them.

Metates may flow through any one of three separate routes into the marketplace and take any one of three alternative routes out of it, regardless of whether they enter as the property of a *propio* or a *regatón.* The first route out of the marketplace (*3a*) is the most direct route to the ultimate destination of every metate, namely, utilization in the food-preparation area of a peasant household: the buyer represents the household and acquires one metate directly from its seller (either *propio* or *regatón*). This seller-to-*comprador* route accounted for roughly 8 percent of total sales by San Sebastián sellers in the Oaxaca City marketplace in 1967–1968, but for 95 percent of total sales by Magdalena sellers in the Ocotlán marketplace during the same period—clearly demonstrating the retail specialization of the latter. The second route (*3b*) is somewhat less direct, having one intervening link between the marketplace and the *comprador*, namely, a stall-based retail vendor (*puestero, casetero, regatón*) who buys from the *propio* or from the village-to-marketplace *regatón* and resells to the *comprador*. This route accounted for about 13 percent of total sales in the Oaxaca City marketplace (by San Sebastián sellers) in 1967–1968, but for only 2 percent in Ocotlán. Finally, the third route (*3c*) is the most circuitous and not only finds the metates passing through another marketplace in the hands of a *regatón* (i.e., the big-lot buyer or intermarketplace trader) but, in many cases, being resold to yet another *regatón* (marketplace-to-village type) before coming to rest in the *comprador* household (*3c₂*). The wholesale specialization of the San Sebastián sellers in the Oaxaca City marketplace is demonstrated by the fact that 69 percent of their sales in 1967–1968 followed this *regatón*-laden path, as compared to only 3 percent of the sales by Magdalenans in Ocotlán.

Unfortunately, this sketch of the *hows* of metate marketing leaves unanswered most of the intriguing *whys*. An important step in seeking to explain why peasant-artisan producers and marketers behave as they do and why the commodities they produce circulate as they do is to scrutinize the pricing process. Price, of course, is never a "prime mover" of economic behavior even in a capitalist economy. But it is the indispensable partner of output in any economic analysis. And in a peasant-artisan economy of the Oaxaca variety, price and pricing are crucial phenomena; price is a basic informational input that feeds decision making and provides the observer-analyst with a measurable index of many forces and conditions. In short, price is not the measure of all things in the peasant-artisan economy of Oaxaca, but it is certainly an essential ingredient of economic performance and analysis.

THE LABOR PROCESS, COMMODITY CIRCULATION, AND PRICE DETERMINATION IN THE METATE MARKET

Granted the importance of the pricing process, it must be emphasized that underlying exchange in any economy is the labor process; pricing does not occur unless labor power has been expended to produce something for use by someone other than the producer himself. In the context of the Valley of Oaxaca economy the peasant-artisan (e.g., the *metatero*) is a commodity producer to the extent that his products (e.g., metates and manos) are produced for other individuals for whom they have a use value. Once the *metatero* has produced a metate for the use of his own household, additional metates he manufactures have no use value to him. As Marx stated: "To become a commodity, a product must pass by way of exchange into the hands of the other person for whom it has a use-value"— that is, the commodity has "social use value" (1930:9–10).

The Valley of Oaxaca *metatero* can make metates for exchange only because, in doing so, he is satisfying a definite social demand in a system of intercommunity specialization and division of labor. As a general rule his labor power can meet the wants of his own household only to the extent that it is exchangeable for the labor power of other producers (in his own or other communities). The market system in this economy serves, therefore, as a mechanism for the equalization of different kinds of labor (e.g., the labor of the metate maker, the potter, the weaver, the basketmaker, the cultivator, etc.); it reduces these to "abstract human labor" and facilitates exchange value by enabling him to obtain, through the medium of the *metatero's* metate, which has no use value to him, becomes his exchange value by enabling him to obtain, through the medium of money, another materialized form of human labor power (e.g., a sarape, pottery, bread, etc.) whose use value he does want to actualize.

If a metate were animate and endowed with the human capacity for speech it would explain this situation to the *metatero* as follows (cf. Marx 1930:58):

My use value may interest you human beings; but it is not an attribute of mine, as a thing. My attribute as a thing is the human labor power I embody—therein lies my value. My interrelations with other commodities in the Valley of Oaxaca economy—with sarapes, pottery, baskets, maize, or mescal—proves this: we are related only as exchange values. From my point of view I consider these and all other commodities which interest you *metateros* to be nothing more than the fundamental form of my own value. When, for example, you exchange me and transform me into money, you don't endow me with value (which I already embody in the form of your own labor); you simply give my value a specific form. And, when you transport me to the marketplace because you want something that is not me—it is only by exchanging me for a bundle of money, that is, realizing my exchange value by seeking another individual who wishes to realize my use value.

This hypothetical metate's view of itself closely approximates reality as my observations and analysis portray it: the metate's actual value is realized only through exchange in the marketplace, a social transaction.

The social relationship between hagglers in the Valley of Oaxaca marketplaces emerges not because of some instinctive urge to trade or propensity to monetize, to perceive and evaluate things and events through the eyes of a trader (see Parsons 1936:12–13, 445; Malinowski and de la Fuente 1957:23; Leslie 1960:67–71); it exists because of the relationship between the peasant-artisan producer and his product. The bargaining situation is one of reciprocal aliena-tion rooted in the fact that producers are producing what they don't need and need what they don't produce; in this economy "useful" objects to each producer are frequently of alien manufacture (cf. Marx 1930:63). All other aspects of the bargaining situation are subordinate to this fundamental reality.

The *metatero*, like other peasant-artisans in the Valley of Oaxaca economy, does not live exclusively on the products of his own labor. Indeed, his participation in a regional marketing system proves that he can only live if he gets rid of his own products (cf. Mandel 1970: 58). As a part-time cultivator he does produce some of his own use values (i.e., those intended for consumption by his own household), but, most importantly, he also produces exchange values or com-modities which are converted into use values for others via the mar-ket mechanism and via the medium of money into use values for himself and his household. Thus, when the *metatero* appears in the marketplace, he does not want to realize the use values of his meta-tes but, on the contrary, wants to dispose of them so as to realize their exchange value—which will enable him to acquire needed complementary goods and services. The following notation describes the transaction by which he accomplishes this:

C — M — C'
commodity—money—commodity

In the marketplace, the *metatero* must encounter a holder of money, M, who is willing to realize the exchange value of the metate, C. Also, this money holder must be prepared to hand over his money if he wants to realize the use value of the metate (as does the buyer for private use—path 3*a* in Fig. 7-1) or if he wants to capitalize further on its exchange value (as does the middleman-trader or reseller—paths 3*b* and 3*c*). Therefore, the sale of the metate, C—M, occurs at the mutual convenience of the transactors. The value of M is, of course, determined by negotiation and is variable (Cook 1968:268–277).

Since the *metatero* sells his metate to acquire other products, for example, a woven blanket (sarape) for home use, he takes the cash pocketed from the metate sale and looks for a sarape seller in the marketplace. When he locates one and initiates negotiations with him, the transaction M—C' can occur. When these two successive operations of sale and purchase are completed (usually on the same trading day) the *metatero* has a commodity (the sarape) which is of use to him rather than one (the metate) for which he has no use.

To summarize this hypothetical, yet commonly occurring transaction: two commodities, the metate and the sarape, have left the market because their exchange value has been realized by their sellers, for whom they had no use value, and their use value has been realized by two buyers, for whom they had no exchange value. The sum of money, M, has changed hands twice—from the buyer of the metate to the *metatero*, and from the latter to the *sarapero* (sarape maker). So long as the *sarapero* is a *propio* he will probably employ this money as savings or to buy some other commodity or service. In other words, money in this *propio*-dominated transaction is merely a subordinate instrument of commodity circulation, even when it renders the producer-seller a value exceeding that of his embodied labor power (cf. Mandel 1970:80).

As might be expected, when *regatones* or other middlemen-traders enter into these commodity transactions, as they often do in Oaxaca, the role of money changes. *Regatones* do not buy commodities simply to realize their use values, like the *metatero* and the *sarapero*. On the contrary, they regularly buy commodities to resell them to others at a profit (i.e., to increase by a surplus value the money invested as in $M—C—M'$). It must be emphasized, however, that there are many *regatones* in the Oaxaca economy, perhaps a majority, who never really transcend the limitations of simple commodity circulation; sooner or later they have to employ exchange value to acquire use values so as to meet the household maintenance and other provisioning requirements of peasant life.

Though ignorant of the writings of Marx, the *metatero* understands his marketing situation from the perspective of a labor or work theory of value. He brings his products to the plaza to convert them into a cash equivalent of the labor and other costs expended in manufacturing and marketing them. This cash equivalent is subject to negotiation and is variable; it may or may not provide a surplus above the estimated cost. To the extent that it does—and the *metatero* enters negotiations to attempt to get the potential buyer to agree on a price that does exceed estimated cost—the *metatero* refers to the surplus as a *ganancia*. But he haggles not so much to maximize *ganancia* (profit) as to convert his product (embodied labor) into cash at a level that minimally covers his labor and other costs. Since the cost of metate manufacture remains more or less constant throughout the year, the *metatero's* MAR (minimum acceptable return) does not vary. However, his MER (minimum expected return) varies seasonally (in accordance with the seasonal demand factor). The *metatero* haggles to maximize the difference between MAR and MER but is willing ultimately to accept an offer which at least equals his MAR.

The *metatero* enters the marketplace as a trader with a producer's orientation; he comes to sell not *a* product but *his* product, his own embodied labor power. "Yo vendo lo que es mío, no vendo el ajeno; yo vendo mi propio trabajo [I sell what is mine, not what is someone else's; I sell my own work]." This is the kind of statement one often hears from the *metateros* in describing their marketing activities. It is the *metatero's* calculation of the money value of the labor he has expended in manufacturing a metate and in transporting it to market that gives him the basic cost ingredient of his MAR. On several occasions I have observed *metateros* refuse to sell a metate to a prospective buyer whose final bid fell only a few pesos short of the *metatero's* final quotation (often equivalent to his MAR). In such deadlocked negotiations (which abort if the buyer does not up his bid) the *metatero* will insist that the price offered by the prospective buyer does not justly compensate his work ("El trabajo no resulta" or "Mi trabajo no vale así [My work is not worth so little]").

The specifics of the process of estimating the money cost of a metate (i.e., its production cost) vary from *metatero* to *metatero*. But a
substantial number of those I interviewed made estimates according to an "opportunity cost" type of formula: they counted the total
number of man-days of labor expended in manufacturing and marketing a metate and assigned it a money cost roughly equivalent to
the going *jornalero's* wage (between ten and fifteen pesos a day).
On one occasion during the slow period in the metate market (May–
October), I saw a *metatero* refuse an offer of thirty-five pesos for a
metate that was part of an inventory held over from preceding
weeks—an action that was surprising under the circumstances.
When I asked why he had refused the offer he stated categorically
that the metate was worth forty pesos (i.e., his MAR) because it
had cost him four days work at an equivalent wage of ten pesos
daily. The following are various ways in which different *metateros*
explained their valuation procedure: "sacarsele los días de trabajo
[to get one's work days out of it]"; "Uno saca la cuenta de cuanto
mete uno en hacer el metate [One makes an accounting of how
much one put into making the metate]"; "Según los días que uno lo
trabaja, saca uno los días [According to the days that one works at
it, one takes out the days]"; "Yo comprendo que tantos días que lo
estuve haciendo y para venderlo barato, pues, el día sale muy barato
y no resulta [I understand that I was making it for so many days and
to sell it cheap, well, the work day comes out very cheap and
doesn't give results]."

While the labor cost component is basic in every *metatero's* computation of the exchange value of his products (including labor time
spent in marketing), many will also include the additional cost of
transporting the product to the marketplace as well as the marketplace surcharge. When a negotiation is deadlocked, with only a few
pesos separating quotation and bid, the *metatero* is usually holding
his ground in an attempt to cover these nonlabor costs (i.e., his
own bus fare plus transport of the metate plus marketplace surcharge), which average about three pesos per metate. I have wit-
nessed negotiations in which the price of the metate was agreed
upon but the sale was not consummated because the buyer refused
to pay the *metatero* a small fee (one or two pesos) for hauling the
metate from the sales area to the buyer's place of departure. Inter-
estingly enough, there are a whole series of production costs that
don't usually enter into the *metatero's* calculation of MAR (e.g., cost
of tools, powder, fuse, pumping water from the quarry, hired labor,

storage in the marketplace). It would, of course, be very difficult—if not impossible—to transfer a portion of these costs to an individual metate; they are simply a part of the overhead.

The implication of the *metatero*'s strategy of embodied labor-to-cash conversion is his immediate need to convert cash into complementary goods and services (e.g., food items for the coming week, clothing, medicine, tools) or to allocate it to other household maintenance expenditures (e.g., payment of debts, rent). As a general rule, the *metatero* prefers to sell his products as early in the day as possible so that he has plenty of time to attend to his other business in the plaza. The difficulty a *metatero* has in breaking out of this habitual plaza involvement as producer-consumer is illustrated by the case of one San Sebastiano, who after years of selling his metates regularly to buyers in the Oaxaca City plaza was persuaded to sell his entire weekly output to a *regatón* in the village. He held to this agreement for several months but then abruptly canceled it, giving the following reasons for his decision:

I felt strange when I no longer took metates to the plaza. I had become accustomed to going to Oaxaca with my metates. It seemed very strange to me that suddenly I was going to Oaxaca only with money. I didn't sell anything there; I only walked around. I felt badly because I got no money in the plaza. I would run into my former patron [a wholesale buyer whom he regularly sold to] and he didn't pay me. What is he going to give me if I have nothing for him? I had become accustomed to the patron asking me when I arrived in the plaza: How many did you bring today? And I would tell him and then he would ask me: How much do you want for them? I felt very ugly going to the plaza to spend money without having sold anything there. One must take something and bring something back. Right? It's like a business. A businessman buys what there is in one place and sells it in another; that's the way I want to operate.

In a strict economic sense, this *metatero* had made a sensible arrangement. He was selling every metate he could produce (unfinished) to a village middleman, who paid him twenty-five pesos per metate and, moreover, would extend him cash advances of up to two hundred pesos in return for a claim to future output. Since he did not have to spend time with finishing operations, the *metatero* was able to devote all of his work to quarry operations—thus increasing his weekly output of unfinished metates. While he was pleased with the economics of this arrangement, he terminated it simply because of his commitment to the plaza routine. As a producer for the plaza he felt that it was necessary for him to sell his own products there so that he, in turn, could buy someone else's.

It is the mythical figure of Juan Garabato, of whom it is said in a popular saying "He buys dear and sells cheap" ("Compra caro y vende barato"), that reminds metatero and regatón alike of their vulnerability as consumers who produce and/or sell in order to consume. On the one hand, the metatero sees himself as Juan Garabato: he is often forced to accept a low price for his products in a buyer's market and then turn around and pay high prices for the complementary goods and services he needs. This is especially characteristic of his situation from May to September, the rainy season, when metate prices decline and corn and other basic food prices increase. During such a slump (few buyers, low prices for metates) I asked one metatero why he continued to quote high prices for his metates, and he responded: "Why are we going to buy dear and sell cheap? That's no joke. One must sell dear, too."

Nevertheless, the metateros consider the regatón to be more likely to fall into the predicament of Juan Garabato because of his obligation to recoup his cash outlay when selling metates. They consider that the risk factor is greater for the regatón than it is for them; given the capriciousness of market fluctuations the regatón can never be assured of a profit margin—something the metatero is not ultimately concerned with.

Although the Juan Garabato theme (which occasionally crops up in casual conversation) reminds the metateros of the risk element in middleman activities, it does not discourage some of them from periodically entering the market in that capacity. These metatero-regatones, in addition to manufacturing finished metates, buy semifinished metates from their coworkers for resale in the marketplace. The following excerpts from an inteview with a metatero-regatón from Magdalena Ocotlán illustrate the salient features of the marketing strategy of this group:

Q: During the past year have you traded metates that you did not manufacture?

R: Yes, I bought some thirty semifinished metates (barreteados) and I finished them.

Q: Why did you do that?

R: Because they brought me a profit. For example, I buy a semifinished metate for forty pesos. I finish it and sell it for eighty, ninety pesos.

Let's discount ten pesos for the mano. That's thirty–forty pesos that I earn in one day. That's money.

Q: Why did you buy metates from others instead of going to the quarry and making them yourself?

R: Because sometimes I'm working at home and they come by and ask me if I want to buy metates from them. From the month of August I begin to buy—I take out about five hundred pesos to buy in September and October; then in November, December I begin to sell. I buy only first-rate metates. I store them and afterwards, when I have time, I take them out and finish them and paint them. And they give me a profit of more than half of my original investment. Rather than having my money in my hands, I invest it in metates.

Q: Where do you get the money to buy metates?

R: I take it out of my own work; I sell something—a hog, a calf, or any animal. And after selling all the metates I bought, I get some more animals and keep the money that I earned. Last year I put aside $500. And I made $950 from selling metates. I earned $450.

Q: Why do you buy metates for resale instead of buying more animals?

R: Because of the weather. Years when the sickness comes, for example, if I have two hundred pesos, to buy a pig is risky. Instead of investing the money in a pig, it's better to invest it in metates—that's safe.

I invest my money in metates. I buy in August, September, October, November. This is preferable to lending money for interest. Because money lent pays no more than 10 percent—one hundred pesos loaned for two months yields twenty pesos. If you buy two metates at fifty pesos each, you invest one hundred pesos—in two months you can sell them for one hundred pesos each. Do you come out better or worse? But many who have gotten into this business have failed. I don't understand why. One must know how much it's worth when he buys it and how much it's worth when he sells it—that's all there is to it. If I buy a metate in August or September, I give forty or fifty pesos; in November or December I will sell these same metates for not less than eighty or ninety pesos. Many have done it and they fall flat on their faces; I don't understand why. When I buy I'm sure that I'll earn half again what I paid for it when the time comes to sell it. There are some who are buying now in this month (May) in order to sell in one or two months from now. But by that time the price will have dropped—it's still high—and they'll be selling when the price is lower. How the fuck? [¿Cómo chingao?] It doesn't come out. One must wait until the price lowers to buy, and sell when the price is right.[1]

Several key elements in the *regatón-metatero*'s marketing strategy emerge from this interview. First, we can infer a profit orientation without a commitment to the appropriation of "processional value" (Marx 1930:140–141; see Part Four). In other words, the *metatero-regatón* operates according to a strategy to earn profit over the short run on a sum of money invested, not a strategy to generate an ever-increasing increment on the sum originally invested over the long run. Second, there is an explicit commitment to arbitrage in accordance with the seasonal variation in the metate trade cycle; metate products are acquired and stored in the village when the price level is depressed (June–October/November) and moved into the marketplace for sale during the season of the year when the price level is high (December–May)—a strategy that some of the non-*regatón* metateros also follow (cf. Cook 1970: 780–785). Third, the *metatero-regatón* has a preference toward the manipulation of highly liquid noncash assets (especially animals) and does not usually invest money to earn interest (via bank savings or lending). This reflects, aside from the relative inaccessibility of formal banking or savings facilities, the peculiar problems and needs of peasant life. Cash on hand, hidden in a trunk for a time of need, is palpably unproductive in the eyes of these petty entrepreneurs; but animals, though susceptible to premature death by disease, are a liquid alternative and also serve an "investment" function. Finally, the *metatero-regatón* emerges as a sophisticated calculator of alternative courses of action: he moves back and forth between metates and animals, according to market and seasonal fluctuations, and usually avoids options like money lending, which can have undesirable social and economic consequences. While he is keenly aware of the risk and unpredictability of metate market behavior in the short run, his experience has taught him that these tend to be minimized over the annual cycle. If he can withstand the impact of short-run crises (of family or market origin), he is confident of the probability of long-run success (i.e., a constant rate of profit).

Of course, the majority of *regatones* are not as successful as this informant says that he is. One thing is clear, however: with respect to his valuational and haggling behavior the *regatón* (whether or not he is also a *metatero*) differs from the *propio*. He does not come to the plaza to convert his embodied labor into cash but, rather, to make a profit on his investment. The products that he brings to the plaza have been purchased at a cost which, except for the possible value added by his own finishing services, represents a cash outlay. Consequently, unless confronted with a crisis situation, he does not sell until he can do so at a price that covers his costs (original purchase price plus value added by labor plus transport plus market-place surcharge) and also yields a profit (*ganancia*) on his investment. He haggles to maximize his profit, often to the point of rejecting bids that do not meet his expected profit margin.

The *regatón* considers his metate-trading activity as a self-sustaining business. After accumulating a sum of capital to enable him to initiate trading operations, he seeks to finance subsequent operations from profits derived from his original investment (which varies from twenty-five to five hundred pesos). A portion of his cash earnings are kept in circulation to acquire products; they are not saved. Typically, the profits earmarked for reinvestment are distributed by the *regatón* to his *metatero* suppliers as "advances" (*adelantos*) or are used to build up product inventory. The most active *regatones* will have several hundred pesos so allocated among various suppliers at any given time.

When hard pressed, *regatones* will sell a metate for a profit of five pesos (sometimes they do absorb losses); however, profits of thirty to thirty-five pesos per metate are not uncommon. In most cases, these earnings are partially spent on consumer purchases in the plaza, with an amount equivalent to the original outlay (for any given metate) earmarked for reinvestment. For example, if a *regatón* purchased a finished metate in the village for $25.00 and spends $1.00 transporting it to the plaza and $.50 for the surcharge, and sells it for $40.00, he will have made a "net" profit of $13.50. The latter sum will usually be spent on consumption articles and the remaining $25.00 will be used to purchase another metate in the village.

In short, while the marketplace is basically a place where the *regatón* does business at a profit, it is important to note that he remains enmeshed in the process of simple commodity circulation together with his artisan companions. He operates to provision his household and to meet all expenditures required to maintain its viability, not to expand his business through increasing profits and investment.

RECAPITULATION AND CONCLUSIONS

In this paper I have outlined the salient features of the economic framework in which metate marketing is conducted. To this end I have identified various market conditions to which buyers and sellers adapt (and perhaps alter as well); and I have indicated certain aggregate statistical results of their behavior during a finite time period. These results were measured as the flow of products (output) between physical sites, and it was assumed that these products circulate through an economic process encompassing production, exchange, and utilization phases—a process integrated and activated by the multiple forces of supply and demand. The metate market was found to be compartmentalized into three site-confined segments through the operation of various imperfections (e.g., location and transport factors, moderate production differentiation); in other words, at the intermarketplace level of analysis the metate marketing process is monopolistically competitive.

At the intramarketplace level of analysis, however, the data indicate that a more perfectly competitive situation tends to prevail— at least in terms of trading behavior (as measured by the degree of control over prices exercised by sellers or buyers, which depends on the number of traders, the uniformity of products, and the freedom of entry for potential traders). Only in the wholesale section of the Oaxaca City metate market do conditions exist that incline the trading situation toward a monopolistically competitive pole. The other, essentially retail markets appear to approximate the perfect-competition model, since activity in them "rests on the free interplay of buyers and sellers, with price established through the interaction of buyers who do not buy enough to set price with sellers who do not control enough of the supply to set price" (Nash 1966:70).

While one important goal of economic anthropology is to explain human behavior in the economic field, we often find it necessary in our analysis to talk about concepts, categories, relationships, principles, and variables several degrees removed from human social reality. As a means for getting at the hows and whys of *human* behavior, the economic anthropologist sometimes finds himself concerned with the hows and whys of *quantity* (output) and *price* behavior. But the analyst must never lose sight of the fact that such commodities as metates are produced, exchanged, and utilized only because individual human beings, singly and in groups, make decisions, organize themselves, and expend energy in particular ways and toward the achievement of specific ends.

One of the aims of this paper, in conclusion, has been to show that commodities circulate between sites and are aggregated and dispersed in regularized ways during the circulatory process only because they are creatures of organized human effort and are objects of patterned human choices and wants. It follows from this that we can learn a great deal about the structure and dynamics of economic performance by studying the circulation of commodities and money, to which men are always directly or indirectly related as producers, exchangers, and users.

8. Zapotec *Viajeras*

BEVERLY CHIÑAS

Since this essay does not deal with marketplaces in the Isthmus of Tehuantepec except briefly and indirectly, a few general comments about these marketplaces (hereafter called plazas) compared to those of the Valley of Oaxaca seem to be appropriate.

There are of course the obvious ecological differences between the Isthmus of Tehuantepec and the Valley of Oaxaca. The Pacific coastal region, the traditional Isthmus Zapotec homeland, is tropical, near sea level, and surprisingly dry most of the year, while the Valley of Oaxaca, with an elevation of around five thousand feet, has a temperate climate, more rainfall, and therefore a very different flora. These differences themselves account for some of the differences in the plazas. A second factor involves a relatively small degree of craft specialization by community in the Isthmus as compared to the Valley of Oaxaca. There is some community specialization (e.g., Ixtaltepec pottery), but its scale is such that craft specialization does not act as a pervasive exchange catalyst as it does in the Valley. Product specialization by community is also much less in the Isthmus, although again it is not completely lacking. There are microniches where certain products can be grown despite a general Isthmus environment unfavorable to them (for example, bananas, mangoes, and coconuts). In the mountainous hinterlands there are numerous products, such as coffee, pineapples, and copal, which pass through the Isthmus plazas for local consumption and redistribution.

Unlike their Valley counterparts, Isthmus plazas are noncyclic and relatively nonhierarchical. Every community has at least a small plaza daily to cater to the needs of the local population. The larger the community, the larger the plaza, but in all plazas Sunday is the busiest day. In the larger communities, *placitas* also exist daily in several of the larger *barrios* or sections of the town where local housewives can shop for necessities without the inconvenience of going to the central plaza, which may be as much as two miles away. Prices are usually a fraction higher in the *placitas*, the choice is limited, and perishables tend to be staler and of poorer quality than in the central plazas. The *placitas* offer hot prepared foods also, and these are often equal to or better than those in the central plazas in quality, although the variety is more limited. There are a few locations where *placitas* spring up in the early morning and again in late afternoon, specializing in prepared foods. These act more as restaurants for working persons who by preference or necessity "eat in the street" than as sources of supply for housewives, and they include a few tables and benches where customers eat.

Historically, one Isthmus plaza has acted as a regional trade center. The location of the regional plaza has shifted within the last ten to fifteen years from Tehuantepec to Juchitán, a shift that is acknowledged with regret in the former and elation in the latter. Most participants in the plazas are not aware of the reasons for the shift— the extension and improvement of the two intersecting major highways, the Pan American and the Trans-Isthmus, together with the decreasing importance of the railroad.

Some wholesaling, bulking, and breaking occurs in the Juchitán plaza, but it is minor compared to that in Oaxaca City. In Tehuantepec large-scale wholesale transactions involving local products are almost entirely in the hands of mestizo and Syrian merchants who operate from their homes or business locations outside the plazas.

In the national cultural folklore of Mexico, Isthmus plazas have a reputation of being operated and controlled entirely by women, but this is not strictly true. About 10 percent of the permanent vendors in Tehuantepec, for example, are men. It is true, however, that Zapotec men traditionally avoid the plazas, whether as sellers or buyers. However, as George M. Foster has noted (1948b), a large majority of vendors in local plazas all over Mesoamerica are women, and I am uncertain whether the Isthmus should be considered at all unique in this respect.

Although I have been discussing mainly differences, Isthmus plazas are similar also to those of the Valley of Oaxaca in a number of ways. Three important similarities involve the functions of the plazas. First, the whole population of the region is dependent upon the plazas as the only source of perishable foods. In a tropical climate where refrigeration is rare, this is no small dependency. Second, the plaza is the redistribution point for most local products that are sold in small quantities to consumers. Since most local products are consumed locally, this function is perhaps more important in the Isthmus than in the Valley of Oaxaca. A third function of importance is that of providing the major outlet for peasant household production, the quantity and flow of which is well suited to retail selling in small lots.

One final point concerns the relationship of the Isthmus market system to that of the Valley of Oaxaca. Beals considers the Isthmus a subsystem of the latter, while I tend to favor viewing the Isthmus as a separate but interdigitating market system. This difference of opinion is not as profound as it at first appears, since Beals is concerned with total production and redistribution, while I take as reference point the plazas and the orientation of the local population. From Beals's vantage point, the Isthmus may be a subsystem of the Valley of Oaxaca, although figures are lacking on the Isthmus end that would support or refute the "subsystem" concept. From my more microscopic vantage point, the idea of the Isthmus system as independent but interrelated produces a better "fit" with the data. Restated, the Zapotec peasant population of the Isthmus, to whom the plazas are so vitally important economically, does not view the Isthmus as a subsystem of the Valley of Oaxaca, interdependent and interrelated to a greater degree than are the Isthmus and the regions to the south or east. Repeatedly informants stated that they did not go to the Oaxaca City plaza because selling prices were too low. They recognize Oaxaca City as favorable to the buyer, but few Isthmus peasants can afford the trip to Oaxaca City merely for buying, although a few storekeepers do so periodically.

The Valley of Oaxaca and Oaxaca City may be becoming more important as a supply source to the Isthmus than the local population realizes. Traditionally, the Isthmus was cut off from direct communication with Oaxaca City by either rail or road, and the main route to Mexico City was across the Isthmus and up through Veracruz, a route which is today only about forty miles longer and much less mountainous than that via Oaxaca City. With the opening of the Pan American Highway in the mid-1940's, Oaxaca City became reasonably accessible for the first time. Nonetheless, there is evidence that a great deal of commerce between the Isthmus and the Valley of Mexico still passes over the traditional Veracruz route, perhaps more than passes through Oaxaca City. As for Isthmus dependence on products of the Valley of Oaxaca, there is no doubt that this dependence is great. Potatoes, peas, carrots, onions, beans, lettuce—in short virtually all temperate-climate products of importance—derive from the Valley of Oaxaca. However, with the exception of onions and beans, these products are not part of the everyday Zapotec peasant diet. Mainly they are purchased and consumed by the rather sizeable mestizo and European population in the Isthmus urban centers. For most of the population of the Isthmus, products of the Valley and Sierra are either never eaten (peas, carrots, and beets for example) or are considered special-occasion foods and eaten perhaps once or twice a year (potatoes and lettuce).

Perhaps another reason for the Isthmians' rather weak identity with the Oaxaca City plaza is that plaza trade has traditionally followed emigration patterns, and Oaxaca City has never been and is not today attractive as a migration point, probably because of lack of job opportunities. The oil industry has attracted many Zapotec migrants to coastal Veracruz, and a variety of factors have served to entice people to Mexico City for at least several generations. Zapotec emigrants normally retain kin and social ties in the Isthmus, often through one and sometimes two or more generations after migration.

Trade with the communities lying along the Trans-Isthmus Highway and with the Chiapas Pacific coastal region is important, although in the case of the Chiapas coast migration has not been great. From the Chiapas coast a significant number of cattle are purchased for Isthmus markets, and this is also almost the only source of dairy products. Pineapples, oranges, and other fruits requiring a moister climate than the Isthmus offers derive from trans-Isthmus communities and the Veracruz-Tabasco coastal regions. Even sugar cane, which formerly was a major Isthmus crop, is now imported from further south. A great many products, including coffee, cacao, copal, and certain *ixtle* products, come into the Isthmus from the mountain hinterland, although some coffee and *ixtle* items especially derive from the north via the Oaxaca City plaza. Thus, while there are strong economic ties with the Valley of Oaxaca, there are also perhaps equally important ones with other regions.

TWO CASE STUDIES

Women traders are common in many peasant economic systems. In some places, such as Haiti and Jamaica (Mintz 1956; 1961; 1964a) and West Africa (Tardits and Tardits 1962; Hodder 1962; Marshall 1964—to mention a few of many sources), women predominate almost to the exclusion of men, as is true among Zapotecs of the Isthmus of Tehuantepec, Mexico. Women traders seems to be one of several possible alternatives to which peasants turn when they are unable to product sufficient food to support themselves, as Wolf has suggested (1966).

Among the Isthmus Zapotecs, while marketing is "women's work," women do not usually consider their market activities as an occupation distinct from other household duties, and they do not find it necessary to label most of the different kinds of trading activities. One exception is the revendor, or middlewoman, who regularly travels. Such women do consider trading as an occupation and are called *viajeras*. Although there are other Zapotec women who travel more or less regularly, as well as many who travel occasionally to sell, the term *viajera* is reserved for revendors who regularly buy products in one location to sell at distant locations as independent operators.

Isthmus *viajeras* spend a good deal of time traveling; yet they are not as itinerant as the Zapotec men traders of Mitla whom Parsons described (1936).[1] *Viajeras* tend to be relatively restrictive in their movements, traveling repeatedly to a single destination. A few have alternate destinations, but it seems to be rare that a woman includes three or more destinations in her plans.

In the following pages, two case studies are presented, representing two distinct types of operation of the *viajeras*. These two types do not exhaust the possibilities. A few other patterns about which less is known, as well as women who travel but are not classed as *viajeras*, will be discussed in the conclusion. Finally, my data should be considered as suggestive rather than conclusive, since *viajeras* were not the main focus of my research.[2]

Viajera A

A is forty-five years old, married by common law to the same man for more than twenty years. She has three daughters between the ages of seventeen and twenty-one and a son, aged thirteen. The eldest daughter is married and lives with her husband's family. A has been a *viajera* for the past twelve years, beginning her *viajes* when the youngest child was weaned. Before this, she bought and sold whatever she could locally, sometimes going to the coastal villages (less than twenty-five miles away) to trade with Huave women for marine products, as do a number of local Zapotec women. Her trading gradually became more continuous and her trips more frequent and regular, and ultimately she became known as a *viajera*. The basis of A's business is still trade with the Huave women on the coast (hereafter called Mareñas) for turtle eggs, shrimp, and fish, in terms highly favorable to A. But where formerly she sold these products locally, she now resells them in Oaxaca City, mostly to wholesalers. The Mareñas could conceivably take their own products to Oaxaca City, thereby cutting out the Zapotec middlewomen, but they are timid and unsure of themselves, and most of them speak little or no Spanish.

A follows a rather precise schedule, which allows her to be home three nights a week. Two of the four nights away from home are spent on the bus going to and returning from Oaxaca City, and the other two nights are passed in her stall in the Huave marketplace, where she sometimes puts up a hammock but more often just sleeps on the *cama de pencas*[3] which in the daytime serves as her counter. Of course, she does not travel fifty-two weeks of the year. During the rainy season there are two or three months when the roads to the Huave village are impassable from several days to several weeks at a time. There are other times when she stays home to attend and participate in various fiestas; she occasionally is sick; and at times family obligations keep her at home. Nevertheless, she travels most of the time, probably not missing more than six or eight weeks total during a year. As she states, she would like to stay home more, but when she is at home she is not earning; so she has no choice but to continue her trips.

Following is a description of a typical *viaje* of a week's duration: At noon on Monday A leaves home for the Huave village on the coast, usually by *urbano*,[4] but sometimes by *redila* (flat-bed truck), whichever happens to be running on that particular day. The trip (less than twenty-five miles) takes a minimum of three hours when weather conditions are favorable and the vehicle does not break down en route. When A arrives at the Huave village she arranges her trade goods in one of the vacant spaces of the open-air market structure. Huave women crowd around, eager to sell and trade their products, but A puts them off, saying she is tired and does not want to do any business until morning. She may sell a few pieces of fruit, or a handful or two of onions for cash, but she does not begin buying until the next day. She may buy a fresh fish for her own dinner and ask the vendor to take it home and cook it for her, then take her evening meal of fish, tortillas, and coffee standing beside her makeshift counter. At dusk she retires.

Tuesday before dawn Huave women begin to arrive with their *mariscos* (seafood) in enamel washbasins atop their heads. A gets up with the arrival of the first Mareña and begins trading by lantern light. Soon the stall is alive with Mareñas all crowding around trying to get A's attention at the same time. Trade is brisk and rapid. A has to make lightning decisions in the half-light of dawn about the quality, freshness, weight, and saleability of the Mareñas' products. Trading proceeds with such speed, and prices and quantities traded and purchased are so variable, that it proved impossible for the field worker to keep records. Quantities and prices, therefore, represent estimates and averages.

A tries to get the Mareñas to take about one-third trade. Sometimes she accepts less, but she never pays all cash. If a Mareña insists on cash, A quotes a price so ridiculously low the woman cannot accept. Sometimes a Mareña will wait around after A has made an offer, hoping she will reconsider and make a higher offer, but I did not witness any such cases. During the time I accompanied A on her *viajes*, maize was in short supply in the Huave village, and the Mareñas were reluctant to accept the apples, onions, bananas, and peaches which A had brought for trading. They wanted cash to buy maize, they claimed. To this, A gave the following sales pitch (freely translated): "Well, tortillas are fine, girls, food of the heart as they say, but what you ladies need are vitamins! These fruits here are filled with vitamins. Vitamins cure you and keep you from getting sick." She was asked to be more specific, what fruits cure what, and how. "Well," A replied, "these apples cure *catarro* and *gripa* [colds and other bronchial ailments]. Just cook them with a little cinnamon, mash them up, and drink them."[5] Several Mareñas decided to try her suggestion and traded their products for a small handful of poor-quality apples.

A's purchases included turtle eggs, in season during the *viaje* herein described, at various prices ranging from ten for a peso to five for a peso, depending upon how much the seller would accept in trade. Eventually A bought about 1,600 turtle eggs the first day, and approximately 1,000 the following day, estimated by the size and number of containers she filled. Turtle eggs sell cooked fresh in Tehuantepec for three for a peso or dried at four for a peso. They will keep uncooked approximately one week.

On this same trip, A bought perhaps a hundred kilos of various sizes and prices of shrimp, all cooked and salted. There are no weighing devices. Occasionally a small basket which is supposed to hold about a kilo is used as a measure, but more often she simply looks at the shrimp and guesses the weight. The Mareñas bring anything from a half-dozen to several kilos of marine products, depending on the luck of the men of the household, who are the fishers and gatherers of most of the sea products.

Fish include several varieties, depending on the season, and sizes vary within each variety. On this trip A bought whole smoked fish at an average price of six pesos per dozen, with one-third of the purchase price taken in trade. Altogether she purchased about fifteen dozen of these, refusing to buy one lot at eight pesos per dozen. Flat, split fish are so variable in size that it proved impossible to determine average price. Her purchases totaled approximately twenty dozen of these latter.

A's sister-in-law, who accompanied her on this *viaje*, decided to return to the home village the first afternoon; so A sent three baskets of turtle eggs, a basket of shrimp, and a live sheep home with the sister-in-law. The sheep was not for resale but was purchased for a coming wedding fiesta in which A and her husband were to act as *padrinos* (godparents). The sister-in-law was to guard A's goods and see that the driver dropped them off at the corner nearest A's home, where, by prearrangement, her husband and son would be waiting to receive them. A's daughters were to cook and sell some of the turtle eggs the following day and put the shrimp out to dry on mats during the daylight hours, adding more salt to hasten the process.

On Wednesday A continued buying and trading, leaving by stock truck in the late afternoon and arriving home about 10 P.M. Again her husband and son were waiting to help her unload. She left about one-fourth of a basket of onions in the Huave marketplace to be sold by the woman in the next stall, also a Zapotec *viajera*.

Thursday and Friday A remains at home doing household tasks and drying, cooking, and packing her products to take to Oaxaca City for the Saturday market. About 11 P.M. Friday she boards a second-class bus bound for Oaxaca City, arriving around 5 A.M. Saturday.

Once in Oaxaca City, A may sell all her goods to a wholesaler early in the day, or she may sell part early and hold out a part for retail selling. She judges the market condition before she makes her decision by selling retail for a couple of hours at least, beginning about 6 A.M., when customers begin to arrive. On the particular Saturday described here, sales were slow. About 9 A.M. A's traveling companion, another *viajera* from A's home town (hereinafter called Viajera C), decided to sell all her shrimp to a wholesaler. This was her entire cargo, consisting of fifty-nine kilos of medium-size shrimp, for which she received $11 per kilo, and thirty-eight kilos of large-size shrimp, for which she received $15 per kilo, a total of $1,219. C reported that she had paid $1,000 for the shrimp in the Huave village. Her expenses, which included a resale permit costing $62.50, amounted to $119.50, not including food, leaving her a net profit of just under $100 *if she had paid cash for the shrimp*. Of course, in all probability she only paid about two-thirds cash ($750) or less. If she traded bananas for the other third, she would have received the shrimp for a cash outlay of only $830, including the retail price of the bananas she traded, making her net profit $270 or about 22 percent. It is also safe to assume that she did not pay retail prices for the bananas, which are produced in her home village, in which case her net profit would be greater still.

C is a single woman of about twenty-five years and has been traveling the same *viajes* (although not necessarily at the same times) as A for the past three years. She exhibited more caution than A by deciding to sell all of her cargo wholesale at an early hour. Judging by the size of her cargo, she worked on a much more restricted capital base than did A. C and A often travel together, but they are not partners. It is convenient and efficient for *viajeras* to travel in pairs so that one can watch the *bultos* (packages) while the other takes care of bus tickets, engages *cargadores* (porters), and handles other necessary details. Traveling companions vary from trip to trip and are frequently determined by chance—those who happen to be waiting for the outgoing bus at the same time. Traveling companions may sell side by side in the Oaxaca City marketplace, watching each other's goods and taking turns selling for each other, or they may not sell contiguously and may even choose different sides of the street.

About a half-hour after C sold to the wholesaler, A followed suit, selling about forty kilos of large shrimp at fifteen pesos per kilo and about eighteen kilos of large fish at twelve pesos per kilo to a revendor from the Isthmus. She held back the amount she judged she could sell retail during the remainder of the day. On this particular occasion, two young women from A's home village selling shrimp directly across the street did not sell to the wholesalers and at the end of the day still had a large stock. A stated that if she did not sell everything on Saturday she took her merchandise to the Tlacolula Sunday market, but added that she seldom did so, preferring to sell to wholesalers and return home.

By about 4 P.M. Saturday A had sold everything except two or three fish and a half-dozen *totopos* (oven-baked tortillas). Earlier in the day A had bought a sack of good-quality apples from a *serrano* (man from the mountainous hinterland) for forty pesos. Now, while C "tended store," A began looking for closing-hour bargains. First she went up the street to the place where apples were sold and bought five more small sacks of poor-quality apples for a total of sixty-seven pesos. Later a woman flower vendor passed offering a bargain, ten bunches for eight pesos. A purchased the flowers, to be divided into smaller bunches and sold for one or two pesos per bunch in the home marketplace Sunday morning for the "cemetery trade."[6]

Purchases completed, A left the immediate area to search for a truck driver to carry her apples back to the Isthmus, since they were too bulky to go by bus. Six or seven bundles, including the flowers and two baskets of Atzompa pottery (purchased for the coming wedding fiesta), were to go on the bus with the women. At the bus station, A and C bargained with and finally agreed to pay a *cargador* three pesos to load their packages when the bus arrived. After the Saturday market in Oaxaca City, outgoing buses are very crowded, making it impossible to load one's own packages and also secure a seat. On this occasion, when the packages were safely loaded and both A and C on board, having secured seats by clever and coordinated planning, A handed the *cargador* two pesos through the window. He, of course, was properly outraged at being short-changed but A determinedly closed the window and settled comfortably in her seat, to sleep through the homeward trip.

About once a month A varies this schedule by going to Agua Dulce, an oil-refining camp near Coatzacoalcos, Veracruz. When she does so, she leaves home Thursday night and returns Saturday night or Sunday because more time is required to sell her merchandise retail there. She stays at the home of a brother in Agua Dulce. Or, as happened at the time of the journeys described herein, she goes to Oaxaca City and sends her eldest unmarried daughter to Agua Dulce.

Unfortunately it is impossible to make any precise statements about A's earnings. Item-by-item accounting is completely foreign to her mode of operation, and since she is illiterate she keeps all her accounts and does all her calculating mentally. She cannot usually recall what she paid for a particular size and kind of fish three days earlier in the Huave village. She may have paid three or four different prices for the same item, depending on how good a bargain she could drive. She knows approximately what her expenses will be to transport her purchases to Oaxaca City, and she knows what prices prevailed in Oaxaca City the previous Saturday and whether the market was brisk or sluggish. Even when she does not go, she gets this information from other *viajeras*. The prices she sets on her trade goods are approximately double the retail price in Tehuantepec, as Table 8-1 of actual prices indicates.

Viajera A does not pay retail prices for the trade items listed above, however. Apples, peaches, and onions are all imported to Tehuantepec from the Valley of Oaxaca, and since A buys these items on favorable terms in Oaxaca City, her cost (as was pointed out for apples) is considerably less.

As an example of what A could earn on a single item on which both the buying and selling price ranges are known, let us consider turtle eggs. Assuming that A bought three thousand eggs at $.20 each (the actual buying prices ranged from $.10 to $.20), paying cash for two thousand and trading bananas at 2 for $.25 for the

Table 8-1

VIAJERA A'S PRICES TO HUAVE VILLAGE COMPARED TO TEHUANTEPEC RETAIL PRICES

Item	Retail Price	
	Tehuantepec	Huave Village
Bananas	3 for $.20	2 for $ .25
Apples, small	3 for .50	3 for 1.00
Peaches, small	each .10	each .25

other thousand, the cost would be $400.00 plus 1,600 bananas (purchased in her home village at $4.00 per 100) or a total of $464.00. If she sold two thousand eggs locally at three for $1.00 and took one thousand to Veracruz, where the price is two for $1.00, she would gross $1,166.00. Allowing $66.00 for shipping, handling, and busfare to Veracruz, she would net $646.00 or 57.8 percent, not deducting anything for her labor of buying, processing, and selling. Turtle eggs are a seasonal item, of course, and she probably profits less on fish and shrimp. Turtle eggs were chosen as an example because they are uniform in size and quality and the price remains stable within the season. They sell well in Veracruz, in contrast to salt fish, possibly because turtles do not nest on the Atlantic coast or do so at a different time of year. Salt shrimp also sell readily in Veracruz, A reported.

A states that her earnings may represent about half of the family income, but I suspect this is a conservative estimate. Her husband farms only five hectares of unirrigated land and works as a day laborer for twenty pesos per day, including his cart and oxen, in his spare time. Except for the team of oxen, the couple own no large animals. Yet they spent twenty thousand pesos between 1965 and 1966 constructing a new house, and they are active in the fiesta system and obviously one of the upwardly mobile families in the status hierarchy that attaches to the fiesta system. A is probably now at the height of her earning capacity because she has two grown daughters at home to help her process and sell. When they marry and move to the homes of their husbands' parents, she will probably not be able to handle the volume she presently handles.

While the type of *viajera* that A represents is not rare in the Isthmus, it is also far from common, considering that virtually all Zapotec women process and sell in the local markets at some time. In the community in which I worked there were about a dozen women following much the same pattern as A more or less regularly (of a total population of about 1,100 households). There were also some women who traded with the Huaves and sold locally, and of these a few occasionally took goods to Oaxaca City. It is well to keep in mind, however, that this community is atypical because farm land is far more plentiful in this *municipio* than in the other Zapotec *municipios*. My observations indicate that *viajeras* are much more common in the larger towns, where a significant number of households are without sufficient land.

Viajera B

Viajera B is a single woman of forty-five years. She is not sure what year she began traveling but states that she has been a *viajera* for "more than ten years." Before this she operated a stall in the local marketplace, selling cacao, beans, eggs, cheese, brooms, brushes, and a few other items. She had endured an incredibly miserable marriage for fourteen years, afraid to leave her husband, who made repeated threats to and attempts on her life. Becoming a *viajera* was her final solution to an unbearable marital problem. She apparently left the Isthmus for a time, but it is not clear where she traveled or what she sold during these first years. She states merely that she traveled "here and there."

About 1960 or 1961 she began going to an isolated mountainous area of Chiapas where the central government had initiated a large hydroelectric project. In 1967 she was still making the 350-mile journey to Chiapas either twice a month, staying a week each trip, or once a month, staying two or more weeks. The important thing was that she be at the project every payday, which occurred twice a month. If she arrived just at one payday and could remain until after the next her traveling expenses were less. This was the pattern she preferred but one that was not always possible for various reasons.

When B was at the project she shared a windowless, rat-infested room without electricity, water, or sanitary facilities with three other women from the Isthmus. Her share of the rent was sixty-six pesos per month. She paid another forty-five pesos for her stall in the small marketplace. A widowed middle-aged cousin also sold in the plaza, and they often traveled together. Sometimes the cousin stayed at the project and looked after B's stall as well as her own while B returned to the Isthmus to replenish her stock.

B bought most of her products in the largest marketplace in the Isthmus. Unlike Viajera A, B never went to the Huave villages to buy because it was too time-consuming and proved not to be profitable for her type of business. She sometimes bought local Isthmus products directly from the producers (for example, mangoes in season), but normally she preferred to buy in the marketplace from revendors who gave her special prices for buying in quantity. Normally she sent her *bultos* (cargo) to Chiapas by truck transport and traveled by first-class bus to the nearest major town, sixty miles from the project, then took the second-class bus that ran to the project. Round-trip bus fare was about one hundred pesos, and freight charges ranged upward from about eight pesos per container, depending on weight and bulk.

At the time of my field work, the hydroelectric project was nearly completed and the population of the construction camp much diminished. There were only about six stalls operating in the marketplace, which had been built to house about forty stalls. B was anticipating the beginning of a similar project near Comitan, Chiapas, and stated that she planned to transfer her business to the new project when it opened.

When B was at the project she sold in the marketplace from 7 A.M. to 8 P.M., when the structure was officially closed and locked. One of her roommates began selling *leche con arroz* (rice gruel) to the breakfast clientele at 5 A.M., and in order to do this she arose at 2 A.M. to start her charcoal fire and begin preparation of the gruel. B and her cousin, who occupied adjoining stalls, prepared their meals together, using whatever they needed from their own stock and buying a few ingredients from other vendors. Cooking was done over a brazier in the stall of the roommate just mentioned.

Because B was cooperative and allowed me to keep a record of daily sales and because I was able to keep records of purchases, B's earnings can be calculated more accurately than those of Viajera A, whose transactions were more complex. Table 8-2 comprises a record of B's earnings for one week in February, 1967.

This trip was atypical in that I furnished transportation for both Viajera B and her merchandise. Had she paid bus fare and freight, her expenses would have been about $300, including a week's rent for her stall and sleeping quarters. An additional operating expense was the $4 per day plus meals which she paid a ten-year-old girl for peeling and selling mangoes on the street in front of the marketplace for six days. Allowing $3 per day for the girl's meals, the total expense would be $42. Thus, under more normal circumstances, B's net profit for the week would have been about $1,280. Her stated aim is to make a profit of 100 percent, a goal she exceeded on this particular occasion. Her highest-profit items, mangoes, were in great demand because they were the first of the season.

Viajera B also carried a small supply of gold jewelry, which she sold outside the marketplace to "private customers." Each day she left the market structure for about two hours shortly after 4 P.M., leaving her cousin in charge of her stall. I was not able to learn the

Table 8-2

VIAJERA B'S SALES FOR ONE WEEK

Item	Quantity	Cost[a]	Gross	Net
Shrimp, giant	5 kilos	$ 100	$ 140	$ 40
Shrimp, large	15 kilos	225	480	255
Shrimp, small	23 kilos	322	644	322
Totopos	8 dozen	16	32	16
Rolls, sweet	15 dozen	30	60	30
Mangoes, green	1,600 mangoes	114	582	468
Chocolate	12 rolls	12	24	12
Cheese	8 blocks	384	576	192
Sour cream	8 *litros*	60	128	68
Panela	25 cakes	25	30	5
Corozo nuts	2,000 nuts	40	200	160
Tamarind	80 balls	16	40	24
Brooms	24 brooms	14	48	34
Totals		$1,358	$2,984	$1,626

[a] Rounded to nearest peso

details of this aspect of her business beyond the fact that she sold the jewelry on the installment plan and that she had about three thousand pesos outstanding in payments. For this reason, she made an effort to be on hand to make her collections on each of the bi-monthly paydays. It is possible that there was some prostitution involved in this aspect of her "private-customer" business.

On Sundays many *serranos* (mountaineers) come from the surrounding area to buy in the project marketplace, even though the prices are high. Their only alternative is to make the 120-mile round trip to the nearest town. Viajera B never lowers her prices or the minimum quantity she will sell no matter how persistent and persuasive the customer may be. One *serrano* tried to get her to sell him one peso's worth of shrimp, but she insisted that the minimum was two pesos. He cajoled persistently, saying he knew it was only because she did not want to sell one peso, not that she could not. Her response was to fold her arms across her chest and stare straight through the man with unseeing eyes until he left (a characteristic and culturally sanctioned Zapotec woman's response to such situations). When a shabbily dressed *serrano* and a boy of about eight wanted to buy one peso's worth of shrimp, she again would not relent. "No, two pesos' worth is the least I sell," she insisted. The man turned and left, pausing at the entrance to count his money and perhaps to decide if he could spend two pesos for the shrimp. After he left she remarked, "Ay, *pobrecitos*, how little they get for their money!"

Except for adding a little water to the sour cream every morning "to make it easier to pour" and selling slightly smaller and broken pieces of cheese to children, Viajera B appears to be honest with her customers.

At the time of the *viaje* described here, Viajera B was deeply in debt and apparently having considerable trouble buying on short-term credit, which had been her usual practice. In this instance she borrowed a few hundred pesos from the anthropologist to make her purchases, repaying the loan from sales receipts before the week was out. Her financial problems stemmed from the fact that she was caring for her bed-ridden mother. Viajera B had borne all the heavy expenses involved in caring for her mother for the past year, although she had two married sisters living nearby. She had also stayed with her mother several weeks at a time on various occasions during the year when the mother's condition worsened, going to Chiapas only long enough to make her collections on jewelry. Her mother died later in 1967. When I returned to the field for a short time in 1968, Viajera B was reported by her sister to be slowly extricating herself from debt. By her own account and that of her sisters, Viajera B had been fairly well-to-do before her mother's illness. She had been forced to sell several thousand pesos' worth of gold jewelry and almost all of her hand-embroidered huipiles and skirts during her mother's illness.

CONCLUSIONS

The two cases just described exemplify two very different modes of operation. Although both women deal mainly or entirely in food-stuffs, as do their stay-at-home counterparts, and also rely heavily on Isthmian products (e.g., salted fish, salted shrimp, turtle eggs, tamarind, mangoes, and *totopos*), Viajera A is able to trade and buy advantageously from the Huave women, a condition that allows her to sell wholesale in the competitive Oaxaca City marketplace and still make a respectable profit, while Viajera B does the reverse, buying much of her merchandise at a relatively high wholesale price from other revendors and selling at elevated prices in the less competitive market milieu of an isolated construction project. Viajera A increases her profits by buying some items at very low prices from producer-vendors at the close of the Saturday market in Oaxaca City, which she then trades to the Mareñas at the rate of about double the Tehuantepec retail price. Viajera B sells jewelry as a profitable sideline and possibly practices prostitution, both activities well-suited to the isolated construction camp with its concentration of steadily employed men, many without families.

Viajera A retains her fundamental and important ties with the home community, where she maintains her home and family and takes an active part in the fiesta system. She views her occupation as necessary to the support of herself and her family but does not enjoy being away from home. She states that she is going to "retire" in a few years and just be la dueña de la casa (the lady of the house).

Viajera B states that she prefers the life she leads to her former occupation of selling in the local marketplace. After her mother's death, Viajera B again began spending most of her time away from the Isthmus, as reported by her sisters. Eventually she may establish a base of operations elsewhere. Prior to her mother's death she had assiduously kept up the household's contributions to fiestas in her home community. She reported that so many people owed her cuotas (contributions) that it was unnecessary to incur more fiesta obligations by borrowing for the mother's burial and funeral masses. If her report was accurate, she could easily have extricated herself from the fiesta obligations in the home community thereafter.

Although successful viajeras earn high profits for their efforts, as compared to local revendors, the work is more strenuous and the risks probably greater, especially for the inexperienced woman trying to gain a foothold as a viajera. Experienced viajeras rarely make serious errors in judging the market conditions, product quality, weights, and prices; but they always face the possibility of losing merchandise in transit, through theft and robbery, risks which are much greater for the viajera than for the local vendor and which are thought to be minimized by traveling in pairs or trios.

Trade by viajeras in Isthmus craft products is negligible, confined mostly to gold-coin jewelry and sometimes a few woven-palm products, such as women's handbags. Many other Isthmus craft products, for example hammocks and pottery, are almost never sold by *viaje-ras* to my knowledge, probably because they must compete with equal or superior products from other regions.

Some *viajeras* specialize in gold-coin jewelry exclusively, usually taking it on consignment from the craftsman, who is often a relative of the *viajera*, and selling on commission. Other women, who are not classed as *viajeras* at all and in fact do not identify themselves as a group, act as jewelers' agents, personally delivering shipments of jewelry to retailers in distant cities. The three cases known to me all involved mature relatives of the three craftsmen, in one case a wife, in another an elderly sister, and in the third a cousin, the latter two living in separate household units from the jeweler. Information about these women was difficult to elicit because of the secrecy that surrounds their activities, ostensibly due to the value of their cargo but probably also because of some illegal aspects of the trade.

Another category of Isthmus Zapotec women who travel but who are not classified as *viajeras* are the many producer-vendors who seasonally sell such products as mangoes in distant markets. These women may make six or eight trips to Oaxaca City during the season, staying away from home one or two nights each time. Often they buy fruit or flowers for resale in the home marketplace, and sometimes they buy some local products to sell in the distant marketplace along with their own; yet the sporadic, seasonal nature of their *viajes* and the fact that the main purpose is to sell the household produce precludes their inclusion in the *viajera* class.

Although my data are inconclusive in this respect, it appears that if a man is involved the woman is no longer considered a *viajera* but rather part of a team of *comercios*, a term that implies larger scale and more prestige than *viajera*. For example, one woman, the cousin of an informant, constantly traveled around southern Mexico buying and selling fruit with her husband, a native of the Valley of Oaxaca. She was never referred to as a *viajera*, presumably because the couple owned their means of transportation, a truck, and bought in truckload quantity. This woman had not lived in the Isthmus for a number of years, but she retained close contact with the home community, visiting relatives and attending fiestas frequently. Since the couple frequently sold fruits locally from the truck, it was probably both advantageous and relatively easy for her to maintain ties with the home community.

What type of selling a woman does and how successful she is depends partly upon the extent of her family responsibilities. Zapotec mothers take the care of small children very seriously and ordinarily do not relegate this duty to grandmothers, older children, or other female relatives except for limited periods. Thus it is rare for a woman with small children to do any selling even locally except for that which can be done from her home. Unmarried girls frequently sell in the local marketplaces and may even be sent to Oaxaca City or Minatitlán or elsewhere to sell products of the household, but in all cases known to me the girls were acting as agents of their mothers. Usually a woman does not become a regular revendor, even locally, until she is middle-aged and her children are at least adolescent.

The amount of capital a woman is able to accumulate also determines to some extent what type of selling she attempts. Evidence suggests that most women who try to establish themselves as *viajeras* fail and lose their capital (i.e., "go broke") in a short time because of lack of experience in a highly competitive occupation. One of my informants had tried to enter the occupation several times over the years at the urging of her sister-in-law, a successful *viajera*. Each time she had quickly erred in one way or another and lost her capital, even under the sister-in-law's guidance, with the result that she refused further opportunities, stating that she was unlucky in trade. The successful *viajera* who retains the home community as her base of operations may be the exception rather than the rule, because a number of *viajeras* were reported to me by informants who could give no information about them other than some remark such as "Fulana's cousin used to be a *viajera*, but I don't know where she is now." In a few cases even informants' siblings had lost touch with their families.

Other important variables in the success of the *viajera* appear to be the type of personality and business acumen of the individual. Whether a woman becomes successful because of these attributes or learns them in the course of becoming successful is debatable, but the fact remains that the *viajeras* are more sophisticated, alert to possible opportunities, open to new ideas, "businesslike" in their customer contacts, and shrewd in calculating their profits mentally than are the vast majority of women who remain in the home community.

In general the *viajeras* are similar to women traders reported elsewhere in that their operations are relatively small in scale and their goods consist mainly of foodstuffs. There appear to be no relations between *viajeras* and their customers or suppliers comparable to

Haitian *pratik* as reported by Mintz (1961), however. Although *co-madre* relations are common among local Zapotec women vendors, both vertical (customer-vendor) and horizontal (vendor-vendor), and are accompanied by cooperation, exchange of favors, and small gifts, none of the *viajeras* known to me had established any binding relations through *compadrazgo* or any alternative mechanism outside the home community.

9. Examples of Stability and Change from Santa María Atzompa

The Valley of Oaxaca, at some distance from the industrial center of Mexico, is steeped in traditional systems of production and exchange. A number of elements in both production and exchange are pre-Hispanic; for example, the coil technique of pottery making, discussed below, and trading trips by professional traders. As government services, industrial processes, roads, new products, and new selling methods penetrate the area, economic activities within the villages are perforce affected. Improved health services and standards contribute to population pressure on food resources. Expansion of opportunities invites shifts in economic strategies in the villages as well as in the city. Traditional industries may undergo changes in work techniques and product form. At the same time, networks of roads and increasing bulk transport affect the character of distribution and the availability of goods. The peasant finds new industrial products in the market in quantity, promoted by advertising and by the possibility of installment buying. As their isolation is broken, rural populations are affected, too, by the value changes that accompany the increased volume of consumer's goods; these are reflected in a rising desire for nontraditional types of wealth and prestige, nontraditional career goals, and, consequently, changes in allocations of time and other resources.

Santa María Atzompa, a pottery-making village situated five miles to the northwest of Oaxaca City, contributes to the study of economic change for two reasons. First, its pottery is widely distributed through the Oaxaca market system and outside the system as well; and second, the product is an aboriginal craft which is being supplanted by industrial counterparts throughout the world. Some aspects of production and marketing that might be examined are the village's adjustment, if any, to prospective displacement of ceramic kitchenware as more durable cookware and new cooking methods are adopted regionally and nationally, experimentation with modern processes, and the impact of modern transport on distribution.

Potters, like other artisans, differ from farmers in that they have a ready supply of cash, minimal though it may be, so that their consumption patterns approximate those of the wage earner rather than the peasant farmer, for example, in installment buying and impulse buying. While our primary interest is in Atzomperos as producers, it is also relevant to inquire whether consumption in Atzompa is changing as consumerism is promoted in rural Mexico and as new facilities, such as electricity, make possible the use of modern appliances and equipment.

STABILITY AND CHANGE IN POTTERY PRODUCTION

Atzompa potters are primarily suppliers of ceramic cookware and other utilitarian ware to the Oaxaca market system and, through it (and sometimes bypassing it), to other regions of Mexico. Some of the ceramic ware is exported. Several of the forms are pre-Columbian, and there are indications, based on color and temper patterns analyzed by Anna O. Shepard of the U.S. Geological Survey (Shepard 1963:19; 1967:478, 483), that pottery was produced in the same approximate area, combining the same clay types and temper sources, during very early Monte Albán times.[1] It has certainly been produced in quantity as far back as oral tradition reaches. Briefly, the pots are molded by the ancient coil method, working up from a base that is pounded out in a flat or saucer-shaped platter, the latter usually being free to rotate on an upended pot. Tubs, flowerpots, ollas, jars, pitchers, casseroles, bowls, and griddles of various sizes are shaped in this way. Decorative ware, principally small animal forms, has been introduced fairly recently with good economic result. Post-Hispanically most pottery is copper-glazed, at least on the interior, exceptions being the griddles, and tubs intended for non-cooking purposes. The latter are slipped with a reddish clay obtained at two sites to the east, San Pablo Etla and San Felipe del Agua. The great popularity of Atzompa pots derives from their considerable porosity, which allows them to be used over open wood fires, still the predominant way of cooking in rural Mexico.

The household continues to be the production unit; its members are detailed to dig clay and the tempering material, pulverize the temper, fetch glaze and possibly grind it, fetch kindling and procure wood, form pots, scrape and polish, fire, glaze, refire, pack, and sell the ware. The division of labor within the household is traditionally established but not immutable: pot forming by the coil method is considered a woman's work, while men are charged with the other tasks; but in several households men participate in pot forming, and women may perform the strenuous task of pounding temper. Specialization is unimportant. There are few processes in pot forming, and these are performed in sequence by a single worker who knows them all thoroughly. While digging clay for resale has become a semispecialization, so that clay may be purchased, fetching materials for a household of one or two potters does not keep a man occupied full time. Only temper pulverization and polishing pot exteriors are daily tasks usually performed by men. Therefore it is difficult to see what could be accomplished by agglomeration of production units that is not accomplished by households except, possibly, reduction of costs through bulk purchase of wood and glaze.

Selling labor for pottery work is not common in Atzompa, since it is more profitable to buy the clay and tempering material and sell the pots unfired. The potter who sells her labor to another household relinquishes the profit taken by the employer and subjects herself to a degree of regimentation. Such a labor strategy is undertaken only by potters too feeble to fetch their materials and too poor to buy them. The principal employer of wage-labor potters is glad to have them, for he pays a potter, on the average, six pesos a day for two dozen pots, invests another peso or two in her meals, and can sell the two dozen pots, after firing, for thirty pesos or more. His profit, even after glaze and wood expenses, is considerable.

In modern times there has been some variation from the coil method of pot forming. The kick wheel was introduced to Atzompa about 1940, when a wheel operator from Cuilapan lived there for a short time. Two Atzomperos, brothers, had been working with wheels in a Oaxaca City pottery shop and taught the technique to a third brother at home. All three improved their skill under the tutelage of the boy from Cuilapan, who was hired as an instructor by other men of the village also. Several of his pupils bought wheels and began to work. After the outsider left, wheel users continued to teach others when requested, particularly their relatives and friends; a few sought instructors in Oaxaca City. However, the poverty of kick-wheel users has had a negative effect. Wheel-made pottery is small and reputedly thick-walled, and prices for it are low. The advantage to the household of owning a wheel is that it utilizes the free time of males (women find wheel use too strenuous),[2] but in most cases it leaves the men too little time for fetching materials, so that clay must be bought from resellers. Added to the facts that pot forming is generally regarded as a woman's work and that learning to use the wheel entails unaccustomed motor habits, its poor demonstration effect has discouraged its spread. There is also a problem of availability of materials: a gross of the jars can easily be produced by one potter daily, but this would require a constant flow of clay and tempering material. Most kick-wheel users produce only three to six dozen jars or cups daily. In a sample of sixty-nine potters' households in 1969, three had used the wheel and given it up, three were using it regularly and two occasionally, and two had tried to learn but failed. Only nine men in the village were using a wheel regularly in 1969.

A more important addition to production techniques is the hand modeling of small animal forms ("toys" in local parlance), introduced two generations ago by a priest who learned the craft in a seminary and taught it to his Atzompa cousin, a nonpotter. It has descended through the cousin's family line and a related line and was adopted by an unrelated family which has brought decorative-ware production to its highest development and elaboration. Since the forms are worked by both males and females, each marriage of a producer may recruit the spouse and all their children to this specialty. At present there are twelve households producing the small animals, ten producing other types of ornamental ware, and a number of others using nontraditional decoration (fluting or appliqué) on utilitarian ware. Some of the new forms de eloped from modification of the animal figures. A few resulted from buyers' requests for particular items; in such a case the potter may use a mold or work from a model or drawing of the desired form.

The level of demand for such potterv is far above the level of production. One potter ships not only to Mexico City but also to three points in the United States with some regularity. Two potters, sister and brother, were selling most of their production to the Folk Art Museum in Mexico City in 1969. Female figures 3½ feet high, elaborately ornamented with appliqué, are usually sold by the sister for $250 but have been seen priced at $700 to $800 in Oaxaca tourist shops. Undoubtedly the trend toward decorative pottery will continue to develop, as it has in the nearby village of San Bartolo Coyotepec, studied by Paul and Henriette van de Velde (1939:40). There, as in Atzompa, some potters were quick to adapt to new demands.

Men who have married into *juguetero* (toymaker) families have generally been eager to learn the technique of toymaking, as production of the small figures is called, since the superior value of these forms is evidenced in the standard of living of the *jugueteros*. It is economically advantageous in that all members of the household, even the children, participate in the molding process, and expenses for materials are fairly low when compared with income, 28 and 33 percent of income for two of the most affluent toymaker households, even though they buy their clay, compared with 54 and 58 percent of income for kick-wheel users in the sample.

Most of the resources Atzompa potters use originate outside their township (*municipio*). For many years a wealthy Oaxaqueño has been the sole purveyor of glaze to the potters, directly or indirectly. Villagers believe that he has an unofficial import monopoly on the glaze, which comes from the Monterrey region. In 1967 he offered a glaze preparation premixed with copper oxide and water, and by 1968 a majority of the potters were buying the prepared glaze (forty-nine in a sample of fifty-nine glaze users), saving three to six hours of laborious hand milling for each firing. A few continued to mix their own glaze in order to obtain a thicker mixture than that offered for sale. Four Atzompa storekeepers resold prepared glaze in the village at a mark-up of $.50 the kilogram.

There were a number of local dealers in firewood who bought the wood primarily from the *propios* of San Felipe Tejalapan (wood is very scarce in dry Atzompa) for seven to eight pesos per burro-load and resold it at ten pesos, usually on credit. In early 1969 a potter acquired what he estimated to be one hundred such loads of wood from an acquaintance at San Juan del Estado in the northeast of the Etla *ex-distrito*, for seven hundred pesos delivered, intending to sell it at the usual dealer's price of ten pesos per load. Due to severe summer floods, which kept San Felipe vendors from reaching Atzompa, he was able to sell at the inflated price of fifteen pesos per load. Wood prices at dealers' homes and stores rose to eighteen pesos per load as the rains and wood shortage continued. As an alternative to buying in the village, a few households spend a nine-to-twelve-hour man-day seeking firewood in the foothills of the western sierra for every firing, once every two weeks for most. The nearer foothills to the east and west have been closed to nonlocal wood seekers because of deforestation.

A need exists, then, to find alternative fuels that would allow potters more control over this important resource. Some are aware that both natural gas and kerosene are possible alternatives, but to date there has been neither experimentation nor inquiry.

Other resources needed for pottery making are of course the clay and the temper. Tempering material—a whitish, friable earth—is available without charge in the *municipio*. "Smooth clay" is also available there, but the most desirable moist clays are brought from other *municipios*, where mine owners charge fees of three pesos and five pesos the burro-load. Most households spend one man-day or part of a day each week getting clay and another half-day getting temper, but there is a trend toward buying the clay from local resellers or sending laborers for it, especially on the part of households which have time-consuming secondary occupations or in which men are pot formers.

Total cash expenses for raw materials vary greatly. For example, griddle makers can use an inferior grade of clay from the *municipio*; they use no glaze and can fire at relatively low heat with kindling rather than large wood, so that expenses may reach zero. For others, the expense of buying clay from resellers, added to glaze and wood costs that can be high for fully glazed pieces, may raise expenditures to more than 50 percent of income.

STABILITY AND CHANGE IN MARKETING

Income depends somewhat on the method of distribution. The potter may sell at the Saturday market in Oaxaca City, where he is surrounded by competitors from the same village and spends hours sitting beside his merchandise on the sidewalk, but where he ekes out 20 to 25 percent more when selling by the piece than he would make by bulk sale to a dealer. On the other hand, he may be approached by dealers and sell his entire production quickly but for less than the retail price. He may take the pottery to another town, usually one with which he or his relatives are familiar, for a slightly better price in the marketplace and less competition (but a higher freight cost).[3] He may sell to regional dealers in bulk on verbal contract, or to a Oaxaca City storekeeper, or to an Atzompa dealer for minimal prices, avoiding freight costs and risk of breakage in transit. His wife may sell some pieces each week to itinerant traders from other villages, and imperfect pieces can be sold to vendors in the small Atzompa marketplace. Many potters sell a few unfired pots to more affluent households when they are short of cash; some potters do it habitually.

In general, demand for traditional ware is at least even with production and sometimes above, so that all production is eventually sold, and income is regular, although not munificent, during most of the year. During the rainy summer season, however, production is reduced because of the difficulty of firing or even storing unfired ware away from moisture, and sales are low because many potential buyers are engaged in land cultivation and are deferring their outlay for such items as pottery until after the fall harvest. During this season potters often sell the chickens, turkeys, and pigs they raise as savings funds. Families that do not have animals to sell may be hard-pressed. Their usual recourse is to request advances from the dealers to whom they sell their pots. The hardships of the rainy season are compensated by the heavy, high-priced buying preceding All Saints' Day, during the month of October, but the Oaxaca City dealers who have stored up pottery or who are now receiving a backlog of pots for which they advanced money in the summer are better off than the potter who has no backlog of merchandise. Also, those potters who deliver to dealers on contract must forego the higher holiday prices.

Decorative ware has a different sales pattern: its sales are steadier during the year and peak before Christmas and Easter. Buyers of this type of pottery are largely urban, including shops that cater to tourists. Dealers from Mexico City and other urban centers send trucks to Atzompa to buy up pottery, principally decorative ware, before Easter; but no one accumulates merchandise for the occasion, not even a major producer of decorative ware who is visited every year by a trucker from Mexico City. (In 1968 the trucker paid $5.20 per dozen above Oaxaca prices for 72 dozen pieces, which were hurriedly produced at the last minute.)

Commercial relationships of distribution are fairly stable but flexible. Thirteen of the thirty-one potters in the sample who were sell-

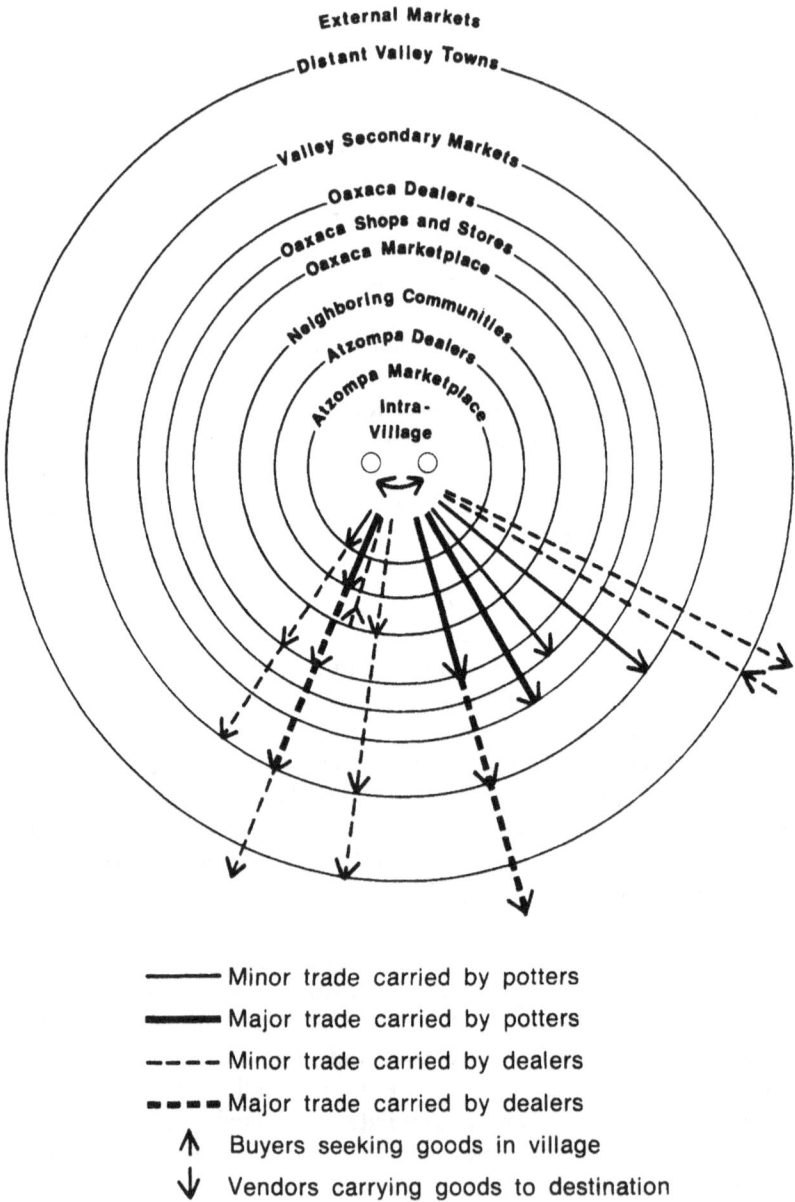

Figure 9-1. Distribution of Atzompa pottery.

ing at least part of their production to dealers in 1969 claimed business relationships with their buyers of ten years or more. Fifty-eight percent of those who came from pottery-producing families and remembered their fathers were selling pottery in the same way and place their fathers had, although some of them had additional methods of distribution. By late 1969, however, eighteen of the sixty-seven remaining potters in the sample had changed their marketing strategy or clientele in a major way, and one nonpotter had become both a potter (by marrying one) and a small-scale dealer.

Two related distribution trends since the previous generation have been the increase of regular delivery to dealers and Oaxaca City shops (49 percent of the potters sampled in 1968 as against 33 percent for their fathers)[4] and a shift away from lengthy selling trips. The primary reason for these shifts is the increase in the number of dealers and Oaxaca City shops. The discontinuance of lengthy selling trips is attributed to the increased commercial traffic in Oaxaca City since the opening of the Pan American Highway, which makes traveling unnecessary, and to the equalization of price levels throughout the region due to the growth of bulk transport, which makes traveling unprofitable. For example, in the late 1930's and early 1940's one potter-dealer alternated his selling trips between Huitzo and Telixtlahuaca in the north, and Tlapacoyan and Ayoquezco in the south, traveling with burros. No one covers such a wide territory now, although some griddle makers travel the highway with burros, sometimes as far as Huitzo, to sell a fragile product that buyers do not like to carry home. Only eight of the sample regularly sell their wares outside Oaxaca City now, but fifteen reported that their fathers did. Atzompa dealers and a few *propios* regularly cover Tlacolula (five, of whom one also covers Mitla and another Zimatlán), Ocotlán (five), Etla (five), Zaachila (four), Nochixtlán (one), and recently Teposcolula (one) (the latter two in the Mixteca). An elderly man goes to Tlaxiaco in the Mixteca irregularly, and a woman over eighty years old enjoys an occasional trading trip to the Isthmus, where she buys mangoes, tamarinds, and coconuts to resell in Atzompa and visits the local shrines. One large-scale dealer makes personal deliveries to a distributor in Mexico City and also attends at least one extraregional fair annually. An older woman, who traveled a good deal in the past and now sells only at Tlacolula, goes to a yearly fair in a Puebla town. Few go so far afield, but the more popular Valley of Oaxaca fairs are attended by some Atzompa potters and potter-dealers, particularly the June fair at San Pablo Huixtepec (thirteen Atzompa *puestos* in 1968). The decline in travel by potters was emphasized by an informant, one of the five presently covering Ocotlán, who said that in the past approximately forty Atzomperos sold pottery in that town.

Atzompa potters and dealers who sell outside of Oaxaca City these days have a good deal of competition from the increasing numbers of regional dealers. Small-scale traders, such as those from neighboring San Lorenzo Cacaotepec, sell at a distance, traveling as far as the Cañada region to the north, seeking higher prices in a few still-remote villages, buying fruit, beans, and other low-priced products of that region for resale in or near Oaxaca City. They buy pottery in Atzompa and bypass the plaza system. Large-scale dealers from Oaxaca City can afford to purchase large quantities of merchandise for low prices in the slow season and store it for seasons of highest prices; therefore they are not at a disadvantage relative to Atzompa dealers.

The extent of the extraregional market is imperfectly known. Agents as well as dealers make large purchases from *propios* at the Saturday market in Oaxaca City. While regular buyers from such Valley towns as Ejutla and Ocotlán and even from the Isthmus are recognized by the vendors, peripatetic agents seldom are. An agent from Mexico City who came to Atzompa in 1968 to recruit three additional suppliers said that he visits Oaxaca only twice a year, since he covers a broad territory including Puebla, Monterrey, and Guadalajara. There are indications that much of the decorative ware is exported to Mexico City and abroad. The above-mentioned potter who exports to the United States calculates that he has sent more than twenty thousand pieces to Boston alone. His daughter, in another household, notes that her ware too is intended for export, since the dealer she sells to tags the figures "Made in Mexico."

While the utilitarian ware reaches Mexico City in quantity and is found in the marketplace of Tapachula, Chiapas, near the Guatemalan border, the greater part remains in the Oaxaca market system. It is ubiquitous in Valley kitchens at all economic levels and has little competition from other cookware locally (see Shepard 1963: 10).

STABILITY AND CHANGE IN EXPLOITATION OF ECONOMIC OPPORTUNITIES

Pottery income can be large for the decorative ware. For example, one childless couple produces about $450 worth of various decorative forms every two weeks, netting about $300 during this period. Since both men and women work at this nontraditional specialty, the household has two potters. With few family expenses, they have a cash surplus for such luxuries as good clothes, a bed with mattress, a modern wardrobe closet, a bicycle, a kerosene stove, a radio-phonograph, and a television set, most of these purchased on installments; and in 1969 they opened a small grocery store, whose profits contributed to the purchase of the television set. Another couple, probably representing the top of the income range for pottery, nets as much as $40 a day without any help from the children. They also chose to invest their surplus cash in a grocery operation, and they too bought a television set. (It is customary to admit the public for television viewing, for a small fee; thus a television set is a source of income.)

Utilitarian ware usually nets less income, for example: $91 a week for casseroles in a family with one potter, and $169 a week in a family with two potters; $93 a week for griddles of various sizes in a family with one potter, and $180 a week in a family with three potters; $72 a week for medium-size jars in a family with one potter; and less than $47 weekly for medium-size tubs in a fatherless family with one potter who sells her ware unfired. (These incomes do not take into account additional expenses that may be incurred for freight or vendors' fees or storage at the marketplace.)

A potter can augment his income within the ceramics industry by reselling clay or other raw materials, buying crude ware to finish and sell, buying finished ware to sell in Oaxaca City or another town, hiring potters to work at his home for a few pesos per dozen pots and meals (as noted, this is not common), and of course by acquiring daughters-in-law, who in this ideally patrilocal community will add their production to the family's budget. Of 392 households in the field census, 346 (88 percent) produced pottery, some in small quantities. Local pottery dealing has increased until, in 1967, 34 households engaged in pottery resale to some degree; at least 11 averaged one hundred pesos or more weekly from this occupation before freight and storage costs.[5]

Most Atzompa households have two or more occupations. Pottery making and farming are the most common combination, although many potter-landholders give their lands for sharecropping to local farmers or to sharecroppers from neighboring villages. Since the haciendas were taken over by the government in the 1920's, government-grant land (*ejido*) has become available to all villagers, but the best *ejido* land generally is passed on to heirs and kept out of circulation. In farming, too, techniques have remained strongly traditional. Tractor use for land preparation is the only technological innovation that has won substantial acceptance.

Some other local occupations are schoolteaching, storekeeping, trucking and truck driving, dressmaking, maize milling, baking, butchering, and house construction. These are preferred to pottery making, which is reduced when a household begins to earn its living in more prestigious or cleaner work.

Most of the nontraditional occupations are only recent possibilities for the Atzompa artisan-peasant. The first Atzompa schoolteachers trace their training to the early 1940's; the first formally trained dressmaker to set up a shop did so in 1960; and the first local trucker commenced operations in 1964. While older residents can recall some sixteen stores that existed before 1930 (never more than five at one time), only half of the storekeepers were natives of the village, whereas in 1970 there were twenty-two storekeepers (fifteen major and seven minor), all but one Atzompa-born. Before 1964, pottery hauling was controlled by outside interests; a favorable demonstration effect (obviously high profits) and increasing village prosperity had led six Atzomperos to invest in trucks by 1970. A new distribution outlet may be opened soon through the efforts of a young man who in 1970 was working in Mexico City, saving toward the purchase of a truck to haul Atzompa ware for resale to Mexico City, where a casserole worth two pesos in Oaxaca sold for five pesos in 1968.

There is a tendency for nontraditional economic activities to multiply in families and lead to a stratification that was not present when land was virtually the only wealth, destined to be fragmented in inheritance. For example, the young man working in Mexico City comes from a family in which there are three large-scale pottery dealers; he will be the fourth. The first trucker began as a potter, then became a pottery dealer, large-scale landowner, storekeeper, and trucker. The largest store of the village belongs to a household that produced three schoolteachers; the store was established with a loan secured by one of the teachers, and with its profits the family has purchased two houses in Oaxaca City as well as unimproved residential property outside the city.

Although there is increasing interest in higher education and professional or white-collar work, Oaxaca's labor market at present is insufficiently developed to absorb large numbers of white-collar employees, or even blue-collar workers. In 1967, twenty-four Atzompa households had members working in Oaxaca City, most of them in factories or with bus companies, and most of them with dual urban and village residence. Wages in the sample ranged from $13.00 to $18.50 daily in ice factories to $30.00 per working day for a long-distance bus driver. Two Atzomperos held responsible white-collar jobs. While men in pottery-making families generally do not seek wage work because they dislike the regimentation, in contrast to self-employment in pottery production, yet as this urban niche expands, more Atzomperos are filling it.

STABILITY AND CHANGE IN CONSUMPTION

For those engaged in pottery making only, especially households with only one potter, producing utilitarian ware, income is meager when measured against the cost of living. Household budgets showed that in 1968 consumption costs approximated $10.50 a day for food alone for a young, lower-income family of four and $19.50 for an older family of six in the middle-income range.

As pottery profits depend somewhat on distribution strategy, similarly, consumption expenditures depend somewhat on purchasing strategy. Now as in the past, the cheapest and best source of goods is said to be the Oaxaca City plaza on Saturdays. Almost every household attends, at least biweekly. Prices at the small Atzompa marketplace are higher, as the result of transport costs, reseller's profit, and low competition. The Atzompa *placita* (little marketplace) had five daily vendors in 1968, of whom two were local; all but one were resellers who acquired produce in the city. On Tuesdays and Fridays, the primary and secondary market days, there were often as many as twenty vendors inside the shed and about ten more (mostly *tortilleras*) outside. A good part of the attraction for nonlocal vendors is the opportunity the *placita* gives them to buy pots for resale. Second, busy women potters are good customers for ready-made tortillas; and, third, there is a good supply of cash in Atzompa after the Saturday pottery sales. Most schoolchildren get a $.20 daily allowance to buy a piece of fruit or a drink during the school's recreation break. A *propio* vendor of flavored ice-water from San Jacinto Amilpas was heard to say that he usually clears $100.00 in the *placita* on Tuesdays.

The local stores are the most expensive source of groceries, with a mark-up averaging approximately 30 percent over Oaxaca City prices, but they are well patronized for such items as soft drinks, liquor, lard, cigarettes, candles, and kerosene. They get their stock primarily from Oaxaca City but also buy cheese, eggs, charcoal, wood, etc., from itinerant vendors and mescal from itinerants who bring it occasionally from Amatengo, south of Ejutla.

Itinerant vendors from hamlets and other villages and installment salesmen from the city swarm through Atzompa on Tuesdays and Fridays, most of the itinerants buying a few pots on each trip for resale elsewhere. *Propios* and a few traders bring poor-quality fruit and wood products from Tlazoyaltepec, Peñoles, and Jalapa del Valle to the west, and a great deal of firewood from San Felipe Tejalapan for pottery firing on Fridays. Four *tortilleras* from one Atzompa hamlet visit the village daily, while others come daily, semiweekly, or weekly from this and other neighboring communities. Four regular vendors from San Raymundo Jalpan bring a home-made maize drink and products from the Zaachila market, mostly meat and fruit. These vendors bypass the Oaxaca City market, but others bring their products from the city—five in a sample of twenty-eight, including two vendors of flavored ices, who enjoy brisk sales in summer. A great deal of buying is done on credit, with promises to pay after Saturday's pottery sales. This is true not only of stores, where credit is extended to selected customers, but even of the Atzompa marketplace and some itinerant vendors. Payments are generally very irregular; thus vendors place a high mark-up on their merchandise to offset bad debts. (A man's shirt and trousers selling for thirty-five pesos in the Oaxaca City marketplace might cost fifty pesos if bought on installments in Atzompa.)

Since Atzompa is traversed by a footpath that connects the eastern edge of the Mixteca with Oaxaca City, it is likely that the trade from the west is of long standing, and villagers cannot remember a time when firewood was not brought in quantity from San Felipe Tejalapan. A certain amount of intervillage trade is attributable to specialization (for example, pottery from Atzompa, baskets from San Lorenzo Cacaotepec, guavas and citrus fruit from San Jacinto Amilpas) and is probably long-established. However, according to informants there were only three or four resellers of fruits and vegetables vending from door to door until 1944, when there was a substantial increase. The latter date follows by one year the extension of the Pan American Highway to Oaxaca City. The *placita*, too, has grown in recent years: a sixty-eight-year-old informant recalled that there were five or six vendors in his youth, who convened only on Tuesdays. Despite changes due to increased traffic, there has been some stability in personnel. Of the sample of twenty-eight itinerants, eleven had been selling in Atzompa for ten years or more, six for twenty years or more. The wife of the aforementioned vendor of flavored ice-water had attended the *placita* for almost forty years.

Some minor intravillage trading was observed. A few households buy soft drinks from city trucks that serve the villages; these may be consumed by the purchaser or sold to others for a profit. Home-produced foods most often sold to fellow villagers, usually by households not engaged in pottery making, are tortillas, milk, cheese, and eggs; less frequently, herbs and *guaje* beans. Maize and vegetables from the fields are not sold systematically on an intravillage basis except by storekeepers selling their own products. Three women (one a potter) make chocolate for sale; two women (one a potter) occasionally sell tamales. Some types of services rendered for cash on an intravillage level are water hauling, barbering, kiln building, plow construction, band music (for religious feasts, weddings, and funerals), candle making for religious observances, traditional curing, marriage brokerage, laundering (very rare, since this service is usually performed by women of other villages), rental of phonographs with records for parties, and television viewing. The latter two are nontraditional and were initiated in 1958 and 1969 respectively.[6]

The status of sharecropping, a major service, has changed significantly since the haciendas were disbanded. Formerly most sharecroppers were attached to the haciendas and were considered servile peons. Now they are the social equals of their employers in most instances and are in high demand because of the number of villagers who hold land but are unable or unwilling to farm it.

SUMMARY AND OUTLOOK

An overview of economic activity in Atzompa shows that, while the technology of pottery making has remained essentially stable, the tempo of commercial activities has increased as other areas of the broadening opportunity structure are exploited.

Technology. For the utilitarian ware, the traditional coil method of pot forming still predominates. The kick wheel has made little headway, due at least in part to the fact that no head-of-household has become prosperous by using one. Molds are used by a few potters in their daily work and by a large number in producing hollow animal forms for Easter. The production of utilitarian pots by coiling is already quite efficient, the bodies of average size pots being formed rapidly at the rate of four to six per hour. (However, scraping a pot smooth may take as much time as forming it, and polishing the exterior, a man's task, requires about four to eight minutes more.) Use of molds might facilitate the spread of decorative ware by obviating the need to learn freehand techniques, but those who know the specialty can shape their small figures very quickly by hand—at a rate of fifteen per hour in one observed instance.

There has been virtually no change in the materials used. Perhaps the most urgent need is for experimentation with other fuels, as wood is expensive and sometimes scarce. There is also room for improvement in the pulverization of the tempering material, presently accomplished by beating with a stick.

Product Modification. The decorative ware may be considered a solution to the foreseeable problem of a decline in the demand for handmade ceramic pots. The spread of esthetically oriented pottery will tend to increase total village income, and demand should continue to exceed supply in the future. Here, a rapidly expanding production niche developed with growing tourism and greater access to external markets, and the animal forms appeared to fill that niche. There has been a proliferation of decorative forms, which now include ornamental ashtrays, casseroles with animal-head handles, liqueur sets, large animal figures, human figures, and miniature pots.

Strategy in Allocation of Resources. The widespread, rapid acceptance of premixed glaze and the dual trends toward buying clay and selling pottery wholesale indicate a prevailing interest in minimizing time and effort. The time saved can then profitably be applied to farming, storekeeping, pottery dealing, or some other enterprise.

Commercial activities afford prestige of a nontraditional type. The major traditional path to prestige, feast giving associated with the sponsorship of a saint, is in decline. Religious brotherhoods, which assumed a large share of such responsibility, declined from ten at the turn of the century to one in 1970. Household sponsorship, which accounted for the remainder, has fallen off commensurately, although there are still a few volunteers each year, usually fulfilling vows made to saints in time of personal crisis. The diminishing attraction of religious service may be due in part to increased dependence on efficacious medicines, which reduces the practice of making vows in return for cures. However, satisfactions provided by the prestige of being a *comerciante* and by ownership of such modern goods as bicycles and television sets are now competing for the resources formerly channeled into the giving of religious feasts. Festive activities are still the primary form of village entertainment, but such parties as are given now (usually on the occasion of one's saint's day) are spontaneous and geared to cash resources available at the time, and they emphasize gaiety rather than piety. These parties have increased greatly since the introduction of phonograph music in 1958.

A growing number of families (sixteen in 1970, including two in modest circumstances) are investing in higher education for their children, a relatively new avenue to mobility and prestige. While some secondary-school graduates do not fulfill their parents' expectations, a number of them have reached white-collar and professional status. In the past two generations the village has produced one lawyer, two engineering technician-instructors (both intend to become engineers), sixteen primary-school teachers, and several accountants. Recent evidence of the attainment of higher living standards through the fairly accessible occupation of primary-school teaching ensures the continued and widening pursuit of this career goal. Thirty percent of the potters sampled who have young children or grandchildren expressed this career aspiration for them.

Other economic opportunities invite the potter's surplus cash. The most profitable, potentially, would be an electric glaze mill, which has become a possibility since electrical service was extended to Atzompa in 1969. Several villagers were eager to see this become a village industry, and forty-five in a sample of seventy-eight expressed a willingness to invest in a glaze-milling cooperative if one should be established. One potter-storekeeper who brings small quantities of glaze from Mexico City intended to electrify his manually operated mill, but to date nothing has come of it. Such a move would require breaking the monopoly of the Oaxaca City importer, who said he would fight any serious competition by reducing his prices to cost for a year.

Another major commercial prospect since the installation of electricity is a tortilla factory. By the end of 1960 two villagers (one a potter) were actively planning to establish *tortillerías*. (The realization of such an enterprise would have repercussions on the current small-scale suppliers of tortillas, just as a change in fuel for pottery firing would have negative effects on present wood suppliers.) Other commercial possibilities recognized by villagers in the sample included a radio-repair shop, a carpentry shop, a chocolate mill, a restaurant, and an irrigation pump for renting.

Increased village income from new types of pottery and from enterprise will undoubtedly lead to increased demand for modern consumer's goods, which potters, with their weekly or biweekly incomes, can buy on installments. The burgeoning demand for industrial products may be observed in radio ownership, up from 56 percent in a sample of eighty (potters and nonpotters) in 1968 to 71 percent in late 1969. Radios are an important element in village life, since they bring villagers into close touch with national and international events and with urban ways of life through the popular soap operas. Also, they convey advertisements for a variety of modern products. One of the two farmers in the sample who have begun to use chemical fertilizer said that he was motivated to buy it by radio advertising. In this case, cash surplus invested in the radio led to improved technology, which in turn produces more surplus.

The Atzompa pattern shows that occupational and production niches are filled as they occur. Improved roads make possible bulk transport, which in turn encourages bulk buying and selling; thus the mushrooming of pottery dealers. Tourist interest in Oaxaca encourages the extension of pottery making to forms that are more esthetically pleasing than traditional cookware, and in Atzompa this niche is being filled. The limited development of factories in Oaxaca has provided new opportunities for wage work; by late 1969 there were eleven Atzomperos employed in factories and two more in mechanics' shops. Increasing numbers of young Atzomperos are preparing for white-collar work, especially for the newly perceived opportunities in schoolteaching. Investments in enterprise have increased, as the growth of regional trade and the availability to villagers of the confiscated hacienda lands have resulted in expansion of the economic structure and greater prosperity; and consumption goals (including conspicuous consumption) have shifted, as new types of goods and services have become accessible and have been found to provide satisfactions in terms of a higher standard of living, or prestige, or both.

On a village-wide basis, the exploitation of an economic role is found to be related to cognition of the opportunity and a perception of its being both attainable and advantageous. Lack of financial means is less of a consideration now than formerly, not only because the village is more prosperous, but also because time-payment plans are available for most types of capital goods. Awareness of possibilities, too, is growing at a rapid rate with increasing literacy and access to mass-communications media. These generalizations are not meant to preclude individual differences in enthusiasm for change or for specific types of change due to differential enculturation within the village. While there is a hard core of conservatism in Atzompa—villagers who consider change unnecessary or undesirable—there are many who willingly change or modify their selling methods or material procurement procedures, learn new pottery forms, and enter new secondary occupations. As in the case of buying prepared liquid glaze, the majority may shift in a short time when there is a demonstrable gain, not only in cash but also in economy of time and effort.

10. The Marketplace Traders of San Antonino: A Quantitative Analysis

RONALD WATERBURY AND CAROLE TURKENIK

As part of a comprehensive study of a village economy[1] in which, among other things, we are attempting to explain household economic strategies by elucidating the socioeconomic conditions determining them, it became necessary to make a quantitatively precise analysis of occupations (here defined simply as ongoing remunerative activities). In other words, before you can explain why people do what they do, you have to know what they do and how many of them do it. This is by no means representative of nor a plea for sophisticated statistical analysis, much of which in recent anthropological literature appears to us to be more scientistic posturing than contribution to the knowledge of people. However, we do agree with an old Malinowskian dictum (without subscribing to all aspects of his particular brand of empiricism) that anthropologists should at least count the countable. We do not attempt here to break down all of the village's occupations—that must await publication of the major work—but rather we focus upon the marketplace-oriented ones. While village specialization is an often-noted characteristic of the regional economy of the Valley of Oaxaca (and other regional peasant economies as well), the actual importance of the specialty to a village's total economy is only vaguely known. In this respect we hope to provide some worthwhile precision.

San Antonino Castillo Velasco (formerly San Antonino Ocotlán) is a large peasant community (1970 population 3,657; see Table 10-1) located contiguously to Ocotlán, the district *cabecera* (head town), some thirty kilometers south of Oaxaca City. In spite of its

Table 10-1

BASIC POPULATION FIGURES FOR SAN ANTONINO

Persons all ages in census	3,579
Persons aged 16 and over in census	2,142
Households in census	918
Average number of persons per household	3.9
Households missing from census	20
Projected total population	3,657[a]

[a] The official 1970 census figure is 3,314, but informants advise us that the census takers overlooked at least two entire blocks.

size, which technically classifies it as "urban" in the federal census, it is still unquestionably rural and peasant in that the vast majority of households obtain at least part of their income from agriculture, and, more importantly, the mode of production is exclusively the undifferentiated household type. Although agriculture is basic, the variety of occupations in the village and even within households is considerable.

Within the regional pattern of village specialization San Antonino has been known for two things: for being the largest single producer of cut flowers and garden vegetables (onions, garlic, lettuce, cabbage, radishes, herbs, etc.) and for being one of the most salient communities of marketplace traders in the Valley of Oaxaca, if not *the* most salient. According to elderly informants the place has spawned traders for generations (see also Malinowski 1940; Malinowski and de la Fuente 1957:63–64, 154, 158–159). Due to increased competition from other villages and, especially, from out-of-state imports, San Antonino's monopoly as vegetable supplier to the regional market system has been declining somewhat (the village still holds firmly to its flower monopoly), but its vegetable traders are increasing in importance, both intra- and extraregionally. San

Antonino is the only village that has an entire street in the Oaxaca City marketplace set aside exclusively for its vendors (see Waterbury 1968:60), and many vegetable-selling stalls in the marketplaces of cities to the south like Tuxtla Gutiérrez, Salina Cruz, and Puerto Escondido are operated by San Antonino emigrants. Market trading, then, is a specialty to San Antonino, as are sarapes to Teotitlán del Valle, metates to Teitipac, green pottery to Atzompa, etc.

The specific data upon which this paper is based were excerpted from a more comprehensive house-to-house census conducted in October, November, and December of 1970. (This schedule also elicited information on demography, household composition, kinship, other occupations, wealth, and migration.) The actual house visits were made by local assistants trained by us. Following the initial data collection, each questionnaire was carefully reviewed with the assistant involved and then again with one or more trusted key informants in order to eliminate errors and/or obvious fabrications. The data specific to marketplace activities were checked with two very reliable informants who themselves were traders and who—in spite of the relatively large number of persons involved—know virtually every trader in the community. The figures utilized here are based upon returns from 918 of the 938 households in San Antonino. This represents a 97.9% sample. The information on the remaining 20 households was judged incomplete or of questionable accuracy and therefore not included in the calculations.[2]

The term *household* as used here should be clarified. It derives from the villagers' own criterion, which is essentially budgetary. Their definition was brought home to us early during the census-taking, when some respondents insisted that certain individuals be entered on separate sheets (the format called for one sheet per household) on the grounds that they were *cuenta aparte* (separate account). This definition of *household* can be rendered technically as "minimal budgetary group" and, as an organizing principle, is analytically distinct from kinship and residential factors. There are some *solares* (living sites or compounds) occupied by extended families, with each nuclear family comprising a separate household. In a number of cases single individuals operate as separate budgetary units, even though they reside in a *solar* with other persons. It is the existence of these single-individual households that accounts for our unexpectedly low average household size of 3.9 persons (Table 10-1).

MARKETPLACE OCCUPATIONS

For the purposes of this paper we have extracted from the occupational complex of San Antonino those occupations that are "marketplace-oriented"—that is, the occupations of persons who regularly buy and sell in the marketplaces and of those who buy, process, and sell in the marketplaces. The term *marketplace-oriented* is to be differentiated from the more general term *market-oriented*, with its more inclusive reference to the price-making supply-and-demand mechanism. In the latter sense, all occupations in San Antonino are market-oriented to some extent.

The specifically marketplace-oriented occupations fall into two broad categories: processor-sellers and marketeers. Processor-sellers are those who buy, process, and sell in the marketplaces, including butchers, bakers, *tortilleras,* and others. Marketeers are those who regularly buy and sell in the marketplaces, including *comerciantes* (wholesalers) and *regatones* (primarily small-scale retailers) (Table 10-2). The word *regularly* should be noted well, because not included in the figures are many persons who occasionally or only during certain seasons of the year engaged in trading activities. Also not counted are those who primarily sold only *propio* (their own household's production). In the case of the processor-sellers, such as butchers and bakers, the wives and daughters who sold the meat and bread were not counted unless they also were engaged in the buying and processing. This was true only for two widows.

Regatones

The 383 *regatones* in the census make this by far the numerically most predominant occupation.[3] The San Antonino *regatones* purchase goods in the village itself, in the plazas, or in both. They usually travel to the plazas by bus and take their basketful or two of goods along with them or send them ahead the night before by truck. The train is used only by a few, because it is more than a thirty-minute walk from the village, is slower, and has a limited schedule.

The efficiency of the trucking service between San Antonino and Oaxaca City merits comment. The night before principal selling days in the city plaza (Tuesday, Friday, and Saturday) a truck makes its way up and down San Antonino's streets loading the baskets that are left in front of each *regatona's* house. The baskets are covered simply by old gunny sacks tied over the top and seldom bear any identifying marks. In spite of the number of individuals

Table 10-2
MARKETPLACE-ORIENTED PERSONS IN SAN ANTONINO

Occupations	Males	Females	Total
Processor-sellers of			
Tortillas	0	72	72
Bread	22	1	23
Sherbet, fruitades, and ices	5	10	15
Chocolate	1	13	14
Atole (maize gruel)	0	11	11
Beef	11	0	11
Tamales, etc.	0	7	7
Pork	6	1	7
Prepared meals	0	3	3
Ground beans	0	2	2
Tortilla dough	0	2	2
Popsicles	1	0	1
Candied fruit	1	0	1
Flavored gelatin	0	1	1
Nicuatole (maize gruel pudding)	0	1	1
Cheese	0	1	1
Blended fruit and vegetable drinks	0	1	1
Subtotal	47	126	173
Marketeers			
Intraregional comerciantes	16	0	16
Interregional comerciantes	20	11	31
Regatones	2	381	383
Subtotal	38	392	430
Grand total	85	518	603

involved, the trucker and his helpers know exactly where each *regatona* sits on the Oaxaca City street reserved for San Antonino marketeers (Calle Mina between Aldama and J. P. García), even though there are no marks on the pavement to indicate the approximately one square meter occupied by each vendor. When the *regatona* arrives between 5:00 and 6:00 A.M. her goods await in her spot.

While *regatones* are principally retailers, occasionally a certain amount of their merchandise is sold to yet smaller resellers. This occurs more frequently in Oaxaca City than in other plazas. For example, one of our informants on one day transported five hundred onions to the city marketplace, sold three hundred retail and the re-mainder in *maletas* (bunches) of fifty or one hundred to revendors.

Of the marketplaces frequented by San Antonino *regatones*, Oa-xaca City is by far the most popular, with 316 persons attending weekly in late 1970 (Table 10-3). This number, however, does not sufficiently express the true magnitude of San Antonino *regatones'* participation in the Oaxaca City plaza, because subsumed in our category of weekly attendance are a considerable number who actu-ally attended two (Friday and Saturday) or three (Tuesday, Friday, and Saturday) days a week.[4] The significance of San Antonino's presence in the Oaxaca City plaza is yet more impressive when one adds the numerous *propios* and occasional *regatonas* who would be present on any market day, and particularly at peak selling seasons of the year (harvest and fiesta times). After the Oaxaca City plaza, the district plazas in the southern branch of the Valley of Oaxaca, due to the factors of time and ease of transportation, are most fa-vored. In addition, in 1970 fourteen San Antonino *regatones* made weekly visits to village marketplaces, and another fourteen were present daily in San Antonino's own plaza (Table 10-3).

The majority of marketeers travel to more than one plaza a week. More specifically, in 1970, 163 *regatones* (42.9%) attended one mar-ketplace a week, 126 (33.2%) attended two, 42 (11.0%) visited three, and the same number went to four. Only five *regatones* (1.3%) traveled to five markets a week, and but two hearty souls made it to six (Fig. 10-1).

Comerciantes

The term *comerciante* is reserved by San Antonineros (or "Toni-neros" as they sometimes call themselves) for wholesale intermediary traders. As indicated above, *regatones* frequently engage in some wholesaling activities on a very small scale (i.e., selling to other vendors rather than directly to consumers), but *comerciantes* are al-most exclusively wholesalers and operate on a much larger scale. Where an average *regatona* may sell approximately two hundred pesos' worth (wholesale cost) of merchandise on a busy market day, an average *comerciante's* inventory might be valued between one and two thousand pesos. In 1970, there were forty-seven *comercian-tes* in the village, sixteen of whom operated on an intraregional basis (within the Valley of Oaxaca), while thirty-one operated in-terregionally (Table 10-2).

Most of the intraregional *comerciantes* are technically *acapara-dores*, or bulking intermediaries. That is, they buy up produce from

Table 10-3
MARKETPLACES ATTENDED REGULARLY BY
SAN ANTONINO REGATONES IN 1970

	Number of San Antonino Regatones Attending	
	Daily	Weekly
Principal marketplaces		
Oaxaca City	5	316
Ocotlán	28	158
Ejutla	0	104
Miahuatlán	0	67
Zimatlán	0	35
San Pedro Apóstol	0	8
Tlacolula	0	6
Zaachila	0	4
Etla	0	0
Ayoquezco	0	0
Subtotal	33	698
Village marketplaces		
San Antonino	14	4
Santo Tomás Jalieza	0	3
San Jacinto Ocotlán	0	2
Santiago Apóstol	0	2
Santa Inés Yatzeche	0	1
Santa Ana Zegache	0	1
San Jerónimo Taviche	0	1
Subtotal	14	14
Grand total	47	712

village farmers, bulk it, and resell by the sack or basket to other intermediaries in the plazas, predominantly in the Oaxaca City marketplace (Table 10-4 and Fig. 10-1). They serve as intermediaries not only for San Antonino producers but also for those of several nearby villages. In fact, San Sebastián Ocotlán (population 335 in 1970) and Santiago Apóstol (population 3,558 in 1970) rely almost exclusively on the *comerciantes* from San Antonino.

The interregional *comerciantes* operate between the Valley of Oaxaca—principally the Oaxaca City marketplace—and more distant places (Table 10-4). Only very rarely do they buy directly from producers rather than from other intermediaries in the marketplaces. The exceptions to this are the four men who in 1970 regularly traveled to Atlixco, Puebla, to purchase vegetables—mostly onions and potatoes—in the fields of large-scale farmers. These interregional *comerciantes* may operate either as *acaparadores* or as *mayoristas* (bulk breakers). The largest of San Antonino's *comerciantes* at the time of the survey was a *mayorista* who, assisted by his family, operated a permanent daily *bodega* (storeroom) in the Oaxaca City market district. He owned a pickup and a ten-ton truck and transported goods between Mexico City, Oaxaca City, the Isthmus

Table 10-4

MARKETPLACES ATTENDED REGULARLY BY
SAN ANTONINO COMERCIANTES

Marketplaces	Number of San Antonino *Comerciantes* Attending
Valley of Oaxaca	
Oaxaca City	36 (one operates daily *bodega*)
Miahuatlán	5
Ocotlán	2
San Antonino	2
Ejutla	1
Zimatlán	1
Zaachila	1
Tlacolula	1
Subtotal	49
Outside Valley of Oaxaca	
Chiapas (Tuxtla, Huixtla, Tapachula, Arriaga)	10
Isthmus of Tehuantepec (Salina Cruz, Juchitán, Tehuantepec, Ixtepec, Matías Romero)	9
Mexico City	7
Coast of Oaxaca (Pochutla, Candelaria Loxicha, Tejemul)	7
Atlixco, Puebla	4
Coatzacoalcos, Veracruz	1
Subtotal	38
Grand total	87

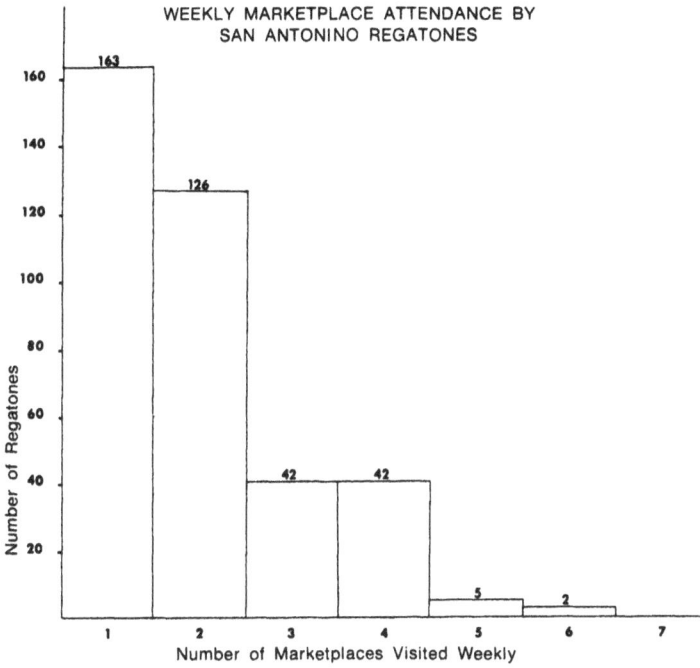

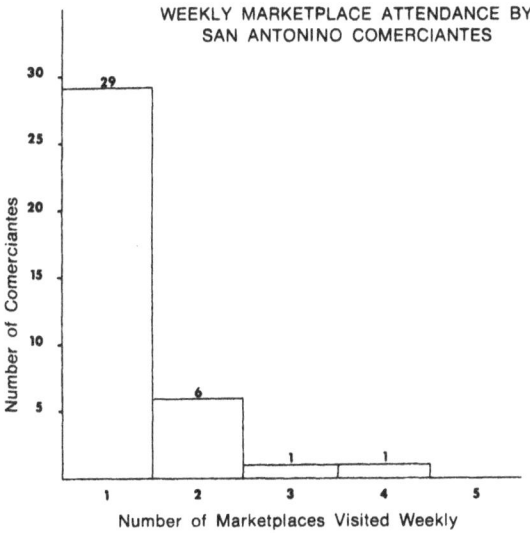

Figure 10-1. Weekly marketplace attendance by San Antonino mar-keteers.

of Tehuantepec, and Chiapas. He had three brothers residing permanently in other regions who were also *comerciantes*. The brothers gave each other information, preferential price treatment, and other forms of assistance, but actually ran separate enterprises. At one time they had worked together in a formal partnership, but, as in every partnership or cooperative venture ever attempted in San Antonino, interpersonal distrust had developed, resulting in dissolution. Another large San Antonino interregional *comerciante* owned a truck with which he regularly bought and transported produce between the coast of Oaxaca, the Valley, and Mexico City.

Processor-Sellers

This category included seventeen specific occupations and 173 persons (Table 10-2). The largest-scale operators were the bakers (*panaderos*) and the butchers, the latter being specialized into *carniceros* (beef butchers) and *tocineros* (pork butchers). These occupations, especially that of the butchers, require the greatest amount of capital and specialized skills. Butchers are among the wealthiest families in the community.

Some processor-sellers, particularly the *tortilleras*, sell a portion of their goods from their houses, but most sell regularly in San Antonino's own plaza as well as in the marketplace of Ocotlán. A few, especially the bakers, attend more distant plazas.

Village Marketplace

Although San Antonino is a community of many traders, its own marketplace differs little from that of any other large village. The plaza is located next to the walled churchyard in a fifty-by-twenty-meter shed with a cement floor and corrugated metal roof. It operates on a daily basis, with the greatest number of vendors on Sunday and the least on Friday. Over the day, vendor attendance fluctuates hourly, the peak times being from 6:45 to 7:30 A.M. and from noon to 2:00 P.M. In 1970 there was a small core of about fifteen vendors with permanent *puestos*: a *fonda* (small restaurant or food-vending stand), a *masa* (tortilla dough) vendor, a blended-fruit-juice vendor, and several vendors each of meat, fruits, and vegetables. In the morning hours, which were the busiest, there was an influx of animal-fodder sellers, a few *propios* of fruit and vegetables, and, most significantly, twenty bread vendors, plus several sellers of *atole* and chocolate. Bread, *atole*, and chocolate are breakfast foods, sold only during the morning hours.

On the average weekday morning there were approximately fifty vendors present in the plaza. Activities dropped off sharply between 7:30 and 8:00 A.M., leaving only the permanent *puestos*. At about 10:00 the three or four regular *agua fresca* (fruitade) vendors arrived. They stayed until about 3:00 or 4:00 P.M. During the noon-to-2:00 P.M. period there was another increase of vendors, including many *tortilleras*, ten to twenty of whom were from the villages of San Sebastián Ocotlán and Santiago Apóstol. This time period corresponds to the increased demand of last-minute buying for the afternoon meal. In the late afternoons only a few vendors remained in the plaza, mostly *tortilleras* and occasional *regatonas* and *propios* of fruit, vegetables, and maize. By early evening the marketplace was empty except for the *fonda* and three or four *tamaleras* (sellers of hot tamales, *empanadas* [meat pies], tacos, soft drinks, and coffee), who catered to the few bachelors, the night police, and the young unmarried boys hanging about the streets in hopes of brief courting sessions with errand-bound girls. On Friday, because of the market day in Ocotlán, the San Antonino plaza was entirely vacant, except for the morning business in breakfast foods. Sunday, with its hundred or so vendors, was the biggest market day. This was in response to the fact that most families eat a somewhat more elaborate meal than usual on that day. Present were a larger number of occasional *regatonas* and *propios* and, of particular note, about twenty flower vendors, most of whom were *propios*.

In his hierarchical scheme of the Oaxaca marketplace system Malinowski classified the San Antonino marketplace as a plaza of "minor importance" (Malinowski 1940–1941; Malinowski and de la Fuente 1957:21). It is indeed of minor importance when compared to the Oaxaca City plaza and the district marketplaces. Moreover, the difference is one of kind and not just degree. Unlike the more comprehensive plazas, the village marketplace almost exclusively serves the consumers of that community. True, it attracts a few vendors from surrounding villages (e.g., the *tortilleras* from San Sebastián and Santiago), but the great majority of vendors and virtually all of the buyers—which is the key—are from the village itself. Furthermore, San Antonino's marketplace serves no intermediary trading functions; and, unlike a true market town, the village does not serve outsiders with ancillary extramarketplace functions of a commercial, political, or religious nature. Thus, in terms of a central place hierarchy of marketplace functions, the San Antonino plaza (even the larger Sunday one) should be classified as simply a "village marketplace" along with those in many other pueblos, e.g., Santiago Apóstol, Santo Tomás Jalieza, San Martín Tilcajete, and Teotitlán del Valle.

MARKETPLACE TRADERS IN THE TOTAL OCCUPATIONAL STRUCTURE

As stated previously, the occupational picture of San Antonino is a relatively complex one, since most households engage in a number of remunerative activities. Although a more comprehensive analysis of this must await a later publication, here we offer a few general comments to provide a context for understanding the importance of marketplace-oriented occupations.

Nonmarketplace Occupations

Agriculture, of course, is the predominant occupation of the vast majority of Tonineros. The villagers subdivide the term *campesino* into two components: *hortelano* and *labrador*. *Hortelanos* are agriculturists who predominantly grow flowers and/or truck-garden vegetables for market sale and who plant only a small portion—if any—of their land to maize. The great bulk of goods that they themselves consume, including food, is purchased with cash rather than self-produced. The *labradores*, who are in the minority, are less market-oriented. They plant most or even all of their land to maize, and they produce more of what they consume than is the case with *hortelanos*. Nonetheless, to acquire cash they sell—among other things—castor beans (intercropped in many *milpas*), the milk of cows fed on their maize, pigs and other animals fattened on maize, alfalfa or sorghum, and maize itself.

A market for agricultural laborers exists in San Antonino, but only for a few Tonineros is wage labor—either inside or outside the community—a significant source of income. Perhaps a measure of the relative prosperity of the community is the fact that in 1970 no more than fifteen San Antonino men were working more or less regularly as *mozos* (hired hands). The community draws upon surrounding villages for its major supply of paid workers.

Other nonmarketplace occupations in San Antonino include storekeeping, milling, blouse embroidering, and clothes making. These occupations are not included in this analysis as "marketplace-oriented" because their selling activities rarely if ever occur in the actual marketplaces; rather, they usually take place in the workers' own homes or establishments. At the time of the survey the only exception was one man who regularly sold the trousers that he made in the Ocotlán plaza.

The recent revival of embroidery is worthy of additional comment. The craft was all but dead ten years ago. With the shift from Indian to mestizo peasant dress style, local demand for embroidery work had declined substantially. Existing traditional blouses were stored away in trunks as heirlooms and worn mostly on ceremonial occasions, and then usually by the conservative-dressing older women. Tourist taste for embroidered "peasant blouses" took an upswing five to ten years ago and in 1974 was still strong. This increased demand was communicated to the village—which is not on the tourist circuit—through two village women who had always traded in blouses on a small scale, and by city tourist-shop operators who came in increasing numbers to the village in search of blouses to purchase. Soon elderly women who still knew the craft were teaching it to younger girls.[5] Now in most households there is at least one female who spends part of her waking hours embroidering. In some households women spend all of their time, apart from domestic chores, at the task; and women embroidering in the marketplace during free time between sales has become a common sight. Most embroidery work is done on a piece or putting-out basis, with the materials provided by a blouse merchant, of whom there are now several.[6]

Marketplace-Oriented Occupations

Marketplace trading activities are by far the most important nonagricultural occupations in the community. In 1970 over one quarter of the population aged sixteen years and older (603 persons, or 28.2%) were engaged in marketplace-oriented occupations of all kinds as defined here. (All subsequent statements concerning "total population" refer to persons of sixteen years and older.)

The 41 butchers and bakers together formed the smallest category: 6.8% of marketplace-oriented persons, and only 1.9% of the total population. Another 132 processor-sellers (*tortilleras, atoleras, neveros,* etc.) comprised 21.9% of marketplace-oriented persons and 6.2% of the total population. There were, then, 173 processor-sellers of all types, forming about one quarter (28.7%) of the marketplace-oriented population and slightly less than one-tenth (8.1%) of the total population (Table 10-5).

Marketeers (*regatones* and *comerciantes*), 430 of them in all, made up 71.3% of the marketplace-oriented population and one-fifth (20.1%) of the total population. Within this category the *rega-*

tones predominated. There were 383 of them, or 89.1% of marketeers, 63.5% of all marketplace-oriented individuals, and 17.9% of the total population. The *comerciantes*, although major contributors to the community's significance in the market system, were but 47 strong and accounted for only one-tenth (10.9%) of the marketeers, 7.8% of the marketplace-oriented people, and a mere 2.2% of the total population (Table 10-5). Their reputation was totally out of proportion to their numbers.

Presented on a household basis, the figures are even more revealing of the importance of marketplace activities in the community. Of the 918 households in the sample, over half (519, or 56.5%) were marketplace-oriented to some degree. That is, they had at least one person regularly participating in a marketplace occupation. Of these households, 379 (73.0% of all marketplace-oriented households and 41.3% of all households) contained at least one marketeer, and 140 (27.0% of marketplace-oriented households and 15.2% of all households) contained a processor-seller. Looking at *regatones* alone, there was at least one in almost two-thirds (64.7%) of all marketplace-oriented households, or in about one-third (36.6%) of all households (Table 10-6).

Many people who emigrate from San Antonino continue in their marketeering ways. Of the 467 names of permanent emigrants collected in the census, over one-fifth (102, or 21.8%) earned their living from marketplace activities. They operated *puestos* and *bodegas* and were traveling traders. Fourteen were in Tapachula, ten in Minatitlán, nine in Salina Cruz, nine in Mexico City, eight in Juchitán, eight in Puerto Escondido, six in Coatzacoalcos, and lesser concentrations were scattered from Chiapas to Nuevo León. Many of the emigrant marketeers maintained relationships with kinsmen and *compadres* in San Antonino, who often shipped them produce from Oaxaca.

Marketplace Occupations and the Sexual Division of Labor

The figures show that not only is home a woman's place but so is the marketplace. Of the 603 marketplace-oriented individuals, 518, or 85.9%, were females. Furthermore, nearly half (46.6%) of all women aged sixteen and over engaged regularly in marketplace occupations, whereas less than one-tenth (8.2%) of males were so employed. Being a *regatona* is considered to be an extension of normal domestic marketing and therefore an appropriate occupation only for women. A man who would resort to being a *regatón* would be thought of as quite odd indeed. The two men among the 383 *re-*

gatones in our census were elderly, and the elderly in San Antonino, as in many other places, are allowed certain eccentricities.

Regatonas contribute significantly to household incomes. As mentioned previously, over one-third of all households regularly derive some income from their activities. For the first few years of marriage most fledgling households are supported substantially by the wife working as a regatona, and there are few adult women who have not been regatonas at some time in their lives. For established households of limited means (little or no land and no remunerative nonagricultural occupation for the husband) the market trading activities of the wives and daughters continue to be an important income source.

The situations of one household may serve as an example. In 1970 it was comprised of a married couple in their thirties; two children, a girl of twelve and a boy of nine; and an elderly woman dependent. The family owned three fields, amounting to between one-half and three-quarters of a hectare, which the husband planted to vegetables. Because they had no grown sons—and thus no field labor other than the husband's—even some of the modest amount of land they owned was frequently share-cropped out. The wife was a regatona who attended the Oaxaca City plaza three times a week. On the average she netted one hundred pesos weekly, which was roughly equivalent to the household's weekly food budget. The income from the husband's agricultural pursuits was used for major expenditures, such as tools, clothing, and house repairs. Except for the times when the husband sold in the field directly to a village intermediary, the wife marketed their produce along with the other goods she sold. And—to corroborate the old adage that a woman's work is never done (at least a peasant woman's work)—the wife also earned additional income by sewing.

Households headed by widows, divorcees, and single women frequently rely upon market trading for income. Three-fourths (74.8%) of these female-headed households were marketplace-oriented in 1970, as against a little more than half (53.2%) of male-headed ones. (There were 143 female-headed households, 15.6% of the total.)

The occupation of comerciante, unlike that of regatona, is quite appropriate for men; in fact, they dominate it (76.6% in 1970). Of the eleven women comerciantes, all but two were married to comerciantes and frequently traveled with their husbands, although they were also involved independently in buying and selling to some extent and thus did not function just as their husbands' helpers. The

Table 10-5

OCCUPATIONS OF PERSONS AGED SIXTEEN AND OVER

	NUMBERS	PERCENTAGES OF		
		Processor-Sellers		
		Butchers, Bakers	Others	Total
Butchers and bakers, male	39	95.1		22.5
Butchers and bakers, female	2	4.9		1.2
Butchers and bakers, all	41	100.0		23.7
Other processor-sellers, male	8		6.1	4.6
Other processor-sellers, female	124		93.9	71.7
Other processor-sellers, all	132		100.0	76.3
Processor-sellers, male	47			27.2
Processor-sellers, female	126			72.8
Processor-sellers, all	173			100.0
Regatones, male	2			
Regatonas, female	381			
Regatones, all	383			
Comerciantes, male	36			
Comerciantes, female	11			
Comerciantes, all	47			
Marketeers, male	38			
Marketeers, female	392			
Marketeers, all	430			
Marketplace-oriented, male	85			
Marketplace-oriented, female	518			
Marketplace-oriented, all	603			
Nonmarketplace-oriented, male	946			
Nonmarketplace-oriented, female	593			
Nonmarketplace-oriented, all	1,539			
Males (total)	1,031			
Females (total)	1,111			
Total population	2,142			

| Marketeers | | | Market- | Nonmarket- | | | Total |
Rega-tones	Comer-ciantes	Total	place Oriented	place Oriented	All Males	All Females	Popu-lation
			6.5		3.8		1.8
			0.3			0.2	0.1
			6.8				1.9
			1.3		0.8		0.4
			20.6			11.2	5.8
			21.9				6.2
			7.8		4.5		2.2
			20.9			11.3	5.9
			28.7				8.1
0.5		0.5	0.3		0.2		0.1
99.5		88.6	63.2			34.3	17.8
100.0		89.1	63.5				17.9
	76.6	8.4	6.0		3.5		1.7
	23.4	2.5	1.8			1.0	0.5
	100.0	10.9	7.8				2.2
		8.8	6.3		3.7		1.8
		91.2	65.0			35.3	18.3
		100.0	71.3				20.1
			14.1		8.2		4.0
			85.9			46.6	24.2
			100.0				28.2
				61.5	91.8		44.2
				38.5		53.4	27.7
				100.0			71.9
					100.0		48.1
						100.0	51.9
							100.0

Table 10-6

OCCUPATIONS BY HOUSEHOLD

	NUMBERS	PERCENTAGES OF		
		Processor-Seller Households		
		Butchers, Bakers	Others	Total
Butchers and bakers, male-headed	39	95.1		27.9
Butchers and bakers, female-headed	2	4.9		1.4
Butchers and bakers, all	41	100.0		29.3
Other processor-sellers, male-headed	65		65.7	46.4
Other processor-sellers, female-headed	34		34.3	24.3
Other processor-sellers, all	99		100.0	70.7
Processor-sellers, male-headed	104			74.3
Processor-sellers, female-headed	36			25.7
Processor-sellers, all	140			100.0
Regatones, male-headed	267			
Regatones, female-headed	69			
Regatones, all	336			
Comerciantes, male-headed	41			
Comerciantes, female-headed	2			
Comerciantes, all	43			
Marketeers, male-headed	308			
Marketeers, female-headed	71			
Marketeers, all	379			
Marketplace-oriented,[a] male-headed	412			
Marketplace-oriented, female-headed	107			
Marketplace-oriented, all	519			
Nonmarketplace-oriented, male-headed	363			
Nonmarketplace-oriented, female-headed	36			
Nonmarketplace-oriented, all	399			
Male-headed households (total)	775			
Female-headed households (total)	143			
Total households	918			

Note: Because of rounding off of percentages, the total percentages do not always equal the sum of the parts.

Marketeer Households			Marketplace Oriented[a]	Non-marketplace Oriented	Male-headed	Female-headed	Total Households
Regatones	Comerciantes	Total					
			7.5		5.0		4.2
			0.4			1.4	0.2
			7.9				4.4
			12.5		8.4		7.1
			6.6			23.8	3.7
			19.1				10.8
			20.0		13.4		11.3
			6.9			25.2	3.9
			27.0				15.2
79.5		70.4	51.4		34.5		29.1
20.5		18.2	13.3			48.3	7.5
100.0		88.7	64.7				36.6
	95.3	10.8	7.9		5.3		4.5
	4.7	0.5	0.4			1.4	0.2
	100.0	11.3	8.3				4.7
		81.3	59.3		39.7		33.6
		18.7	13.7			49.6	7.7
		100.0	73.0				41.3
			79.4		53.2		44.9
			20.6			74.8	11.6
			100.0				56.5
				91.0	46.8		39.6
				9.0		25.2	3.9
				100.0			43.5
					100.0		84.4
						100.0	15.6
							100.0

[a] A marketplace-oriented household is defined as a household having at least one marketplace-occupied person.

two completely independent women *comerciantes* were widows, one of a *comerciante*, the other of a baker.

Butchering and baking, occupations requiring considerable skill and capital, are clearly men's work. These are, of course, household enterprises, with the women helping in activities supplemental to the primary processing. In the case of butchering, men buy the animals, slaughter, and butcher them. If hired helpers or apprentices are used, they are also men. Once an animal is butchered, women help to prepare the meat by salting *tasajo* (long, thin strips of beef), cleaning *menudo* (tripe), etc. Corresponding again to the maxim that the marketplace is woman's place, the all-important task of meat selling is carried out entirely by wives and daughters.

The sexual division of labor for baking is similar to that of butchering. Men buy the materials, prepare the dough, and bake the bread. The women help pack bread into baskets and do the selling.

The one female butcher and the one female baker in our census were widows of a butcher and a baker respectively. Although they managed the enterprises, the tasks traditionally performed by males were done by their sons or by hired male helpers.[7]

The other processor-seller occupations—particularly those that are commercial extensions of customary female domestic tasks—are pursued overwhelmingly by women. Males who engage in them are considered slightly odd. This is true of the two *regatones*, the *chocolatero*, and even more so of the single *dulcero* (maker and seller of candied fruits), who also happened to be a bachelor.[8] The case of tortilla making is, of course, archetypical. There are no male *tortilleras* because no male knows how to make tortillas—or if he did would not admit to it nor be caught dead doing it.[9] In fact, the term *tortillero*, frequently accompanied by tortilla-making hand gestures, is used derogatorily for effeminate or suspected homosexual males.

The other processor-seller occupations engaged in by men are *paletero* (maker and seller of ice cream bars, popsicles, etc.) and *nevero/refresquero* (maker and seller of ice cream, sherbet, and fruit-flavored iced drinks). These involve skills not possessed by every housewife and are thus open to men.

CONCLUDING REMARKS

Local or village specialization is one outstanding characteristic of the peasant market system of the Valley of Oaxaca. In attempting to understand the dynamics of this regional economy it is important to know in some detail how—from the village perspective—a community participates in the market system. To this end we have provided a descriptive statistical analysis with an eye to substituting precision for presumption as to the significance of the specialty occupation—in this case market trading—in the total occupational structure of a large specialized village.

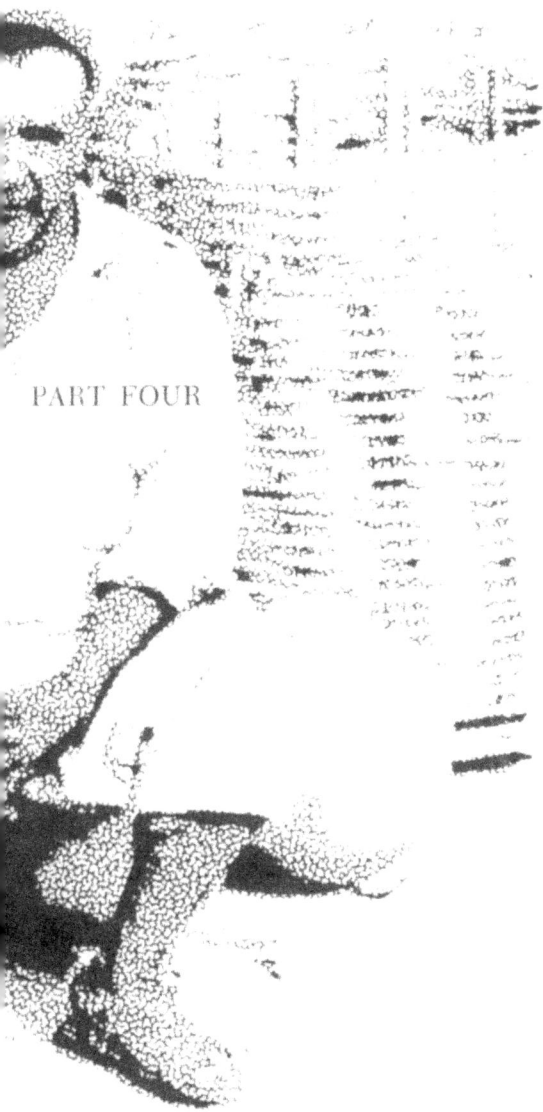

PART FOUR

Problems in Retrospect
and Prospect

In this concluding section, we try to follow several leads suggested by the preceding empirical accounts of plazas and society. First, Diskin sees the Valley of Oaxaca regional system as the outcome of an adaptive process within specified circumstances of environment, social structure, and economy. In general evolutionary terms, the result of this process is the region, a coherent socioeconomic entity composed of smaller units (local systems) that constitute the "atoms" for economic analysis. Methodologically, a key problem in understanding this adaptive process is to ascertain the various types of contradictions or constraints which exist at the local and regional levels and to identify the alternatives these contradictions or constraints (internal or external) present (or presented) to individuals and to groups. Only in this way can we hope to approximate an understanding of the present structure and past transformations of this complex system.

In the last essay in this volume, the editors try to understand the experience and findings of the Oaxaca project in the light of present concerns. The five problems mentioned range from those of concept clarification (e.g., *economy, market, system*) to the broad issues of economy-ecology distinctions and finally the historical dynamics of capitalist penetration.

Ideas from economic anthropology, geographical locational analysis, and economic history are used to elucidate our five problems. We borrow these notions, not because any one satisfactorily "explains" this region or to contribute yet another accretion to the taxonomic enterprise, but rather, because we see the regional social-economic system of the Valley of Oaxaca as an outstanding human achievement, and existing analytic tools may help us understand its particular genius over time and, we hope, for the future. While terms like *precapitalist* do not imply any fixed historical sequence, the Marxist view of economic change is quite helpful. Its emphasis on the monetization of labor and its ideological consequences points out the real pressures that weigh on such systems as those discussed here. Monetization, a well-established fact in rural Mexico, tends to erode the regional definitions of economic activity and emphasize the relation of individual actors to the largest definition of *market*. Under such circumstances, decisions regarding production and consumption become detached from the local moral order and reflect emergent values of profit seeking and economic development. Economic activity ceases to be influenced or modified by local sociocultural factors.

We mention several explicit research directions that could be profitably examined to further our understanding of this and similar systems. They range from quantitative accounts of nutritional status to consideration of the "moral order" of techniques of distribution. Their goal is to develop a reliable data base that will serve as an aid to policy formation.

Our hope is that a diachronic, dynamic approach to a complex, creative institution, such as the system of plazas, can enable us to do more than preside over their imminent destruction. Perhaps, through insights that emerge from works such as these, real progress can occur without its ubiquitous, destructive trauma.

11. A Historical-Ecological Approach to the Study of the Oaxaca Plaza System

MARTIN DISKIN

The Valley of Oaxaca is a "key area" in Mesoamerica (Palerm and Wolf 1957:29–30). Impressive evidence of the long, continual occupation and cultural growth of the region makes it clear that creative adaptations have occurred over time and have left traces of all the steps of evolutionary development in Mesoamerica as well as in many other locations of pristine evolution. Since the system of cyclically convening marketplaces (plazas) also has considerable antiquity (Whitecotton 1968), this essay will treat it as one mechanism of adaptive response in the area. It will be seen as one of several responses to circumstances in the physical and social transformation of Oaxaca, but also, at a later stage of development, as a condition that shaped and stabilized the articulation of the units that make up the region. This approach, diachronic and evolutionary—generally within the perspective of cultural ecology as elaborated by Julian Steward and others (Steward 1963)—is the best way to understand the significance of this institution. In addition, I hope that it will help direct research toward the creation and the ethnographic testing of hypotheses, and stimulate ethnohistoric research as a way of analyzing the evolutionary meaning of such sociocultural systems.

The perspective of cultural ecology helps to identify units and systems and seems to reflect more accurately the material realities lived by the people we study. Within the over-all plaza system, depending on particular research goals, we might want to consider as the essential unit of study the household management unit, the specialized village production system, the complex of satellite villages and market towns that comprise a weekly plaza, or the whole arrangement of plazas throughout the entire Valley, including Oaxaca City, that serves as a link for many other kinds of economic activity. Further, it is of great interest to consider the relation of the entire Valley system with that of the Sierra Juárez, the Mixería, the Isthmus of Tehuantepec, the Mixteca, perhaps the cycle of large fiesta markets of Veracruz. By being clear as to the nature of the units under study, we can design empirical, quantitative measures for purposes of description and analysis. Each of the units sketched above can be observed as it creates and uses valued goods and services. Also, each of these units is related to other units through exchange relations in the plazas and elsewhere. While any of these units may be the focal point for study, within the Valley of Oaxaca I will describe two units, really two clusters of behaviors, whose regular interaction over time seems to account for much of the character of the greater system.

I distinguish here between the *local system* and the *regional system*. For present purposes the local system is a group of villages and the town they habitually use as a plaza. The regional system is the totality of the local systems in the entire area. These two systems perform different jobs: the local system converts, uses, and exchanges energy so as to be able to satisfy culturally defined requirements for life for all the participants within its limits, and the regional system coordinates the operations of sets of local systems to form a more extensive and qualitatively different entity.[1] While both of these units, the local system and the regional system, satisfy the formal requirements of systems (see the concluding discussion), they vary greatly with respect to their coherence, stability, "maturity," and other aspects of their behavior. We may ask, for example: Is there any difference between the goods that move within the local system and those that move within the regional system? What are the characteristics of the populations served by each? What are the modal roles (both social and economic) that inhere in each one?

By attending to the central question of cultural ecology—the relation of different human populations in a given habitat to the sources and distribution of energy—our focus is directed toward these operative units as well as the regular mechanisms that make for smooth interaction and exchange between them. The significance of these mechanisms becomes clear only when they are considered against a broad time perspective. That is why there must be a close relation between the definition of units, clear ways of describing or measuring their functional effectiveness, and observation of them over long periods of time.

CULTIVATION AND DEPENDENCE

In the Valley of Oaxaca we may study the pristine development of the agricultural way of life. Recent works permit the reconstruction of the development of agriculture and the social mechanisms that widened the exchange possibilities of Valley production. The Valley of Oaxaca, by which is meant the limits of the drainage of the Atoyac River, has, since the beginning of our geological epoch, been a zone hospitable to human occupation. Kent V. Flannery's study of cave sites near Mitla (Flannery 1968) shows complexes of food procurement systems that provide for a well-regulated correspondence between plant and animal populations, with human adaptations through nomadism and technology. The systematic mechanisms of regulation that Flannery discusses, in keeping with his ecological systems approach, he calls "seasonality" and "scheduling" (ibid.:74–76).

Seasonality refers to the uses of time and energy "imposed on man by the nature of the wild resources themselves" (Flannery 1968:74). Here the annual migratory round was determined by the movements and maturation of the animal and plant populations. Sedentary community life was difficult, and population size was severely restricted. Human mobility, foraging, hunting, and collecting were the major adaptive responses to the food quest. *Scheduling*, on the other hand, is a process that involves evaluation and reaction to the changing proportions of the different food-procurement systems. These devices operate on food-procurement systems in a manner implying both negative and positive feedback, dampening or amplifying changes in the systems. One such change, involving the procurement system based on the use of wild annual grasses, including maize, came to predominate over other systems, with maize assuming overwhelming significance while simultaneously undergoing a genetic transformation. Other procurement systems were altered and accommodated to the new requirements of care and time that maize required. During the rescheduling time, the transition to sedentary agriculture (8000–1500 B.C.), not only were higher yields made possible, but also the subsistence base was stabilized through patterns of kinship (Flannery and Coe 1968), settlement patterns (Chang, ed. 1968), particular technologies (mainly associated with agriculture, such as irrigation, manuring, and terracing), and a pattern of interzone exchange that William T. Sanders and others call "symbiosis" (Sanders 1968). This pattern, probably the result of the complex interplay of the factors mentioned above, gave tremendous stability to the whole region. It is the contemporary form of this historic situation that we are studying today.

Two historic shifts, from nomadic hunting and collecting to cultivation, and from localized, subsistence cultivation to community specialization and regional trade, have their "costs" and advantages. Each new mode of subsistence, through the rescheduling mechanism, tends to render previous patterns of food procurement less and less possible, both because of the realignment of time and because of environmental change that eliminates certain food sources. The movement from simple cultivation, under conditions of low population density and size, to exchange over larger areas, with more complex political structure, probably represented the burning of bridges for the population. Here, not only did the rescheduling of effort result in more intense cultivation, but also effort must have been invested into the exchange system. That is, the transfer of goods of various kinds from place to place should be seen as a systematic mechanism that helps in rationalizing the total environment of the whole region. There is a qualitative aspect to this shift. With the growth of a regional system, probably in the middle or late Formative, the rescheduling that seems apparent is not merely the more intense favoring of one procurement system over the others, but the realignment of time in accord with the growing demands of a more comprehensive polity, possibly involving regular labor or corvée and, quite conceivably, the regular convening of a market or other exchange mechanism.

It is really not possible at this time to say whether sociopolitical pressures or environmental and economic forces were most influential in shaping the pattern of community specialization and regional exchange. A reasonable speculation would be that, with political unification and integration perhaps on the level of chiefdoms, village communities subject to town centers had their production adjusted so that tribute flows would be in keeping with the needs and requirements of the ruling sector. Joseph W. Whitecotton describes the basic unit of Zapotec polity at the time of the conquest as a "lordship" (Whitecotton 1968:140), consisting of a series of hamlets that were tributaries of a ruler living in a large nucleated town. From time to time larger entities were formed, consisting of several lordships. These larger confederations (called tributary states) did not endure and were rather unstable. This political structure seems to parallel the present local system–regional system setup.

The Preclassic period probably saw the mutual reinforcement of several social areas—economic assimilation of new entities by emerging political elite groups, organized interregional and intraregional trade, growth of social complexity, and proliferation of distinctions both reflecting and influencing the growth of an elite that required imported luxury goods—whose total impact is visible in the urban developments that mark the Classic period. This is to say that the exchange system, as one social invention or technique, is an integral part of the whole process of social and cultural development. Further, one result of this evolutionary development is that the basic unit of subsistence is no longer the Neolithic village but is rather the local system as considered here.

The plaza system, the modern manifestation of this process as a "mechanism of social articulation" (Mintz 1959), then, is both a product and a cause of social development. More research is necessary to determine the nature of this exchange and its relation to political authority, but for our present purpose it is sufficient to note that the plaza system is probably one of the crucial historic developments in the history of the Oaxaca region. This system, a part of the cultural core (Adams 1966:14–17), has survived a variety of political and social changes, so that Ignacio Bernal may say of the area, "The valley of Oaxaca has had a common history and is an ecological unit in which the same cultures have succeeded one another throughout in the same order" (Bernal 1965:759–796).

ECONOMIC DIMENSIONS

Under conditions of village specialization, simple reciprocal arrangements would quickly prove inefficient. For a regional network, the most likely possibility is a marketplace system like that of the central Mexican highlands, perhaps combined with some sort of redistributive system. Thus far there is no clear evidence of the underlying exchange principle of the ancient regional system. The fact of central places—be they ceremonial centers or accumulation points for the redistribution of goods—does not permit any finer dis-crimination archaeologically. When Flannery and Coe talk about a market system they seem to be referring not to an exchange mech-anism based on supply-demand factors but simply to the existence of plazas and evidence of trade (Flannery and Coe 1968).

Whitecotton (1968:72–102) reconstructs the plaza system at the time of the conquest as consisting of a series of plazas within sub-regions as well as between such zones, integrating the whole valley. Each subregion seems to correspond to a contemporary plaza town and its dependent villages. He relates this exchange system to the wide range of productive diversity based on microenvironmental differences and to the pattern of community specialization, as evi-denced in the records of tribute paid to the various lordships, indi-cating very little overlap from community to community. Many questions still remain to be answered from existing archival sources. The relation between lordships and local irrigation systems is im-portant: did water control provide for integration of the lordships, or was it itself a manifestation of centralized political control? (Ad-ams 1966:74). Was specialized village production connected to irri-gation systems? With respect to patterns of land use, it seems not only that specialization was maintained during the early colony but that pre-Hispanic crops were continued as before.

While it is likely that some of the economic exchange was sub-ject to state (or lordship) control, certainly for tribute payments and possibly for long-distance trade, there is no evidence that this system was a classical instance of redistribution, with state control of production, records, and warehouses. Rather, the plaza locations probably had the multiple function of facilitating exchange between the producing communities at different levels of the system and serv-ing as a device used by the state for the collection of tributes and possibly for their redistribution.

Now, if the plaza system is a series of places through which goods flow under a variety of arrangements that may include reciprocity, redistribution, and market principles, perhaps what we should be asking is not how to characterize the exchange system but rather, what are the internal regulatory mechanisms that help perpetuate it? The auto-consumption pattern that pertains to the village level undoubtedly accounts for a fair percentage of basic needs. What is not clear at present is the extent to which villagers could be entirely self-sufficient without the plaza at all. If the bedrock level of activity in the plaza requires the exchange of subsistence items, and if this level alone were considered, then it would be reasonable to see the plazas as places where goods and services must be exchanged at any price. That is, participation in the plaza, at the local-system level at least, would be evaluated by the participants not solely on a profit-loss basis but rather according to whether a person or a community could adequately obtain provisions there.

However, we know ethnographically that for the village buyer or seller the plaza functions as a locus of activity where the market principle, or, as Cyril Belshaw puts it, "compendium of principles" (Belshaw 1965:8–9), generally applies. Supply-demand forces determine price. Yet village communities do not alter their production schedules in accordance with price shifts. Within the local system, the characteristic unit is, following Max Weber, the budgetary unit, with its emphasis on provisioning and replacement, and the accommodation between production decisions and price events in the plaza occurs through the adaptability of the consuming public. In this manner production may remain constant, or relatively constant, and the plaza may still be the locus of true bargaining activity. This situation reflects the motivations of the various actors at the level of the budgetary economy whose goal is to participate in the plaza each week in a way that enables participation the following week.

But the plaza as we know it in its regional aspect has another dimension. That may be seen by considering the range of actors who look to the plaza for a profit and whose behavior embodies the awareness and skills of accounting, profit computation, and strategies for maximization, that is, people and organizations that may be called firms. Typically, that includes those who do not produce but specialize in selling. For such actors (*regatones* in general) the plazas must satisfy a somewhat different series of characteristics in order to make their participation worthwhile. The plazas must attract a large enough buying public that has enough cash left over after provisioning its basic wants that other goods may be bought. Merchants regularly express this in the rich terminology they use to describe given plazas (*muerte, triste, viva, regular*). For such participants in the plaza there is a yearly cycle that corresponds to the agricultural cycle, the success of the harvest, and the round of ritual observances (cf. Nash 1961; Cook 1970). Their movements and buying strategies reflect these details, and their reactions must be quicker and more sensitively adjusted to these circumstances than those of their peasant buying public.

The plazas, then, actually represent the interaction of two systems in the same location. The basic level, the one that justifies and continues the institution, is the local system. It integrates the production of peasant communities within a relatively fixed ecological zone, where the emphasis is on traditional subsistence and consumption patterns. The mechanism of flexibility and deferral of consumption on the part of the peasant participants serves as a "negative feedback device" and gives the system considerable stability and continuity. With this level constant, another kind of activity is permitted, that of the firm, with a different set of actors holding different goals and motivations. The interaction of the two systems, the local and the regional, or the peasant sector and the capitalistic firm, the budgetary unit and the profit-making enterprise, has been sketched for the modern period, but one might speculate that a similar interaction occurred during the pre-Columbian period as well. In fact, the interplay of the two systems suggests, to me, some reasonable hypotheses concerning the development of this region from relatively self-sufficient village communities to political entities (perhaps chiefdoms) based on principles we see in operation on the local-system level. The development of the regional system is the equivalent of the formation of larger political entities (tributary states). Hypotheses generated from ethnographic information await validation from archival and archaeological research. Still, we can see how the interacting subsystems, with a host of internal adjustment mechanisms (feedback), operate to solve the problems of regional socioeconomic articulation.

SOCIAL DIMENSIONS

The repetitive enactment of marketplace activity can be and has been considered from an economic-ecological point of view. However, if the exchange of goods is factored out of this regular interaction between social sectors, then we have an interesting perspective for the study of social communication, the formation of social strata, and mobility.

The repetitive association of social units in the plaza handles two important tasks. First, it clarifies the units that comprise the society. This is obvious to any observer of plazas in the different patterns of interaction that may be seen between villagers with respect to language etiquette, the "strandedness" of relationships (Wolf 1966), and the affective component (e.g., the hand-kiss greeting still employed by many villagers). In the plaza, people from the same village or neighboring ones exhibit a great deal of cultural similarity, while between people from different local systems relations tend to be more specific to the economic tasks, with less interest in personal matters. Between city folk and peasants there is often a large measure of incomprehension.

The second function served by the plazas is that of articulation between units. By this I mean that the members of each stratum participate in the plaza in a legitimate way. The minimal rule for participation seems to be the acknowledgement of the validity of the total system. That means that villagers coming to the plaza are not despised as they are in other Mexican marketplace systems, such as in highland Chiapas (San Cristóbal Las Casas) or Tlaxiaco in the Mixteca (Marroquín 1957). An individual either can take part in the plazas as one with status security and no mobility aspirations or can use this weekly social map as a way to seek opportunity and mobility through experimentation with different economic roles, different products, or, to a lesser degree, different production processes.

One indication of this simultaneous participation and identification with one level and place, with movement and the search for opportunity, is found by talking to internal migrants, people who live in a community in order to establish a niche in the system and to capitalize on the sale of a skill they have. In Tlacolula there are *metateros* from San Juan Teitipac, ropemakers from the Cajonos of the Sierra, and fireworks makers from Miahuatlán. They identify themselves as belonging to their natal communities and express this by saying that someday they will return. The above merits more careful study, but it points to a situation where the rhythm of the plazas provides mobility within the system while maintaining comfort with community affiliation and identity. The integration of this system is in part maintained by the constant reaffirmation of social boundaries.

The clarity of the units that articulate to form this system helps to rationalize and explain the social world to its members. However, from the vantage point of the outsider, the system suggests channels of movement of goods, people, and ideas. Merchants can accurately gauge the market (in the sense of the aggregate demand for a commodity). In addition, since the social organization of the region is demonstrated each week, the goals of the agents of national society can be best carried out by using the plaza schedule. This is what happens when marketplace days are used for a large variety of functions, such as tax collection, the administration of justice, religious observances, and organizing activities of national political parties. It appears that the regional system is most susceptible to influence from outside its limits at those times when it is working at a peak of involvement for its members. The more people that come to plaza at a given time, that attend mass, or that pay taxes, the more access a central political force has to the population. What this might mean in turn is that, during periods of intense marketplace activity, on either a seasonal or a long-range basis, the region is in most intimate contact with entities outside, such as other chiefdoms or states in the pre-Columbian period and other regional entities or the central government in the present time. It is thus very likely that there is a close relation between the internal integration of this region and its "incorporation" into larger social units. Perhaps because of this, in the Valley of Oaxaca, both in its dealings with the outside and in the field of internal colonialism, there has been a feeling of a regional culture that maintains its integrity and pride.

THE MODERN ECONOMY

Here I am concerned to assess the potentiality for change created by a system that has at its disposal modern means of communication, access to efficient productive techniques, capability to create demand, and great economic withholding power. All of this is a description of the operation of modern businessmen in standard quantitative terms as well as a sense of their manner of operation. An analysis of this regional system must yield some idea of its capability for change so as to incorporate the modern sector. The complexity of internal adjustments that makes of this system an embracing environment for want satisfaction and not a supermarket means that it is difficult to accomplish readjustments of wants and production schedules and still maintain the subsistence orientation of the primary producers. The process of rescheduling that Flannery talks about does not happen easily, since subsistence is being met and there is no alternative procurement system that seems attractive enough so that, in exploring it and developing it and adapting it to the local scene, a positive feedback loop is developed that intensifies this change until the entire region is irreversibly transformed. The most static feature of the system is the slow rate of change of subsistence production. This reflects the present level of agricultural and craft technology.

There seems little doubt that the interaction of this regional system and an ever-growing, nationally centered economic system will create severe strains and forces for dislocation and change. Although one line of inquiry into future change in the region is based on extrapolating evolutionary trends, an analysis of internal forces will not aid in understanding as much as a consideration of fiscal and political decisions made by the central government. The issue of "secondary development," that of the nation-state and international environment in which regional and local cultures such as this one exist (cf. Adams 1966), is not easily settled by the usual tools of anthropological study. Change in this region may come about as a byproduct, many times removed from the scene, of considerations totally independent of it.

Although futurological speculation may be a vain task, perhaps the broad survey of the Valley of Oaxaca can yield an insight that bears on the present. By understanding the local-regional system interaction, we become aware of its utility as a powerful and flexible mechanism of social articulation. The coherence and cultural integrity of this system should not be destroyed by "planning" or needlessly tampered with. Instead, attempts to improve the welfare of the region should begin with the understanding that there is already a substantial base on which to build that has been developed over the centuries.

12. A Concluding Critical Look at Issues of Theory and Method in Oaxaca Market Studies

SCOTT COOK AND MARTIN DISKIN

Our purpose in this concluding section is to critically examine and clarify our thinking about certain fundamental theoretical and methodological problems that have arisen in the course of our work with the Oaxaca material. A failure to ascertain and then deal with these problems in the past has been a major barrier to progress in our understanding of the structure, functioning, and evolution of the Valley of Oaxaca economy. The recognition of these problems and the stimulus to confront them and to evaluate or rethink our data in terms of them has been one of the most significant results of the Oaxaca Market Study Project.

Two broad areas of theory and method require systematic attention if we are to make real progress in the analysis and interpretation of the data already collected and in future research: (a) the need to clarify and codify such basic concepts as *economy, market,* and *system* in order to determine how they may be best employed in studies of regional peasant economies of the Oaxaca type; and (b) the need to relate a formal, restrictive focus on markets and marketing to broader political-economic and social-anthropological concerns of economy-society articulation and socioeconomic development. While it is only in retrospect that the scope and significance of these needs is fully appreciated, our intention here is to suggest how their consideration helps to sharpen and organize our thinking about the data on hand—and, we hope, to provide our tentative interpretations with broader relevance. Finally, we will suggest specific operational procedures and empirical tests that should facilitate the future resolution of some of the important questions that inevitably remain unanswered.

CLARIFICATION OF CONCEPTS

"Economy," "Mode of Production," and "Ecosystem"

When, for analytical purposes, we speak of the Oaxaca *regional economy*, the Valley of Oaxaca *economy*, or the *economy* of a given local community, we are referring to a particular culturally mediated field of human activity in which specific populations interact with their physical and social environments in the calculated attempt to acquire a living through production for use and exchange (see Cook 1973:808–814). This conception of the economy has the advantage of emphasizing process, not stasis; it conveys the idea that at a particular time and place economic activity occurs only on the basis of movement, exertion, and interaction of human labor and other material means. The economy is reduced to a process—empirically identifiable as flows of materials, energy, products, and information —in which people, individually or in groups, calculate and act to acquire or dispose of material wealth.

The disadvantage of this view—which also specifies the components of the economy as production, transfer, utilization, and distribution (see Cook 1973)—is that, while facilitating the analysis of specific parts or fragments of social process (or the results of a specific kind of social process), it may inhibit the holistic analysis of social process as a totality. For example, it provides a framework for the analysis of commodity flows in terms of output, pricing, and marketing in the regional economy, but not for the analysis of the political-economic relationships between the various classes of people in regional society who facilitate or participate in the production and circulation of commodities; it enables us to identify and analyze problems internal to the economic process (e.g., costing, pricing) but inhibits the identification and analysis of contradictions within and between this and other dimensions of the social process (i.e., infrastructure/superstructure relationships).

To overcome this disadvantage we recommend that the *economy* concept be articulated with the *mode of production* concept; the latter, as a structural component of a "socioeconomic formation," has built into it the crucial element of infrastructure/superstructure correspondences and contradictions (Terray 1972:97–105; cf. Godelier 1972:77–104). More specifically, a *mode of production* is defined as an infrastructure comprised of *forces* (material means and technological organization) and *social relations* (classes arising from property ownership/control) of production, related to a superstructure consisting of *juridico-political* and *ideological* components. This conceptualization implies nothing other than a set of functionally differentiated, yet articulating, relationships. No stipulations are made concerning the types of components that assume certain functions or the number of functions a particular component may have. For example, kinship or *compradazgo* (coparent) relations may be involved in the organization of the forces of production as well as in the ideological patterning of social relations; or juridico-political elements (e.g., the *ejido* program as legislatively formulated in the Código Agrario) may correspond to certain social relations of production (*ejido* functionaries as rural bourgeoisie versus *ejidatarios*, and the latter versus *propietarios*) and to a certain organization of the productive forces (e.g., land designated for ejidal tenure; production geared to ejidal rules, regulations, and facilities). Finally, this conceptualization implies that contemporary social reality and political-economic arrangements are products of the past and embody the constantly changing expressions of contradictions and other relationships of previous historical periods. Consequently, a specific mode of production is a localized structural component of a socioeconomic formation that integrates local and supralocal processes and institutions in a historically distinctive way. And, as Claude Meillasoux argues, it is the task of economic anthropology to "go in to the analysis of each specific mode of production, the secret of their functioning and how they evolve" (1972:97–98).

In the Valley of Oaxaca economy, or for that matter in any empirical economy, the labor process is the hub of activity or the motive force underlying the production and circulation of wealth. "The labor process," observed Marx, ". . . is . . . purposive activity carried on for the production of use values, for the fitting of natural substances to human wants; it is the general condition requisite for effecting an exchange of matter between man and nature; it is the condition perennially imposed by nature upon human life, and is therefore independent of the forms of social life—or, rather, is common to all social forms" (1930:177).

Given this theoretical orientation a salient problem is to determine how various ecological and technological processes relate to economically productive social activities—those involving labor power and other energy expenditures, together with flows of material resources, commodities, and information, in calculated and planned acts of appropriation, transformation, transfer, and utilization. We must also take into account the unplanned, unintended consequences of such activities. This view is compatible with the identification of the local or ecological population as the basic unit of analysis (Rappaport 1969:184–185). What we mean by the local or ecological population, following the usage of Roy A. Rappaport, is an aggregate of human beings sharing a set of distinctive means by which they adapt to their environment. As it turns out, in the Valley of Oaxaca, these local or ecological populations correspond to groups of local territorial corporate communities, which claim more or less exclusive rights to exploit the resources located within their jurisdiction, and which interact with each other through the mechanism of the town plaza.

However, since we are not exclusively concerned with trophic relations (i.e., food chains) in the analysis of our Oaxaca data, we will not use the term *ecosystem* as it has been used and elaborated in recent ecological work. The reality of life in the Valley of Oaxaca is that no village is self-sufficient; each exchanges raw materials, people, commodities, and information with other communities. We agree with Rappaport that in situations of economic interdependence among populations the ecosystem concept (defined as a system of trophic exchanges between species) is not appropriate as an analytical tool and that "we recognize that local populations are likely to participate in, and form component parts of . . . a system composed of all the local populations that occupy a geographical area" (1969:185–186). For our purposes, we distinguish between the local system—the minimal self-sufficient unit—composed of a group of villages and a town plaza, and the regional system— the widest socioeconomic structure that integrates the component local systems.

Another reason we offer for the nonapplicability of the ecosystem concept to the Oaxaca situation is that the local systems in the Valley are no longer "adapting" primarily to a natural environment; rather, they are adapting to an environment that incorporates many extra-ecological elements (e.g., government programs, credit services, national and international market fluctuations). This reflects the increasingly complex involvement of local populations in the Valley of Oaxaca with national and international activities and emphasizes the greater relative weight we attach in their daily lives to political-economic and other sociocultural features, as opposed to purely ecological or biological factors (cf. Steward 1955:32; Bennett 1969: 12).

On the "Market" Concept

A necessary point of departure for any study of marketing is the fundamental distinction between "site-confined," or locational, and "site-free," or nonlocational, notions of market (LeClair 1962:1185–1186; Firth 1967:5–6). In Oaxaca, for example, the term *plaza* has both meanings. It refers both to the physical location of marketing activity (this is usually the municipal plaza in the community that hosts the marketplace) and to *market* in the site-free transactional sense (as in the phrase *la plaza pone el precio*, "the market sets the price"). A substantial portion of marketing activity in Oaxaca is channeled through these marketplaces, although marketing possibilities are not exhausted by the plazas. Extensions of the site-confined notion are useful in understanding the distributive function of marketplace trade. Here William G. Skinner's term *market area* (Skinner 1964), referring to the distributional area of a particular product or to the dependent territory of a particular marketplace, could be used.

The site-free, or nonlocational, sense of *market* refers to a "theoretical or ideal state of affairs relating to transactions between abstract categories of suppliers and demanders and focusing on the behavior of prices and quantities, as well as on the allocation of rewards to producers and marketers" (Cook, Essay 7 above). This notion enables the investigator to cope analytically with the fact that the peasant economy of Oaxaca is essentially a money economy, in which pricing operates to guide factors of production into uses that meet consumer (or producer) wants as expressed through the consumers' willingness and ability to buy (i.e., effective demand). In such an economy the transactional market distributes among the working population the aggregate product of their labor through its determination of prices of the various factors of production. In the peasant economy of Oaxaca the marketing sphere is guided by the convention that transactions are made in terms of money—but they are influenced by such factors as patterns of autoconsumption, non-monetary exchanges, and public consumption (e.g., on ceremonial occasions) (see Beals, Essay 2 above). These latter factors in turn are prevalent in the economic life of the peasant village and inevitably have an impact on the supply and demand of goods and services in the regional economy.

In considering the spatial attributes of regional marketing organization, we find a considerable amount of ambiguity generated by the profusion of labels to denote one basic concept. In the Mesoamerican literature the following terms are used interchangeably (often by the same author in the same publication) with reference to the same system: *market system, solar market, regional market system, regional system of interchange, periodic markets, rotating markets, sectional markets,* and *cyclical markets.* Whatever the term given in a particular context, the marketing arrangement referred to is usually an organization of marketplaces interrelated spatially (i.e., they include separate central places within a geographic region) and temporally (i.e., the calendar dates on which they meet are sequentially staggered).

A classic example in Mesoamerican studies of the site-confined market is the Malinowski–de la Fuente study (1957) of the Valley of Oaxaca marketing system. Although a principal concern of this study is with the behavior of buyers and sellers in their exchange of goods and services through the price-integrated market mechanism, these authors employ the term *market* in its locational sense (1957: 15–32 and passim) and define the *market system* as an organization of interrelated marketplaces whose relations are defined by where and when the component plazas meet (ibid.:20–21). In elaborating their approach, Malinowski and de la Fuente construct a taxonomy of marketplaces (using such additional criteria as population size, political-administrative status, and trading volume) under the headings "principal," "principal regional," "secondary district," and "important minor." While this taxonomic approach has some classificatory utility, it has little analytical or explanatory value.

Such taxonomies should merely serve as departure points for inquiry and should not be accepted per se as definitive interpretations of the dynamic and complex reality to which they refer. In the contributions by Beals and Diskin above (Essays 2 and 3), an effort is made to classify the various marketplaces in a more comprehensive and analytically suggestive way. Beals, with more complete ethnographic data than Malinowski and de la Fuente, presents a scheme for ranking many more plazas, still using their criteria. Diskin, on the other hand, tries to divide the region into "levels" according to sociocultural criteria and to show how the plazas operate in the sociocultural milieu. His scheme is not empirically exhaustive but represents an effort to determine categories of sufficient generality that any plaza, of any size and at any locale, could be assigned a place.

The use of concepts and principles of locational economics (see Berry 1967) does not enable us to approach the intermarketplace organization of the Valley of Oaxaca in terms of economic process (i.e., using the transactional, model-building notion of market as outlined by Belshaw [1965:6-9]) or social process (e.g., focusing on the social implications of what Marx refers to as the contradiction between exchange for the sake of exchange and exchange for the sake of commodities [1973:148-149], one example of which may be a transformation in the role of women [see Mintz 1971; Johnson 1973]).

In neoclassical microeconomic theory, a market system is not an organization of episodic marketplaces but an interactional network of buyers and sellers. Particular groups of buyers and sellers are connected (via communication) into a system of price and production decisions through time on the basis of buyer-seller interplay (with mutual interdependence of buyers and sellers recognized in varying degrees). In this model situation, then, prices are viewed as the outcome of buyer-seller interaction. The only meaning that can be attached to the term *market system* in the light of these propositions is that it consists of a series of more or less interconnected markets *in different commodities*. Economists have long recognized that prices of different commodities are interrelated with one another, rather than being independent of one another. This grows out of the fact that, so long as the individuals who appear either as buyers or sellers in one market also appear as buyers or sellers in another market, all commodities are to some extent substitutes for one another. At the very least, if the supply of one commodity changes, it is likely to have some influence on the supply of other commodities; and, if the demand for one commodity changes, it is likely to have an influence on the demand for other commodities, at any given time (Fraser 1947:131-133; Dorfman 1964:Chaps. 1, 4).

To consider the Valley of Oaxaca marketing organization as a price-integrated market system requires that the researcher use the tool kit of microeconomic theory. Accordingly, the principal integrative factor in that organization is price; the relevant analytic units are no longer marketplaces inhabited by flesh-and-blood peasant traders, but rather markets inhabited by bloodless categories of buyers and sellers. Consequently, the system that emerges as the focus of analysis is not a land-locked organization of rotating marketplaces but a free-floating, interrelated network of markets; the relevant parameters are not time and place but supply and demand. Given this theoretical orientation the researcher can address himself to a whole series of new questions. For example, he can look into the possible relationship between marketplaces and nonmarketplace trade through the pricing system (e.g., are there commodity markets that cross-cut marketplaces and localities? If so, what are their characteristics and how do they operate?). In short, by framing questions of this type, we can proceed to analyze our data, and can no longer be satisfied with a poetic search for new and ingenious ways to describe it. While the application of this approach to Mesoamerican marketing studies is only in the preliminary phase (e.g., Cassady 1968; Cook 1970 and Essay 7 above; Swetnam 1973; Plattner 1973; Berg, Essay 5 above), most of us now realize its fruitfulness as well as its limitations (cf. Beals, Essay 2 above). Among the limitations of this approach in the present case are the fundamental questions of the applicability of the root assumptions of microeconomics concerning motivation and the image of peasant economic actors as "firms." For example, in the Oaxaca plazas, we note that there is a relatively constant participation of peasant buyer-sellers, with a variable amount of produce. This results in fluctuation in price over time. But, contrary to expectations about the integrative effect of price, production decisions that underlie market participation are not influenced by these fluctuations. That is, principles other than those of the price-integrating market seem to be at work in perpetuating the pattern of community specialization of production.

By contrast, in Marxist economic analysis, the abstract notion of *market* is recognized as a necessary category for dealing with relative prices, their interrelationships, and the role of supply and demand forces in determining these (e.g., Marx 1935:24–26; 1973:279–281; cf. Godelier 1972:60–77). However, in Marxist analysis the source of the value of commodities is not synonymous with their price as determined in the market through the interaction of supply and demand. On the contrary, the value of a commodity is measured

by the socially necessary labor embodied in it (see Marx 1935; Mandel 1970: Chaps. 1, 2). As Marx expressed it, "Supply and demand
regulate nothing but the temporary *fluctuations* of market prices";
they "explain . . . why the market price of a commodity rises above or
sinks below its *value*, but they can never account for that value itself" (1935:26; italics in original). For Marxist analysts, then, the
process of price determination is where the value of commodities is
realized, not where it *originates* (cf. Godelier 1972:62), and the
deeper significance of the market lies in the class relationships it re-
inforces in its capacity as a social mechanism that facilitates the appropriation of surplus-value (see Marx 1935; 1930, vol. 1, part 1).
One of the ways in which this problem can be approached in the
Valley of Oaxaca is to analyze the plazas in terms of the kinds of circulatory routes of products that flow through them (see Cook, Essay
7 above). There are several variants that should be considered (cf.
Meillasoux 1971:80): (*a*) products are transferred from *propios*
(producers) to *regatones* (traders), thus being transformed into
commodities as their exchange value is partially realized; (*b*) commodities are sold by one *regatón* to another, thus realizing even
more of their exchange value; (*c*) commodities pass from *regatones*
to private consumers, thus completely realizing their exchange value
as they acquire their final use value; and (*d*) commodities are exchanged directly between *propios* as use values (*cambio* or barter).
   Suggested by the Marxist approach to commodity circulation is a
consideration of the differentiation among commodities produced
by peasant-artisans with respect to their potential for generating surplus value. Our research suggests, for example, that certain artisan
products, such as sarapes or pottery, carry more capitalist circulatory potential than metates; and a similar situation prevails in the
agricultural sector. We lack systematic comparative data of sufficient
scope and depth to demonstrate conclusively how the structure of
production, exchange, and consumption of commodities produced in
the regional peasant economy relates to their differential capacity
for generating surplus value or for becoming objects of capitalist
development.

The Regional Economy as a System
   In the preceding discussion we have dealt with different notions
of the market concept and outlined some of their implications for
analysis. Now we address ourselves to the *system* concept and to its
application in market studies. First, we must emphasize that social
anthropologists, as natural scientists, are committed to the proposi-

tion that phenomenal reality external to the observer is characterized by regularities and that these regularities are ascertainable,
may be conceptualized as patterns, and are amenable to operational
analysis (Rapoport 1965). Where does this general orientation lead
us in our attempt to understand a specific set of problems about
economic process in a regional peasant-artisan economy? One realization we are led to is that it is likely to be quite some time before
our understanding of the complexities of the regional sociocultural
process approaches definitiveness. Another is that it might be wise
to proceed piecemeal, to first acquaint ourselves with the least abstract and most concrete parts, segments, aspects, and dimensions of
the whole before we attempt to cope with the process in its entirety.
A third realization is that our knowledge of this whole (i.e., a sociocultural formation) will not be certain or fixed; like the reality that
is its object, our understanding will emerge dialectically and will
proceed as a dialectic—a method of approximation which employs
concepts and models to temporarily stop processes that are in mo-
tion and which relies upon abstractions to approximate concrete
reality (cf. Cook 1973:803–808).

The assumption of the systematic patterning and interrelatedness
of human social behavior was axiomatic in the functionalist approach of Malinowski and de la Fuente. Indeed, their view of the
Valley of Oaxaca economy as a system was a pioneering contribution to the scientific study of the Mesoamerican rural economy. Yet
in several crucial respects their analysis failed to penetrate the surface events of market schedules, transportation routes, movements
of people, marketplace layouts, product inventories, prices, and
some sample bargaining sessions. They give some idea of the geographic rationale of the system but do not identify mechanisms that
link marketplace activities to production activities. Nor do they give
us any indication of the relative size of the marketplaces except on
an impressionistic basis. They allude to the systemic nature of the
markets, but they can be interpreted to mean by this nothing more
than convenience of location on bus lines between the various subsidiary marketplaces and Oaxaca City. Their treatment of the "system" (*sistema de mercados*) conveys no sense of its indispensability
to the people of the region or of its internal dynamics; they offer
no explanation for the remarkable durability of the system in the
face of severe stresses and strains throughout the history of this
region.

The notion of a marketing system implies to us a series of regularized relationships of interdependence between people, commodities, and sites in a circulatory process coordinated and animated by human communication, decision-making, and work. In the regional economy of the Valley of Oaxaca, marketing involves many exchange-specialized sites (plazas) and many exchange-specialized roles (e.g., various kinds of middlemen-traders, many of whom are lumped together as *regatones*). The Valley of Oaxaca marketing system manifests itself empirically as a series of plazas and trading crowds operating on a coordinated periodic (seven-day) schedule. A network of highways, roads, and paths links these marketplaces together and also links each marketplace to a multitude of production sites and utilization sites—thereby facilitating the coordination of periodic activity (i.e., the cyclical flow of commodities and people). The sites themselves, including the marketplaces, contain many concrete embodiments of human cultural activity (e.g., buildings, tools, and other facilities and equipment) which inevitably affect the course of marketing events.

When we add the dimension of people/commodity circulation to this concrete, inanimate scene and view the resulting mix as a dynamic, animate system, we immediately complicate our task by injecting a series of nonlocational, nonmaterial variables—decision-making, economizing, price formation, allocation, competition, communication, cycling, scheduling, rationality, supply and demand, opportunity costs, ceremonial and ritual requirements, preference scales, etc. In other words, we are now faced with the task of attempting to understand relationships between overt, explicit, visible, objective manifestations of phenomenal reality and covert, implicit, invisible, subjective manifestations. Thoughts, messages, ideas (the symbol element); intended versus unintended consequences of action, manifest versus latent functions (the functional element); adaptive strategies and problem-solving (the decision-making element); planning and foresight, memory and hindsight (the time element); positive versus negative feedback (the general systemic element); contradictions and correspondences (the dialectical element), etc.— all of these indirectly observable phenomena now present themselves to us as factors to be described and analyzed. The reality of the situation is that all of these variables ultimately impinge upon material flows in ways that can be scientifically approximated.

Given these complexities of observation and analysis, how should we proceed in studying a regional economic system? A logical and necessary point of departure is to clarify and codify basic concepts and units of analysis. We have done this above for the market concept but now must do so for the system concept.

First, let us agree that a system is a "set of objects together with relationships between the objects and between their attributes" (Hall and Fagen, cited in Haggett 1966:17). More specifically (and with the Oaxaca region as our object of concern), according to the general theory of systems, a system is a set of objects (e.g., central places), attributes of the objects (e.g., population, facilities, types of economic activity, velocity of circulation, volume), interrelations among the objects (e.g., distance) and among the attributes (e.g., graphical relationships), and interdependencies of objects and attributes (e.g., the central place hierarchy) (cf. Berry 1967:76–77). General systems theorists identify two basic kinds of systems: closed (which are completely self-contained) and open (which exchange materials and information with a surrounding environment).

It will be noted that in establishing our general notions of systems analysis we are utilizing examples from central place theory—the study of the location, size, nature, and spacing of human activity clusters (Berry 1967:3). While economic anthropological inquiry assumes many of these locational variables to be given, the spatial dimension of the Oaxaca regional economy—as exemplified through the plaza organization—is the most obvious and operationally accessible element or aspect of the systemic, regionally operative economic-ecological-social process. Or, put differently, to approximate an understanding of the hidden realities, the crucial nonlocational attributes and processes, it is most logical to proceed from the overt realities (i.e., locational attributes and processes) of the regional system. Moreover, this approach is consistent with our view of the economy as operating through its production infrastructure.

One of the crucial points emerging from the analysis of a central place or nodal region as an open system (see Berry 1967:78–79 for a summary of this kind of analysis) is the emphasis on positive feedback mechanisms involving circular and cumulative causation (Maruyama 1963). Kent Flannery (1968) has identified some of these mechanisms in his consideration of the shift from a preceramic hunting and gathering adaptation to incipient cultivation in the Valley of Oaxaca between 8000 and 2000 B.C. In the postconquest development of the market system in this region, one change-amplifying mechanism appears to be represented by the tendency of producers and consumers to prefer to conduct trade in the Oaxaca City marketplace and to bypass the smaller marketplaces—a tendency which, of course, permits the former to grow while constraining the growth of the latter.

In analyzing the Valley of Oaxaca region as a system from the perspective of economic anthropology, we must proceed through various stages. The central place theorist begins with *movements* of energy, which lead in turn to a consideration of *networks* (the channels through which energy flows), nodes on the networks and their organization as a *hierarchy*, and, finally, *surfaces*, or recognizable landforms (Haggett 1966:18). This progression is not incompatible with the aims of economic anthropological inquiry but must be adapted to the foci of that inquiry. Whereas the cultural geographer's quest is for the patterning of materialized space, the economic anthropologist focuses on the patterning of movements in his quest for sociocultural (nonlocational) forms. Networks, nodes, hierarchies, and surfaces have meaning to the economic anthropologist only in reference to the circulation of commodities, people, raw materials, information, and money.

It is not misrepresenting reality to characterize the Valley of Oaxaca as a nodal region operating as an open system. Given our knowledge of movements and of transportation and communication networks (roads, telephone, telegraph), we know that Oaxaca City is the principal node in a hierarchy. But we are less certain of how other nodes in the hierarchy (i.e., the various towns and villages with plazas) relate to each other. It is clear that all of them are subordinate to Oaxaca City, but it is less clear how the subordinate units can be ranked among themselves—although some reasonable suggestions are offered by Diskin in Essay 3 above.

Peter Haggett (1966:18–19), following R. J. Chorley (1962:3–8), suggests that an open system must have some of the following six attributes, not all of which need necessarily be present in a regional nodal system: (*a*) the need for an energy supply for the system's maintenance and preservation; (*b*) the capacity to achieve a "steady state" in which the inflow and outflow of energy and material is not by "form adjustments"; (*c*) the ability to regulate itself by homeostatic adjustments; (*d*) the ability to maintain optimum magnitudes over periods of time; (*e*) the ability to maintain its organization and form over time rather than trending toward maximum entropy (as closed systems do); and (*f*) the ability to behave "equifinally," in the sense that different initial conditions may lead to similar end results.

In the Oaxaca case we encounter most of these six conditions. The regional market organization requires a constant movement of people, commodities, resources, money, and information to maintain it; there is evidence in recent decades to suggest that an excess of inward movements may bring about form changes (e.g., expansion of Oaxaca City and development of squatter settlements along its peripheries), just as certain historical periods suggest that decreased movement led to contraction and decline (e.g., of Oaxaca City and other towns, and of haciendas). What this indicates is that the first two conditions stipulated above are met in the Oaxaca regional system. The third condition is apparently also met by the system in that historical evidence suggests that the Oaxaca City hinterland may expand or contract to meet increased or decreased flows. Drawing upon archaeological, historical, and ethnographic data, we know that the Valley of Oaxaca has exhibited both urban and rural settlement patterns, relative cultural homogeneity, marketplaces, and trade in forms not unlike the present ones from pre-Columbian times; this suggests that it meets the fourth and fifth requirements, since the form and function of the urban center–hinterland configuration tends to be relatively constant across space and through time.

The advantages of viewing the Valley of Oaxaca region as an open system, in sum, are that it focuses our attention on the relationships between process and form and that it enables us to include diachronic and synchronic data from a wide range of disciplinary perspectives.

The division of labor and specialization in Valley of Oaxaca society and economy has reached a point in its evolution characterized by an unprecedented degree of functional differentiation and interdependence of differentiated parts—a point at which the corporate village is no longer a viable basic or minimal unit of adaptation (i.e., "operating unit" [Adams 1970:48]) and has been replaced in that role by the town plaza–village system (i.e., local system). However, as Oaxaca becomes increasingly integrated into modern industrial-commercial Mexico, the regional interplaza system (i.e., regional system) may eventually emerge as the basic "operating unit" in Oaxaca—an evolutionary process which is already underway. At the present time, Valley of Oaxaca society and economy, from the systems perspective, are best understood as a bi-level system in which the corporate territorial communities are involved in a local system (with its principal node being the plaza town); and, at a higher level, these local systems are integrated into a regional system, whose principal node is the urban center, Oaxaca City.

The *region* is an abstraction, reflecting not only observable behavior and activities that occur in a variety of circumstances but
also historical, archaeological, and statistical descriptions. The region is composed of a wide range of elements: village production-
consumption units, specialized occupational groupings, reciprocal
exchange arrangements for commodities and services (*guelaguetza*),
ceremonial distribution (*mayordomías, fandangos,* fiestas, etc.),
plazas, labor markets, and others. Linking these elements together
are a number of feedback principles, such as the "market principle"
(Belshaw 1965:8–9), *costumbre,* subsistence requirements of the
budgetary unit, the profit-making enterprise, the ritual cycle, and
what we may call the "morality of trade." Our decision to study particular segments of the system or certain regulatory mechanisms is
a function of the problem we are investigating. For example, in
studying the "market" in the dual sense discussed above (site-
confined and site-free) we would have to select different attributes
of the whole system for intense investigation. Thus, in considering
the locational market we would focus on the plaza cycle, the spatial
relation between plazas (i.e., distances and traveling times), the
movement of goods from production sites to consumption sites, and
so on. The dynamic aspects we seek are those factors that affect the
above variables, such as physical or social accessibility, routes and
costs of movement. The results of this kind of analysis can be summarized in a diagram like the one presented by Cook above (Fig.
7-1). On the other hand, if we are interested in such processes as
the integrating effect of the transactional market, we must study the
pricing system and the supply-demand mechanism. These may be
studied in the plazas, in nonplaza negotiations, and in the abstract
through the serial comparison of output and price fluctuations over
time (Cook 1970). In undertaking such a study, our emphasis shifts
from the movement of people or commodities to the movement of
information through the system, the way actors interpret it, and its
return or feedback into the production sector.

The components of a system (i.e., objects and attributes) represent ways that clusters of behavior or units of analysis can be isolated for study. As we have shown, these components can be
grouped in different ways, depending on the nature of the problem
we are studying. Indeed, the several papers in the present volume
show how varied the conception of units or components can be.
While we do not reject alternate conceptual schemes, we have proposed that, by looking at the Oaxaca region as being comprised of a

bilevel system (the local system and the regional system), we have taken one meaningful step toward the construction of a model of some explanatory power. There are several reasons we can enumerate in support of this approach. First, the two levels posited connect to each other in a dependent manner, that is, the success of the local level is the necessary precondition for the existence of the regional level. There is strong reason to believe that this relationship explains why the system, at various times in the past, has expanded and contracted, grown and decayed. Second, each level, while on occasion behaviorally identical with the other (i.e., in examining the behavior of any given actor it will not be possible to determine which level he is operating at), in general there are different norms for conduct, different motivations for action, and different measures of satisfaction, as well as symbolic and cognitive differences; in short, the two levels represent separate phenomenal realities.

The local system, which combines agricultural with craft-service production, is the basic provisioning mechanism. Its constituent village production units, many of which are specialized in what they produce, direct energy toward activities that are consistent with their natural-resource endowments and cultural experiences. This local system, spatially represented by the network of villages and their town plaza, because of its relative completeness (i.e., full representation of socially and culturally necessary productive roles, commodities, and services) may be viewed as relatively stable. It is a homeostatic system in that it uses energy internally to preserve the same relative proportions of participation of its constituent sections. In practice this means relative fixity of the contribution from producing villages. Although there is undeniably some change over time in crops planted and products manufactured for the plaza, short-range inequities in supply of given commodities, usually reflected in higher prices, are offset by the curtailment of consumption by the peasant consumers. Systemically, the variability of consumption can be interpreted as negative feedback acting to dampen the possible deviation occasioned by the vagaries of supply. Furthermore, perhaps to compensate for these inequities, the various redistributive and reciprocal institutions in the local communities come into play to provide some subsistence goods to the population. In essence, the local level of the system serves to provision village and town populations, to facilitate their achievement of the culturally acceptable minimum inventory of goods and services required for their subsistence; this in turn permits these populations to produce the commodities and services necessary to sustain their participation in the regional system.

The regional system is sustained through the regular interaction of the populations involved in the various local systems within the Valley of Oaxaca as well as some others from areas lying outside the drainage of the Atoyac river (e.g., Ayoquezco, Miahuatlán). This regional system is itself but one subsystem of a larger interregional system that embraces the Sierra Zapoteca, the Isthmus of Tehuantepec, the Mixteca, the Mixería, and the upper Pacific coast. The activities of the regional system are carried out in the same plazas and on the same schedule as are those of the local systems. In general, the same people participate in both. The regional system, to reiterate, exists through the movement of goods and services between the various local systems.

There is a series of marketing roles specific to the regional system: those of traders who specialize in handling goods imported either from outside the system or, in any given plaza, from another local system. These traders are generally competent in handling the strategy and tactics of the business firm and are profit-oriented. The organization of their activities depends on economies of scale. They have considerably more market staying power (e.g., they maintain inventories in warehouses, have large cash reserves) than the typical peasant producer-seller and, consequently, can turn market fluctuations to their advantage through abitrage. Profits, usually measured in cash but sometimes in inventories, are the strict measure of success among these interplaza traders. And, as might be expected under these conditions, competition is severe and the attrition rate is fairly high. The most durable and successful traders appear to be those who stress flexibility and adaptability in buying and selling, and who are sophisticated in the collection and use of information about price, quality, and availability of goods. Among these middlemen, consumption is segregated from business; they seldom produce their own food or other use values for their own consumption. By and large, they are involved in what Weber has called the "profit-making enterprise" (1947:199).

The regional system imports commodities, people, and information from outside. Some of its actors respond to market information (i.e., demand and supply conditions) by accommodating to the situation. They may, for example, try to use their techniques more efficiently to provide customers with goods or to compete through price reductions. Some of these traders deal in commodities traditionally absent from all of the local systems: salted fish, dried chilies from the sierra. Other merchants may seek new niches, either by the introduction of new products or by trying new marketing modes (e.g., specializing in the fiesta plaza circuit). These innovative or entrepreneurial traders, because they engage in relatively high-risk activities, often fail—or introduce systemic changes. The participants in the regional system are also more mobile than participants in the local systems; this is so physically, as in the case of the bolt cloth sellers who travel in panel trucks, and socially, as in the case of traders who have changed their permanent places of residence from hinterland communities to Oaxaca City.

It is important that we elaborate more on those mechanisms that operate to facilitate the interaction of the constituent sections of the system, as well as the articulation of levels within it. The regional system is viable only to the extent that the local systems are viable. The local system supplies the products, the potential buyers, and the cash to make the participation of the interplaza middlemen worthwhile. Villagers don't come to the plaza unless they have products to sell or cash with which to buy. And it is the concentrated supply of products and cash that makes the plaza. In the absence of these conditions at the plaza level, the regional system would collapse. The converse of this relationship also holds: as the supplies of commodities and cash in the local systems expand, the scope and intensity of activity in the regional system will expand. We can express these relationships in terms of schemes already in use. For example, we can say that, as the sections of a "sectional market" (Wolf 1966:40–41) experience productive abundance, the "network market" expands in scope and intensity; or that, when "obligate symbiosis" adequately meets the subsistence needs of a given population, the proper atmosphere is created to sustain "facultative symbiosis" (Wagner 1964:71–74); or, finally, that the horizontal movement determines the course of the vertical movement (Mintz 1959).

While we contend that the local system is a functional prerequisite for the operation of the regional interplaza system, many of the details of this relationship are by no means clear to us at present. In practice the boundary between the two levels of the system dissolves, even though the personnel and operations for each are clearly defined. In some cases, for example, peasant-artisan *propios* shift out of the production sector and undertake reselling, middleman (*regatón*) activities. This shift can be interpreted, at least partially, as a response to the level of output from the villages as well as to the existence of growing consumer demand throughout the system. When the economic pace slackens because of a diminution of cash and effective demand, these opportunistic traders will either shift back to their *propio* activities or seek wage-paying jobs. There is evidence that such shifts now occur on a seasonal basis (e.g., the role shifts during the Day of the Dead markets [*la plaza de los muertos*]) (see Diskin, Essay 3 above).

Another way to get at this relationship is to compare the role and "level" breakdowns of the plazas on regular trading days and special (e.g., holiday or festive) trading days. It appears, for example, that the local systems can vary their contributions of personnel and roles considerably. Undoubtedly some of the personnel increment evident on special trading days derives from people who usually participate as *propios* but who shift into *regatón* roles under favorable market conditions. This not only makes the plaza system a possible channel for social mobility but also, by the ease with which participants shift between roles, provides a means for "correcting" imbalances in the economy. We can speculate that, on the local level, negative feedback operates to staff economic roles. In other words, given the basic stability of production requirements at the local level, when conditions attract more people into plaza participation, some of them will participate at the level of the regional (interplaza) system. The relative stability of conditions at the local level contrasts with the volatility at the regional level. There is more flux and movement of personnel, at the regional level, between kinds of market involvements. In effect, conditions at this level are more highly competitive, with the middleman-trader population fluctuating in size and composition more abruptly than the *propio* population. This relative instability of the regional system reflects its greater sensitivity to economic cycles, shifts in demand, and changes in world market prices.

The articulation of these two levels of the regional system raises an important issue regarding the nature of socioeconomic development. The plaza, as we have argued, permeates all aspects of regional economy and society. It follows, then, that if any segment of the system changes, there must be some corresponding adjustment in other segments. This may be illustrated by examining the historical question of the penetration and expansion of the hacienda in the Valley of Oaxaca. As argued in the introduction (cf. Taylor 1972), it appears that the hacienda system did not become established here to the extent that it did in central Mexico or elsewhere in the New

World. This is explained, in part, by conflict between the crown and various creole landowners (particularly in the aftermath of the divestiture of the Marquesado del Valle). It also seems quite likely that the bilevel nature of regional structure played a role in this. The haciendas were locked into a round of production focused on regional demand, with plaza exchange as a necessary part of the process. To successfully proletarianize the village populations, the hacendados would have had to alienate people from the land. This would have destroyed the productive base of the regional economy, led to the collapse of the local system, and forced the hacendados to assume the complex task of distributing products to provision the rural proletariat. This, of course, would have transformed the hacendados into a new class of middlemen to collect products (from where?) for distribution throughout the region. Aside from the logistical complexities of such an assignment, this would have required the hacendados to place themselves between the flow of tribute from the villages to the Spanish colonial authorities and would have represented a direct threat to the crown or, perhaps, a usurpation of crown privileges. The subject Indian population, whose indigenous production and exchange system was so compatible with "indirect rule," was protected by the crown against expansion-minded private landowners to maintain the flow of tribute.

The approach taken in this section—the definition of units, delineation of the components of a system, and interrelation of the parts of the system—helps to elucidate the richness and complexity of the phenomena under study. It also shows us that rather than merely studying plazas or village economies, we must come to grips with nothing less than a regional socioeconomic formation. The system of plazas is but a surface marker of a subtle process of integrating people of different class positions, types of communities, and life chances.

POLITICAL ECONOMY OF REGIONAL DEVELOPMENT: CAPITALIST/PRECAPITALIST RELATIONS IN THE VALLEY OF OAXACA

To slightly rephrase a statement by Lenin in his classic study, *The Development of Capitalism in Russia* (1964:380), the essence of the problem of "the destiny of capitalism in Latin America" is often presented as though the most important question is *how fast?* (i.e., how fast is capitalism developing?). Yet questions of more fundamental importance are *how exactly?* and *where from?* Certainly one of the most basic and controversial issues confronting students of economic process in Latin America is the nature of the relationship between precapitalist and capitalist modes of production and circulation in the evolution of regional and national economies. This is an issue which has often been circumvented or muddled through the use of such concepts as *dual economy, plural society,* or *multiple society,* or of such conceptual dichotomies as *traditional-modern, centripetal-centrifugal, folk-urban, open-closed, subsistence-exchange,* or *market-nonmarket.* It is also an issue with ramifications in the realm of political ideology; the position that one takes reflects the strategy one advocates for reform or revolution. Among Marxists, whether or not one advocates socialist revolution (as opposed to coalition with the bourgeoisie) as a solution to a given nation's problems depends upon one's judgment as to the relative status of "feudal" and "capitalist" institutions in that society (cf. Frank 1969: esp. Chap. 23).

It is clear to many students of economic history that, once the capitalist mode of production gains a foothold in a precapitalist economy, its influence on the latter is neither ineluctable, irreversible, nor unidirectional but, on the contrary, is subject to constraints and may be characterized by "regressions." As Eric Wolf cautioned in his pioneering essay on the Latin American peasantry, "It would be a mistake . . . to visualize the development of the world market in terms of continuous and even expansion, and to suppose therefore that the line of development of particular peasant communities always leads from lesser involvement in the market to more involvement" (1955:462). Moreover, Wolf draws two conclusions from his analysis that are as pertinent today as they were when he wrote them two decades ago:

First, in dealing with present-day Latin America it would seem advisable to beware of treating production for subsistence and production for the market as two progressive stages of development. Rather, we must allow for the cyclical alternation of the two kinds of production within the same community and realize that from the point of view of the community both kinds may be alternative responses to changes in conditions of the outside market. This means that a synchronic study of such a community is insufficient, because it cannot reveal how the community can adapt to such seemingly radical changes. Second we must look for the mechanisms which make such changes possible (1955:463).

Our data on the development of community and regional economic life in the Valley of Oaxaca since the sixteenth-century Spanish intrusion completely reinforce the thesis that the career of capitalism

—in its mercantile, liberal, or industrial phases (Aguilar Monteverde 1968)—has not been uniformly "progressive" and omnipotent in its impact on precapitalist modes (cf. Lenin 1964:317). Indeed, in its current phase of development in Mexico, it appears to us that precapitalist modes continue to survive because of—rather than in spite of—the needs of capitalist reproduction.

In scanning the trajectory of Mexican economic development from 1500 to the present, no one can deny the profound and pervasive impact (e.g., in terms of land, labor, markets, money) of capitalism (mercantile capitalism during the colonial period, liberal "free-enterprise" capitalism during the second half of the nineteenth century, and industrial capitalism during the postrevolutionary period of the present century—see Aguilar Monteverde 1968). But it should be equally evident that capitalist production and circulation have not completely subverted the content and development of local/regional economic process in Mexico—although there is no area of Mexico in which detribalization has not occurred and in which the rural population has not undergone at least partial "depeasantization" and proletarianization (cf. Lenin 1964:172–187). Dynamic precapitalist modes of production exist in juxtaposition with or as enclaves within a dominant, if periodically indifferent, capitalist system; and these local/regional modes have an evolutionary rhythm and adaptive dynamic that is at least partially their own (e.g., use-exchange value mix; differing sector/level mixes in class differentiation). The task of economic anthropology is not to mechanically explain the economic life of these local/regional modes as creatures of predatory capitalism but to analyze their internal processes and relationships and the origins of these (cf. Laclau 1971; Meillassoux 1972). Even though money, wage labor, rent, interest, profit, investment, and credit are systematically operative in the Mexican economy and are present in varying degrees at the local/regional level throughout Mexico, precapitalist elements continue to operate in regions like Oaxaca. In essence, economic anthropologists should identify, describe, and analyze these elements without losing sight of the larger reality of over-all capitalist domination, i.e., of the "subsumption" or subordination of some forms of peasant economic activity at the local/regional level to principles and processes determining the functioning of the national (and international) economy (cf. Galeski 1972:22).

When the contemporary Mexican economy is considered as a whole, it is apparent that it contains sectors that are noncapitalist in organization and recent (e.g., state-owned enterprise sector, state redistribution sector, collective agriculture) or ancient (corporate village sector) in origin. These elements, as in most other national economies of the contemporary world, are intertwined in complex ways. Maurice Dobb (1963) has formulated a rule for classifying such economies. According to him, in examining the evolution of a particular economy, we can label a developmental phase by a new name when "the new form has grown to proportions which enable it to place its imprint upon the whole of society and to exert a major influence in moulding the trend of development" (p. 11). Applying Dobb's rule to the Mexican economy—and assuming that it is not simply a neocolonial appendage of the U.S. economy—we can infer that it is embarked upon a capitalist development trajectory which may, indeed, have entered a "monopoly capitalist" phase dominated by multinational corporate interests (cf. Aguilar Monteverde 1968). However, the Mexican capitalist development process is sectorally and regionally differentiated and segmented into "mercantile" and "industrial" spheres; and in certain regions like Oaxaca it is still essentially an intrusive rather than an indigenous process—though it is easy to overlook manifestations of indigenous capitalist development. Not all economic phenomena in the Valley of Oaxaca express the "struggle and antagonism of interests" characteristic of the capitalist mode (Lenin 1964:172). The system of socioeconomic relations prevailing among the Valley of Oaxaca peasantry manifests some of "those contradictions which are inherent in every commodity economy and every order of capitalism" (ibid.) (e.g., competition, the struggle for economic independence, the grabbing of land [purchasable and rentable], the hiring of farm laborers) but not others (e.g., the concentration of production in the hands of a minority, the forcing of the majority into the ranks of the proletariat, their exploitation by a minority through the medium of merchant's capital).

Whether we examine the Valley of Oaxaca regional economy from the perspective of commodity circulation (i.e., the destination of peasant products into use or exchange routes [Marx 1930:part 1; Mandel 1970:79–82]) or from that of the "social existence-form of labor power" (i.e., serfdom, free wage labor [Takahashi 1967:31]), we are justified in classifying it as a petty (or simple) commodity mode of production—emancipated from "feudal" exploitation—which is subjected to capitalist relations of production (cf. Dobb 1967:25). As Marx observed, "The production and circulation of commodities may occur although the overwhelming mass of products (being primarily produced for the producers' own use) are not transformed into commodities; and although . . . the social process of production is a long way . . . from being dominated throughout by exchange value" (1930:157). While we do not have sufficient data to enable us to make an accurate estimate of the proportion of total output in the Valley of Oaxaca economy which is transformed into commodities (i.e., exchange values) rather than moving directly into consumption as use values, we do know that most artisan output and a substantial volume of agricultural output flow into commodity circulation. (Incidentally, we agree with H. W. Takahashi [1967:32] that there is a real danger in focusing on the relations obtaining between producers and their markets or on exchange relationships to the exclusion of production relationships—a tendency that Takahashi calls "circulationism.")

In generalizing about how commodities are produced in the Valley of Oaxaca we find that a substantial proportion of members of the peasant-artisan population own the essential means of production (e.g., land, tools, oxen) and that, by and large, commodities become the immediate property of the direct producers for disposal as they see fit. Yet there is definitely substantial inequality in the ownership of productive means in the Valley; and, in fact, many peasants are dependent on others for access to these means. These dependency relationships underwrite a process whereby a portion of the "surplus product" of the peasantry is appropriated (e.g., through rent in labor or rent in kind) by the owners of the productive means, most of whom are also peasants, albeit of a different class level (i.e., petty or middle bourgeoisie). And there is, of course, widespread evidence of incipient or small-scale industrial capitalist relations (e.g., *molinos de nixtamal*, sugar-cane grinding mills and *panela* factories, mescal distilleries), together with wage labor in the local agricultural sector. While many peasants are temporarily or partially involved in these capitalist relations of production, it still appears that relations based on producer control of the means of production predominate. In short, surplus value is appropriated by petty traders and other merchants as a regularized part of the circulation process, but true capitalist accumulation (i.e., the investment of profits in production, acquisition of labor power, etc.) is the exception rather than the rule in the Valley of Oaxaca economy (cf. Marx 1973:253).

As mentioned above, there is an internal labor market operating in the Valley of Oaxaca economy, and most peasants work for a wage at one time or another during their careers, either on a seasonal basis each year or more irregularly. This labor market has not developed to the point of being indicative of a capitalist transformation of the social process of production—in which the entire economy would be polarized between a group of propertyless "free" workers who sell their labor power as their only means of livelihood and a group of owners of the means of production. Only in the towns and cities do we find evidence of a true proletariat; in the rural areas the labor force is only partially proletarianized.

Likewise, while there are many middlemen-traders in the Valley of Oaxaca, we cannot speak of them collectively as a merchant capitalist class (i.e., traders who aim at the "never ending process of profit-making" [Marx 1930:138]), though they are creditors (and usurers) in an economy with many peasant debtors. A product that is the source of profit for one Oaxaca trader may be a source of use value for another (or for the same trader on a different occasion). This is, in essence, an economy in which the distinction between value in use and value in exchange is basic in the production system, but in which commodities circulate to provide for the satisfaction of fundamental social reproductive needs (cf. Mandel 1970:67–68), not to underwrite the creation of "value in process" (i.e., capital) [Marx 1930:140–141]).

The distinctiveness of a peasant-artisan market economy of the Valley of Oaxaca type is not that production for exchange, like production for use, is geared primarily to the producers' subsistence (i.e., reproduction of labor) but that the economy contains within it the embryo of capitalist accumulation and is itself embedded in a national (and international) capitalist economy. The peasant-artisan producer-seller (*propio*) comes to the marketplace to convert the labor power embodied in his products into cash: C (commodity)→ M (money); he does so because it is the most direct and practical means for him to acquire products that he needs: M→C. In other words, he realizes the exchange value in the commodities he produces so as to acquire other commodities that have use value for him. If the commodities he brings to market are sold to middlemen-traders (and not directly to buyers for private use), then these commodities enter a route in which additional exchange value will be appropriated from them before their use value is realized (i.e., before they are acquired by a user). It is in this process of circulation through a series of trading (or exchange-value) circuits that a peasant-artisan commodity may contribute to capitalist accumulation. The *regatones* who deal in such commodities start out with a sum of cash which is employed to acquire the commodities for resale at a profit: $M \rightarrow C \rightarrow M'$. Whereas a portion of M' may be converted by the trader into use values to meet his (or her) own subsistence needs, some portion of it will be re-employed for subsequent profit-seeking transactions. The typical Valley of Oaxaca *regatón* does not accumulate sufficient capital to enable him to become an employer of labor power and technical means for the production of commodities (though such cases are on record for the metate, pottery, basket, and sarape industries); rather he appropriates surplus value *within a framework of simple commodity circulation.* Nevertheless, the potential for such development is omnipresent. And there are capitalists operating in the Valley of Oaxaca economy whose careers began with or are sustained by capital appropriated and accumulated from the circulation of commodities produced by peasant-artisans (e.g., owners of *molinos de nixtamal*, mescal distilleries, vegetable-oil processing factories, or sugar-cane processing plants [*trapiches* and *panela* factories], commercial farmers, dairymen). These capitalists own the technical means of production, hire labor power, and manufacture products to sell at a profit; and their subjective aim, the processional increase of exchange value, coincides with the objective purpose of their transactions. While for many *regatones* the need for use values (i.e., for household provisioning purposes) may inhibit the expansion of the surplus values they acquire, this is never the case among the indigenous capitalists, whose business interests are never subordinated to or incompatible with their subsistence needs.

As we shift from a microscopic analysis of the regional economy to a macroscopic survey of the Mexican national economy and the place of Oaxaca in it, we must cope with the complex dialectic of regional/national economic process. On the one hand, we are on firm ground in emphasizing the unequal nature of the relationship that obtains between a provincial, agrarian economy like that of the Valley of Oaxaca and the metropolitan economy of urban-industrial Mexico. From this perspective, the dynamic of regional/national relations would appear to lead inevitably to the transformation of the former into a pale carbon copy of the latter. On the other hand, we are confronted with the fact that the development of the metropolitan capitalist economy is partially generated from its dominant relationship with hinterland peasant economies like that of

Oaxaca—a need which appears in direct conflict with the transformation (and disappearance) of the latter. This is a contradiction of capitalist development identified and analyzed by Rosa Luxemburg, who wrote that ". . . the accumulation of capital, as an historical process, depends in every respect upon non-capitalist social strata and forms of social organization" and that ". . . the noncapitalist social environment . . . absorbs the products of capitalism and supplies producer goods and labor power for capitalist production" (1968:366). Accordingly, she argues that "Historically, the accumulation of capital is a kind of metabolism between capitalist economy and those pre-capitalist methods of production without which it cannot go on and which . . . it corrodes and assimilates" (ibid.:416). In a similar vein the Russian scholar Evgenii Preobrazhensky wrote as follows: "The transition of society from the petty-bourgeois system of production to the capitalist could not have been accomplished without preliminary accumulation at the expense of petty production, and would thereafter have proceeded at a snail's pace if additional accumulation at the expense of petty production had not continued alongside capitalist accumulation at the expense of the exploited labor-power of the proletariat. The very transition presumes, as a system, an exchange of values between large-scale and petty production under which the latter gives more to the former than it receives" (1965:88).

One of the principal ways in which the unequal exchange of values between capitalist and petty production occurs in Oaxaca is through the system of seasonal wage labor, by which a portion of the labor force is maintained in a semiproletarian state (i.e., the mode of social reproduction of labor power remains essentially noncapitalist). We lack accurate statistics on the extent and types of migratory labor in Oaxaca, but we do know that there is a substantial out-migration of Oaxacans to other, more "developed" states. For example, between 1960 and 1968 the average annual rate of this out-migration is estimated at .6 percent of the total population (UNDP/FAO 1972:11). It is not clear what percentage of these emigrants established permanent residence outside of Oaxaca, nor which regions of the state they represent; however, in 1960 there were more than 210,000 Oaxacans residing outside of the state (11 percent of the Oaxaca-born Mexican population)—and during that same year the census shows a net out-migration from Oaxaca of 156,028 persons (ibid.:52). Whether these emigrants were settling permanently outside Oaxaca or not, they represent, in effect, a contribution by this "underdeveloping" peasant-artisan market economy to the developing capitalist sectors in other Mexican states. Those who are seasonal migrant laborers remain rooted in a domestic economy in which they provide for their own means of reproduction—a burden which would otherwise have to be absorbed indirectly by the capitalist sector through increased wages. The permanent emigrants represent a loss to the Oaxaca economy in terms of social reproductive costs (including costs of education) incurred up to the time of emigration. This is a concrete example of the unequal exchange of values alluded to above.

In a process of capitalist development like that underway in Mexico, it is clear that profits are enhanced by allowing the costs of the social reproduction of labor to be absorbed by the precapitalist regional economies (or through a public-welfare or social-security system). (See Wolf 1957; Geertz 1963.) Consequently, it can be in the interest of the developing capitalist sector in the Mexican economy to perpetuate (rather than eliminate) elements in the regionally segmented precapitalist sector. This means, of course, that the capitalist sector (through its state apparatus) must establish and maintain programs to assure the availability of productive means to domestic production/reproduction units in the regional peasant economies. Land reform programs of the *ejido* type—to the degree that they promote equal distribution of land—are crucial in this regard. Likewise, income or wealth-pooling mechanisms and reciprocity arrangements (e.g., *guelaguetza*) which are indigenous to regional society and culture contribute to the capacity of the Oaxaca peasantry to reproduce labor power (cf. Wolpe 1972).

Meillasoux concisely summarizes the importance of the labor reproductive role of the peasant sector within a developing capitalist economy of the Mexican variety and shows how the "dual-economy" model serves to mystify it:

It is convenient for the capitalist economist to . . . explain away underdevelopment by attributing it to the sexual incontinence of the natives or to their devious mentality. Failure to perceive the real situation leads them also to such contradictory conclusions as that underdeveloped countries are 'dual economies' consisting of two different and noncommunicating sectors and that the primitive sector is slowly blending into the capitalist one. The 'dual' theory is intended to conceal the exploitation of the rural community, integrated . . . as an organic component of capitalist production to feed the temporarily unproductive workers of the capitalist sector and supply them with the resources necessary to their survival. Because of this process of absorption within the capitalist economy, the agricultural communities, maintained as reserves of cheap labor, are being undermined and perpetuated at the same time, undergoing a prolongated crisis and not a smooth transition to capitalism. (1972:103)

It is clear to us, in conclusion, that we must combine a macroscopic (metropolis-down) view of the Valley of Oaxaca economy with a microscopic (village-up) view if we are to avoid distorting the real nature of its evolution and present structure. Obviously this regional Mexican economy is not experiencing a smooth, normal, autochthonous transition from petty commodity production to the capitalist mode of production. Rather, its evolution and structure have been partially skewed to meet the demands of increased development and prosperity in the metropolitan capitalist economy, and its future course is inextricably linked to the developmental fortunes of the latter. In the meantime, it continues to facilitate production and circulation for use and exchange among the regional population.

HYPOTHESES AND SUGGESTIONS FOR FUTURE RESEARCH

In this final section we recapitulate central themes in preceding sections for the purpose of isolating a series of problems for further empirical (ethnographic and historical) investigation. Again, we do not approach these problems in a definitive way or with the intention of exhausting the possibilities, but simply as another step toward the improved understanding of a complex sociocultural and political-economic process.

Ecological Units

The units that interest us here are describable in terms of activity patterns and movements of people both in productive processes and plaza routines. Do these units have ecological coherence? What aspects of the natural environment are perceived and used by people as a guide to the specialization of production?

Hypothesis: The local system (i.e., a plaza community and a series of satellite producing villages), when viewed in terms of aggregate production and distribution mechanisms, constitutes a natural unit in the sense that something approximating self-sufficiency can be achieved within the boundaries of the system. Contemporary evidence exists in the fact that each of the local systems has, either in active or remnant form, all the historically necessary cultigens and the important craft items (e.g., pottery, basketry, weaving). This indicates that within the environmental limits of these zones a high degree of self-sufficiency is possible through internal symbiotic exchange (cf. Kirkby 1973: esp. Chap. 2).

Research Directions: Of interest here is the nutritional return obtainable by confining food procurement to the various units (i.e., the household production unit, village, and local system). Of interest too is the level of nourishment of the traditional menu and the possibility of attaining it, given mean income. Further, we should study the marginal benefit of nonplaza distribution (e.g., food distributed at *mayordomías*, as part of labor contracts, and through balanced reciprocity between households).

Production Specialization

Is the pattern of village production specialization conducive to greater productivity, or output, for the whole region? What is the specific relationship between the microenvironment and the technology employed in agricultural production (cf. Kirkby 1973: Chap. 9)? Is the expertise necessary to cultivate a given crop so specialized as to prevent diversification or movement between different productive roles?

Hypothesis: The pattern of production specialization, especially in agriculture, results in greater output for the total region because of greater efficiency of energy use through technologies that are finely adapted to specific microenvironmental niches. Although the technological level may be considered uniform throughout the area in gross terms (digging stick, hoe, or plow agriculture), considerable advantage can be obtained by the use of techniques that capitalize on peculiarities of the microenvironment, such as pot irrigation (*riego a brazo*)—practiced today as well as aboriginally in the zone of the high-water-table alluvium (cf. Flannery et al. 1967:450; Kirkby 1973). Moreover, the intensification of such techniques tends to fix the agriculturalists in their physical and cultural sections, thus rendering them less and less likely to be self-sufficient in the future.

Research Directions: In order to learn more about the use of microenvironments, we must expand our knowledge of the ethnoecology and ethnogeography of the Valley landscape. The recent study by Anne V. T. Kirkby (1973) provides an important basis for understanding correspondences between niches with respect to water availability, temperature, and soil types, and gives us an excellent preliminary analysis of the advantages of specialization in terms of yields.

Rescheduling of Production and Consumption

How is a new cultigen or product incorporated into the preference scales of peasant households? How does a new crop become integrated into schedules of planting or replace other crops or other food procurement activities, such as hunting and collecting of wild foods? (Messer 1972).

Hypothesis: Since production must be planned not only for immediate local consumption needs but also to insure a level of plaza participation, the replacement of one procurement activity by another will depend upon the feasibility of integrating the new product into the regional or local system—or into the local round of activities—without displacing plaza-targeted production.

Research Directions: It should be possible to ascertain whether plaza-oriented work is distinguished from subsistence-oriented work through an analysis of time disposition within separate household production units. With respect to the plaza orientation, we want to be able to distinguish changes in household production that stem from changing requirements of the plaza from local physical and social changes.

Exchange Spheres in the Plaza

Is it possible to separate products and activities earmarked for subsistence—whether produced and consumed by the same household or obtained through the plazas—from those products that are "extrasubsistence" (e.g., luxury or prestige) items? What are the principles of allocation that operate within or between these categories (e.g., "conversions" or "conveyances" [Bohannan 1955])?

Hypothesis: By analyzing peasant production—perhaps in terms of Wolf's "funds" (i.e., replacement, ceremonial, and rent [1966])—it should be possible to distinguish between goods and activities in a subsistence (use-value) and a market (exchange-value) sphere and to ascertain the surplus-value differentials of various commodities. The allocation principle in the subsistence sphere will involve both reciprocity and market exchange, while in the "market sphere" the principle of money pricing will predominate.

Research Directions: Peasant household budgets, including the apportionment of commodities, cash, and labor time, should be recorded to determine the relative importance of each "fund" vis-à-vis subsistence, as well as the elasticity of demand for various items. It might be possible to obtain a rank order of products required by the household that represents movement from the subsistence to the market sphere. Historically oriented research possibilities include the use of documentation on prices and quantities of products for the colonial and independence periods to determine if regular patterns in fluctuations and plaza structure can be identified through time and also to determine what infrastructural and superstructural events affected the plazas.

The Ideology of Distribution

Is there a generalized code of conduct or a common set of standards of behavior operating in the plaza? Do all actors in the plaza seem to conduct themselves in accordance with these? Are their behavioral goals equivalent?

Hypothesis: The plaza behavior of those whose participation falls within the local sections of the total system will be oriented toward the adequate fulfillment of certain social roles that are specific to their class position in a community. They will often participate in the plaza in a targeted fashion, that is, having a specific purpose for the cash they derive from the sale of goods in the plaza. Those who operate on the regional-system level will generally seek to enlarge their capital through trading in the plaza. They will try to develop competitively strong positions and to maintain large inventories. They will be relatively free of the obligations of allocating their wealth to ceremonial or rent funds.

Research Directions: Is there a definition of success and failure at all levels of the marketing system? For the larger *regatones*, the idea of bankruptcy seems to have meaning. For smaller-scale plaza traders it would be interesting to ascertain whether there is a higher frequency of entering and leaving and re-entering the plaza due to needs for cash, temporary lack of funds, or withdrawal from marketing in favor of production specialties.

Markets, Capitalist Accumulation, and the Peasant Economy

One question which recurs throughout this monograph is that of the extent to which regional economic development in Mexico (and elsewhere in Latin America) converges with or diverges from the earlier development experiences of Western Europe and Anglo-America—and, therefore, the extent to which the study of the latter can provide insights for understanding the former. Such an approach justifiably arouses skepticism, if only for the obvious reason that Western European and Anglo-American development involved the nations of these areas in colonialist-imperialist relations with most of the rest of the world—relations which most of today's "developing" nations in Latin America can't replicate (cf. Mintz 1964b:1). Yet the question remains as to the existence of developmental parallels in specific areas or instances. For example, does the development of capitalism in the Valley of Oaxaca involve the isolation of one branch of industry after the other from agriculture for the introduction of capitalist production operations and the substitution of capitalist factory products for peasant-artisan products in local markets? How is this reflected in commodity and social relationships within the marketing system? To what degree is regional and local economic process determined by extraregional (national and international) forces?

Hypothesis: If the present trend toward high unemployment and underemployment in the urban-industrial sector of the Mexican economy continues, then, other things remaining equal, the depeasantization and proletarianization of the rural Valley of Oaxaca population will become less intense, but the volume of traders and commodities circulating through the marketing system will expand. The social reproductive capacities of corporate peasant communities will be taxed to their limits, and the peasant-artisan population —faced with diminished possibilities for migration—will turn increasingly to the marketing sector for remunerative employment.

Research Directions: Of importance here will be reliable statistical-survey data on labor migration, together with general socioeconomic and demographic data pertaining to the population of the Valley. It would also be helpful to arrive at reasonably accurate estimates of "carrying capacities" for different ecological zones and plaza districts in the Valley. Likewise of interest here will be marketplace inventories (products and personnel) and their tabulation and analysis in terms of various criteria (e.g., type of product, where produced, how sold; prices; role of seller, seller's place of residence, sex, work history). An evaluation should be made of the positive and negative functions of marketing roles to determine if they are parasitical, superfluous, or constructive with respect to regional socioeconomic development (cf. Mintz 1964*b*). Does the expansion of the marketing sector intensify or dampen the contradictions of capitalist development? How does the growth of activity in the internal marketing sector affect "national" as opposed to "local/regional" capitalist accumulation? Does the role of producer-sellers (*propios*) in marketing increase or decrease during periods of trade expansion? What is the impact of this on productivity in local peasant-artisan industries?

POLICY IMPLICATIONS?

A fundamental question here is this: If the integrity of this regional system depends on maintaining a certain subsistence level, would developmental policies that ignore the intricate adjustment between communities and social roles cost more in terms of dislocation and dissatisfaction than they are worth? Is there a set of policy recommendations that can operate through the channels created by the plaza network? Is this network—given its past and present social reproductive indispensability—obsolete because of its possible incompatibility with the needs of capitalist expansion or because local production cannot be increased at the present level of technology? Finally, does this system, as it is now structured and as it now functions, serve the greatest good for the greatest number of Oaxacans— or does it promote and reinforce socioeconomic inequalities and serve the interests of a minority at the expense of those of the majority?

At this juncture in our research, the data do not suggest definitive answers to these difficult questions. Indeed, the Oaxaca project was not designed to adequately answer such questions—though we are now convinced, in retrospect, that it should have been so designed. Only recently has anthropology recognized the connection between "research" and its multiplicity of potential implications for researchers and researched alike and begun to cast its own concerns accordingly, not shrinking from the implications—political, ideological, or other.

This volume represents a temporary and arbitrary stopping place in the process of studying a complex regional sociocultural formation. Its contents give a sample of the kinds of material already collected, which the editors have tried to relate to relevant work in Mesoamerican studies and economic anthropology. We have also tried to introduce a certain amount of internal criticism, based on hindsight, for the purpose of assisting us in the continuing enterprise of data collecting and analysis. This is, then, a collection of working papers, not only because of the necessary tentativeness and incompleteness of the analysis, but also because of the dynamism and vitality of the phenomena under study. Indeed, we will count ourselves successful if our preliminary sense-making efforts convey some of the creativity and liveliness of the people and the region we have devoted our time to researching.

Appendix

MAPS AND DEMOGRAPHIC TABLES

CECIL R. WELTE

The following demographic tables (Tables A-1 and A-2) are based on the system of *distritos* (districts) and *municipios* (municipalities) through which most of the governmental functions of the state of Oaxaca are administered. There are thirty districts, all of which are listed in Table A-1, and whose *cabeceras* (district towns or seats) are shown on Map A-1. Oaxaca is unique among the states of Mexico in retaining the district-level organization on an official basis. The district *cabeceras* are important centers of fiscal, judicial, and general administrative functions. Each *municipio* of the 570 in the state is assigned to a district for administrative purposes, but politically the municipal officials are directly responsible to the state governor. Districts as political entities were abolished in 1917. From then until 1970 they were referred to as *ex-distritos*, although they were in active use for administrative purposes, as they continue to be. Reinstatement of the term *distrito* was announced in August, 1970.

The *municipio* is a territorial unit and each has within its boundaries a *cabecera de municipio* (head town or village) and usually other villages, hamlets, and ranches. The *municipios* listed in Table A-2 are those that contain a town or village that has a plaza in one of the market systems covered by the market studies. *Municipios* take the names of their *cabeceras*. With three exceptions noted at the foot of the table, the markets are in the *cabeceras*; so the *municipio* names correspond to the names of the market towns or villages. The locations of the plazas are shown on Map A-1 with the exception of those of the Central Valleys system and the Sierra Zapotec system, which are shown on Map A-2. The *municipio* is the unit for the national census. The population counts shown in Table A-2 are for the totality of populated places within each *municipio*.

Map A-1 shows the entire state of Oaxaca and its position relative to the surrounding states and to Mexico City. The state is very mountainous, with the exceptions of the Pacific slopes, the Isthmus of Tehuantepec, and the lowlands to the north adjoining the state of Veracruz. Altitudes of the higher mountain peaks range from ten thousand to thirteen thousand feet. The floors of major valleys vary from about three thousand to seven thousand feet. The greatest concentration of high mountains is in the Mixteca Alta, in which lie the district towns of Coixtlahuaca, Nochixtlán, Teposcolula, and Tlaxiaco. This region is immediately to the west and northwest of the Central Valleys region, which is the most extensive valley area in the state. The rectangular outline in the center of Map A-1 frames the

Central Valleys region, which is shown at larger scale in Map A-2. The Pan American Highway (Carretera Interamericana) crosses both the state and the Central Valleys from northwest to southeast. The section of it from Mexico City to Tuxtla Gutiérrez, capital of Chiapas, is shown on Map A-1. Also shown is the Trans-Isthmus Highway (Carretera Transistmica), which runs from Salina Cruz through Tehuantepec and Juchitán to the Gulf ports of Minatitlán and Coatzacoalcos in the state of Veracruz.

Map A-2 shows the Central Valleys as bounded on the north by a portion of the Sierra Madre de Oaxaca mountain range and on the south by part of the Sierra Madre del Sur. The section of the Sierra Madre de Oaxaca in the vicinity of Ixtlán is known as the Sierra de Juárez. These mountains and those to the east, in the Villa Alta district, are inhabited by the mountain Zapotecs, so the entire area may be referred to as the Sierra Zapotec area. The towns and villages of the Sierra Zapotec market system are shown on the map as an adjunct to the depiction of the Central Valleys region. The watersheds or divides encompassing the Central Valleys are shown at the mountain ridges to the north and south, at the divide to the west where the Mixteca Alta begins, and at the divides to the east that flank the exit of the Río Grande where it flows through a gorge to become the Río Tehuantepec. Representative altitudes are as follows: Oaxaca City, 5,100 feet; Ocotlan, 4,850 feet; Ejutla, 4,750 feet; Miahuatlan, 5,300 feet. There are peaks in the northern divide with altitudes of up to 11,200 feet, and those in the Sierra Madre del Sur rise to 13,200 feet. The ridge of the Mixteca Alta to the west is at about 9,000 feet, while the ridges to the east are at about 7,000 to 8,000 feet.

Of primary importance among the Central Valleys is the Valley of Oaxaca. This is the traditional name for the upper drainage basin of the Río Atoyac, which terminates at a gorge twelve kilometers south of Ayoquezco. The shape of the valley is shown on Map A-2 as outlined by its watershed. The alluvial plain of the valley floor has an area of about 700 square kilometers, but the area of the basin as a whole is about 3,600 square kilometers. It is the most densely populated of the Central Valleys, and its high density does not depend entirely on the presence of Oaxaca City. Here are the population counts and densities per square kilometer of the basin over the past thirty years:

	Total for Valley of Oaxaca	Oaxaca City	Valley less City	Density for Valley	Density, Valley less City
1940	184,900	29,300	155,600	51.4	43.2
1950	223,400	46,600	176,800	62.0	49.1
1960	279,500	72,400	207,100	77.6	57.5
1970	348,800	99,500	249,300	97.0	69.2

Population densities for the districts are given in Table A-1. It will be noted that the densities in the districts outside the Central Valleys are substantially lower than the density of the Valley of Oaxaca as shown above. The grouping of districts in the table conforms only approximately to market areas, but it serves to give the general picture of growth or decline in the vicinity of the various market systems. There is no official division of the state into regions. None of the various regional divisions currently in use is satisfactory for other than limited purposes. The "traditional," "geo-economic," and "sociocultural" regional schemes all take into account the major geographical features of the state: the isthmus, the coast, the Mixtec mountains, the northern mountains, and the central valleys; but the ways in which these are delimited and subdivided varies with the purpose of the scheme.

When using Tables A-1 and A-2 (or the publications of the Mexican national censuses on which they are based) certain peculiarities of the administrative divisions of the state should be kept in mind. The first of these is that the districts and *municipios* are subject to change. *Municipios* are sometimes changed from one district to another, and villages may be shifted between *municipios*. New *municipios* have been created, and old ones have been suppressed. Such changes are infrequent and, in the case of districts, have little impact on the over-all population figures, but the abrupt changes in a few of the population counts for *municipios* in Table A-2 can be attributed to the removal or addition of a village. The second peculiarity is that the districts take the names of their *cabeceras* in all cases but two. These are the districts of Mixe, whose *cabecera* is Zacatepec, and Centro, whose *cabecera* is Oaxaca City. Since *municipios* also take the names of their *cabeceras*, and the *cabeceras* of districts are also *cabeceras* of *municipios*, confusion sometimes arises as to what it is that a name refers to. For example, "Zaachila" may refer to a district, a *municipio*, or a town, and the town of Zaachila is both the *cabecera* of a district and the *cabecera* of a *municipio*. As a further complication, some *municipios* are larger than the smaller districts. The *municipio* of Nochixtlán has an area of 820 square kilometers, while the district of Zaachila has an area of only 504. At the other extreme there are *municipios* as small as 8 square kilometers. The third peculiarity is that population counts for *municipios* and their *cabeceras* are sometimes identical, but more often are not. In 156 of the *municipios* of the state there are no populated places other than the *cabecera*. In these cases confusion between a *municipio* and its *cabecera* causes no misinterpretation of census figures, but for the remaining 414 *municipios* such confusion can cause serious errors.

Table A-1
STATE OF OAXACA: POPULATION BY DISTRICTS

	1940	1950	1960	1970	Area Km²	Density (1970)
Districts of the Central Valleys						
Centro	57,633	78,732	112,455	158,497	643	246.5
Ejutla	25,206	27,229	32,594	35,984	1,146	31.4
Etla	41,291	48,930	56,414	61,761	1,750	35.3
Miahuatlán	51,017	57,244	71,072	71,947	3,752	19.2
Ocotlán	35,182	37,821	41,873	46,295	1,008	45.9
Sola de Vega	27,204	33,350	38,825	41,311	3,719	11.1
Tlacolula	45,980	51,050	62,373	73,638	2,922	25.2
Zaachila	12,878	13,946	17,047	19,574	504	38.8
Zimatlán	23,877	31,251	36,768	40,553	790	51.4
Districts of the Sierra Zapotec and Mixe						
Ixtlán	32,353	33,786	39,704	39,503	2,922	13.5
Villa Alta	31,697	32,804	34,867	34,002	1,498	22.7
Mixe	33,842	38,172	49,260	60,156	4,929	12.2
Districts of the Isthmus						
Juchitán	88,729	114,458	146,631	186,311	13,300	14.0
Tehuantepec	40,182	56,240	77,112	101,451	6,675	15.2
Yautepec	16,964	20,854	24,758	28,092	4,772	5.9
Districts of the Coast						
Jamiltepec	53,383	65,954	81,371	103,471	4,237	24.4
Juquila	28,463	33,476	42,178	55,528	4,236	13.1
Pochutla	37,718	46,185	60,802	77,642	4,029	19.3
Putla	34,906	41,351	47,414	54,321	3,250	16.7
Districts of the Mixteca Alta						
Coixtlahuaca	19,661	18,090	17,722	15,853	1,835	8.6
Nochixtlán	51,549	54,037	61,340	57,960	3,183	18.2
Teposcolula	35,549	41,715	38,095	32,405	1,534	21.1
Tlaxiaco	64,142	75,869	80,756	85,493	2,689	31.8
Districts of the Mixteca Baja						
Huajuapan	56,895	67,027	81,584	85,939	3,167	27.1
Juxtlahuaca	30,948	32,258	36,417	45,162	1,707	26.5
Silacayoapan	31,004	33,620	41,246	36,720	2,219	16.6
Northern districts						
Choapan	11,645	14,647	20,318	27,735	3,167	8.8
Cuicatlán	33,978	40,664	44,534	45,011	2,272	19.8
Teotitlán	63,116	80,399	95,786	103,289	2,000	51.6
Tuxtepec	75,772	100,154	135,950	189,820	5,512	34.4
State totals	1,192,794	1,421,313	1,727,266	2,015,424	95,364	21.1

Table A-2

MUNICIPIOS WITHIN WHICH PLAZAS OF THE
MARKET STUDIES ARE LOCATED

	Population				Area	Density
	1940	1950	1960	1970	Km²	(1970)
Municipio containing the Oaxaca City plaza						
Oaxaca de Juárez	31,839	49,953	78,639	116,388	85	1,361.6
Municipios containing central town plazas of the Valley system						
Ayoquezco	2,704	3,019	3,529	4,349	59	74.1
Ejutla	8,252	12,041	13,861	15,822	283	55.9
Etla	1,693	2,446	2,864	3,438	18	192.5
Miahuatlán	8,367	11,943	16,857	16,606	327	50.8
Ocotlán	6,128	7,845	8,040	9,613	124	77.7
Tlacolula	6,483	7,084	9,041	10,554	245	43.1
Zaachila	5,012	5,734	7,039	8,332	55	151.9
Zimatlán	5,335	8,688	10,788	11,276	255	44.2
Municipios containing village plazas of the Valley system						
Atzompa	1,908	1,839	2,428	3,073	23	133.8
Mitla	4,799	4,149	5,122	6,296	83	75.9
San Antonino	3,074	3,611	3,682	3,314	33	99.9
San Lorenzo Cacaotepec	2,305	2,942	3,556	4,322	13	338.7
San Pablo Huixtepec	3,659	4,612	5,132	5,927	18	331.9
San Pedro Apóstol	3,269	2,555	2,679	2,434	23	106.0
Santa Cruz Mixtepec	1,885	1,771	2,218	2,642	66	39.8
Teotitlán del Valle	2,596	2,831	3,231	3,894	82	47.7
Tlacochahuaya	2,454	2,853	3,404	3,654	47	77.4
Totolapan	1,109	1,202	1,887	2,499	392	6.4
Municipios containing Sierra Zapotec plazas						
Capulalpan	1,131	1,186	1,401	1,269	19	66.3
Ixtlán	3,890	4,237	4,348	4,889	549	8.9
Lachirioag	1,761	1,675	1,748	1,679	24	69.3
Lalopa	1,011	1,240	863	676	112	6.0
Natividad	805	896	1,079	1,165	28	41.5
San Juan Yaeé	1,719	1,696	1,650	1,549	93	16.6
San Pedro Cajonos	1,549	1,721	1,287	1,276	77	16.7
Talea	2,383	2,554	2,946	2,654	55	48.4
Villa Alta	1,801	2,383	2,525	2,799	137	20.5
Yalalag	3,020	3,000	3,117	2,848	36	79.7
Yavesía	686	777	1,680	927	38	24.2
Zoogocho	1,004	1,052	1,083	965	23	42.0

	Population				Area	Density
	1940	1950	1960	1970	Km²	(1970)
Municipios containing Sierra Mixe plazas						
Atitlán	1,182	1,712	1,595	1,795	83	21.6
Ayutla	2,516	3,293	3,865	4,636	108	42.8
Cacalotepec	2,059	2,401	2,243	2,344	108	21.6
Juquila Mixes	2,734	2,889	3,040	2,828	227	12.5
Mixistlán	1,543	1,634	1,815	1,766	191	9.2
Quetzaltepec	2,087	2,123	2,436	2,900	199	14.6
Tlahuitoltepec	3,382	3,993	3,715	5,263	75	69.9
Totontepec	3,846	4,387	4,527	4,377	319	13.7
Zacatepec	2,338	3,757	3,815	3,707	143	25.9
Municipios containing Isthmian plazas						
Guichicovi[a]	9,620	11,693	14,433	16,960	564	30.1
Ixtepec	7,069	11,684	12,908	14,469	230	63.0
Jalapa del Marqués	1,587	3,234	5,063	5,946	563	10.6
Juchitán	15,089	16,811	23,870	37,686	415	90.9
Matías Romero	7,023	10,967	15,849	24,671	1,460	16.9
Salina Cruz	5,201	8,974	15,514	23,970	114	211.1
San Mateo del Mar	2,862	3,611	4,771	5,991	75	79.6
Tehuantepec	7,969	12,207	16,682	22,833	966	23.6
Municipios containing major Coastal plazas						
Candelaria Loxicha	3,467	4,330	5,818	5,733	87	66.1
Jamiltepec	4,056	4,819	6,782	10,984	623	17.6
Juquila	4,422	4,726	6,191	6,753	811	8.3
Pinotepa Nacional	10,020	11,903	18,221	22,141	720	30.8
Pochutla	6,334	8,763	10,474	13,599	421	32.3
Putla	9,059	14,145	15,407	16,975	884	19.2
San Pedro Mixtepec[b]	1,731	2,577	4,117	9,423	332	28.4
Tututepec[c]	5,296	8,255	11,239	18,454	1,249	14.8
Municipios containing plazas of the Nochixtlán Cycle						
Coixtlahuaca	6,336	5,314	4,938	4,824	279	17.3
Jaltepec	3,318	3,538	4,219	4,036	185	21.8
Nochixtlán	6,079	7,934	7,406	7,514	820	9.2
Tamazulapan	3,590	4,107	4,308	3,752	102	36.8
Teposcolula	3,812	4,514	4,489	3,558	162	22.0
Yanhuitlán	1,954	2,055	2,136	1,894	23	82.5
Totals	271,212	342,015	449,610	568,911	15,960	35.6

[a] The plaza for this *municipio* is in Mogoñé.
[b] The plaza is in Puerto Escondido.
[c] The plaza is in the village of Río Grande.

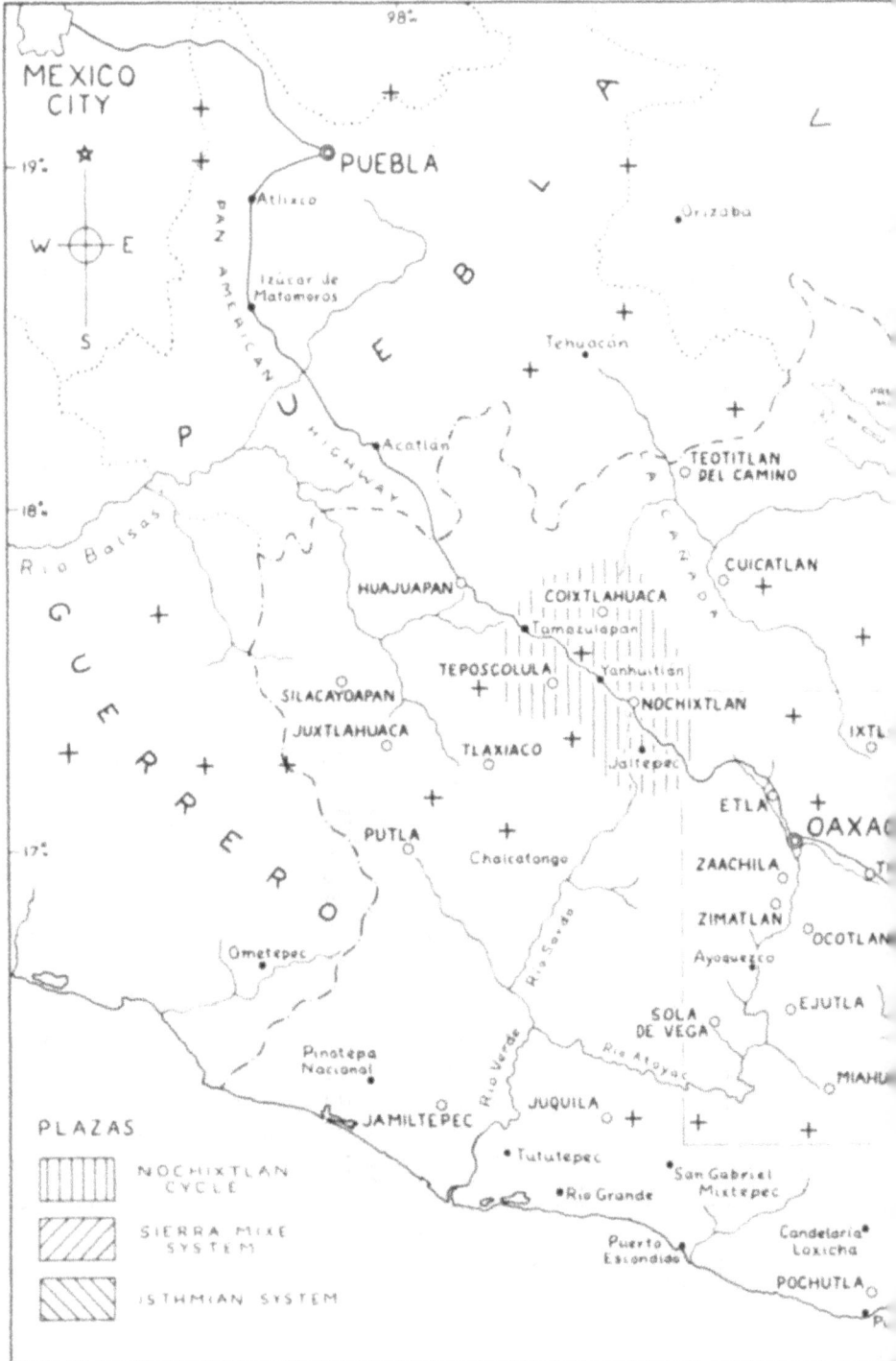

Map A-1

PLAZAS

NOCHIXTLAN CYCLE

SIERRA MIXE SYSTEM

ISTHMIAN SYSTEM

State of Oaxaca and Surroundings

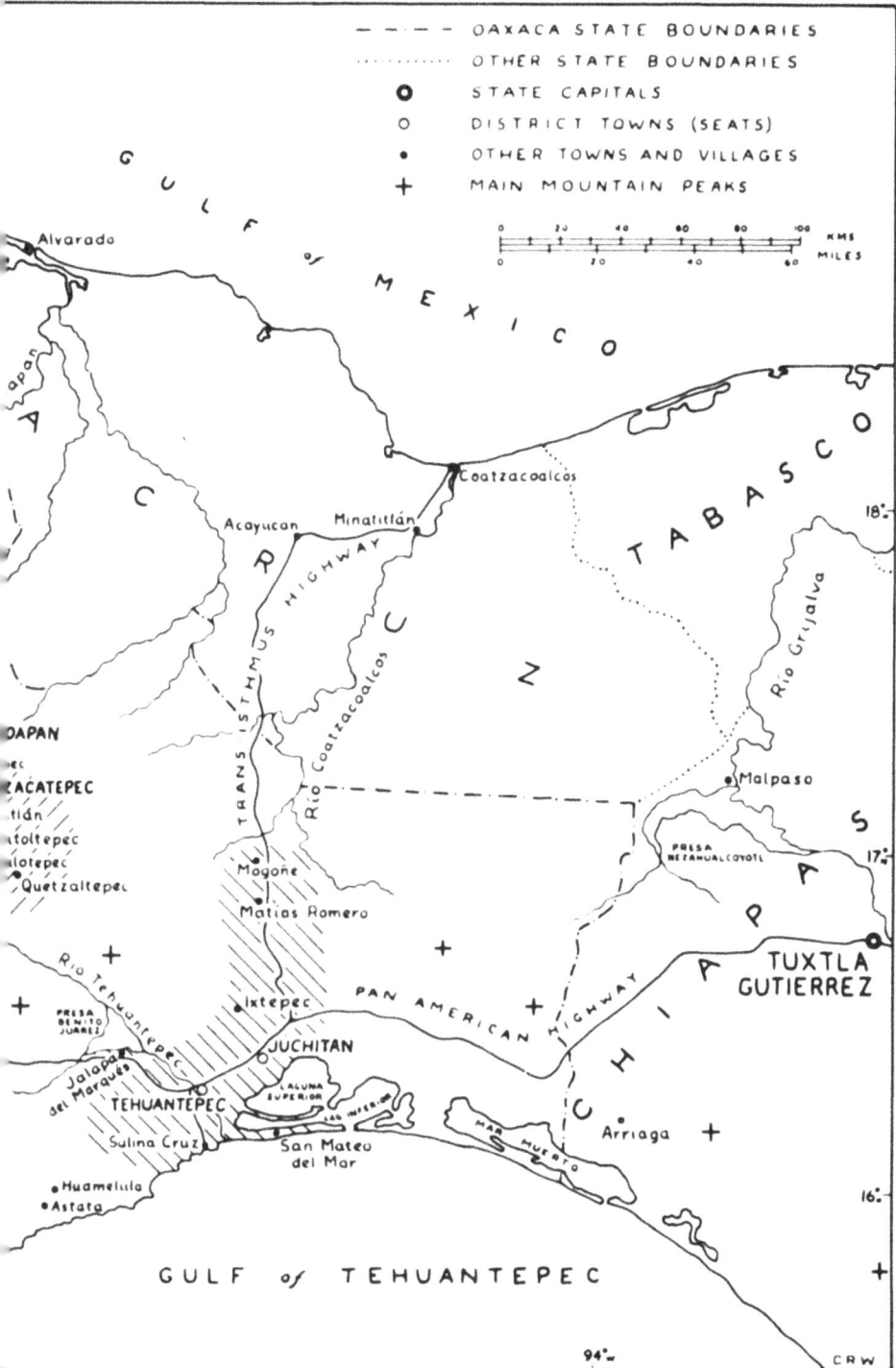

Map A-2 The Central Valleys of Oaxaca

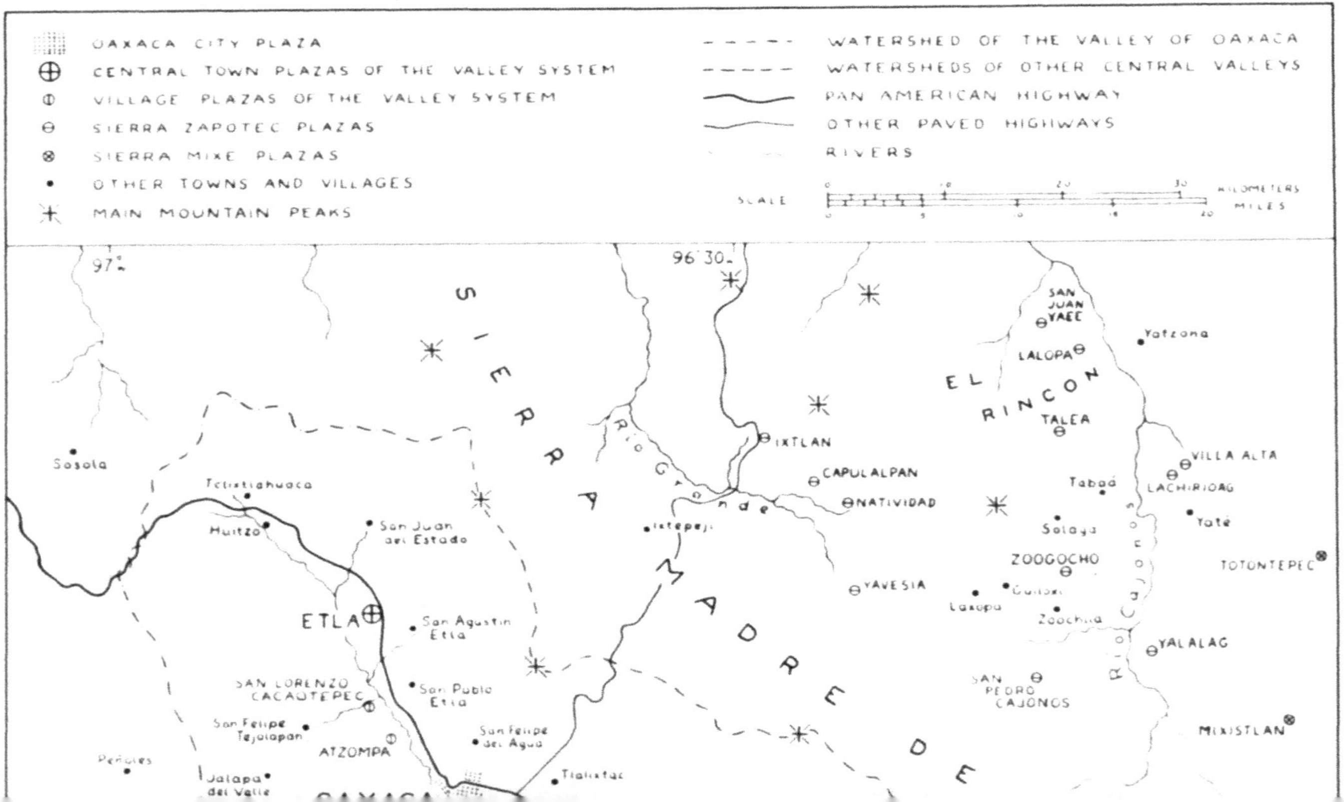

Legend:

- OAXACA CITY PLAZA
- CENTRAL TOWN PLAZAS OF THE VALLEY SYSTEM
- VILLAGE PLAZAS OF THE VALLEY SYSTEM
- SIERRA ZAPOTEC PLAZAS
- SIERRA MIXE PLAZAS
- OTHER TOWNS AND VILLAGES
- MAIN MOUNTAIN PEAKS

- — — — WATERSHED OF THE VALLEY OF OAXACA
- — — — WATERSHEDS OF OTHER CENTRAL VALLEYS
- PAN AMERICAN HIGHWAY
- OTHER PAVED HIGHWAYS
- RIVERS

SCALE

KILOMETERS
MILES

Sosola

97°

Teitipac

Huixco

San Felipe
Tejalapan

Jalapa
del Valle

Peñoles

ETLA

SAN LORENZO
CACAOTEPEC

ATZOMPA

OAXACA

San Juan
del Estado

San Agustín
Etla

San Pablo
Etla

San Felipe
del Agua

Tlalixtac

SIERRA

MADRE   DE

96 30'

Río Grande

IXTLAN

CAPULALPAN

NATIVIDAD

YAVESIA

EL   RINCON

SAN
JUAN
YAEE

LALOPA

TALEA

Tabaa

Solaga

ZOOGOCHO

Lachiroag

VILLA ALTA

Yatee

Yatzona

Yalalag

San Pedro
Cajonos

Lachiroag

Zoochina

TOTONTEPEC

MIXISTLAN

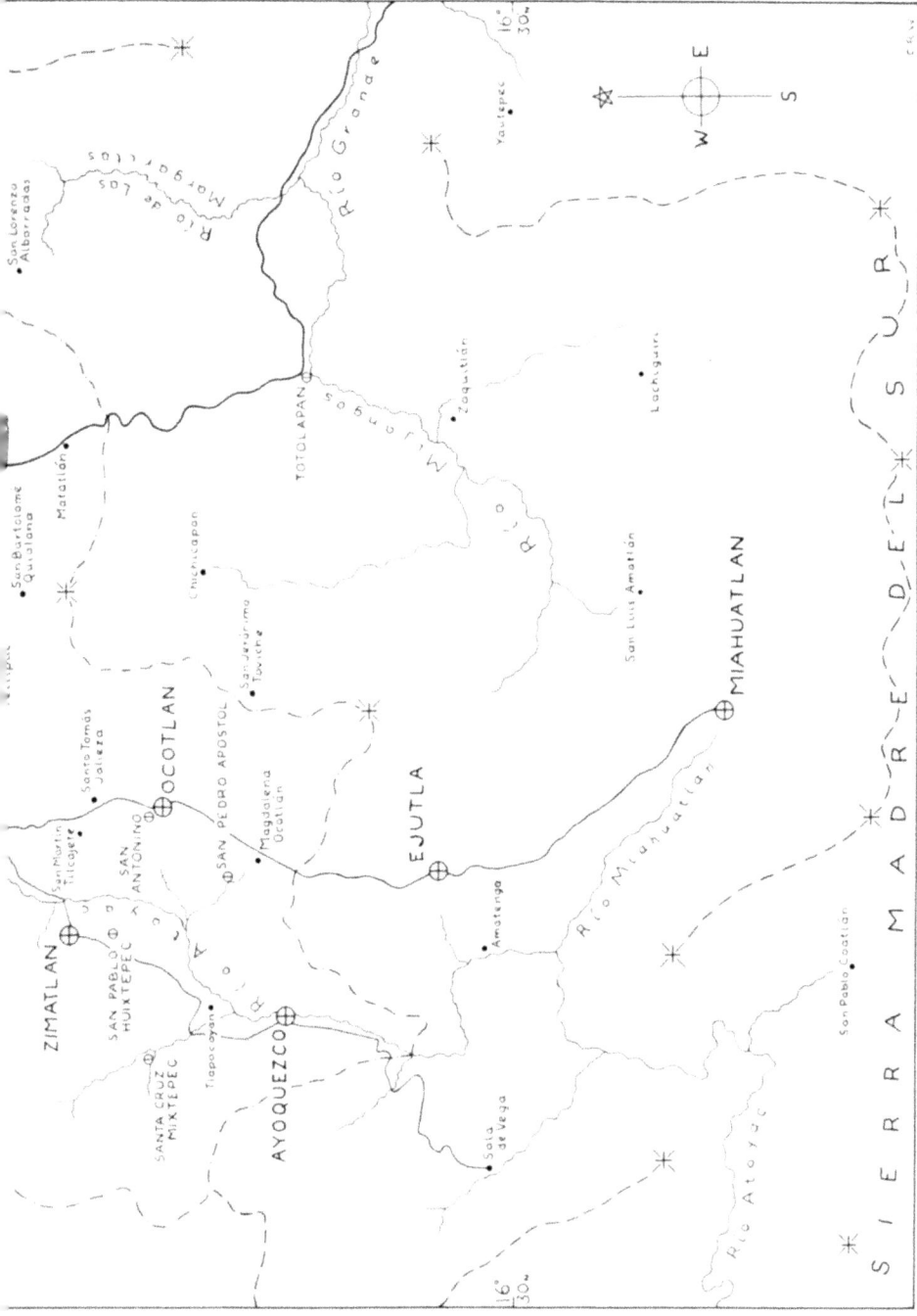

GLOSSARY

alcalde mayor: a civil administrator of Indian areas (*provincias*) through the end of the eighteenth century (1786). *Alcaldes mayores* were notorious for their abuse of the indigenous population and for their efforts at self-enrichment at the expense of the crown.

alfarero: potter.

ambulante: hawker who carries his stock in the marketplace.

atolera: seller of *atole* (maize gruel).

barbacoa: barbecued meat (either beef, pork, lamb, or goat).

barreta: crowbar, used for agriculture as well as for the roughing out of metates.

barrio: named subdivision of a community.

bodega: storage place for a merchant's inventory of goods.

bulto: bundle.

cabecera: head community of an administrative land division, such as a *municipio* or *distrito*.

campesino: peasant; generally used to refer to someone engaged in agriculture.

casatienda: small store, run out of a house.

caseta: permanent market stall.

casetero: seller who operates out of a *caseta*.

casta: general term for a variety of sociophysical types in the colonial period. These people were considered as intermediate between Spaniards and Indians.

comadre: "comother," the relationship between two women created through the *compadrazgo*. It has the social force of solidifying a friendship and sometimes facilitating business dealings.

comedor caseta: food stall.

comerciante: businessperson; often implies one who operates on larger scale than the person who brings an occasional small quantity of goods to the marketplace.

compadrazgo: the institution of ritual coparenthood. Usually, two adults solemnize a relationship that implies responsibilities to children (at whose baptism, birth, or marriage the ceremony usually takes place), mutual support, and respect.

comprador: buyer; usually in another part of the valley.

costeño: native of the coastal zone.

distrito: an administrative territorial division that includes several *municipios*; called *ex-distrito* from 1917 to 1970.

dominical: process of domination whose major outlines were developed during the colonial period.

ejidatario: a member of an *ejido*.

ejido: a form of government-regulated collective and individual land use established after the Mexican Revolution.

encargo: special orders placed with itinerant peddlers or artisans; neighbors shopping for each other in the weekly market.

encomienda: the colonial institution of labor exploitation in which a Spaniard was granted the use of the labor of a number of Indians as well as the obligation for their Christianization and education. The abuses of this institution provided a significant tension between the Spanish crown and Spanish settlers in Mexico.

ex-distrito: the term in use during the period 1917–1970 for the *distrito*.

fandango: wedding celebration.

guelaguetza: the custom, in the Valley of Oaxaca and other parts of the Zapotec zone, of exchanging goods, in the arrangements of weddings and saints' celebrations (*mayordomías*); also, the reciprocal exchange of labor for harvests and other large tasks.

hortelano: one of the various terms used to denote a person whose occupation is agricultural.

huehuete: a ritual spokesman whose services are used on various occasions, such as weddings and *contentadas* (peacemaking rituals preparatory to weddings, particularly where there has been bride capture).

ixtle: the fiber of the maguey plant, used for rope and netting, among other purposes.

jornalero: day laborer.

labrador: worker; finisher of metate products.

mayordomía: the celebration of a local saint. Generally the *mayordomo*, a man picked to organize and finance the celebration, undergoes considerable expense, part of which he raises through the *guelaguetza*.

mayorista: wholesaler.

mercado: the municipal, daily marketplace; usually a large one, such as that in Oaxaca City.

metatero: maker of metates (grinding stones for maize and other grains).

milpa: plantings of maize.

molino de nixtamal: the mill in which maize is ground into *maza*, a dough from which tortillas are made. It is prepared by being soaked overnight in lime and in that state is called *nixtamal*.

municipio: the most significant unit of local administration, consisting usually of a *cabecera* (head community) and several smaller communities.

nanche: a fruit native to tropical regions of Mexico.

nevero: one who makes and sells ice cream (*nieve*).

nopaleras: stands or plantings of the nopal cactus.

palma: palm.

panela: brown sugar.

petate: woven straw mat, for sleeping or displaying merchandise in the marketplace, as well as many other uses.

propietario: a small landowner.

propio: a seller who is also the producer of the goods sold.

propio solar: metate propio's house lot.

puesto: market stall.

puestero: person who sells from a stall in the marketplace, distinguished from *ambulantes*.

recaudero: collector of fees for marketplace space.

reducciones: the Spanish policy of relocation of the indigenous populations.

regatón, regatona: seller of goods that are bought from someone else, often a *propio*.

repartimiento: a colonial institution whereby Spaniards were given the right to levy the labor of Indians for public and private projects. This was abused and finally terminated.

requa: string of cargo animals.

rumbo: zone or area.

salineros: salt workers.

solar: house plot.

tasajo: slightly salted beef strips, popular in the Valley of Oaxaca.

temporal: farmland that depends on rainfall exclusively; not watered either by irrigation or by a high water table.

tenate: a soft woven basket of palm.

tianguis: the Nahuatl term for *cyclical marketplace*. Used mainly by the newspapers and various people and agencies outside the Valley of Oaxaca.

tienda: store.

tienda de rayas: the company store of the Mexican hacienda. All goods were purchased through this store by the working force, and all accounts were kept by the manager. Hence, the workers were in perpetual debt.

tierra caliente: the hot country, usually tropical coastal lowlands.

tortillera: a woman who makes and sells tortillas.

trapiche: sugar press. These are sometimes small, unmechanized operations.

viaje: a trip, made regularly by a merchant.

viajera: common term for a woman merchant in the Isthmus of Tehuantepec.

vías de penetración: roads.

NOTES

FOREWORD

1. While there are many examples of this, a particularly revealing case is Gillin 1947. The community of Moche is revealed for what it really is by the aerial photographs Gillin provides: a rural proletarian village surrounded by sugar-cane plantations. Yet these important facts are not explicitly adduced anywhere in the monograph itself, which—in my opinion —conveys a somewhat spurious, local, and bounded quality to the community, imparted by the way that the data are organized and used.

2. This foreword was written while the writer was a member of the Institute for Advanced Study; he is indebted to the Institute for the opportunity to write and to study while in residence there.

PREFACE

1. The symposium, "Market Systems and Economics of the Oaxaca Region," was sponsored by the Southwestern Anthropological Association. It was held in Tucson, Arizona, on April 30, 1971, at the joint annual meeting of the American Ethnological Society and the Southwestern Anthropological Association.

ESSAY 1. THE PEASANT MARKET ECONOMY OF THE VALLEY OF OAXACA IN ANALYSIS AND HISTORY

1. Translations are ours unless otherwise indicated.

2. The name of the state is also that of its capital, Oaxaca de Juárez, a city founded in 1486 as an Aztec garrison. The name derives from the Aztec word *Huaxyacac*, which means "the place of the *guajal*, or *huajal*"— referring to the abundance throughout the region of the Central Valleys of the *guaje*, or *huaje*, tree; the latter yields edible beans that are still harvested and is classified botanically as *Leucaena esculenta* (UNDP/ FAO 1972:4).

3. The remaining six regions are as follows: El Istmo, La Cañada, La Costa, La Mixteca, La Sierra de Juárez, and Tuxtepec. This sevenfold division reflects in part the characteristics of the different regions from the

"geoeconomic" point of view (UNDP/FAO 1972:5). A recent UNDP/ FAO study—following a precedent set by the Bank of Mexico—includes the following "districts" within the Central Valleys (designated "Centro") : Centro (Oaxaca City and the surrounding area—about 643 square kilometers, or twenty-five kilometers north-south by twenty-five kilometers east-west, extending to Tule to the east and to Coyotepec to the south), Ejutla, Etla, Ocotlán, Sola de Vega, Tlacolula, Zaachila, and Zimatlán (1972: 94). In aggregate these districts encompass a total of 470 separate localities (15.5% of the state total) with a total area of 12,480.47 km² (13.1% of state total) and a population of 477,613 (1970 census). See Appendix, Tables 1 and 2, for further demographic and cartographic information on this and other Oaxaca regions.

4. All 1960 census figures were computed from Welte (1966). Mr. Welte also kindly provided 1970 census figures. Consult the Appendix by Mr. Welte for further census tabulations and other related information.

5. This index of socioeconomic development, which compares the levels of development for each of the Mexican states in 1950 and 1960, shows that while there was a substantial improvement in the nation's living standards during this decade, the disparities between the prosperous areas and the depressed areas grew. The index is interpreted and discussed in *Mexico: The New Government's Economic Policy* (Banco Nacional de Comercio Exterior 1971:51–63, 218–221). According to this source: "The index of socio-economic development is determined using the factorial method of analysis, considering the following variables: a) gross domestic product per inhabitant; b) literate population; c) consumption of sugar per inhabitant; d) infant mortality; e) houses with piped water; f) the population using shoes; g) use of electricity per inhabitant; h) the use of gasoline per inhabitant; i) area under irrigation; j) percentage of industrial activity within the gross product of the entity; k) non-agricultural population; and l) index of agricultural capitalization."

ESSAY 2. THE OAXACA MARKET STUDY PROJECT: ORIGINS SCOPE, AND PRELIMINARY FINDINGS

1. These categories, together with Cecil Welte's demographic résumés (Appendix, Table 2), suggest the possibility for a more precise locational analysis, such as was done by Carol Smith for western Guatemala (Smith 1972*a*; 1972*b*; 1973). Our typology (elaborated more fully by Martin Diskin in Essay 3) lays the functional basis for a more accurate delineation of subsystem boundaries.—Eds.

ESSAY 3. THE STRUCTURE OF A PEASANT MARKET SYSTEM IN OAXACA

1. Coe (1961:67) argues that this kind of environmental differentiation,

coupled with adequate transportation possibilities, is consistent with and supportive of organic civilizations.

2. Oaxaca City as a locus of market activity will not be included in this study. A separate study of city merchants was done by Ronald Waterbury and F. Jiménez Caballero as part of the project. What is treated here as the system consists of the eight towns in which the plazas are held and the territory directly served by them. There are several other plaza systems that relate to the Valley of Oaxaca. The Sierra de Juárez, including Zapotec-speaking communities, is one. Another is in Mixe region and yet another in the Mixteca Alta. The Sierra de Juárez system has been studied by Richard and Myrna Berg.

3. Mintz puts it in a slightly different way: "Queries concerning the relationships between goods and goods, and between goods and money, lead inevitably to further queries—this time about the relationships between goods and people, and between people and people. That is, within the marketplace human beings are dealing with each other through the instrumentality of things—agricultural products, handicrafts, food and drink, the measures of quality and quantity employed in establishing equivalences, etc.,—and a map of the people as sociological "persons" is essential to an understanding of the market system as such" (Mintz 1964b:4). This point of view results in a very thorough and complex picture of a market system. It differs from my approach in two respects: (a) it describes a *market system*, rather than a region whose major expression is a market system, and (b) it is not clear how it might be rendered operational in the field, and quantified.

4. Sr. Marcos González, my friend and assistant, also helped me in a sample survey of Tlacolula.

5. I was able to extend my knowledge of the area through the kind cooperation of Professors Siegel and Hotchkiss of the Stanford University Summer Field Program in Anthropology. Their receptivity to suggestions about the setup of the program and the chance to speak at length to the students who were working in villages were most valuable.

6. These levels are not unlike Steward's levels of sociocultural integration (Steward 1963:Chap. 3). One difference is that embodied in the levels as I describe them is the impact of national institutions, where applicable. Steward seems to feel that such institutions are not properly studied by ethnographic methods. Also, these levels are not meant to describe widely occurring "sociocultural segments," such as occupational groupings, but are seen to be valid for one region only.

7. This is true of Tlacolula but has not been verified for every town in the system. Tlacolula may be more differentiated than other towns because of its nearness to the Pan American Highway.

8. It is not clear to what extent wage earners participate in this secular, rational ideology.

9. I wish to thank Dr. Gerald M. Platt and Mr. William Ingham for their help in the preparation of these data.

10. This information is summarized by Nash (1966:64–70) and Belshaw (1965:54–62).

11. Very suggestive here is the relation between the sectional market and the closed community; likewise, the network market and the open community.

12. There is evidence suggesting the pre-Columbian existence of plazas in this region. The Spanish crown found it useful to use these plazas as collection points for the profitable colonial trade, especially in cochineal. In fact, the plaza appears to be a useful indicator of the institutional response to colonial rule (Diskin 1967: Chap 2).

ESSAY 4. MARKETS AS MIRRORS: REFLECTORS OF THE ECONOMIC ACTIVITY AND THE REGIONAL CULTURE OF COASTAL OAXACA

NOTE: A draft of this essay, entitled "Notes for a Cultural Geography of Coastal Markets, Oaxaca, Mexico," was predistributed to symposium participants. An oral synopsis was given at the Southwestern Anthropological Association symposium, "Market Systems and Economics of the Oaxaca Region," in Tucson, Arizona, April 30, 1971. I wish to thank my colleagues J. Campbell, B. Golomb, J. J. Parsons, C. L. Salter, W. L. Thomas, and R. C. West for reading the original manuscript and making suggestions for improvement; imperfections remaining in the paper are the responsibility of the author.

1. For noteworthy studies of folk economics and regional marketing systems, see Foster (1948b), Malinowski and de la Fuente (1957), Skinner (1964), Beals (1967b), and Diskin (1969; 1971).

2. Cultural geographers who have turned their attention to the phenomena of markets and their economic regions are McBryde (1947), West (1948), Mikesell (1958), Hodder (1965), and Symanski and Webber (1974), among others.

3. Supported by funds from ONR Contract Nonr-3656 (03) Project NR 388 067, Department of Geography, University of California, Berkeley, J. J. Parsons, Principal Investigator.

4. Supported by the Foreign Field Research Program, NAS-NRC, sponsored by ONR Contract N0014-67-A-0244-0001.

5. One academic-quarter sabbatical and a travel grant from the Center for Latin American Studies, University of California, Berkeley, allowed me to return to the field for December, 1968, and January–February, 1969.

6. For an excellent and rarely cited article on the cultivated and collected plants of southern Mexico that appear in the marketplaces, see Whitaker and Cutler (1966).

ESSAY 5. THE ZOOGOCHO PLAZA SYSTEM IN THE SIERRA ZAPOTECA OF VILLA ALTA

1. Villages that participate in the five plaza-areas are listed by number in Table 5-2. The Camotlán–Villa Alta area includes villages 17, 21, 24, 27, 28, 33, 34, 37, 38, 42, 43, 46, 48, and 51 (a two-plaza area); the Yaté–Yalalag area includes villages 16, 22, 40, 41, and 45 (a one-plaza area); the Cajonos area includes villages 29, 30, 31, 32, 39, and 50 (a one-plaza area); the Rinconado area includes villages 18, 19, 20, 23, 25, 26, 35, 36, 44, 47, and 49 (a three-plaza area); and the Zoogocho *rumbo* includes villages 1–15 (a one-plaza area).

2. The sum of the total number of percentages is greater than 100% because several of the same type of products move through more than one marketing channel. Each marketing channel represented in rows 1–13 must be treated as a separate entity.

ESSAY 6. SURVEY OF THE MARKET SYSTEM IN THE NOCHIXTLÁN VALLEY AND THE MIXTECA ALTA

NOTE: The material presented in this essay is based on data gathered by the author from May 1 to October 20, 1970, as one of several related investigations for a project entitled "The Mixtec Community and Intercommunity Relations in the Valley of Nochixtlán, 1000 B.C.–A.D. 1970," directed by Dr. Ronald Spores of Vanderbilt University and funded by the National Science Foundation.

1. In this study, I have been concerned with the region's specialization and market networks as instruments of production and distribution of goods and services, and my objective is a structural and functional analysis of these networks. Further, primarily because of the lack of literature on the area, attention has also been devoted toward providing an ample descriptive analysis of the results of the investigation.

2. Yolomécatl is chosen by some Tlaxiaco and Teposcolula cyclical market vendors as the Sunday market of their circuit.

ESSAY 7. THE "MARKET" AS LOCATION AND TRANSACTION: DIMENSIONS OF MARKETING IN A ZAPOTEC STONEWORKING INDUSTRY

1. This informant is describing price patterns in the metate market which are widely understood among the *metateros*. My market data verify their understanding to be correct. (See Cook 1970:784.)

ESSAY 8. ZAPOTEC *VIAJERAS*

NOTE: This essay, excluding the introductory section, was presented in the symposium "Market Systems and Economics of the Oaxaca Region," at the joint annual meeting of the American Ethnological Society and the Southwestern Anthropological Association, Tucson, Arizona, April 30, 1971. Field work was carried out during a period of fifteen months, beginning in August, 1966, and was supported by National Sciences Foundation Research Grant GS-1064.

1. Webster's Seventh New Collegiate Dictionary defines *itinerant* as "one who travels from place to place" or "one who covers a circuit," both of which seem to imply more continuous travel over a wider geographical area than the travel of the *viajeras* described herein.

2. My research problem centered around household economics and the relationship of women's market activities to family structure and interaction and to the wider community.

3. A *cama de pencas* is a bed or table made of the stems of palm fronds placed close together across a support of two or three sawhorses.

4. *Urbano* is the local term for the third-class local buses, also called *camiones*.

5. The efficacy of vitamins as preventive medicine and even the idea of preventive medicine itself are not commonly held beliefs among the Isthmus Zapotecs. Vitamins are sometimes prescribed by medical doctors for pregnant women but are seldom taken, because folk belief has it that they increase the size of the fetus and make for difficult births. I have never encountered A's remedy for *catarro* or *gripa* elsewhere in the Isthmus. She may have invented it on the spot.

6. "Cemetery trade" refers to a local custom of taking flowers to the cemeteries Sundays and Thursdays to decorate the graves of deceased relatives. This is always "women's work."

ESSAY 9. EXAMPLES OF STABILITY AND CHANGE FROM SANTA MARÍA ATZOMPA

1. Shepard states that diorite tempering material similar to that found in Monte Albán I and II pottery is used in present-day Atzompa (1967:479) and that diorite temper is highly associated with a buff-firing clay at Monte Albán. Present-day Atzompa uses a buff-firing clay mined near San Lorenzo Cacaotepec. A low association of the diorite temper with *café* or red-firing clay in the Monte Albán sherds is congruent with Atzompa's use of a dark red-firing clay, principally for ollas and jars that are not given exterior glaze, mined at San Felipe Tejalapan farther to the west. Whether these same mines were worked in ancient times is a moot ques-

tion. The San Felipe mines are deeply worked, giving evidence of long use.

2. George Foster suggests that studies of energy input requirements for kick-wheel operation might shed some light on the resistance of women potters to the wheel (1959:117).

3. Atzompa dealers selling in Tlacolula and Ocotlán reported profits of 33%, whereas those selling in Oaxaca City reported 20 to 25% above purchase prices for the pots which they buy for resale.

4. In Jean Hendry's 1955 sample, 24% regularly sold to dealers (1957: 173).

5. Hendry reported that in 1955 there were four local pottery dealers (1957:173).

6. Also, two pool halls were opened in 1969.

ESSAY 10. THE MARKETPLACE TRADERS OF SAN ANTONI-NO: A QUANTITATIVE ANALYSIS

1. Research in San Antonino has been carried out in several periods beginning in December, 1965. The senior author participated for two years (August, 1964–August, 1966) in the UCLA Oaxaca Market Study Project (under the direction of Professor Ralph L. Beals). During the last seven months of that time he divided his efforts between research in San Antonino and Oaxaca City. Subsequently both authors have worked together in San Antonino during the summer of 1969, July through December of 1970, and the summers of 1972, 1973, and 1974. Further research is planned.

2. The analysis presented here is preliminary in that it involves a manual compilation of only a portion of the data collected in the census. We plan to computerize all of the data, after which a more thorough statistical analysis will be undertaken. We would like to express our thanks to two student research assistants, Barbara Bleiweis and especially Geraldine Grant Friedman, for the tedious task of extracting the data from the census forms.

3. Proper Spanish grammar dictates use of the term *regatones* (masculine plural) for mixed-gender references, even though females overwhelmingly predominate in the occupation. *Regatonas* (feminine plural) will be used in general situations not specifically involving males.

4. The absence of precise figures on those who regularly attend the Oaxaca City plaza more than once a week derives simply from an oversight in constructing the schedule. However, according to informants, probably more than half of those who regularly attend the Oaxaca City plaza do so two or three times a week.

5. In 1965 the sewing teacher attached to a Cultural Mission operating in

the village at the time attempted to stimulate interest in embroidery along with interest in cutting and sewing city-style skirts and dresses. Her seeming success in the former contrasted sharply with her modest accomplishments in the latter.

6. The blouse merchants are not included in the figures on marketplace traders because they primarily sell directly to tourist shops in the city or to other intermediaries who come directly to their houses.

7. As mentioned earlier, the wives of butchers and bakers were not counted as marketplace-oriented persons because, while they do the selling, they are not significantly involved in buying and processing. In other words, their activities are dependent upon their husband's occupation, which is not the case with *regatonas* and *comerciantes*, who can and do operate independently.

8. The *chocolatero* and the two *regatones* are old men who work along with their wives. They sell in the Oaxaca City market, where male vendors are more common.

9. The only time male informants ever admitted to making tortillas was in their accounts of barracks life while working as braceros in the United States.

ESSAY 11. A HISTORICAL-ECOLOGICAL APPROACH TO THE STUDY OF THE OAXACA PLAZA SYSTEM

1. The division of the phenomena under study into two principal subsystems reflects, but does not resolve, two issues in ecological theory. First, I have used the term *local system* instead of *ecosystem* because of the narrow scope given that term by Rappaport, who defines it to mean only intraspecies trophic exchange. In Oaxaca the local system is already too complex to accommodate this definition, involving as it does nontrophic exchanges in the form of craft goods and services, all ultimately based on the domestication of plants and animals. The second issue concerns the grouping of all possible constituent subsystems into units that reflect the phenomenal realities experienced by the people of this region. The two units proposed do this fairly well but inevitably exclude certain important manifestations, such as the flow of goods and services through channels other than the system of plazas. Examples of this are magical services, illegal alcohol, yearly plazas during pilgrimages or patron-saint celebrations, more capitalistically organized native industries, such as sugar production, and perhaps certain intermediate groupings of local systems that we presently know little about (Santiago Apóstol, Miahuatlán and its hinterland). I recognize the importance of these phenomena; however, for the present purpose—evolutionary ecological explication—this bipartite scheme is parsimonious and convenient and accounts for much of the data.

REFERENCES CITED

Adams, Richard Newbold
  1970 *Crucifixion by power: Essays on Guatemalan national social structure, 1944–1966.* Austin: University of Texas Press.
Adams, Robert McC.
  1966 *The evolution of urban society.* Chicago: Aldine.
Aguilar Monteverde, Alonso
  1968 *Dialéctica de la economía mexicana.* Mexico City: Editorial Nuestro Tiempo.
Aguirre Beltrán, Gonzalo
  1967 *Regiones de refugio.* Mexico City: Instituto Interamericano Indigenista.
  1970a "Símbolos étnicos de la identidad." *Anuario Indigenista* 30:101–140.
  1970b "Comentario." *Anuario Indigenista* 30:280–294.
  1970c *El proceso de aculturación en México.* Colección del estudiante de Ciencias Sociales 2. Mexico City: Editorial Comunidad, Instituto de Ciencias Sociales, Universidad Iberoamericana.
Avila, Manuel
  1969 *Tradition and growth: A study of four Mexican villages.* Chicago: University of Chicago Press.
Banco Nacional de Comercio Exterior
  1971 *Mexico: The new government's economic policy.* Mexico City.
Barnes, John A.
  1954 "Class and committees in a Norwegian island parish." *Human Relations* 7(1):39–58.
Beals, Ralph L.
  1945 *Ethnology of the western Mixe.* University of California Publications in American Archaeology and Ethnology, vol. 42, part 1.
  1967a "The structure of the Oaxaca market system." *Revista Mexicana de Estudios Antropológicos* 21:333–342.
  1967b "Un sistema tradicional de mercado." *América Indígena* 27:566–580.

1970 "Gifting, reciprocity, savings, and credit in peasant Oaxaca."
     Southwestern Journal of Anthropology 26(3):231–241.
Belshaw, Cyril S.
1965 *Traditional exchange and modern markets.* Englewood Cliffs,
     N.J.: Prentice-Hall.
Bennett, John W.
1969 *Northern Plainsmen.* Chicago: Aldine.
Bernal, Ignacio
1965 "Archaeological synthesis of Oaxaca." In *Archaeology of south-
     ern Mesoamerica: Part two,* edited by Gordon R. Willey, pp.
     788–813. Handbook of Middle American Indians, edited by
     Robert Wauchope, volume 3. Austin: University of Texas Press.
Berry, Brian J. L.
1967 *Geography of market centers and retail distribution.* Englewood
     Cliffs, N.J.: Prentice-Hall.
Bohannan, Paul
1955 "Some principles of exchange and investment among the Tiv."
     American Anthropologist 57:60–70.
Bohannan, Paul, and George Dalton
1962 Introduction to *Markets in Africa,* edited by idem, pp. 1–26.
     Evanston, Ill.: Northwestern University Press.
Bonfil Batalla, Guillermo
1966 "Conservative thought in applied anthropology: A critique."
     Human Organization 25:89–92.
Brandenberg, Frank
1964 *The making of modern Mexico.* Englewood Cliffs, N.J.: Prentice-
     Hall.
Cámara, Fernando
1966 "Tianguis y mercados en Oaxaca." In *Summa anthropologica en
     homenaje a Roberto J. Weitlaner,* edited by Antonio Pompa y
     Pompa, pp. 273–280. Mexico City: INAH.
Carrasco, Pedro
1951 "Las culturas indígenas de Oaxaca, México." *América Indígena*
     11:99–114.
Cassady, Ralph
1968 "Negotiated price-making in Mexican traditional markets: A
     conceptual analysis." *América Indígena* 28:51–78.
Chang, K. C., ed.
1968 *Settlement archaeology.* Palo Alto: National Press Books.
Chayanov, A. V.
1966 *The theory of peasant economy.* Edited by Daniel Thorner, Ba-
     sile Kerblay, and R. E. F. Smith. Homewood, Ill.: Irwin.
Chevalier, François
1963 *Land and society in colonial Mexico.* Berkeley and Los Angeles:
     University of California Press.

Chorley, R. J.
1962 "Geomorphology and general systems theory." United States Geological Survey, Professional Paper 500-B.
Coe, Michael D.
1961 "Social typology and tropical forest civilizations." *Comparative Studies in Society and History* 4(1).
Cook, Scott
1968 *Teitipac and its metateros: An economic anthropological study of production and exchange in a peasant-artisan economy in the Valley of Oaxaca, Mexico.* Ann Arbor: University Microfilms.
1970 "Price and output variability in a peasant-artisan stoneworking industry in Oaxaca, Mexico: An analytical essay in economic anthropology." *American Anthropologist* 72:776–801.
1973 "Economic anthropology: Problems in theory, method, and analysis." In *Handbook of Social and Cultural Anthropology,* edited by John J. Honigmann, pp. 795–860. Chicago: Rand McNally.
Cortés, Hernando
1962 *Five letters.* Translated by J. Bayrd Morris. New York: Norton Library.
Dahlgren de Jordan, Babro
1963 *Nocheztli, la grana cochinilla.* Nueva Biblioteca Mexicana de Obras Históricas, no. 1. Mexico City.
de la Fuente, Julio
1947 "Los zapotecas de Choapan, Oaxaca." In *Anales del Instituto Nacional de Antropología e Historia,* II, 143–206. Mexico City: INAH.
1949 *Yalalag, una villa zapoteca serrana.* Mexico City: Museo Nacional de Antropología.
1965 *Relaciones interétnicas.* Mexico City: Instituto Nacional Indigenista.
1967 "Ethnic relationships." In *Social anthropology,* edited by Manning Nash, pp. 432–448. Handbook of Middle American Indians, edited by Robert Wauchope, vol. 6. Austin: University of Texas Press.
Díaz del Castillo, Bernal
1956 *The Bernal Díaz chronicles: The true history of the conquest of Mexico.* Translated and edited by Albert Idell. Garden City: Doubleday.
Diskin, Martin
1967 *Economics and society in Tlacolula, Oaxaca, Mexico.* Ann Arbor: University Microfilms.
1969 "Estudio estructural del sistema de plazas en el valle de Oaxaca." *América Indígena* 29:1077–1099.
1971 "Persistence of tradition in the urbanization of the Oaxaca val-

ley." In *Race, change and urban society,* edited by P. Orleans and W. R. Ellis, pp. 191–213. Urban Affairs Annual Review 5. Los Angeles: Sage Publications.

Dobb, Maurice
1963 *Studies in the development of capitalism.* New York: International Publishers.
1967 "A reply." In *The transition from feudalism to capitalism,* pp. 21–29. New York: Science and Society.

Dorfman, Robert
1964 *The price system.* Englewood Cliffs, N.J.: Prentice-Hall.

Eder, Herbert M.
1969 "Turtling in coastal Oaxaca." *Pacific Discovery* 22:10–15.
1970 "Palms and man in coastal Oaxaca, Mexico." *Yearbook of the Association of Pacific Coast Geographers* 32:41–58.

Firth, Raymond
1946 *Malay fishermen: Their peasant economy.* London: Kegan Paul.
1967 "Themes in economic anthropology: A general comment." In *Themes in economic anthropology,* edited by idem, pp. 1–28. London: Tavistock.

Flannery, Kent V.
1968 "Archaeological systems theory and early Mesoamerica." In *Anthropological archaeology in the Americas,* edited by Betty Meggers, pp. 67–87. Washington, D.C.: Anthropological Society of Washington.

Flannery, Kent V., and Michael D. Coe
1968 "Social and economic systems in formative Mesoamerica." In *New perspectives in archaeology,* edited by Sally R. and Lewis R. Binford, pp. 267–284. Chicago: Aldine Press.

Flannery, Kent V., Anne V. T. Kirkby, Michael J. Kirkby, and Aubrey Williams, Jr.
1967 "Farming systems and political growth in ancient Oaxaca." *Science* 158:445–454.

Flores, Edmundo
1970 *Vieja revolución, nuevos problemas.* Mexico City: Joaquín Mortiz.

Foster, George M.
1948a *Empire's children: The people of Tzintzuntzan.* Washington, D.C.: Smithsonian Institution.
1948b "The folk economy of rural Mexico with special reference to marketing." *Journal of Marketing* 13:153–162.
1959 "The potter's wheel: An analysis of idea and artifact in invention." *Southwestern Journal of Anthropology* 15(2):99–119.

Frank, Andre Gunder
1969 *Latin America: Underdevelopment or revolution?* New York: Monthly Review Press.

Fraser, L. M.
1947   *Economic thought and language.* London: Black.
Galeski, Boguslaw
1972   *Basic concepts in rural sociology.* Manchester, Eng.: Manchester University Press.
Geertz, Clifford
1963   *Agricultural involution: The processes of ecological change in Indonesia.* Berkeley: University of California Press.
Gillin, John
1947   *Moche, a Peruvian coastal community.* Smithsonian Institution, Institute of Social Anthropology, Publication 3. Washington, D.C.: Government Printing Office.
Godelier, Maurice
1972   *Rationality and irrationality in economics.* New York: Monthly Review Press.
González Casanova, Pablo
1965   *La democrácia en México.* Mexico City: Serie Popular Era.
1966   "The Mexico which has and the Mexico which has not." In *Is the Mexican Revolution dead?* edited by Stanley R. Ross, pp. 217–227. New York: Knopf.
Haggett, Peter
1966   *Locational analysis in human geography.* New York: St. Martin's Press.
Hamnett, Brian R.
1971   *Politics and trade in southern Mexico.* Cambridge: Cambridge University Press.
Hendry, Jean
1957   *Atzompa: A pottery producing village of southern Mexico.* Ann Arbor: University Microfilms.
Hodder, B. W.
1962   "The Yoruba rural market." In *Markets in Africa*, edited by Paul Bohannan and George Dalton, pp. 103–117. Evanston, Ill.: Northwestern University Press.
1965   "Some comments on the origins of traditional markets in Africa south of the Sahara." *Transactions of the Institute of British Geographers* 33:97–105.
Ibarra, David, I. M. de Navarrete, L. Solis, and V. I. Urquid, eds.
1972   *El perfil de México en 1980*, vol. 1. 4th ed. Mexico City: Siglo Veintiuno Editores.
Johnson, Eleanor
1973   "The capitalist adaptation of marketwomen in rural Benin (Nigeria)." Unpublished manuscript.
Kaplan, David
1965   "The Mexican marketplace then and now." In *Proceedings of the Annual Spring Meeting of the American Ethnological So-*

ciety, edited by June Helm, pp. 80–94. Seattle: University of Washington Press.

Kirkby, Anne V. T.
1973 *The use of land and water resources in the past and present Valley of Oaxaca, Mexico.* Memoirs of the Museum of Anthropology, no. 5. Ann Arbor: University of Michigan.

Laclau, Ernesto
1971 "Feudalism and capitalism in Latin America." *New Left Review*, no. 67 (May–June):19–38.

Lamartine Yates, Paul
1965 *El desarrollo regional de México.* 3d ed. Mexico City: Banco de Mexico, Departamento de Investigaciones Industriales.

Landa Abrego, María Elena
1962 *Contribución al estudio de la formación cultural del valle Poblano-Tlaxcalteca.* Mexico City: INAH.

LeClair, E. E., Jr.
1962 "Economic theory and economic anthropology." *American Anthropologist* 64:1179–1203.

Lees, Susan H.
1973 *Socio-political aspects of canal irrigation in the Valley of Oaxaca, Mexico.* Memoirs of the Museum of Anthropology, no. 6. Ann Arbor: University of Michigan.

Lenin, Vladimir I.
1964 *The development of capitalism in Russia.* Moscow: Progress Publishers.

Leslie, Charles M.
1960 *Now we are civilized: A study of the world view of the Zapotec Indians of Mitla, Oaxaca.* Detroit: Wayne State University Press.

Lorenzo, José L.
1960 "Aspectos físicos del Valle de Oaxaca." *Revista Mexicana de Estudios Antropológicos* 16:49–64.

Luxemburg, Rosa
1968 *The accumulation of capital.* New York: Monthly Review Press.

McBryde, Felix Webster
1933 *Sololá: A Guatemalan town and Cakchiquel market center.* Middle American Research Publication, no. 5. New Orleans: Tulane University.
1947 *Cultural and historical geography of southwestern Guatemala.* Institute of Social Anthropology, Publication 4. Washington, D.C.: Smithsonian Institution.

Malinowski, Bronislaw
1922 *Argonauts of the Western Pacific.* London: Routledge.
1940–1941 Unpublished field notes.

Malinowski, Bronislaw, and Julio de la Fuente
1957 *La economía de un sistema de mercados en México.* Acta Anthro-

pologica, Epoca 2, vol. 1, no. 2. Mexico City: Escuela Nacional de Antropología e Historia, Sociedad de Alumnos.

Mandel, Ernest
1970   *Marxist economic theory*, vol. 1. New York: Monthly Review Press.

Marroquín, Alejandro
1957   *La ciudad mercado (Tlaxiaco)*. Colección Cultura Mexicana 19. Mexico City: Imprenta Universitaria.

Marshall, Gloria
1964   *Women, trade, and the Yoruba family*. Ann Arbor: University Microfilms (no. 65–7878).

Martínez Ríos, Jorge
1964   "Análisis funcional de la 'guelaguetza agrícola.'" *Revista Mexicana de Sociología* 26(1):79–125.

Maruyama, Magoroh
1963   "The second cybernetics: Deviation-amplifying mutual causal processes." *American Scientist* 51(2):164–179.

Marx, Karl
1930   *Capital*, vol. 1. London: Dent, Everyman's Library.
1935   *Value, price and profit*. New York: International Publishers.
1973   *Grundrisse*. London: Pelican.

Meillasoux, Claude
1971   Introduction to *The development of indigenous trade and markets in West Africa*, edited by idem, pp. 49–86. London: Oxford University Press.
1972   "From reproduction to production: A Marxist approach to economic anthropology." *Economy and Society* 1(1):93–105.

Mendieta y Núñez, Lucio, ed.
1949   *Los zapotecos*. Mexico City: Imprenta Universitaria.

Messer, Ellen
1972   "Patterns of 'wild' plant consumption in Oaxaca, Mexico." *Ecology of Food and Nutrition* 1:325–332.

Mikesell, Marvin W.
1958   "The role of tribal markets in Morocco." *Geographical Review* 48:494–511.

Mintz, Sidney W.
1956   "The role of the middleman in the internal distribution system of a caribbean peasant economy." *Human Organization* 15(2): 18–23.
1959   "Internal market systems as mechanisms of social articulation." In *Intermediate societies, social mobility and communication*, edited by V. F. Ray, pp. 20–30. Proceedings of the 1959 Annual Spring Meeting of the American Ethnological Society. Seattle: University of Washington Press.
1961   "Pratik: Haitian personal economic relations." In *Proceedings of*

the 1961 Annual Spring Meeting of the American Ethnological Society, pp. 54–63. Seattle: University of Washington Press.

1964a "The employment of capital by market women in Haiti." In Capital, saving and credit in peasant societies, edited by Raymond Firth and B. S. Yamey. Chicago: Aldine.

1964b Peasant market places and economic development in Latin America. The Graduate Center for Latin American Studies, Vanderbilt University, Occasional Paper No. 4. Nashville.

1971 "Men, women and trade." Comparative Studies in Society and History 13(3):247–269.

Nader, Laura
1964 "Talea and Juquila: A comparison of Zapotec social organization." University of California Publications in American Archaeology and Ethnology, vol. 48, part 3, pp. 195–296.

Nahmad, Salomon
1965 Los Mixes. Mexico City: Ediciones del Instituto Nacional Indigenista.

Nash, Manning
1961 "The social context of economic choice in a small society." Man 61:186–191. Reprinted in Tribal and peasant economies, edited by George Dalton, pp. 524–538. New York: Doubleday, Natural History Press.

1966 Primitive and peasant economic systems. San Francisco: Chandler Publishing Co.

1967a Introduction to Social Anthropology, edited by idem, pp. 3–11. Handbook of Middle American Indians, edited by Robert Wauchope, vol. 6. Austin: University of Texas Press.

1967b "Indian economies." In Social Anthropology, edited by idem, pp. 89–102. Handbook of Middle American Indians, edited by Robert Wauchope, vol. 6. Austin: University of Texas Press.

Paddock, John
1966 "Oaxaca in ancient Mesoamerica." In Ancient Oaxaca: Discoveries in Mexican archaeology and history, edited by idem, pp. 3–25. Stanford, Calif.: Stanford University Press.

Paddock, John, ed.
1966 Ancient Oaxaca: Discoveries in Mexican archaeology and history. Stanford, Calif.: Stanford University Press.

Padilla Aragón, Enrique
1969 México: Desarrollo con pobreza. Mexico City: Siglo Veintiuno Editores.

Palerm, Angel, and Eric R. Wolf
1957 "Ecological potential and cultural development in Mesoamerica." In Studies in human ecology, pp. 1–37. Social Science Monographs 3. Washington, D.C.: Pan American Union.

Parsons, Elsie Clews
1936 *Mitla, town of the souls.* Chicago: University of Chicago Press.
Paso y Troncoso, Francisco del
1905 *Papeles de Nueva España,* vol. 4. Madrid: Real Academia de la Historia.
Peterson, Frederick A.
1959 *Ancient Mexico: An introduction to pre-hispanic cultures.* New York: Capricorn Books.
Plattner, Stuart
1973 *The economics of peddling.* Center for International Studies, University of Missouri, Occasional Paper No. 734. St. Louis.
Polanyi, Karl, C. S. Arensberg, and H. W. Pearson, eds.
1957 *Trade and markets in the early empires.* Glencoe, Ill.: Free Press.
Pozas, Ricardo, and Isabel H. de Pozas
1973 *Los indios en las clases sociales de México.* 3d ed. Mexico City: Siglo Veintiuno Editores.
Preobrazhensky, Evgenii
1965 *The new economics.* Translated by Brian Pearce. London: Clarendon Press. First published in Russian in 1924.
Rapoport, Anatol
1965 *Operational philosophy.* New York: Wiley.
Rappaport, Roy A.
1968 *Pigs for the ancestors.* New Haven: Yale University Press.
1969 "Some suggestions concerning concept and method in ecological anthropology." In *Contributions to anthropology: Ecological essays,* edited by David Damas, pp. 184–188. Ottawa: National Museums of Canada Bulletin 230.
Ravicz, Robert S.
1965 *Organización social de los mixtecos.* Colección de Antropología Social 5. Mexico City: Instituto Nacional Indigenista.
Redfield, Robert
1939 "Primitive merchants of Guatemala." *Quarterly Journal of Interamerican Relations* 1(4):42–56.
Romney, Kimball, and Romaine Romney
1966 *The Mixtecans of Juxtlahuaca, Mexico.* Six Cultures Series 4. New York: John Wiley and Sons.
Sahagún, Bernardino de
1950 *General history of the things of New Spain: Florentine Codex, Book 9.* Translated and edited by Arthur J. O. Anderson and Charles E. Dibble. Santa Fe: School of American Research.
Sahlins, Marshall
1962 *Moala: Culture and nature on a Fijian island.* Ann Arbor: University of Michigan Press.

Sanders, William T.
1956 "The central Mexican symbiotic region." In *Prehistoric settlement patterns in the New World*, edited by Gordon R. Willey. Viking Fund publications in anthropology, no. 23. New York: Wenner Gren Foundation for Anthropological Research.
1968 "Hydraulic agriculture, economic symbiosis and the evolution of states in Central Mexico." In *Anthropological archaeology in the Americas*, edited by Betty J. Meggers, pp. 88–107. Washington, D.C.: Anthropological Society of Washington.
1972 "Population, agricultural history, and societal evolution in Mesoamerica." In *Population growth: Anthropological implications*, edited by Brian Spooner, pp. 101–153. Cambridge: MIT Press.
Sanders, William T., and Barbara J. Price
1968 *Mesoamerica: The evolution of a civilization.* New York: Random House.
Secretaría de Industria y Comercio, Dirección General de Estadísticas
1963a *Localidades de la república, entidades federativos y municipios*, vol. 2. *VIII censo general de población: 1960.* Mexico City.
1963b *Estado de Oaxaca*, vol. 2. *VIII censo general de población: 1960.* Mexico City.
1969 *Anuario estadístico de los estados unidos Mexicanos 1966–67.* Mexico City.
Shepard, Anna O.
1963 *Notes from a ceramic laboratory, part 2: Beginnings of ceramic industrialization; an example from the Oaxaca Valley.* Washington, D.C.: Carnegie Institution.
1967 "Preliminary notes on the paste composition of Monte Albán pottery." In *La cerámica de Monte Albán*, edited by Alfonso Caso, Ignacio Bernal, and Jorge Acosta, pp. 477–484. Mexico City: INAH.
Simpson, Leslie B.
1970 Foreword to *Land and society in colonial Mexico*, by François Chevalier, pp. v–ix (paperback ed.). Berkeley and Los Angeles: University of California Press.
Singer, Morris
1969 *Growth, equality, and the Mexican experience.* Latin American Monographs, no. 16. Austin: University of Texas Press.
Skinner, G. William
1964 "Marketing and social structure in rural China: Part 1." *Journal of Asian Studies* 24:3–43.
Smith, Carole A.
1972a *The domestic marketing system in western Guatemala: An economic, locational and cultural analysis.* Ann Arbor: University Microfilms.
1972b "Market articulation and economic stratification in western Gua-

temala." *Food Research Institute Studies in Agricultural Economics, Trade and Development* 11(2):203–233.
1973 "Determinants and consequences of local system types in the region of western Guatemala." Paper presented at the Mathematical Social Sciences Board Conference on Formal Methods in the Analysis of Regional Systems, Santa Fe, New Mexico. Mimeographed.
Spores, Ronald
1965 "The Zapotec and Mixtec at Spanish contact." In *Archaeology of Southern Mesoamerica: Part two*, edited by Gordon R. Willey, pp. 962–987. Handbook of Middle American Indians, edited by Robert Wauchope, vol. 3. Austin: University of Texas Press.
Stavenhagen, Rodolfo
1965 "Classes, colonialism, and acculturation." *Studies in Comparative International Development* 1(6).
1970 "Social aspects of agrarian structure in Mexico." In *Agrarian problems and peasant movements in Latin America*, edited by idem, pp. 225–270. Garden City: Doubleday-Anchor.
Steward, Julian H.
1955, 1963 *Theory of culture change*. Urbana: University of Illinois Press.
Swetnam, John
1973 "Oligopolistic prices in a free market—Antigua, Guatemala." *American Anthropologist* 75(5):1504–1510.
Symanski, Richard, and M. J. Webber
1974 "Complex periodic market cycles." *Annals of the Association of American Geographers* 64:203–213.
Takahashi, H. K.
1967 "A contribution to the discussion." In *The Transition from feudalism to capitalism*, by Paul M. Sweezy, Maurice Dobb, H. K. Takahashi, R. H. Hilton, and C. Hill, pp. 30–55. New York: Science and Society.
Tamayo López Portilla, Jorge
1960 *Proyectos de integración vial en el Estado de Oaxaca*. Mexico City: UNAM, Escuela de Economía.
Tardits, Claudine, and Claude Tardits
1962 "Traditional market economy in the south Dahomey." In *Markets in Africa*, edited by Paul Bohannan and George Dalton, pp. 89–102. Evanston, Ill.: Northwestern University Press.
Tax, Sol
1952 "Economy and technology." In *Heritage of Conquest*, edited by idem, pp. 43–75. New York: Macmillan.
1953 *Penny capitalism: A Guatemalan Indian economy*. Institute of Social Anthropology, Publication 16. Washington, D.C.: Smithsonian Institution.

Taylor, William B.
1969   *The Valley of Oaxaca: A study of colonial land distribution.* Ann Arbor: University Microfilms.
1971   "The colonial background to peasant economy in the Valley of Oaxaca." Paper submitted to the symposium "Market Systems and Economics of the Oaxaca Region," at the joint annual meeting of the Southwestern Anthropological Association and the American Ethnological Society in Tucson, Arizona, on April 30.
1972   *Landlord and peasant in colonial Oaxaca.* Stanford, Calif.: Stanford University Press.

Terray, Emmanuel
1972   *Marxism and 'primitive' societies.* New York: Monthly Review Press.

Tibon, Gutierre
1961   *Pinotepa Nacional: Mixtecos, negros y triques.* Mexico City: UNAM.

UNDP/FAO (United Nations Development Program and the Food and Agricultural Organization)
1972   *México: Estudios de los recursos del estado de Oaxaca; Diagnóstico socio-económico del estado de Oaxaca.* ESE:SF/MEX 10, Informe Técnico 1. Rome: United Nations.

van de Velde, Paul, and Henriette Romeike van de Velde
1939   *The black pottery of Coyotepec, Oaxaca, Mexico.* Southwest Museum Papers, no. 13. Highland Park, Calif.

Wagner, Philip A.
1964   *The human use of the earth.* Glencoe: Free Press.

Warman, Arturo, M. Nolasco, G. Bonfil, M. Olivera, and E. Valencia
1970   *De eso que llaman antropología mexicana.* Mexico City: Editorial Nuestro Tiempo.

Waterbury, Ronald
1968   *The traditional market in a provincial urban setting: Oaxaca, Mexico.* Ann Arbor: University Microfilms.
1970   "Urbanization and a traditional market system." In *The social anthropology of Latin America,* edited by Walter Goldschmidt, pp. 126–156. Los Angeles: Latin American Center, UCLA.

Weber, Max
1947   *Theory of social and economic organization.* Glencoe: Free Press.

Welte, Cecil R.
1966   "Index of populated places in the Valley of Oaxaca listed in the census of 1960." Oaxaca City: Oficina de Estudios de Humanidad del Valle de Oaxaca.

West, Robert C.
1948   *Cultural geography of the modern Tarascan area.* Institute of Social Anthropology, Publication 7. Washington, D.C.: Smithsonian Institution.

Whitaker, Thomas W., and Hugh C. Cutler
1966   "Food plants in a Mexican market." *Economic Botany* 20:6–16.
Whitecotton, Joseph W.
1968   "The Valley of Oaxaca at Spanish contact: An ethno-historical study." Ph.D. dissertation, University of Illinois.
Wittfogel, Karl A.
1957   *Oriental despotism*. New Haven: Yale University Press.
Wolf, Eric R.
1955   "Types of Latin American peasantry: A preliminary discussion." *American Anthropologist* 57:452–471.
1956   "Aspects of group relations in a complex society: Mexico." *American Anthropologist* 58:1065–1078.
1957   "Closed corporate peasant communities in Mesoamerica and central Java." *Southwestern Journal of Anthropology* 13, no. 1.
1959   *Sons of the shaking earth*. Chicago: University of Chicago Press.
1966   *Peasants*. Englewood Cliffs, N.J.: Prentice-Hall.
1967   "The Valley of Oaxaca and its Zapotec-speaking hinterland." In *Social Anthropology*, edited by Manning Nash, pp. 301–308. Handbook of Middle American Indians, edited by Robert Wauchope, vol. 6. Austin: University of Texas Press.
1969   "Mexico." In *Peasant wars of the twentieth century*, by Eric R. Wolf, pp. 3–48. New York: Harper and Row.
Wolpe, Harold
1972   "Capitalism and cheap labour-power in South Africa: From segregation to apartheid." *Economy and Society* 1(4):425–456.
Zavala, Silvio, and José Miranda
1954   "Instituciones indígenas en la colonia." In *Métodos y resultados de la política indigenista en México*, by Alfonso Caso, Silvio Zavala, José Miranda, Moisés González Navarro, Gonzalo Aguirre Beltrán, and Ricardo Pozas, pp. 29–112. Memórias del Instituto Nacional Indigenista, vol. 6. Mexico City: Ediciones del Instituto Nacional Indigenista.

INDEX

www.ingramcontent.com/pod-product-compliance
Lightning Source LLC
Chambersburg PA
CBHW020334270326
41926CB00007B/178